NIGHT'S
CIRCLE

BY
DUNCAN HAUGHEY

This book is published by
Grosvenor House Publishing Ltd
28 – 30 High Street, Guildford, Surrey, GU1 3HY.
www.grosvenorhousepublishing.co.uk

A CIP record for this book
Is available from the British Library

ISBN 978-1-905529-29-2

Dedicated to
John Queen and Alan Tooby.

My gratitude and thanks to my loyal family and
friends, especially Rosemary and Pete.

Thanks to Margaret Whitelaw for her invaluable
help in editing this book and to those who have
helped get it published.

CHAPTER ONE

The earphones were creating a distorted sound that was unacceptable. The nurse thought that the Bach violin concerto deserved better and quickly removed the offending pieces of crudely shaped plastic from his ears.

A draft of cold air blew through the half-open window, the water in an antiquated cistern bubbled away trying to release the trapped air, and the equally ancient water pipes rang and rattled while singing a discordant phrase. The male nurse threw away the half-smoked cigarette onto the floor of the sluice; it landed in a wet patch of urine and quickly extinguished itself. He turned onto the unit and moved quickly across the hard tiles, his shoe heels striking the over-polished floor creating a staccato-like sound that echoed around the old-fashioned unit. A patient had pressed his bell and unusually the nurse attended without delay, hoping that something would break the monotony of what had become a boring night, without any interesting incidents that might alleviate the tedium.

The night had suddenly become cold and although Harry was sleeping, the cold had partially awoken him leaving him in that dazed state between sleep and awareness.

His mind, not unusually, was meandering about without any real sense of purpose.

To his surprise, he suddenly thought that he could no longer walk. Due to this surprising situation, he quickly managed to fully awaken himself only to find out that his thoughts were unfortunately accurate. No matter how hard he tried getting his legs to function they would not move, and a feeling of intense fear that was bordering upon panic enveloped him when he realised that he definitely could not walk. Small droplets of perspiration had formed on his forehead while dreaming which he quickly wiped away with his sleeve.

He took a few deep breathes, and then sighed while trying to regain some control over his thoughts.

He knew that he had been dreaming but he was still surprised. In truth, he was very worried by the stark realism of the event. He took a few more deep breaths hoping to clarify his thoughts. He knew that he had to think very clearly and not allow himself to panic.

He carefully looked around him, but he could see nothing that might initiate any memory patterns that could suggest why he was dreaming that he could not walk. It seemed, for want of a better word, bizarre, or illogical, given that he had been unable to walk for a number of years. His head was now clear and he decided that he would try once more to get to sleep hoping that the dream would not recur as he had found the experience very unpleasant. Moreover, Harry did not want to concern himself with anything that might be considered unpleasant at a time when his main desire was for sleeping.

He surreptitiously looked under the sheets for some reason as though an answer might be found there. His hand reached down and instinctively gave his catheter a slight shake while he tried to focus his eyes upon the recumbent tube that was a constant worry to him, and when he could see properly he watched it for a moment as though some significant act might be about to happen. He watched carefully as an air bubble rose to the top of the tube; he shook the tube once again. Nothing occurred so he grunted in recognition that things appeared to be functioning correctly, he then placed his head back upon the pillow while quietly threatening any thoughts that might prevent him from sleeping.

Like a motionless pachyderm, the whole building was laying in a dormant state during those quiet eventless times between the early hours of the morning and the break of day. Unusually the lighting on the unit seemed brighter than was normal for the early hours, casting a strange, cold glow that lacked any warmth or comfort.

She was relatively slim with dark brown hair that was losing its colour and shape. She sighed loudly for no apparent reason. The middle-aged nurse looked as though she had worked too many nights without a break, her hair was in a desperate state and in need of a good hairdresser; her face was gaunt and lined, there were dark shadows under her eyes. Her complexion appeared neglected giving the impression that she had no one she needed or wanted to impress, or she no longer cared about such things.

She looked strained and her lips were held tight as though she was well accustomed to frowning. She was sat quietly at her station on a less than comfortable chair engrossed with a malevolent computer; she was working on the patients care plans while tentatively sipping at a cup of less than palatable coffee. The taste was disgusting and as she snorted involuntarily, a small amount of saliva appeared to form a small globule in the corner of her mouth, which she wiped away. She pushed away the cup of coffee at the same time trying to fathom out how to bring a new record onto the computer screen without losing the existing records. She sighed loudly, and then cursed in exasperation as once again, she had pressed the wrong key and the error box defiantly appeared on screen.

'You have committed an illegal operation', the box stated aggressively.

"Fuck you!" she said aloud, unable to contain her pent up anger.

Her patience with computers or any devices that supposedly contained a memory chip had long since disappeared, she did not understand how such items worked and she did not know what a memory chip even looked like, but she recognised the reality of the situation, they were a necessary evil and they were here to stay. Such was progress; there was no way of avoiding them. She was of an age where she had been taught how to write things down in an orderly manner that was clear and simple and, in her opinion, it had always worked. Computers were supposedly faster and better at everything, and in the mind of some, it seemed almost a panacea when it came to organising a more efficient structure. At that moment, she did not believe it as she struggled to obtain the required information. In her mind, a computer was nothing but a spiteful enemy without any real cognitive ability; it was something one had a constant battle with in order to accomplish the simplest of tasks. The best you could hope to do was to agree a truce in one's own mind. That way the machine did not seem to win the war but just the odd battle.

She swore under her breath as the screen once again displayed the box stating error. She briefly fantasised that if computers ever obtained the ability to feel pain she would inflict a great deal upon the first machine that offended her. Why does it keep doing the wrong things she wondered, what is wrong with the bloody thing! She took a deep breath, "roll on retirement," she said quietly, if only she could afford to give up work or manage working shorter hours then it would be goodbye to the bloody computers for good. She sighed deeply once again, seemingly resigned to the situation knowing that defeat was almost inevitable. It was then her thoughts changed, as though it was a simplistic form of psychological protection against computers, her mind automatically switched to thinking about her dead husband.

No one thought Diane and Henry Hartley was a perfect couple. And a few of her friends thought that their getting together was an impulsive decision on both their parts. Her first marriage had failed and after being divorced and lonely for some time she had thought that Henry was better than nothing. Not a great deal better, but at least he walked and talked and on occasion he worked, albeit slowly and, at a pace that he had created that caused him the least exertion.

Henry was of little assistance in life, and of less assistance in death. Unfortunately, he had died after a long illness leaving her without enough money for her future.

She deeply resented having to return to work after looking after him for his last four years on this earth, although a few who knew him said that he wasn't really of this planet, but they didn't mean it unkindly. He had acquired a disabling condition that meant he needed someone with him for most of the time. And in the last months of his life he needed care both night and day. 'If only he had the common sense and had taken out life insurance I would have been comfortable like some of my friends', she thought. But they, or more accurately he, assumed that they could not afford it. "Money down the drain," he used to say, "And, who knows, you might die first and then it will not be needed." Why he thought he would not need money, she had no idea. And when they finally realised that they needed it unfortunately it was too late. He was not a bad husband in some respects but he had made no provision for her when he died.

She knew that he was lazy, thoughtless, and lacking in imagination but she had made her decision and despite his faults, she had stayed with him. She had forgiven him when he had lost his job and had not told her. She even forgave him when he showed a liking for her friend's daughter, and could not remember what he had spent money on; she suspected other women but was not sure, as he was not the most romantic of men to say the least. Her friends were only too happy to inform her that they could not understand why she had married him. Hearing such comments annoyed her but in truth, she could not understand either. 'How did I get into that situation with my eyes wide open?' she often asked herself. He was supposed to take charge of some things like most other men seemed to do. That's what husbands are supposed to do, share the problems, deal with things. She always felt angry when these thoughts returned, which was quite frequently.

She was unwilling to take on any responsibility for the situation she found herself in. And she now deeply resented his lack of forethought. It was too late now, she realised, the ship has gone and left the port while she is still standing on the dockside; 'the story of my life', she thought, always too late or in the wrong place at the wrong time. 'Luck is not balanced out and life is not fair and never will be in this world', she concluded, sighing deeply once again. Why do I always get the crap end of the stick? she thought. She sighed again knowing that her future promised her nothing but work, drudgery, and unless a miracle happened, loneliness. She looked at her watch and decided that she would go for her break a few minutes early if another member of staff agreed to sit at the nurses' station. She knew from experience that they would sit there gazing at a well thumbed magazine looking into the coffee pot to see if a cupful remained, while hoping that the telephone would not ring with instructions from the high command that required some change or modification that upset the routine.

She shuddered for a moment and her face contorted slightly. The draft from within the unit brought with it the smell of disinfectant and stale urine that emanated from the out-of-date sluice; these were odours that she had become accustomed to over the years. To outsiders they would have been more noticeable and unacceptable but time and familiarity had brought about a strange acceptance. It crossed her mind that on the news it had mentioned how many billions had been ploughed into the health service in recent years. We have not seen much of it around here, she thought, while looking around her at the decaying inner fabric of the building. This place looks no better than it did years ago when I first started here, it's just an old decaying dump and it needs pulling down.

Something instinctively suddenly attracted her attention; she looked up almost in relief and listened to the sounds emanating from the unit as she thought that she had heard someone speaking.

The sounds came from the section that was off to the right; a light had been switched on by someone indicating that something was happening. The nurse working on that section was obviously dealing with the matter and would soon indicate if help was required. After a few moments of not hearing anything other than a muffled dialogue between the patient and the nurse, she once again attempted to get the computer to cooperate, by threatening it with everlasting damnation and a good kicking. Surprisingly this seemed to have the desired effect and the patients records appeared on screen. She shouted out in delight then allowed herself to smile with satisfaction at this small, if fleeting, victory.

She had once read somewhere that old buildings seemingly can have a life of their own, and can communicate different feelings and emotions to the individuals living or working within them; some individuals can find that this form of synesthesia can at times be both comforting and disturbing. Was synesthesia the correct word, she wondered, she wasn't sure. She thought about it for the moment then allowed her mind to do what it normally did at such times if she wasn't thinking about her deceased husband and her unhealthy financial situation.

Her thoughts drifted along on a carefully trodden path dwelling upon some of the patients and staff who had occupied the unit over the years. She reached for the pack of biscuits that she always had available while on nights; these were a true source of comfort to her. Until a few weeks ago, she had eaten bars of chocolate but she recognised that she was comfort eating and she had somehow found the will power to stop. She thought biscuits were more healthy than chocolate even though they were half coated in chocolate, but in her mind that still meant less fattening calories. She wondered what stupid person had invented sliming diets, or what stupid person thought that being slim was good for everyone but especially women. Obviously someone who wanted to make money out of selling something nobody needed, she thought. She concluded that it would be a man, a slim man, with a slim wife. And slim children whom you would never get tired of hitting. Although she no longer believed in hitting children, she decided that given the correct circumstances she would make an exception.

Her mind once again drifted into thinking about her future. She thought she really needed a man with his own home and a reasonable income. She would settle for security and a very simple lifestyle, it did not matter what age he was or what he looked like. If he were not too bright that would be better because she could then make the decisions that were in her interest. Given the chance, the next one will be well insured, she was sure of that.

A mouse searching for food ran undisturbed along the old heating pipes spreading untold diseases. In some surrealistic way, even the vermin that had made their home in the buildings seemed tired in their pursuit of morsels of discarded and rotting food.

There was very little sound from anywhere except for the odd murmur from the central heating system which had seen better days. It seemed that the whole of the hospital had fallen into a deep sleep with the exception of those small creatures that inhabit the dark corners of such buildings.

Harry turned over once again and grunted something incomprehensible; the duvet had slipped from its original position and was hanging just above the floor leaving him cold once more. This had caused him to once again awaken temporarily in order to readjust the situation. The sounds emanating from around the unit were familiar and did not add to his disturbed sleep. Although not fully awake, his senses informed him that there was nothing happening that motivated him to remain awake; he could hear the nurse attending a patient but it seemed uninteresting. Harry did not like to miss anything but he quickly decided that as nothing was happening that was out of the ordinary, trying to get back to sleep was the only correct and sensible option. He was grateful that amongst the patients there was not a heavy snorer. That was a sound, or to be precise a series of sounds, that he could not contend with. He grunted once more and snuggled down trying to recapture some of the warmth and comfort that had been his experience until the past few minutes.

Getting back to sleep was an effort that irritated him. Harry knew without looking at his watch that it would be a long time before he would be offered the first cup of tea of the day, and that until that moment sleep was his only sensible option. He had briefly thought about asking the nurse who was sat at her station if she would make him a cup of tea or coffee, but he decided against the idea as it would have been met with a negative response that he would have resented. He had drifted off into a particular form of sleep where he could normally allow his mind to meander and drift wherever it wanted to take him, although when he awoke earlier to find that he could no longer walk this thought had surprised him. Although Harry prided himself in the belief that he could direct his dreams and use them constructively on occasion, for some inexplicable reason, he was unable to do so that night, making the hours seem interminably long. And he still retained the thoughts of dreaming that he could not walk which he had found very disconcerting, or to be more precise, bloody frightening.

Harry was not the most patient of men at the best of times, he was getting bored, and this caused him to be irritated with himself. He had been a patient for some weeks now and although it was not his first visit back to the unit he was feeling it was time to be allowed up out of bed, and getting ready to go back out into the real world. He continually told himself that he had many things to do that could not wait forever; time was money and Harry did not like wasting money. In addition he knew that time was moving on too quickly with regard to achieving some of the projects that he had decided were his priority. The oncoming cold weather would soon prevent him from doing some of the things he intended, but he had reasoned that if he could get some of his plans into shape and ready to have them implemented when the opportunity arose it would be sensible.

Harry, it should be pointed out, was a believer in good,

sensible planning; life had taught him that it was better to have plans available for most eventualities and then you were never surprised or placed at a disadvantage. "Get the buggers before they get you," was a favourite saying of his. There was only one perceived weakness to this idea and that was the hidden variable, that unknown item that can throw the best of plans into disarray when least expected, which is commonly called 'sods law', the most familiar of all laws whether sleeping or awake.

Harry grunted as he fell asleep thinking that the time he was having to spend in bed was unfortunately necessary in order to solve a simple medical problem. He had unwittingly acquired a small pressure sore that had become infected and it had required medical attention from the unit's staff.

His thinking was, on the surface, logical but his thoughts were not as structured as they usually were. He was getting very frustrated with everything around him but he tried to keep calm and reasonable, as he knew any other attitude was pointless. He also felt that it seemed such a waste of time laying in bed with regard to being unable to move events forward or to be in control of events. In addition, he knew from experience that some unexpected events in a person's life could occur when they are definitely unwelcome. The most careful planning could never eliminate those events he thought, but Harry still liked to believe that he could eliminate most of them with some appropriate thinking and decision-making. It only required common sense and a modest amount of effort, he liked to say to himself and to anyone else who was willing to listen. Harry was not short on confidence or reluctant when giving his opinions on any subject, whether he knew anything about the subject or not did not seem important to him; to hold forth at length was a suitable conclusion in Harry's mind.

He was soon back asleep although his mind was still turning over as though subconsciously analyzing the various options that were available to him once the night was over. One thing Harry had decided was that he would do whatever was necessary to keep himself out of the spinal unit in the future, and he would attempt to apply extra vigilance to those areas of his condition that were always vulnerable and ready to cause him the problem of not being in full control of his body and his wellbeing. He drifted away dreaming and meandering on an ephemeral plane that caused him a modicum of recreation without the threat of any real distress. This was to Harry's taste during the hours of darkness, a simple meandering without any emotional cost.

Andy Davis had been awake for most of the night, which was not unusual for him. He had heard Harry but had not cared to talk to him, as he knew from experience that Harry only talked at night when something was concerning him. And he knew that Harry had no interest in anything that might be causing immediate concern to anyone else. Harry was, by nature or design, often insensitive to others' needs or feelings. Although on occasion he did surprise those who knew him by doing something unusually generous but that was a rare occasion and definitely not the norm.

Since Andy's accident, it appeared that the days and nights ran into endless circles of minimal events, which were interspersed with uncomfortable and unwelcome instances that usually arrived unexpectedly, and he had quickly realised that such incidents were seldom positive or enjoyable.

He did not like nights, it would be true to state that he hated them; he recognised that it wasn't sensible to allow himself to feel that way about nights but he could not help it. The nights' circle he thought was everlasting, it was not a cycle of time but a circle which for some reason sounded easier to accept and more applicable.

The days ran into nights without any appreciable changes, unless they were of a detrimental nature, he had concluded. However, he was feeling both negative and irritable at that particular moment and boredom was setting in on a regular basis during the long uninteresting nights. In fact, most of his thoughts at that moment were negative with the odd exception. He had watched the sky slowly brighten through the small window that was within his field of vision. His bed did not face east. This was something of a major disappointment to him while to others it might have seemed insignificant. For some reason he always felt a little better once the darkness started to disappear; he wondered if it was to do with the lack of light, currently one of the more popular beliefs for people feeling miserable.

He then remembered that such effects usually occurred during the winter months. A new day brought with it an unwarranted level of optimism, which he was always glad to hold onto for as long as possible. Usually this was only a matter of a few hours each day, but it was important to him and he believed that it assisted in keeping him progressing in the right direction, albeit there could justifiably be an argument over which was the right direction in the existing circumstances. For some reason, he started thinking about a popular tune, *Knights in white satin*. The old ones are the best, he thought. He then realised that the tune was being played on the radio and the sound was coming from the headphones at the back of his bed. They are trying to brainwash us in our sleep by subliminal means, he thought, this mildly amused him. He strained to listen to the next tune that was being played but he could not make it out.

He thought that they would not be playing anything that he liked on the radio at that time anyway; they seldom played anything during the night that was worth listening to. Bloody discordant jazz type rubbish that had no tune, melody or beat that you could listen to. Who listens to that crap through the night?, he said to himself while resenting the existence of such people.

Andy had been on the unit for some sixteen weeks and he was now fully aware of the daily routine. Due to his mood at that particular moment, he had no time for nurses, or nursing auxiliaries and domestics. Bunch of time servers some of them, they would not hold a job down in a real business where you have to get results, he said to himself as he observed a care assistant who had expertly been doing nothing worthwhile for the past hour. They are always going on about being overworked and underpaid; some of them should give money back to the patients due to the damage they inflict, he thought. Andy was not at this instant given to any charitable thoughts. He was having a difficult time. He somehow felt lodged tightly between ignorance and being drip-fed morsels of information that he did not really understand. Therefore, everything was on an obtuse scale of difficulty and this annoyed him as it affected his understanding of so many things. At times, he felt a lone traveller in a distant land.

It seemed to him that very little changed from day to day except on a Sunday. Sunday, he thought was always more boring and tedious than most days, he could not understand why we had to have Sunday anymore, let us have two Saturdays, that would be better. The government seems to be able to change anything - let them get rid of Sundays. He knew that the long Sundays were something you just had to get through as best you could, you had to survive them somehow, as they demanded a certain state of mind that accepted what could be described as a state of 'benign limbo'. The other difference was that there was always fewer staff on duty on Sundays. This was usually because some patients went home for the weekend, and therefore in theory there was less work to do.

Thank God that it's not Sunday, he thought. Sundays were as bad as Monday washdays when he was very young, always miserable with washing drying slowly around the coal fire. He shuddered when he thought that it always cold, damp, and devoid of any vestiges of comfort for a child. He remembered how the clothes had been carefully and orderly dried around the coal fire ensuring that any heat had little chance of escaping or adding warmth to the kitchen, which meant he could not get close enough to feel any of the fire's warmth or comfort. All through the winter the clothes were washed and then dried indoors. He shuddered again at the thought of the cold damp atmosphere. He then wondered why they were the last family in the district to still dry their clothes around a coal fire when everyone else had tumble dryers; those were miserable days, he thought, he then shuddered one final time as though he could still feel the cold dampness that had permeated every ground floor room of their modest house. He remembered his father's words of economic wisdom regarding coal fires: "That you had to use them for drying clothes, cooking, and heating the house, otherwise all the heat was lost, money going up the chimney and wasting good money was something he was unaccustomed to doing, so keep that in mind."

Andy thought that his father's voice was something that he would never miss hearing, the local wit and wisdom he extolled which was usually centred around saving or thrift or being careful, left him anaesthetised. That's the trouble, he thought, with some working class families who are demonstratively proud of being working class, they wear it as a badge of honour and do not accept it for what it really is. A social and financial situation that they would prefer not to be in, anyone with common sense would prefer to be better off with all the comforts and trappings of the middle classes, but not those proud fools. Stupid buggers, thought Andy, they had not emerged from the nineteen thirties, which then had him thinking that such a state was strange because they had no experience of such times, as they had not been born then. So why take on such an attitude? He thought about it, then decided it was possibly beyond reason, which was on the surface inexplicable, it must have a genetic connection somewhere, he assumed. Half of them look inbred anyway, - incestuous bunch, he concluded.

He was now feeling very uncomfortable and he felt that it was time someone came and turned him over; in his current position he was aching and feeling a lot of niggling discomfort. He had mentioned this some hours earlier to a member of the night staff who then complained that she had tried to get him into the position he had wanted earlier. This was said with some obvious resentment which included a facial expression similar to a goat chewing a wasp. This conveyed her annoyance as she had already adjusted his position to her satisfaction, and she had made it obvious that she was not going to risk any damage to her back by moving him again, no matter how uncomfortable he might be.

Her parting shot was, "I've had major surgery you know."

She glared hard at him almost defying him to comment. That accounts for your idleness and insensitivity, he thought. Before she had chance to leave the room he was already uncomfortable again. He thought about asking her to move him once more but he changed his mind. He did not feel like having to observe her expression, or listen to the sighs and large intake of breath that would be the response to his request. He realised that she was a miserable example of humanity, always complaining about something or other. He finally concluded that she should not be allowed near patients as she had no feeling or understanding of their needs. And as for her having surgery, he thought that she should get another job if she cannot do this one, let some one else have the job more suited. He had also learned that some members of the staff had formulated their own rules when it came to health and safety, usually deciding that there was so many things that they were not allowed to do anymore. This, more often than not, tended to work disadvantageously with regard to the needs of the patients.

The last few weeks had been a difficult learning curve for him. He was paralyzed from just below his shoulders and this affected his hands and fingers and the rest of his body. He had quickly come to recognise his vulnerability and physical dependence upon others. After a few fruitless arguments, he had also learned that once positioned and turned in bed he was not expected to complain; it was almost an unwritten rule that on nights you received care and attention in small controlled packages requiring a minimum of effort. That to ask or expect anything more than what is considered the basics is not something that is looked upon kindly by some members of the nursing staff.

He had come to the conclusion that as soon as people went on nights a strange thing occurred, a metamorphosis; they had a personality change and they all became miserable, idle sods who wanted to get into the nursing station and put their feet up. When he told them this, he was told in no uncertain terms how difficult it was on nights with such a limited number of staff.

"I'm not stupid," Andy quickly said

"Everyone knows that it's a nice steady number that paid a good hourly rate. And while everyone rushes around for first couple of hours appearing to be busy, then it is the kettle on and the feet up and sod the rest of us in here."

The nurse was very indignant at his outburst and was starting to feel angry. She then realised that Andy was looking forward to seeing her angry so she resisted his taunts and walked away, but only after telling him

"Don't ring your call button as I'll be asleep and will definitely not hear it."

"That would be nothing new, you've probably had to go on a course for it at the public's expense," said Andy ensuring that he had the last word.

He told himself that he hated hospitals, he hated

uncooperative nursing staff, also the administrators and the cooks who prepared the less than appetising food, and he hated everyone at that moment.

"Fucking bastards," he said loudly in desperation but no one heard.

Andy gave a thought to what it was that was making him uncomfortable but he was unsure. He was paralysed from just below his neck, and had no real sensation from below this level although his body seemed to him to ache and hurt from time to time. He had complained about the pain and discomfort and it had been explained to him carefully that what he was feeling was not real direct pain. It was phantom sensation similar to the sensations amputees sometimes get when they believe that they can still feel their non-existent limb. He had listened to what had been said, and while it sounded logical he still thought that whatever it was that was causing it was of no interest to him as it still hurt.

He decided that he was also very thirsty. Over the past few weeks he had drank more water than he was used to drinking. He had got into the habit of drinking more and he believed that he felt better for drinking on a regular basis. During the first few weeks that he was in hospital, it seemed as though every time a nurse passed his bed she was telling him to drink more. On enquiring why he had to drink more water he was told that it was good for his kidneys and bladder, and especially his catheter.

"You have to keep the urine running clear," they said, while looking at him in a manner that was almost threatening.

At that time, this did not mean a thing to Andy but he obliged everyone by trying to drink in a dutiful manner. Yet for the past couple of weeks no one seemed to bother regarding his fluid intake. This was of some relief to him as he was tired of being told what to do by everyone who passed the bottom of his bed.

It did however come as something of a surprise, or shock, when he first saw his catheter; he had never seen one before and the thought of someone inserting a pipe into his penis, that delicate, precious part of his body made him shudder. But now he was used to seeing the catheter and he almost felt that such an appendage was natural in the circumstances. He thought that it was strange how he no longer felt squeamish when it was changed and observed the process with some degree of interest, if not fascination. He would not have believed it a few months earlier if he had been told that a stranger would be pushing a pipe up his penis and into his bladder without him being comatose or tied down.

It was a similar situation with his bowels. They now seemed to require the expertise of a physicist to get them to work effectively at the appropriate time. The use of suppositories and enemas were new experiences, experiences that were at times daunting, but he went along with them simply through lack of choice. And on first having a manual evacuation, he was almost in a state of shock. He had never heard or read of people inserting their fingers into someone's rear end to assist in emptying their bowels. It then crossed his mind that strangers were inserting things into his body almost every day for some reason, which he decided could not be normal, and could, in the right circumstances give a sensitive person a complex. He was also surprised at the fact that his own bodily functions had seemingly turned against him in order to make life just that little bit more difficult.

He did not miss going to the lavatory, as he had never found it a recreation but more of a time consuming necessity, except when he was younger when he had recognised that during the day in his household it was a good quiet place in which to masturbate. Now he missed all such events as he quickly recognised that his body was no longer acting in a friendly manner towards him, and if anything could go wrong then it was likely to do so. He also recognised that in the recent past he had simply not appreciated the seemingly intricate workings of his bladder and bowels. He was surprised at the difficulty in getting them to function in a manner that was acceptable. One elderly patient who had visited the unit had said quite bluntly that he would donate his mobility allowance to his worst enemy if he could get his bladder and bowels to function reasonably. He was not bothered about them being normal, nothing so profound. Andy thought that 'profound' was not the correct word but did not say anything.

"I just want them to function on a regular basis without making life bloody miserable," he said.

When Andy asked him what he actually meant, he realised that he might have made a mistake as the elderly patient went into great detail regarding his lack of suitable bowel actions. Details were forthcoming regarding all the diets and concoctions that he had been encouraged to take over the years.

"And as for bladders," he said, while contorting his face

"One day everything is running freely and you feel fine, a few hours later you are shaking like a leaf with a bladder infection."

Andy tried to interrupt but it was to no avail.

"Over the years they keep trying different things, but at the end of the day it's best if you find the simplest route for yourself and stick to it. But don't think you will get away with it. One day you are fine the next day something has gone wrong and you have not a clue why. What you do need to learn is how to cope with the problems when they occur, for occur they will, that is something you can be sure of."

"Fucking infections," he continued, "I've been riddled with them, the bastards creep up on you. As soon as you suspect you have one, get some antibiotics. Your Doctor will probably say that you should not take them as you will become immune, but take my advice: if you are feeling ill take them as soon as you can, because when a bladder infection flares up it bloody hard going, you are hot and then cold, a nightmare."

That's good advice, thought Andy, who was glad when his visitor left the side of the bed. He thought that you only needed someone like that every day and you would be totally depressed. However, he had taken on board some of what was imparted.

He was being given advice upon how he should go about sorting out his future a few days earlier which on the face of it seemed very reasonable, until he had chance to think upon how the young fellow on a work experience scheme who had come to measure up the curtains around the bed space had suddenly become an expert upon rehabilitation.

He had decided to nod and grunt as a sign that he had taken on board the advice and appreciated it. The man fitting the curtains smiled in the knowledge that he had done his bit for humanity for the day. Andy quickly recognised that there was always advice available on how to go about doing almost everything; everyone had an opinion on the most obscure issues when it came to knowing what was good for you. The cleaners were great sources of information if they were asked, and if they were not asked they would still proffer an opinion, which was often of little value. They could tell you the best cleaning fluids or any new product that was supposed to remove dirt and grime with a minimum of effort. Unfortunately, their other information tended to be always useless or nearly useless with the exception of finding cheap holiday flights and cheap cigarettes. For some reason they had an exceptional understanding of such things. They had seen patients come and go over the years and they had conditioned themselves to that reality. Over time, patients seemed of little importance, they just happened to be residing at their place of employment. They did, on rare occasions, remember who had died in which bed. And such discussions were not prolonged, as it was not unusual to forget someone who had been admitted but had unfortunately passed away without causing a ripple so to speak.

What was important was knowing when the supervisor might be on her way round as she had the unpleasant habit of exerting her authority in front of everyone if something was not quite up to standard. This did not happen too often, as the standards were not very high; dirt and infections were rife, standards having drifted low over the years ensured that they were easy to attain. As the building aged and decayed, it seemed almost acceptable that it was not possible to clean the place; the visitors usually sighed deeply and blamed the government cuts on spending. When this was mentioned to a member of staff, they also sighed and nodded to indicate that they were trying to do their best in very difficult circumstances. Some visitors remarked that when matrons were in charge of things hospitals were much cleaner and standards higher. But in recent years it seemed as though no one really cared, and everyone just went around with the idea that whatever it was that might need doing, it was someone else's job and responsibility. Everyone therefore looked at one another and sighed in agreement and with a modicum of contentment. This was because they had recognised the perceived problems that pervaded the system, and thankfully, it was not their problem when it came to finding answers.

Andy could hear the nurses talking as they were about to change shifts. He was wide-awake by now and still uncomfortable, but he was in a mood for thinking as long as the thinking did not make too many demands upon his intellectual powers. A few weeks ago, he had unexpectedly had a visit from the hospital social worker who had brought with her another social worker from the Local Authority. He wondered if he would receive three upon their next visit, and tried to think of the collective noun for a number of social workers.

A confusion of social workers, that sounds reasonable, he thought, while instantly smiling. In fact it is better than reasonable - it's bloody good! The hospital social worker had already discussed with him his future housing needs:

"We need to move quickly as these things often take too long as different departments don't always get their meetings to coincide."

Andy had not given it a great deal of thought at the time but he now realised that housing was a major issue. The young women from the Authority seemed positive and helpful, but Andy was unsure as to her ability to get things moving. He had already learned that Local Government moved at its own speed, which did not really serve the publics interest, but tended to serve the interest of those who were already employed by the system. And if things were not going fast enough it was easy to blame the elected members, who in turn blamed the government of the day. When the two social workers were leaving, they had promised that they would prioritise his needs right away.

"As soon as something materialises, we'll inform you."

He politely thanked them and almost forgot what they had agreed within minutes of their departure; he had other things on his mind, nothing of real importance it should be stated but at the time the conversation did not seem particularly significant.

Wendy, one of his regular nurses, had informed him the day before that the social worker was coming down to see him later the following day. Andy had thought that he had better think clearly, as to what he thought he required or he might be pushed into something that was totally unsuitable.

"Do you know the social worker?" he asked Wendy.

"You know what social workers are like," said Wendy, at the

same time shrugging her shoulders, which supposedly indicated something, although Andy had no idea what.

Harry, who was in the adjacent bed, had already warned him that he had to be assertive now. "Tell them what you want before someone in the system decides what's suitable for you," Harry said, adding "clearly the system finds the simplest solution for them, and if you're not careful, you'll be stuck with something that you dislike from day one. And that's definitely not the right way to start out," he said.

This was said while emphasising the point by nodding his head and contorting his face into a scowl. Andy had come to recognise that a scowl from Harry indicated that he was being serious, and what he was imparting was factual. He had tried to scowl back to show his appreciation when he had first encountered Harry's scowls, but for some reason he could not achieve the desired effect. And he thought that Harry would think that he was taking the piss, which would definitely not assist matters as Harry's sense of humour was limited if he thought that he was at the receiving end of a joke or quip.

The week earlier big Freddy had also told him that he must find suitable accommodation, otherwise he might finish up like him, in the shit. Andy obviously asked him to expand, which had always been Freddy's intention whether he had been asked or not. He started in a moderate and controlled voice. "When I went home, it was a nightmare. My mother died and the family wanted their share of the house, and to cut a long story short I finished up in a home for the disabled.

"Social services said: 'Don't worry, they have a good record and they can look after you properly until we find you a suitable place and arrange a care package'. That was two years ago, I'm still waiting."

Andy was about to ask a question but Freddy was already ahead of him.

"The place is a prison, the staff are like warders yet they smile when the visitors appear, they're bloody hypocrites. It's a nice building in a very nice area but that's it, no one bloody cares, we're the residents and that's it. Once inside these places you lose your right to anything.

"Believe me," he said with some passion, "argue with one of

them and within minutes none of them'll speak to you. They can make your life a misery and they know it, they only relate to you as some kind of alien who should be grateful. Your family will pretend to themselves that you're there because it's the best place for you, social services will agree because it solved their problems, so they'il not be in a rush to get you out. Everyone closes their eyes to reality, no matter how the system bullshits the public, these places are crap, a national disgrace." He paused for a few seconds. "Having said that, I've come across a few people who actually enjoy the place but that's because they don't know any better, or they're so worn out trying to struggle on without any support. So take note: don't let the bastards send you to such a place saying it's only until they find something suitable.

"And I'll tell you something that might surprise you. In a short matter of time you lose any drive, assertiveness or dignity, When you get a visitor you hardly listen to what they have to say, at the back of your mind you're almost pleading with them to get you out of the place, but your self-respect won't let you, so you smile and say:, 'it's not so bad'. You have less real freedom than a criminal does, you're incarcerated out of sight of the public and no bugger cares. But of course you can't say anything no matter how desperate you become."

Andy responded as tactfully as he could. "I think I've got the gist of what you have said." Andy did not want to disagree with Freddy who at that moment looked menacing. Andy wondered if Freddy had been accurate and when he mentioned it to Harry, he was told that most residential or nursing homes were a disgrace but everyone pretended that they were fine and that way you could incarcerate people without feeling guilty.

"No one really wants to live in such places, we all want to stay at home with suitable care packages - it's not complicated, it's all very simple," at that point Harry laughed cynically.

Andy was about to say something when Harry indicated that he had not yet finished. "All governments have been unwilling to fund care in the community, they don't care about disability as basically we're a cost on society and we don't add a great deal to society by our existence." He scowled in a manner that suggested the appropriate level of accuracy was forthcoming.

"That's how they see it, we're not a threat to anyone, we're just a bloody problem so you can't expect much in those circumstances can you?" He did not allow Andy to reply. "And you'll never be surprised by something really good happening because one thing is certain, you're not going to get much from society; society is not understanding or generous but you'll find this out very quickly: forget any rubbish you might have seen on television, we're not wanted or desired - that is the reality. Of course, what I've said would be seen as the ramblings of a bitter and twisted disabled fellow who hasn't come to terms with his disability. If society cannot minimise what you're saying legitimately they'll try and ridicule you personally." He shrugged his shoulders at that point.

"You'll soon find out when people will tell you it's different now. Or you're bitter and that you're not being fair, etc. One other thing you'll soon find out is that fairness and life are strangers both outside and within this unit." Harry turned over feeling satisfied that he had delivered a very important message that was suitably depressing but accurate. "And one last point - those buggers who are supposed to keep a check on nursing homes and such like, they know what's going on and they're not willing to make any waves. They have their careers to think about. There are two main items that you must remember. The first being, how much is your care going to cost; the second is, where can we push him out of the way in order that the problem is solved? The politicians know that care in the community is a disgrace but if anyone complains all you get is a half-witted lying bastard of a minister stating how much the government has spent, and how wonderful everything is."

"Thanks, Harry, I really needed that."

That's really cheered me up and started the day off on a light note, thought Andy, any more bits of information like that and I might as well throw myself under a bus.

Harry told him "You need to understand the way things are, that way you might be able to prevent yourself being pushed around by the system. It's very similar to the old Soviet Gulag system. Once you're in the system you have to accept what is given out to you; you have no real choices, you have no power. But everything will be done with your best interests in mind."

Harry burst out laughing at that point. "I honestly think that some of the buggers who organise your life believe that it's for your own good," he said while shaking his head as though he could not really believe his last statement. "Try to keep out of the residential and care homes; they exist to make money; they're not interested in your wellbeing, they just need to keep the beds full. I knew a homeowner who gave his staff a pay rise. A couple of residents suddenly died and he didn't manage to get the beds filled right away. So he stopped the pay rise, which is how it works, sad really."

Andy was not happy with what he had heard so he allowed himself to think of other things. Time was slowly moving on and Andy then pondered upon the most pressing of questions. What would it be for breakfast? He already knew the answer, but for some masochistic reason he enjoyed toying with the idea that for some reason today it might be different. That a strange supernatural being with mystic powers had descended upon the kitchen, and decreed a full English breakfast for anyone whosoever desired one. This would include real fresh orange or tomato juice, not the stuff that comes in packets or tins. He then briefly thought about two smoked haddock fillets with two poached eggs on top, the yolks carefully split open and the golden liquid with a suitable viscosity would ooze over the lightly smoked fish. This, he had decided, was his favourite breakfast right now. He also would have a few slices of toast with thick cut marmalade that was dark and almost exotic in appearance, all very simple but healthy and tasty, he concluded, perhaps some fresh fruit would be appropriate. Breakfast could be the best meal of the day if it was prepared correctly, which was not difficult he thought, as he had always enjoyed cooking his own breakfast. He liked grapefruit with his breakfast but recently someone had told him how grapefruit could affect many drugs by increasing their potency, and not enough people were aware of this problem. He wondered how accurate this was and he decided that sometime he would look it up, as no one on the unit had heard about it when he had mentioned it, but until he knew for certain, he had decided that grapefruit was out, which was not a problem as such an item never appeared at meal times or any other time.

His mind temporarily allowed itself to drift onto pleasant thoughts. Waking up fully refreshed and feeling healthy, then getting up on a bright summer's morning and having a nice breakfast on the terrace, while watching the fishing boats coming back into the small harbour after spending the night out at sea. That's how it should be, he thought, the simple things in life are the best. He was going to allow himself to think along those lines when he realised that many of the so-called simple things were not at that moment within his reach, so he changed his train of thought before he had to face reality, which was not quite so desirable. Although he knew that he was paralyzed he did not like it or even thinking about it at times. Such thoughts affected his moods so he tried to put them to the back of his mind. However, he was intelligent and he recognised that at some period, he would have to think about his future, but for the moment, he was not going to allow such thoughts into his mind and disturb his limited comfort.

Caroline and Wendy suddenly arrived at his bedside, and without speaking pulled the curtains around him with a noise that startled him. Caroline then pulled the bedcovers back exposing his upper body and abdomen. Wendy was at the same time pulling the bedclothes up from the bottom in order that they met in the middle conferring a modicum of dignity on the unusually undignified proceedings.

"Take your hands from out of the covers we don't know what you might get up to. What a horrible sight! Is it still alive?" said Wendy, while sighing loudly. She grimaced.

"It looks as though it has decomposed. It should have a health warning; it must be toxic!" added Caroline while laughing.

Andy was not the sort of person who accepted someone having a laugh at his expense. "Good morning you churls, you mindless minions and poltroons," said Andy sarcastically, but this was ignored. "I can see it is my lucky day - it's the dream team again, the mighty duo Noddy and Big arse. Or Laurel and Hardy might be more appropriate considering your shapes and state of physical decay, and not forgetting your ages," continued Andy.

They did not rise to the bait and his comments were duly ignored but he would persist until he obtained a suitable response that would illicit an atmosphere for an argument. Wendy had to ask the question while looking at Caroline.

"What's a poltroon?" Caroline looked bemused for a moment, "I think they live in caves, or perhaps the jungle."

Andy just groaned out loud.

Wendy placed the partially full drainage bag on the bed. The urine quickly flowed to the end that slightly hung over the bed. The bag started to move but Wendy caught it before it had chance to slip off the bed. "Got it just in time! That could have damaged you a bit," she said triumphantly while looking at Andy.

She continued, "I should have emptied it first to be on the safe side, but who cares about little items like that nowadays?"

Andy just shuddered at the thought of the partially full bag quickly descending to the floor while still firmly attached to his catheter. He had by now become familiar with such occurrences but when they happened it still remained a frightening experience. He had a terrible vision of the catheter being ripped out and blood flowing profusely from his mutilated penis, which was an appendage he treasured and would have gone to great lengths to maintain in good working order.

"Just try and be careful will you! Just look and think what you are doing, that could have been damaging," said Andy, not able to disguise his concern.

Wendy reassured him that he had nothing whatsoever to worry about. Noddy and big arse were in full control and she had caught the bag easily. And if he asked her nicely, she would juggle with it just to show him how good her hand coordination was.

"I was captain of the schools netball team. I could toss this urine bag at least fifteen feet through a hoop if necessary!."

"Presumably, you obtained some kind of qualification in that pursuit that allowed you to take up nursing?" said Andy sarcastically.

Andy was definitely not impressed by her flippant attitude and her inability to respond in a reasonably reassuring manner to his genuine concern.

They just do not give a bollocks, they could have ripped my dick off, he said to himself. He once again winced at the thought. He did not mind the sight of blood as long as it was someone else's. Caroline quickly pulled Andy towards her pressing his face and shoulders against her body while Wendy pulled hard upon the turning sheet. Andy's senses were briefly aroused; he thought Caroline must have been using baby powder, or something similar that he had not smelled for years. He liked the feminine smell of her. Before he could mention it, Caroline interrupted.

"The top sheet is in a mess it will have to be straightened out - god knows why you cannot keep tidy in bed," she said in mock exasperation.

"It'll be fine when I pull the turning sheet through a bit further," said Wendy, while at the same time pulling as hard as she could.

"Protecting ones back is sensible," she said, "but these turning sheets are bloody useless for turning someone right onto their side." Her anger was genuine knowing that patients spent a long time in one position and getting them comfortable was important.

"I'm not comfortable at all, it's a mess, the whole bed's a fucking mess" protested Andy very loudly and angrily.

Neither Caroline nor Wendy said anything. He was starting to feel very angry, sensing that they were totally ignoring him and about to leave him in an unacceptably dishevelled state.

"If I had a bowel action in bed you would have done a proper job," he muttered belligerently but loud enough for them to clearly hear him. He then thought that even in such circumstances they still might still have left him. At that moment he was not feeling very happy with the world.

"What, little man has woken up the wrong side out?" said Wendy mockingly.

Wendy then turned and asked Caroline: "Did you buy the new coat you mentioned at the weekend?"

"No," Caroline said, "I just couldn't make my mind up about the colour."

"I cannot believe what I'm hearing!" said Andy loudly.

"Bugger your coat, and concentrate upon my needs, and do not talk over me in future! It's bad manners - or didn't anyone inform you when you did your training? Training, I nearly forgot, you have a cycling certificate and a certificate for the hundred yards breaststroke."

Wendy said "I have a badge for lighting campfires by rubbing two boy scouts together. And I had special individual training from our guide leader. She was the first to teach me how to be a good nurse; she used to let me rub all the sore places on her body."

At that point Wendy just smiled. "I rubbed her sore bits so hard one day I thought that I'd killed her." Andy and Caroline suddenly took notice. Wendy, keeping a straight face, said, "She suddenly shouted out, 'Oh god I'm coming'."

A look of incredulity passed across Caroline's face. Andy just groaned loudly. Wendy just stared at them and shrugged her shoulders.

"I thought it was funny; the problem with you is that you don't have a sense of humour."

Andy and Caroline looked at each other, but said nothing. Caroline paused and then asked:

"Andy, do you want to be washed before breakfast?"

She also added "Your language has deteriorated in recent days and that if you required a response then interact accordingly and not like a spoiled child."

He just grunted thinking that they were enjoying themselves. She then added that they were going to be short staffed and it was going to be a busy day. Andy's first thought was to say:

"No, I bloody well would not get up! I just wanted to be more comfortable," but it dawned upon him that if he agreed he would at the same time be able to get his sheets sorted out. To their obvious satisfaction and surprise Andy agreed, everyone smiled a satisfactory smile and Caroline went to get the hot water. Washing was generally one of the more pleasurable experiences as far as Andy was concerned. Although he could only feel a relatively small percentage of his body, it was an important percentage, his head and shoulders.

"Hell," he exclaimed loudly. The warm water made him flinch as though he had been half expecting cold water. His flesh for some reason now seemed more sensitive to most kinds of stimulation. Wendy was as gentle as possible, trying hard not to let her fingers press the face cloth into Andy's eyes but somehow she did not quite succeed. Andy did not bother saying anything; he knew that resistance of any kind was useless.

Complaints during the procedure of being washed or any other regular process were always rather pointless. He had quickly learned this lesson when he complained to a male member of staff who was feeding him.

"Y'know you'd do better to look what you're doing, and you might then get the food into my mouth."

It must be said that the member of staff did have the most disconcerting habit of constantly straining to listen to other people's conversations while feeding a patient. Andy's complaint had for some reason annoyed the member of staff who then promptly tried to shovel the food into Andy's mouth as quickly as possible. Some of the food spilled and ran down his chin. This was wiped off and the process would begin again. It had crossed Andy's mind that if the positions were reversed what would the nurse say? He would be furious, knowing his personality, thought Andy. But he was not in that position and probably never would be. Therefore, in his view justice would never be seen to be done. He thought this was definitely an unfair aspect of life but something to be expected.

He had plenty of time to think about these things and they constantly irritated him. He would definitely have enjoyed some suitable form of painful retribution. And for the life of him he could not understand why such individuals were so insensitive and bloody-minded, they must be born like that he concluded. He said to himself angrily after another incident that they are 'insensitive fucking morons', who gravitate to positions where they have a level of power over vulnerable people that is unwarranted by their ability. He was not really happy with that thought, although deep down he believed it to be true in some cases. He then tried to be fair and reasonable by saying to himself that he would not want their job looking after difficult individuals who were never satisfied, but he knew that he did not really mean it.

Then his mind drifted back to his studies which now seemed a long time ago, although it was only a relatively short time ago. He thought about what he had read about institutions and the practices that existed in some establishments. He had originally thought that many such insensitive and stigmatising practices existed because of the ignorance of the carers or those in charge. He now realised that the insensitivity was brought about by many variables, which were probably a little more complicated than he had previously thought. He also knew that irrespective of any variables there was no excuse for staff to treat patients in such an off-hand manner as though any action was acceptable, and that nothing really mattered anymore as though almost anything was good enough. Andy tried to comfort himself with the thought that their actions could be excused because that was the way they lived and acted at home, and they just did not know any better. However much he tried, he could not convince himself that this was true, as he often overheard staff members describing events that were in direct contradiction to their practices while at work. He had argued the previous day with Harry about the illogical and unacceptable practices in the health service while adding,

"If they talked to you, or treat you like this when you were not a patient, you just would not tolerate it."

Harry thought for a moment then said

"The health service is different, you are expected to be grateful. God has placed you in this grovelling position and you have to accept it. You have found your place in society. It's the old protestant work ethic!" added Harry, while laughing.

"You have been disabled because God decrees it and subsequently it's justified to treat you like shit. Unless you have a lot of money of course, that tends to make a difference. These highly trained individuals are not employed like ordinary beings; theirs is a vocation," he said with sarcasm.

"Except, of course, in certain circumstances, which might effect in some small way their wellbeing or interests. Just try to get someone to do something for you a few minutes before they're due to go off duty."

He stared at Andy and gestured with his hands.

"I accept that I'm generalising. Some are better than others, just sensibly and quietly getting on with their work in a reasonable manner. That's all that I want from them and perhaps a little appreciation, we are after all providing them with a living. They don't work for nothing, otherwise we should be duly grateful; they're not volunteers working free for a charity," said Harry who was content with his words of wisdom.

Wendy held tightly onto his legs, which suddenly wanted to bend instead of laying flat on the bed. One leg suddenly retracted fast and glanced against the side of Caroline's cheek, she pulled back quickly and winced in pain.

"Wendy, hold his legs firmly! I don't want to explain how I got a black eye from someone's knee while attempting to wash their scrotum!."

Wendy laughingly agreed

"That could take a bit of explaining," adding "it's the nearest you've been to a man's balls in some time."

"That's totally unprofessional of you! You shouldn't talk like that in front of young innocent patients who expect a high standard from us," said Caroline in mock horror.

"I know" Wendy said, placing her hand over her mouth, at the same time smiling at Andy in an apologetic manner that lacked any degree of sincerity.

Andy liked Caroline; he felt comfortable with her attending to him but for some perverse reason he still wished that, his knee had caught her a little harder even if it wasn't very hard. He put his thoughts down to his present frustration and relative helplessness.

"You need your toe nails cutting," said Wendy. "Cut them, then, or is it beyond your ability?" replied Andy with some disinterest.

"You need the chiropodist to do it properly and she usually takes about a week to get here once we've notified her."

Andy was tempted to ask How far does she have to travel?, but once again he refrained, realising that it would be pointless. It seemed such a simple task to have ones toenails cut he thought, but evidently, once in hospital, the whole process takes on a different level of importance. Must be something to do with time and relativity, he thought. He continued his inane thoughts: Perhaps it could be the mass of the nails in question and their gravitational pull upon other objects that require expertise to deal with them.

He tried hard to remember a simple formula concerning gravity, mass and distance, and what was it? He could not think for the moment and then wondered how something like that, which he had known for years, had slipped his mind.

"Why cannot one of you highly trained and highly paid 'Angels of Mercy' cut my toenails?" asked Andy in mock humility.

"Don't be such a little clever sod, we're not supposed to. I cannot stand young ungrateful patients who know little or nothing about our profession," said Wendy.

"You're getting the best possible treatment that the health service provides, and in all modesty you have the finest of nurses looking after every whim of yours."

"Well, nearly every whim," added Caroline while at the same time giving Andy a knowing look, which told him not to add anything to her remark.

"What a load of crap! Have you rehearsed that rubbish or do you trot it out for all the patients who can see your inadequacies?."

Caroline explained: "Your nails are not in good condition, and they really need the attention of a chiropodist."

He quickly replied "Yeah, they're only in a bad condition 'cos I've been in hospital over four months and nobody's bothered to do anything with them, or haven't you realised that small point?"

He was feeling annoyed at their unwillingness to take on any responsibility for something that he thought was within there remit.

"Just shut up will you and stop moaning! I'll do them when we have finished washing you," said Caroline, while pretending to be annoyed.

Caroline liked Andy; he had a distinct personality that made him just that bit different to many of the younger patients, and she was happy to do whatever was necessary in order to make him comfortable. Her experience told her that many of the frequent problems and disagreements between staff and patients existed because of a general lack of understanding, which was often coupled with a disinterest in the needs of the individual. She was not happy about this situation but she knew that there was little that she could do to change matters. If there were to be changes, not only had they to be imposed from above, they also needed the full co-operation of the staff. She also knew that some members of staff would never co-operate on the principle that they might be required to think a little harder about the patients needs. The same thoughts kept coming back into her mind. It was just a job to many of them, and patients' needs were incidental. A few years ago, this situation would have made both her and Wendy angry, but their anger had dissipated over time. She had made her mind up that she would try to retain a good standard of care irrespective of whatever anyone else did.

She had not found it easy to sustain this self-imposed standard, as everything seemed to be against it. More often or not the major problem was those members of staff who could always find a difficulty where one did not exist. It was as though life had somehow deliberately treated them badly, and now they existed only to make other peoples' lives as miserable and meaningless as their own, if they were given the opportunity. They were very sad people, she thought, but they were also a liability and at times even dangerous. What was even worse was her belief that such people were on the increase.

She had often asked herself why such people had chosen nursing as a profession when they seemingly disliked ill or disabled people. She had concluded reluctantly that it gave them a sense of power when they were in control of people who were relatively helpless most of the time. She also thought that they were lacking something in their lives, but she was not a psychologist and she did not know what it was that was lacking. When she was thinking along those lines, she also kept asking herself: Why was she allowing the same thoughts and questions to go through her mind? It was almost the same thoughts day after day and it had started to worry her. These thoughts were not doing anyone any good, least of all herself. She knew that she had to find a life outside of the hospital. There was a world out there, with lots of things happening, and she wanted to be part of it. But when it came to thinking about any radical steps, she could not bring herself to take that necessary first step.

She had recently pondered on what she was really missing in her life. She had recognised that time was moving quickly and no matter how much thought she had given to the situation she was not really sure what she wanted. It would sometimes be nice, she thought, if someone would take an interest in her and help her make a few decisions. She wanted some support and some understanding. She also desired some gentle tender care.

When she felt like this, it made her quiet and withdrawn for a while. She wanted to think at length about her situation during these times. Fortunately, she thought the lack of time and the pressure of her work prevented this from happening, which was almost a relief to her.

At the same time, the thought came into her head that times had changed and women were no longer passive individuals; if you wanted something then you had to go out and get it, and if you did not then it was not anyone else's fault. The thought of this was of no comfort to her as doing something of that nature was just not her style. She had listened to her colleagues talking about their domestic lives and their love lives and decided that she would be more discriminating than most of them. She wasn't being critical or judgemental, it was just how she felt. Sometimes when she was feeling lonely, she wished that she could be different. If she could think differently, life might become easier. But if that meant lowering her standards and beliefs, she then quickly thought that it was not worth it in the long run. I'm chained down and imprisoned, trapped with my attitudes and my beliefs, she said to herself in exasperation. I'm not a child of my generation, but a Victorian throw-back trapped by an out-of-date morality. That was the way I was brought up; those were the standard values that I had to listen to day after day. She pondered for a while upon her last thought. If necessary, she thought that it might be possible to change one or two things as she was a realist, and she knew that in most circumstances she was quite capable of change. But she always decided that in the long run you have to be true to yourself otherwise you will not be really happy, it will be a form of pretence and living a lie. She shrugged her shoulders and said something under her breath that could not be discerned by those near by.

Wendy had moved on to the next bed while Caroline set about cutting Andy's toenails.

"You are a witness to the great toe nail cutting ceremony. Do you know of a good solicitor?" said Andy in a loud voice hoping that Harry could hear him.

"You can save the clipping and make a necklace out of them if you want."

There was no response from Harry.

"He's never awake when you bloody well need him, but if you don't want to talk he'll talk forever," said Andy in frustration.

He turned towards Caroline. "What's it like outside?" he enquired in a tone of voice that did not imply any serious interest

But Caroline obligingly replied, realising that spending a few months in bed in the same room must be tedious and boring in the extreme. Subsequently, any information regarding what was going on outside had to be welcome.

"It's not a brilliant day, a bit colder than it should be, but it's not going to rain, at least I don't think so, as my washing is out," she added.

"I don't really give a toss," said Andy under his breath.

Caroline heard him and told him that she had to go out later that afternoon and if it rained, she would not enjoy it one little bit. She emphasised the last phrase, which was intended to be a mild rebuke. This did not bother Andy as he was now looking carefully at Caroline without her knowing it. He scrutinised her well-defined bone structure and wondered why he had not really noticed this before. She has good bones, he thought and she will age well. He then looked at her eyes as best he could although she was sideways on to him. For some reason he could not recall their colour. Her hair is nicely shaped, he thought, cleverly cut in a style that clung to her head and yet it appeared longer than it really was when she moved. He was indulging himself now and enjoying it in a somewhat modest kind of way; it did not obtain a level that could be called exciting, but it was pleasurable for all of that. He recognised that he was starting to fancy her and wondered why he had not given this much thought on previous occasions.

He indulged himself, he thought that he would really like to slowly take her clothes off and fuck her, just there and then; his present feelings were such that he was not into making love or anything so subtle, and there was nothing about his thoughts that exuded sensitivity or even affection. It's probably the crisp white sheets and the warm smell of her body, he thought. He also thought that she looked somehow almost innocent, clean and wholesome, he imagined that in his hands she would be passionate and giving and totally unable to resist any of his demands. He was going to add the word rampant, but he realised that was over the top even for such a short-lived fantasy. Perhaps one day he might surprise her. However, he was sure that it was better than just thinking about breakfast, which was imminent.

His mind quickly jumped back to Caroline. Andy then wondered what she looked like in normal clothes. He tried to imagine it but for some reason he was unable to do so. It seemed that the nurse's characterless uniform had become embedded in his mind. It was as though this is how these people are supposed to look, and subsequently they cannot look any different. He knew that this was illogical and that the young woman before him changed her clothes before going home. She looked and dressed similar to her peers. It was just that the uniform was what it said it was: 'uniformity'; a shapeless garment that helped categorise a group of people. He tried once again to visualise her in normal clothing and then in some sexually attractive underwear. He wanted to see her in black stockings; he then thought about black leather, which he realised, was very predictable and therefore lacking in imagination. He kept trying different combinations of garments while having her pose for him provocatively. He deliberately wanted to feel aroused while looking at her.

He was surprised when for some unknown reason he found that he just could not do it, his mind would not allow him the concentration that was required, and it then dawned on him that he should not have to concentrate as such thoughts normally arrived automatically. What is wrong? All the bits and pieces are still there, he said to himself. This really disappointed him and brought about a moments concern. He had heard rumours that when in the army they had added something to the tea that lowered the sex drive. He thought that they might be doing the same on the unit. He then decided that such a thought was ridiculous. What would be the point and the system would not waste the money just to minimise a person's stress due to sexual abstinence. Caroline suddenly realised that she was being carefully observed and asked

"What are you looking at?"

Andy at that moment could not think of a sharp witty response, and he was reluctant to tell her the truth as he thought that he might not like her response.

"Have you ever thought of lightening your hair? Going blond for a while?"

He was reasonably pleased with his answer, which was nice and quick without disclosing his recent desires.

Caroline could not answer right away as his answer was unexpected because of its ordinariness. This caused her some momentary suspicion knowing from experience how young male patients tended to think, and Andy was often quicker with a riposte than most. She was thinking about asking him why he had asked her. For some unknown reason she was interested in his interest in her, even if it was something as tentative as the colour of her hair. She put her hand up and touched the side of her hair.

"I used to have a few blond highlights a couple of years back, but I didn't like the look of my hair when they were fading or growing out," she said.

Andy groaned to himself, then wished he had never mentioned her hair. He tried to think of something that would turn the conversation onto something more interesting. Caroline continued without noticing the obvious bored expression on Andy's face.

"I used to have my hair long, in fact I've been thinking of growing it long again," she continued.

"That's wonderful, really nice. I used to have a beard," said Andy with some obvious sarcasm.

Caroline made a gesture of slapping his leg. "Don't be so rude or I won't cut your nails on the other foot, in fact my fingers might just give a little twitch and slice off the end of your big toe if you're not careful."

"You can slice off my balls if you want," said Andy childishly while quickly descending into a darker and more miserable mood.

Caroline had recognised Andy's change of tone as she had witnessed this before with many other patients. She had to decide whether to let it pass or should she ask him what was wrong. She thought that she should ask him but she also knew that she had not really the time to listen to his problems. Besides, she had more than likely heard it all many times before.

She finally decided that she would ignore the remark but if the opportunity arose then she would listen to him later during the day. She said this to herself, knowing in reality that it was more than likely that she would find a reason not to do this. She had a good idea of what he was going to say and what line he would take. She knew that she had no answers that would help him. She never enjoyed sitting and talking with relatively new patients. It was hard for her to evade some of the leading questions that were always going to be asked, even if the were hidden behind some innocuous sounding enquiry. As she liked Andy, it would be more difficult for her to discuss anything in depth that was to do with his disability or his future. She thought that she could possibly deal with some of the emotional issues that he would more than likely present her with during the coming weeks as she had the ability to be warm, gentle, and understanding. And she knew that a little understanding was often what a patient wanted, just someone to talk or show an interest in his or her feelings at that moment.

Her experience had taught her that patients did not really expect or require complete answers to all of their questions. They often wanted someone to listen, someone to share their immediate fears and apprehension. To be there to listen without criticism or dismissing what they were saying as being of no consequence. And to recognise that to that patient at that particular time their thoughts and fears were felt very strongly regarding whatever it was they were concerned about. To them it was very important and they felt the need to express their feelings to someone in whom they could some trust. Caroline thought that if she had the time and the skills to do the job as it should be done the patients would have a more acceptable understanding of their future trials and tribulations.

She had realised a long time ago that communication and understanding were a major problem on the unit. It had been discussed many times over the years with no successful outcome. In discussion, there was even a minority of nurses who said that it was not part of their job to discuss such things with patients; they employed a psychologist to deal with such problems. They said that there was little enough time to do what they already had to do without seeking any extra work. She could not agree with them on this point. Nor could she come up with a suitable solution to the problem, as she did not have the time or the expertise. She also knew it was easier for her if she avoided some issues, but that did not help the patients and this lack of a solution to what seemed a simple problem frustrated her. She had argued the point that talking to a psychologist in some cases was just off-putting to some patients as they equated psychologists with psychiatrists and adverse mental conditions. Subsequently they were automatically very careful when talking to a psychologist about anything in the belief that the psychologist would label them, or pronounce that they had a particular mental condition that required a dose of something that would increase any stigma they might already be feeling.

At times like this, she often thought that the unit was similar to a large rowing boat with two sets of people operating the oars, but pulling in different directions. The boat was remaining afloat but it wasn't getting anywhere irrespective of how hard they pulled.

Andy had wished that he had not made the remark about cutting his balls off, as it seemed a childish response to a relatively normal situation. He wondered why he had said it. For a moment, he could not decide if he wanted some form of sympathetic response, which in the circumstances he would more than likely have found patronising. On the other hand, was he just trying to shock Caroline in order to see what her reaction would be? He thought about it for a short while and decided that he had said it out of boredom. That it just might, given a bit of luck elicited, a novel or different response that he could at least argue over. He still felt annoyed with himself as it had made him sound immature and stupid.

"How about washing my hair?" he asked. Caroline looked at him thoughtfully.

"Can you wait till after breakfast?" she replied.

"Of course I can, that is if you won't forget" said Andy.

He continued, quickly getting back into his stride,

"It's surprising how often, when someone wants something doing other than the everyday routine, he or she never sees you again for the rest of the day. That is, except when you are obviously busy with meals or another patient. It's as though there is a magic formula, which comes into operation when someone ask for something."

Caroline gave him a scathing look unsure whether or not he really meant what he said or whether he was just trying to wind her up.

"There are other patients who require attention," said Caroline in a harsher tone.

Andy was pleased that she had taken the bait and had given him the opportunity to respond at length.

"That's bloody rubbish! Absolute crap!" said Andy, while becoming more animated and starting to enjoy himself.

"Anything slightly off of the routine and you just don't want to do it, that's the truth," said Andy, who was starting to enjoy himself even more as he was now really getting into his stride.

Caroline was about to say something but he continued before she could respond.

"You might as well all be packing Mars bars here or picking turnips," he continued.

"We're supposed to be individuals with individual care plans yet we're all treated the same. One of you lot happens to be my key nurse, or has the system changed through the night? One of you is supposed to instruct the others with regard to my needs and desires, or have I got it wrong."

Caroline saw her opportunity and jumped in. "Are you saying that you should not all be treated the same and that some patients should get better treatment than others?" she said, looking at him directly.

She said this knowing that this was not what he really meant, but turning the situation around so that he would have to explain what he meant. She also knew at the same time he would be becoming irritated by knowing that she fully knew what he really meant. He was irritated at her quick response as it left him with no advantage. He attempted to recover the situation.

"If you don't fully understand what I mean, then I'm wasting my time trying to discuss it with you" he replied,

"Perhaps you should ask one of your fellow workers to explain it to you in simplistic terms."

She smiled at him, which annoyed him considerably. "In that

case, you've had your treatment! There are others who are waiting to be turned and washed."

With that, she smiled again at Andy and then quickly moved down the room and joined Wendy before he had chance to say anything else.

Andy knew that he had let her off the hook, which was not his usual style. He could have tightened his grip on the argument but he had not done so. He thought 'bugger it!'. There will be time before the day is over. He closed his eyes and thought that in a few minutes breakfast would be coming round. He was feeling hungry although previous experience had told him that the food was always lacking in taste and there was no real choice at breakfast. In fact, breakfast was usually awful. Later during the day, someone might venture to the shops where something decent to eat might be obtained. He comforted himself with that thought.

"When I receive proper attention, and I look clean, and decent I'll venture down town and do a little clubbing one night," he said, while awaiting a suitable response.

"I might take one of you socially under-privileged types with me if you're lucky and cooperative," he added.

Caroline was about to say something when her better judgement restrained her, she knew that he was waiting to have an argument.

Andy was expecting a suitable response but nothing was forthcoming which really disappointed him but he was not willing to give up easily.

"I might take one of you born-again virgins down town if you're good," he said loudly.

There was still no response, which disappointed him even more so, but he was still not willing to give up, so...

"Looking at you both, you'd better take up my offer as others won't be so charitable" he then quickly added,

"You're all nearing your sell-by-date! Don't forget that the offer won't be there forever."

"You should be so lucky! You've never been out with anyone as sophisticated as us, you just would not come up to our standards" said Wendy unwilling to let him have the last word.

At that point, Andy burst out laughing before telling her that they had no standards worthy of mention.

"And one other point you should know about, we've carefully observed all of you and we all know who does the work and who doesn't. We recognise the shifty and the work-shy types who pretend that they're busy. And when it comes to nominating the nurse of the year, we know who will and who won't get our nominations."

Harry's attention was gained at the mention of the nurse of the year award.

"What's this nurse of the year thing?" said Harry.

"Don't worry about it!," said Andy quietly, then added,

"It doesn't exist. I've just thought of it."

Harry understood, and for some reason felt pleased at Andy's action.

"It's good to see that you are slipping into the correct frame of mind when trying to converse with the paid help," he said while smiling.

"Actually, this nurse of the year award is a bloody good idea. It doesn't exist. I just thought of it," said Andy looking bemused at Harry's comment.

"It's a good idea. Just listen, take note, listen, and learn, this is a valuable lesson. We get the patients and ex-patients to vote for whom they think is best nurse. And we give a prize, well, say three prizes, otherwise it won't work."

Andy still looked bemused.

" What are you going on about? Your mind isn't functioning properly, explain your thoughts," he asked while wondering what the hell Harry was talking about. Harry smiled a smile of satisfaction,

"It's simple really, so bloody simple. We tell them there are good prizes awaiting the best three nurses, something worthwhile and desirable and they'll try like hell to win while pretending that they are not interested. Obviously, it'll only work for a few weeks before someone asks when the judging will take place."

Harry placed his hands at the back of his head and smiled to himself.

"We can offer a weekend for two in Paris, and a shopping weekend in London, plus for third place a couple of nights somewhere else, it doesn't matter really." said Harry pleased with himself.

"It sounds good very good but there seems to be a small flaw in this interesting proposal. Who's going to provide these not inexpensive prizes?" asked Andy while looking worried at the possibility that he might be asked to contribute.

"What prizes?" said Harry looking surprised.

"There are no prizes! Don't be silly. You won't get me providing prizes for this bunch. They only need to think that there are. Just long enough until I get out of here, it's a bloody good idea! You deserve credit for it," said Harry laughing.

"We'll announce it tomorrow. Give it a full roll of drums. Well actually it'll be better if we get some other poor bugger to announce it then he can take the shit when it all falls through. It's a good start to the day; I'm now going to tease them with my gold vote."

"What on earth is a gold vote?" said Andy looking confused again.

Harry smiled at him a smile of superiority.

"I've just thought of it. A brilliant idea, even if I say so myself. But don't worry, the main idea is ours, but the credit is yours. I don't want you to think that I'm usurping your idea. The golden vote applies to patients who are on the unit now but have been disabled over ten years, which gives them three votes to ordinary voters' one vote. It's bloody good isn't it?" said Harry feeling pleased with himself

"It sounds better the more I think about it. It means that they're more likely to be nicer to us older patients than you new ones."

Andy did not like the sound of that and protested right away. "If it's my idea, then I also should have a golden vote," he said with suitable conviction.

Harry pulled his face a few times murmured something then finally agreed, as it seemed fair in the circumstances.

"We'll need a specimen voting slip. We can run one off a computer at OT – it'll help give credibility to the scheme. We could enjoy this," said Harry, who looked content at the prospect.

"I'd like to be a fly on the wall when they find out, god, they'll not be pleased. "

"Slow down! We've only just thought this up and you've already reached the conclusion," said Andy trying to keep up with Harry's thoughts.

"Don't worry! This is the sort of thing that I'm good at. It'll work like a well-oiled machine. Just remember, we don't want to be here at the end, because they'll seek retribution from some poor bugger, and one thing is sure, it's not going to be me."

"Do you want two sausages, or one with your beans?," asked Tony in a loud booming voice that carried throughout the main unit area.

"Can you shout a little louder?" said Andy, "So the whole fucking hospital can hear you."

"You'll not get any breakfast if you go on like that, you naughty rude little man," shouted Tony in response.

"Give him two large sausages - he's just that difficult side-out this morning" added Caroline."

"The beans will do him good. Give him plenty of beans, they'll add to the wind he's already expelling."

"We'll tell you where to insert the sausages," added Wendy who had heard some of the proceedings. Andy was annoyed that everyone was getting in on the act at his expense.

"They probably make better suppositories than they make food anyway," he added quietly.

He could not let statements of that nature go unanswered.

"What wind am I already expelling?" he asked.

Tony thought before answering. "You're full of wind. You never shut up and you're always complaining."

"Bollocks!" said Andy expressing a level of indignation,

"You're talking a load of bollocks as per usual, besides you're just an untrained minion, a male scullion from bellow stairs, a member of the lower classes, a distributor of sausages and urine drainage bags, so what do you know or understand about anything?."

He would not like, that thought Andy, with some modicum of satisfaction.

Tony brought over the plate and sat himself down at the side of the bed. He glared at Andy and said.

"Before you start to say anything, don't. I had a hard night last night, and I'm not in the mood."

"He was a big boy was he?" said Andy sarcastically. He continued, "be honest you went without again, he got away and you didn't get any."

"Who in their right mind would go with you"?. Fortunately Andy was used to Tony and his somewhat different personality which meant that he could take Tony seriously or not, whichever he chose the result would usually be the same. After some prolonged banter they would both settle down to the task in question and Tony would feed Andy his breakfast.

"You couldn't find yourself a decent fellow then" said Andy in a more accommodating tone. He continued,

"If I was gay I wouldn't fancy you either." He paused for a few seconds and gazed at Tony. "In fact you could be described as being somewhat ugly, not the sexy raw ugly that some individuals display, but just plain ordinary ugly."

"But don't take it personally! Someone out there might be short-sighted and think you look almost acceptable, or they might be charitable."

Tony just grunted knowing that there was some truth in what Andy had said. Tony and Andy were very different, but they had become used to each other. They enjoyed the banter that went on between them, generally insulting each other but it was harmless and lightened the proceedings for anyone in earshot.

"We might get you up early today," said Tony in a tone that he knew would gain a negative response.

Andy said "I've already been told that the staff are busy, therefore I'm not getting up early, so you're talking a load of bollocks."

Tony continued "They'd go out of their way just to ensure that you'd be the first to get up." He said this while missing Andy's mouth with the fork that then caught Andy's left cheek.

"Sorry about that," said Tony who was trying to listen in to someone else's conversation.

"How can you manage to miss a mouth so big?" shouted Wendy who had once again observed the proceedings while feeding someone across the room. Andy muttered an obscenity under his breath while at the same time threatening to stick the fork in her arse if he had the opportunity. Someone from further down the unit shouted that the target was impossible to miss.

Andy was about to respond, but Tony stopped him from saying anything else by pushing more beans into his mouth.

"My bottom is not so big," said Wendy, while trying hard to peer over her shoulder just to convince herself.

"Like a young Hippo!" said someone further down the room.

"You have a wonderful bottom, just like a Gibbon or a baboon," said a passing male nurse who was wheeling a patient down to the sluice. There was a consensus that her bottom was of a shape and mass that had a gravitational pull similar to the moon. And that she should never be allowed near the coast as she would affect the tide. Her only response was to threaten everyone with an enema. Whereupon, all the patients said 'yes please'.

Tony said "Although I'm not a patient I'll go first to set a good example upon how to receive such forms of treatment to ones rear end in a proper and dignified manner."

"There, there," said Tony "didn't you enjoy your beans then?"

"Just fuck off! will you," muttered Andy who would have liked at that moment to hit Tony over the head with the plate.

"Talk to me like that and I'll not feed you again," said Tony, adding emphasis to his statement by distorting his face while others within earshot all said, boohoo! in unison.

"I should be so lucky, and make sure you wash your hands before feeding me next time. I don't know what you have been doing and to whom," added Andy as his parting shot.

"I wouldn't dare tell you," said Tony while attempting a smile.

"You don't have to tell me you only dream of it. No one out there would come near you. The only time you'll get your share of any action is when you go on holiday to those resorts full of perverts." Andy was satisfied that he had managed to have the last word.

Thank God another breakfast is over he thought, he had originally almost stopped eating some weeks back as he had found the whole process degrading. He simply hated the idea of having to lay there unable to feed himself, while some seemingly non-caring individual shovelled whatever the fork came in contact with into his mouth. Not every forkful managed to enter the appropriate aperture, and to his total dismay and anger, this usually caused some amusement to the carer. Who, it must be said in fairness, was bored by having to feed people. Feeding now seemed a chore, something that had to be done, but it was more boring for some carers or nurses who did not fully understand its importance.

Tony stood up at the side of the bed and shouted to Caroline and Wendy who were washing another patient at the far end of the room.

"What are we doing with him now?" shouted Tony while pointing down at Andy.

"He cannot get up yet," shouted Caroline in a voice that echoed around the room. "His skin was red last night and it needs watching."

Andy's attention was instantly on beacon two. "No one told me that," he said, looking bewildered but quickly joining in the conversation.

"I'll leave him until later on," replied Tony.

Andy felt perplexed for the moment. "Just a minute you two," he said in a tone of voice that commanded attention. He continued in a loud voice, "nobody mentioned to me that my skin was red," he said this while containing his anger.

"Don't blame me," said Wendy, "it's in the book and presumably it'll be in the report." She quickly added that Caroline and she had left the office before the report was finished, but it had been mentioned that it was in the book under 'Andy's red arse'. She found it impossible to stifle a laugh at that point and neither could Caroline who explained to Andy that evidently he must have been a bit red last night.

She added that "Everything seemed fine this morning and it was probably a one off. But we'll keep an eye on it."

"You should have told me what the situation is. It's my body and I want to know what's happening to it," said Andy.

Caroline moved to the bottom of his bed and told him "If there'd been anything I would've told you." To make sure that there was not going to be an unwanted response, she added "I wouldn't allow anything of that nature to happen without telling you. And if you think that I'd keep something like that from you, then I'm disappointed in your opinion of me." Andy tried to think of a suitable reply without it making him look foolish, but he could not think quickly enough. He could not be absolutely sure whether she was being very honest or just bullshitting him. This uncertainty irritated him as he suspected that she was actually bullshitting him, but he could not be certain. Although on past occasions, they had held a few good conversations, which were enough to allow Andy to think that she was a sincere and caring person. It was in this particular context that gave him doubts, but he thought that it made little difference. It was up to him to a large extent to watch out for himself. The problem was that he was not always sure what it was he was supposed to be watching for. Caroline then was heard to say something to the effect that his rear end would glow similar to Aladdin's lamp if it was rubbed, but they would look after it no matter what it looked like. He thought not to be drawn any further on this matter as the rest of the room was starting to enjoy themselves once again at his expense.

Over the past weeks, he had listened to patients in the beds near to him and some further down the unit. All had entered the system at different times. Three of the individuals had come back onto the unit for surgery after being home for some years. They had all proffered advice of one sort or another. Most of it was of little value, as it seemed to be tainted by what could only be described as very odd or strange experiences, which the older patients seemed to take great pleasure in recounting. However, some of the patients who visited the unit did on occasion have something worthwhile to say, but it was fragmentary. They seemed pre-occupied with their own particular needs and gave the appearance that talking at length to new patients wasn't of any particular interest to most of them.

Andy had listened carefully to what he had heard and tried hard to put the ideas and thoughts into some order. But there were considerable gaps in his understanding of his condition which he knew that he needed to fill as soon as it was possible. There were also times when he was feeling miserable when he thought that an improved understanding was a waste of time, a futile exercise in which he had no interest. But his curiosity and thoughts upon minimising pain and discomfort caused him to enquire and to think about his condition. And most importantly his future, whether he had one or not. For the time being he wasn't sure about this. No one had given him enough information and there were times when he wasn't sure whether or not he really wanted to know. Everything depended upon his particular mood swings, which for some reason he had little control over. This was also a source of annoyance for him; he had always been highly motivated and positive in his approach to problems. Now many of the problems seemed too large and complex, he recognised with some reluctance that he was out of his depth and that he needed help. When his thoughts were running in this direction, he just wanted to pull the sheets up and drift into a sleep hoping that upon waking up it had all gone away, that it was a prolonged bad dream and it had not happened to him. He wasn't really on a spinal unit but somewhere else, and it was all a mistake. Sometime someone would come along and tell him to go home; that he should not really be there and that it was all over and he could resume his life. Deep down he knew that would never happen and such desires were illogical; the way ahead was not one leading to the sunlight or any glittering prizes. He felt a tear forming and he closed his eyes tight in order to remove such an offending object, he already knew that he could no longer afford even the smallest sign of weakness. He was now different and he thought that he might always be different, it was not his choice but he could no longer effect such matters. It was as though his lifestyle was out of his hands and he had lost the ability to control anything that might affect him. This negative thought pattern for the moment seemed alien to him. A few minutes later, he knew that he would change his mind and clutch at an emotional straw if it drifted his way.

Caroline felt that she might have been unfair and dismissive with Andy when he was obviously concerned. She knew that it warranted a bit more explanation.

"It was the night staff who'd put it in the book," said Caroline, in a deliberately dismissive manner that was intended to state that it was of no importance and just a precaution.

"Why didn't they tell me? It's my skin, my body," said Andy a little louder.

"Don't get at us. It's not our fault. We're keeping our eyes on it," she said in a calm softer voice, "you're staying in bed a bit longer as a precaution. What more can we do?."

"But how did it get there? How long has it been there?" said Andy, once again concerned. He had observed older patients coming back to the unit with pressure sores and he knew that they were something that should be avoided at all costs.

"I wasn't here yesterday," replied Caroline, "but don't worry it's not bad and it'll go away. It was just a bit red as we've already told you. I honestly doubt that there's any damage and we will watch it. Just trust us," she said while laughing, hoping to lighten the atmosphere.

"Trust you? Trust you?" Andy repeated. "It's my arse not yours!" he said with some indignation, "if it was yours I might trust you to look after it, but on the other hand perhaps you wouldn't. You don't seem to give a toss the lot of you."

He was now feeling miserable again and was wondering how bad his skin really was. Had the redness gone during the night? It could not have, he thought, otherwise they would not be keeping me in bed. He then wondered if he was laying on it creating more pressure. He turned to ask: "Tony, where about is the reddened skin?" but Tony had moved away quickly and quietly, making his way to the side entrance where he could have a smoke without being seen by his superiors. Andy then remembered that Caroline and Wendy had asked him if he would get up early as they were short staffed. The left hand does not know what the right hand is doing, he thought. Andy was feeling argumentative and any situation would suffice. Andy looked around to see if there was anyone about whom he could vent his frustration upon.

"What a bloody stupid and insensitive idea it was to bring in a no smoking rule," said Tony quietly to himself. It was fine for him as he could easily slip away for a smoke, but what about the regular smokers who were confined to their beds gasping for a cigarette? He knew that some of the older men and women had smoked for fifty years and now just because they were at the mercy of non-smokers they were forced to stop.

Tony was not over-sensitive or caring as an individual. The system had removed any vestiges of sensitivity some time ago. In fact, he now cared little for his job or most of the patients; it was just a job to him - a monthly cheque was his main motivation. He had applied for the job some years ago when he had been made redundant for the third time in as many years. It seemed a good idea at the time. He thought the job was, for all intents and purposes, relatively easy. It did not require any real training to do the job, just a bit of common sense and doing what he was told. This seemed fine for a few months, almost ideal, but he was soon bored. He could no longer muster the energy or motivation to find any other employment, so here he remained, something of a reluctant fixture. Although he was normally lacking in sensitivity he also thought along with some others that the no smoking policy on such a unit was cruel and thoughtless. He had heard many patients complain, especially the older ones, that a good smoke was the only pleasure they now had left to them. He stubbed the cigarette out under his foot and muttered to himself that it was not his problem, so why should he worry. And if his superiors had little or no thought for the needs of some of the patients, why should he be concerned. At that time he remembered how, only a few weeks back, an elderly patient who smoked had been brought onto the unit. It was obvious that he had only a short time to live but when he asked for a smoke, he was quickly and seemingly sadistically told that there was a no smoking policy in operation. A nurse attempting to be humorous at the time told him that it was bad for his health. Tony hoped that when his time came someone would be compassionate enough to give him a last smoke. He shuddered at this last thought, hoping that such an event would be a long time off. He once again wondered if he should try to obtain another job. He knew that he was as intelligent as the average person was, and it should not be too difficult to get something else. But he then reverted to his usual position. He thought that it might be wise just to stay where he was a little longer. It has its good points he thought. No one really bothered him or pressurised him. There was something to be said for the familiar, it was easy to cope with and there was little pressure from anyone. He had soon convinced himself, and he was now sure that he should stay a little longer. He had no other person to consider; this thought tended to bring about a wave of sadness, he wanted to be in a position where someone else counted; he desperately wanted to have another person in his life. The major part of his life had been spent alone, his relationships seldom lasted long. He knew that there were many men out there who did not find him attractive, and he was unhappy at such a situation. When he was younger, it had been relatively easy to form a relationship or simply have sex. It was everywhere and all so easy but things had changed. He was now years older and he regretted not forming a lasting relationship when he had the opportunity. He knew that he could never recapture those earlier years and he was possibly destined to live alone, unless he was lucky; he shuddered at the thought before a touch of optimism came his way, something might just be waiting around the corner he said to himself. Work was not so bad really he thought, he knew everyone and everyone knew him; he was part of the furniture. He thought about the patients, which was unusual for him. I'm better off than they are he thought, then thought that there was no comfort to be gained by such reasoning.

CHAPTER TWO

Amanda was in charge of the unit and she was always concerned with its efficient running; she did on occasion take her work home with her but that was never a problem, yet the thoughts of her patients were not in the forefront of her mind at that moment.

The night was a long one for Amanda who had little belief in predestination or fate. However, the forthcoming day would turn out to be different as fate had taken a hand in her life, and to some extent had chosen the path for her. She drank the last mouthful of coffee that was almost cold, the sweetener had not fully dissolved and she grimaced as she swallowed what liquid remained. Amanda was both tired and weary, a strange combination that is often difficult to articulate with any accuracy, but a condition that almost everyone has experienced at some time or other. Although she was very tired, she had still found it hard to fall asleep. It had been a long and difficult day at the hospital, much like most other days had been over the past few months. There was nothing new in that as such days at the hospital were now normal. The work was usually enjoyable, and being a nurse was also still enjoyable at times; this was despite what seemed like the politicians' and the medias' unwitting but constant attempts to lower morale, but her mind and body were now telling her that she really needed to rest.

If it were not for the increased paperwork and all the dubious forms that had to filled in the job would be so much easier for everyone, she thought. Nursing was simple, most of it was common sense but the paperwork, most of which was unnecessary except to provide the government of the day with statistics that were lacking in real content. It used to be so much better. Why have they messed about with something that worked? she asked herself. When will they realise that the whole system is moving away from the patients' needs? She sighed in exasperation. She wondered if it had been better or was it that she found the changes difficult to contend with?

The bed was unusually uncomfortable as it was forming shapes and contours of its own volition in such a random fashion that ensured her discomfort. She had tried drinking her favourite wine earlier but to no positive effect. Somewhat illogically, she had made herself a cup of coffee that she knew would not assist her in getting to sleep. But she was not as particularly concerned as she would normally have been by the lack of her ability to fall asleep; many of her thoughts and actions that day had appeared contradictory. Her hand briefly touched her inner thigh as though wanting to provide her with some physical comfort, but her skin was not soft or quite as smooth as she knew it should feel. She quickly withdrew her hand at the same time sighing in frustration. Her body and mind were not functioning in unison. Her mind was unwilling to let her rest; her thoughts were almost moving at random, apparently uncontrollable, and this irritated her. She had always been controlled, calm, decisive, and effective, but for the moment that had changed. She could admit to herself that she was afraid, and fear was something she had not experienced for a long time. And she was unsure as to what she should do to improve what she thought of as an unacceptable situation. She knew that people were to some extent depending upon her judgement, her decisions were important and she had never treat any situation involving others lightly. The whole of her life had been involved with other people. This is what she had wanted. This was what she was usually good at, but not today. Today she had found it very hard. She had suddenly to deal with her own problems as well as those of the patients. She sighed deeply once again and thought that perhaps she should not have had the coffee after all; she did not like the idea of smoking in bed she was aware of the dangers, but nevertheless she reached for a cigarette. She thought about rolling herself a joint as she had a small amount of cannabis left over from a trip she had made to Amsterdam earlier in the year. She then decided that in her present state of mind that there would be little point, and that it would be a waste recognising that smoking a joint would only enhance her existing mood.

The book she had been reading had not initially helped, it only added to her confused emotions. But she was compelled in her efforts to understand what it was saying. She closed the book after reading the short passage once again; the atmosphere that had been created in the passage somehow enhanced her train of thought, full of half-submerged meanings that can strike a chord at an inappropriate time when one's mood is receptive to the more negative aspects of any text or image. She then thought about a patient who was on the unit - someone she had known all of her life; she was worried about him, she felt closer to him than many of her relatives. He was not at all well and he was loosing ground very quickly and she could not accept this; by any of the standards she had created for herself, it was wrong. It was both frustrating and depressing, as no one had found anything specific that would account for his decline. She tried to put these thoughts out of her head but without too much success.

She sighed loudly and stared at the ceiling for a few seconds trying to empty her mind of all the thoughts that had drifted in without her realising, or knowing. The book attracted her attention again. She decided to attempt to read a particular chapter one more time in the hope that the essence would remain in her thoughts for a while longer. She knew that this was bordering upon the masochistic but that did not stop her. She slowly read out loud to herself hoping that somehow this might assist, sometimes dwelling upon a particular phrase that appealed to her, knowing that the correct phrase could still strike a chord with her that deeply affected her present emotions, while allowing her the simple pleasure and the brief luxury of a small tear, or a moist eye. Anyone who thought they knew her would say that this was out of character. Such was her perceived need at that moment. Amanda read the words slowly; she had stopped reading aloud as it seemed a futile gesture. Unintentionally her mouth formed the words as her eyes scanned across the page.

She held the book at an appropriate distance unwilling to use her recently obtained reading glasses. The words were now clear on the page and they drifted around her mind as she read:

'Time slowly drifted by, like a deep meandering stream, carrying with it fragments of misshapen grains of dust that acted like prisms while occasionally catching the light.

A thought fleetingly crossed my mind and then departed. I raised the glass high and tilted it towards the flickering candle light while allowing multicoloured prisms of light dance their way round the rim. Just like a thousand miniature rainbows, I thought.

My eyes dimmed as I followed their sensuous movement while the unknown couple on the dance floor moved to the rhythm of a Spanish guitar. They threaded their way around the room entwined like two serpents unaware of their surroundings.

They were totally entranced by the enticement of their bodies moving and swaying to a hidden tune that pervaded their desires.

The thought of the pleasure of a warm body moving next to mine was negated by my dark Indulgent mood that obscured all but thoughts of despair.

I placed the empty glass upon the stained wooden tabletop and I beckoned the waiter across. I told him to pour more wine and leave the bottle. He walked slowly away in a manner that seemingly indicated contempt.

I needed to dull my senses to the endless tedium of the day. How long the music played I cared not, without me realising it the dancers had suddenly disappeared, and only the smoke of a spent cigar drifted across the empty room creating shapes and patterns that momentarily transfixed my gaze.

The candle flickered its last pearls of light. The dawn was only a few minutes away. It had been the longest of nights and it was now to be the longest of days. I threw a few coins onto the table and left the dismal establishment. I walked slowly towards the early morning sun. For a brief moment, a light breeze touched my cheek as though it was a whisper from some past time, telling me that it was once a different time and a different place. I gazed up to the fading stars and clenched my fist as though they were within my grasp, I almost laughed in self-indulgence but it was very different now. I'm carried back and forth by an unseen tide. I shout out loud in anger and despair, as I'm powerless to resist, I look for some distant welcoming shore hoping to gain a land where time embraces me without hostility. I need a land where I have a true purpose, where I can climb the hills and shield my eyes against the warm sun as I gaze down upon that distant but fair plain. But it is said to dream such dreams is the way of all travellers who are lost, and I still have some way to go before I can rest. I will move forward slowly knowing that the path I tread will lead me out of the forest and finally into the light of fearful and terrifying acceptance. Such contradictory actions lack reason but drive me on with an optimism known to be deceptive and false.

The effects of the cigar smoke and the wine are no longer comforting me. I constantly ask myself 'How many miles must I go?' for I have no way of knowing. My eyes can see very little through the overhanging branches that block out the light.

Perhaps I have time and I can shed a small tear, I but then I must depart; time will await me no longer and I must once again seek the best of paths. A figure emerges within my mind and a silent friend points me to the far off land, I will heed the advice without knowing why. I thank my friend who then looks directly at me, he does not speak; he just smiles knowing that the path I have chosen is the right one. The thoughts somehow came into my head these were thoughts I had many years ago. We need friends as we need sweet water, and clean cold air we need to breath, and to live to take the journey, to dream.

"And so we will my friend" I quietly said to myself, "so we will for an eternity, for the world is ours if we but knew it. So I say to you with sincerity let the pure water quench your thirst and drink your fill for the journey before you is not finite. And the pages of your journey are not yet open to you."

She briefly mused upon the words she had read: "The journey before you is not finite." The text had the desired effect and her eyes began to close. The book slipped out of Amanda's open hand first onto the bed, and then onto the floor. Amanda slept a troubled sleep, sometimes dreaming, sometimes almost awake with troubled thoughts constantly tormenting her. After this unreasoned torment for a brief period, she finally fell asleep. Like many similar nights, there was no peace to be found in sleep, but she had become accustomed to such nights. Nights when you pray for the comfort of sleep only to be distressed by uncontrollable dreams, dreams that are inhabited by mysterious creatures of the night whose inane ramblings and actions are devoid of logic. She was frightened by her dreams as they seemed meaningless, but they implied darkness and pain, also torment and suffering that was convoluted and indecipherable.

Her husband was always there in her dreams; he was always fighting her, laughing at her as he dragged her down and brutally ravaged her seemingly helpless form. He tore at her clothes and at the flesh on her naked body. He squeezed the reason from out of her mind while she only stared into his eyes, but she could not see him there, it was a different person. She was hurting and for some reason he was hurting her. She did not understand why she was in so much pain and why he wanted to hurt her, all of her attempts to plead with him failed. For a moment, she thought that he looked at her and yet he seemed not to recognise her. She was sweating a dank cloying liquid, which she could both smell and taste, yet she was deathly cold.

Her dreams continued to torment her; they seemed almost painful but unrecognisable in the sense that there was no structure or recognisable continuity. New faces appeared briefly only to depart unrecognised. It was then that Bernard spoke to her in a tone that made her feel increasingly strange and very vulnerable. He smiled unconvincingly before he spoke which made her feel even more apprehensive. She could hear him clearly, as he attempted to speak.

"I'm tired very tired," his voice trailed away.

She asked him to stay and talk to her; she told him that she did not understand. He slowly shook his head and said that it was not possible. He continued to look at her as he spoke. His voice was suddenly weak and distant. At that moment, she desperately wanted to tell him something but she could not speak. He continued as though he knew what she had wanted to say. He smiled as he spoke her name, but this time his voice was soft and gentle; she reached out to touch him but she could not reach him or get any closer. He paused for a moment as though he wanted to choose his words carefully before he continued. Suddenly and in a stronger tone of voice, he said.

"But this is not the time to worry about the past, it is gone and there are so many things that I would change if only I could... "

He sounded angry for the moment but the anger quickly disappeared as though he had not the time nor desire to waste on something as negative as anger.

He continued slowly as though he was imparting a message yet at the same time reminding himself of something of importance.

"We seldom obtain those things we desire, those things in life that are really important will nearly always be out of our reach, this is one of the few things I have learned." And we have desire; we're inflicted with desires, the irony is that those who do not desire are already lost to this world. For to desire is to drift away into dreams, and to dream is the only doorway that is left available to us that makes us worthy of our existence. I know that will sound pretentious or even meaningless to you now but you will understand sometime, and if you don't, I'm unsure as to what I mean anymore, it is all so meaningless, and does it really matter."

His face slowly disappeared and she could feel herself crying, she did not want him to leave her and she did not understand what he had meant, she just wanted him to hold her close and comfort her at that particular moment. She wanted him to help her understand what was happening to her, yet she knew he was also in a state of despair and suffering and she did not want to see him in that situation. She did not know what she needed to do. She looked around for help, and there was non-forthcoming, she was alone and she felt helpless. She also knew that she was dreaming although it appeared so real. While knowing she was dreaming she found it difficult to assess what was possibly valid and held some meaning and what was irrational and fragmented in the way some dreams are, and although she tried, she could make little sense of what she had experienced.

'Bloody gibberish; total rubbish', she said to herself, 'childish dreams that create within them characters that are unrealistic and simpering'. She was not in a happy frame of mind and she recognised the need to be pragmatic. She had always dreamt, and occasionally her dreams had given her an insight into her own thoughts and feelings, but more often than not dreams were confusing scraps of events and interactions that defied logic and time.

The bedroom had become cold during the night and the windows were steamed up only allowing in a glimmer of the early morning light. The noise of a car engine sounding louder than usual in the cold air rescued Amanda from her cheerless sleep.

At the same time, it irritated her. She still felt tired and did not want to move. It seemed to her that only minutes had elapsed since she had been reading. She could not fully remember her dreams, but she could still see Bernard talking to her. She couldn't remember what he had said, it couldn't have been so important, she concluded, otherwise she would have been able to remember. With some reluctance, she reached out from underneath the bedclothes and fumbled for the bedside lamp. The light caused her momentarily to place her hand over her eyes in order to shield them from the unwelcome glare.

She glanced over towards the alarm clock, which had once again failed to awaken her. She could not decide whether the alarm had actually gone off or not. There was not the slightest recollection on her part of hearing it. 'I need a new clock' she thought, at the same time dismissing the thought almost instantly from her mind, having no patience at that moment to think about alarm clocks. She then gave a large, somewhat exaggerated, sigh in desperation; this was something she had started to do more often in recent weeks. The most trivial of things caused her to sigh. She had frequently promised herself that she would stop doing it. She allowed herself a few seconds in which her mind slipped into action upon realising that she had over-slept once again, although fortunately it was only for a few minutes. The duvet was slowly pushed further down away from her face, her hand reached out for the packet of cigarettes that were on the bedside table, automatically placing one between her lips. It was quickly lit. Her first breath of smoke was eagerly drawn into her lungs. Her body was still not fully responding to the fact that she was now awake her; limbs felt dull and lifeless and unwilling to move. But that first smoke of the day was the signal for life, it now ordered her body to start responding even if it was only slowly.

Her limbs refused to move for the moment knowingly defying logic. She stared ahead looking towards the window not thinking of anything in particular but enjoying the smoke. This brief period of calm and relaxation was only temporary. She was already a few minutes behind the time that she had pre-set for herself. Her experience told her exactly how long was needed to get out of bed, to wash and to shower, to make breakfast and to be on her way to work. Every task had been carefully broken down to a manageable size in order to see if any saving in time could be made. Her motives for this exercise were quite simple; it was a desire to stay in bed as long as possible now that it was starting to get colder.

It always seemed difficult, almost painful, but with some reluctance she forced herself to walk the few yards to the bathroom. Her bare feet felt instantly cold now that they were out from under the warm bedclothes. The small bones in her feet cracked and she winced at the noise half believing that it was the first signs of arthritis although she knew that it was just the stiffness. The central heating has knocked itself off at the wrong time again, she thought. She wondered how it was that in the cold weather the first thing you wanted to do was go to the bathroom. Her period had started during the night, it was early and she felt miserable as her stomach ached and her back ached. She grimaced as the cold seat of the lavatory met her warm flesh. She sometimes mused upon the thought that it would have been more convenient if women could have been created without the need for periods, they were useless, even stupid, and always inconvenient, there must be a better system in nature. The same rule applied to bladders, she concluded. We should have bladders that only needed emptying once every few days, she said to herself. She thought that the need to keep going to a toilet was a waste of time, and that for some reason the human body had not developed far enough in this particular area. She also concluded that evolution had not developed in line with modern day needs and the lack of time that almost everyone seemed to have to face. For some reason her thoughts continued somewhat aimlessly thinking along these lines. Perhaps there was a flow of some kind in the theory of evolution, perhaps we now need another theory. She was sure that Darwin had not taken into account the effect of scientific changes on the lifestyle of humans. She gave another sigh in frustration at allowing herself to even bother thinking about such things. It's too early to think about such gibberish she decided. Besides, what did she care about Darwin or evolution, and revolution, or any other form of evolvement; although she did not like the word it seemed appropriate. She thought, Who gives a toss about such things?' It was bloody stupid even to consider such things she told herself. And what the hell did she know about evolution anyway. She stubbed her toe and shouted out in pain while once again, in anger, kicking the offending object and inflicting more pain upon herself. She quickly concluded, as if it was an excuse, that she was still not fully awake and thinking properly.

Amanda sat still for a few seconds hoping that her mind and body would start to function in conjunction with one another. She reached out automatically to find that her tights were missing. She searched around for a new pair of tights that she knew was there only a few hours earlier but now they were missing. Where the hell have they gone?

"It's always when you are in a hurry!" she gasped. She spotted them on the floor at the side of the linen basket. She thought that it was time that she found a new location for the basket as it was something of a nuisance where it was standing. She would have to deal with it later, baskets were of little importance at that moment as she was getting later behind her self-imposed schedule. The kettle was filled with water out of the warm water tap and plugged in without thinking. The bread was placed into the toaster, and the cereal was placed into the bowl that had been purposely left out the previous night. A glass of orange juice was quickly consumed, the kettle was soon boiling and the coffee was made. Only a few minutes behind time now, thought Amanda who was now feeling a little better at making up some of the time that she had lost by over-sleeping. She did not really taste the breakfast cereal. And did not even know why she still bought it, as she did not particularly care for any breakfast cereal, to her it tasted disgusting, only fit for cattle. She had been brought up in the old-fashioned manner of eating a full cooked breakfast every day. Her mother had insisted upon this being the right and proper way to start the day.

"If you do not have a proper breakfast, you'll have spots, and no one wants a girl with spots" her mother used to say.

'Bloody rubbish' she remembered thinking at the time. However, Amanda would have liked to carry on doing this, but time and fashion dictated that this was no longer appropriate. Healthy eating was now a social requirement and this did not include a traditional fat saturated breakfast, no matter how good it tasted.

She lit another cigarette which was more enjoyable than her breakfast. She was still feeling miserable and angry but she knew there was nothing that she could do about her situation at that moment. She wondered what she would do, how she would manage without the comfort and support of a cigarette or two in the morning. Smoking did not do her any good with regard to her general health, but she reasoned that she would be a lot worse without a smoke, almost incapable of functioning, in a morning. To admit such a dependency was embarrassing but she was fully aware of her weakness. And in the great scheme of things, it was probably only a small weakness compared to others. This thought comforted her on occasion, although it was increasingly difficult to convince herself that it was true.

Her mind reluctantly then drifted on to the subject of her husband Athol, this was his fourth night away from home. He was now spending more and more time away from home since he had obtained promotion. When it had been offered to him they had both readily agreed that it was in their interest, and that he should take the promotion. It would mean a better standard of living. And after all, they agreed, that was what it was supposed to be about, getting on in life, moving upwards, even if it was moving up only a little. It was still supposed to mean something in the greater scheme of things. Amanda pondered upon this thought and knew that she was now indifferent to moving upwards or even sideways at the moment. She had other, more important things, on her mind. She was now of the opinion that following the direction of others, or what society deemed as taking the right path or moving upwards, was a total waste of time. She was certain that it was usually an exercise in futility, avidly pursued by those poor sods without any imagination, or who simply knew no better. This realisation, or to be accurate acceptance, did not make her feel any better. On the contrary, she was very disappointed that she had not accepted this perceived reality earlier. She had known for a number of years that she had little interest in competing with friends or the neighbours. Or some of her socially conscious relatives. She was not in the least interested in obtaining a new kitchen or new car, a larger house or going further a field for a holiday, in order that they might impress someone with their tales of exotic places which she knew bored everyone who had to listen to them. But it was all part of the process of getting on in what she perceived as a crass, superficial world. Her thoughts suddenly changed.

"I must be feeling bloody miserable! God am I pissed off!" she exclaimed out loud, What the hell's happening to me? She shuddered at her last thought. The irrational anger came back and she decided that if anyone told her that someone was really getting on, or doing well for themselves she would tell them what 'getting on' meant to her. She promised herself she would ensure that they were insulted. Only that way would she be certain that they would never mention the subject again when she was present or within earshot.

"Bunch of arseholes!" she muttered under her breath.

Her mind was, for some reason, turning over at a rate of knots. It was hard for her to comprehend at times how insensitive and stupid some people were. Due to these less than charitable thoughts and her outburst, she had quickly introduced a flow of adrenaline into her system that had raised her anger and her pulse rate. The anger was surprisingly therapeutic in its effects. This made her feel better equipped to face the day ahead. Only a couple of years back Athol would have made love to her in the early morning knowing that the feelings of pleasure and security would help take her through the day. She had enjoyed those early morning sessions of love and laughter. She thought for a moment and realised that she could no longer remember when they had last laughed together.

Amanda quickly stubbed out the cigarette and put her coat on, picked up the car keys and went to the door. The sky was now becoming much lighter and she thought that she could just feel a hint of frost in the air although it was still a bit early for frost. Her mind wondered onto some of the recent documentaries she had seen on television. These had led her to think that it's something to do with the climatic changes we're supposed to be experiencing. 'It's all doom and bloody gloom', she thought, but at that moment that suited her fine; 'bring on the doom and gloom, pile it high', she said to herself. It appeared to her that there is either a famine in Africa, or floods in Asia, and occasionally a new killer disease is waiting around the corner.

She recognised that she was not feeling very positive at that moment. She formed the word 'positive' with her lips and took in a large breath of cold air. On the contrary, she was feeling both miserable and under stress and ready to argue with anyone who displeased her. Recently she had started to hate the word 'stress'; it appeared that everyone had decided that they must be under stress, as though it was some new disease that rapidly infected everyone. It was a legitimate excuse for doing as little as possible. Or having others sort things out for you. And if you were lucky, you might even go to court and obtain compensation. Amanda had always felt strongly about people taking responsibility for their actions, or lack thereof. She recognised that she was opinionated, but had decided that it was better to have opinions than to go through life as though anaesthetised. Even her father had warned her about keeping her opinions to herself when young, but she had always failed to do so. Now that she was older, she still held strong opinions, but she knew that over the years she had become less aggressive in her arguments.

The car was definitely of the male gender, she had decided. It was cold and damp and for a moment refused to start, but it finally gave in after being cursed and threatened with castration and the scrap yard. The engine spluttered and coughed into life almost cynically in order that she felt insecure regarding its ability to continue to function. She shivered with the cold and the damp; the inside of the car seemed as cold as it felt outside. It was, however, only a few miles to the hospital where she worked. She knew that by the time she arrived at the main entrance the car's heater would just be starting to work effectively in a perverted act of defiance.

"Probably, I do need a new car" she said out loud whilst hitting the steering wheel in annoyance at being delayed at the traffic lights, at the same time shouting at the driver opposite. Even so, she would be sad to see this one go as she had purchased it from an old lady who had carefully looked after it. She smiled to herself as it almost sounded like a salesman's pitch. "It has had only one owner, a little old lady." With a feeling of regret, she concluded that it had served her well. And after all, it was only a car made out of metal and plastic, it wasn't as though it was alive. She thought that it was somehow illogical to have some form of affection for an object like a car, but this was the case, illogical or not. She finally decided that she would give it some serious thought. Probably she would mention it to Athol, who she knew would be only too pleased to advise her upon the most suitable car for her specific needs. At the same time he would have conflicting feelings as he would want to see a car of appropriate status on their drive. Yet he would not want to spend too much money, as he would not be the main driver.

'He had become a tight bastard' she thought. Amanda laughed to herself at the dilemma she was going to place him in. 'It would ensure a classic situation of cognitive dissonance theory' she thought as she smiled to herself. She also realised that this was indicative of their present life together. That such an item would take on a level of false importance while the important matters were seldom discussed at length anymore. She now found it almost impossible to discuss anything with Athol. To her constant annoyance he always seemed as though he had a clear idea of what was desirable and what was not in his life. Everything seemed simple and clear to him. Life could be planned as though you were taking a holiday. All that was required was good sensible planning and everything would fall into place.

'Life was like a journey', he often said in a patronising tone, 'there is a beginning and an end; all that you have to do is carefully, and with forethought, fill the gaps in between'.

Every time he said this it angered her, and she wanted to physically hit him. Even the tone of his voice made her wince. "The arrogant bastard," she said out loud.

Amanda knew that her ideas and needs were becoming further and further apart from those of Athol's. This was once a source of deep regret to her but now she was generally indifferent. She knew that things had gone too far for them to have any real chance of improving their relationship. Their marriage was just something that they were 'in'; it no longer meant anything other than the legal and financial obligations they might share. For a moment Amanda felt sad at that thought, but this quickly passed. She knew that she no longer had any real feelings for Athol; unfortunately he just happened to share the same accommodation. 'I just wish that he would go away from home one morning and not come back' she thought, 'What if he killed himself while driving?' She took in a deep breath and thought that she would not really want that to happen. She wondered if other people lay in bed thinking about their husbands and wives dying. She assumed that people did, but did not mention it for obvious reasons. She then decided that she would want him to telephone in order that appropriate details could be tidied up with the solicitors. She shook her head as if to remove the last thought from her mind, and to bring herself back to reality.

"Why did such trivial thoughts drift into her mind? Why couldn't she concentrate anymore?" she asked herself.

She thought that her inability to be as focused as she had been would affect her job if she was not careful. And within a short time her colleagues would recognise the change and to her that was totally unacceptable. She needed to be on top of her work, and fully in control, anything less would not be tolerated by her personality that always demanded that those difficult standards which she had set herself had somehow to be retained.

The hospital gates soon appeared and Amanda drove into the nearest empty space in the staff car park. The car's heater had warmed the vehicle just as it was time to get out. Amanda felt the cool wind and shivered slightly, now regretting not wearing the thermal underwear she had bought the previous week. She hurried through the automatic doors and headed towards the corridor leading to the unit office.

Caroline Baker was already in the office enjoying a smoke before she started her day's work.

"You're not supposed to be smoking in here," said Amanda.

Caroline grunted something to the effect that she was giving up, she looked up and carried on smoking.

"Is there anything new?" asked Amanda expecting the usual negative reply.

Caroline sighed which meant that if there was something new it was not anything to get excited over. She then told Amanda that she had heard that Andy was uncomfortable and she and Wendy would attend to him first. The night staff could have done something to make him more comfortable but they were busy, evidently two of the patients' catheters blocked a short while ago and they were changed, otherwise they would have made Andy more comfortable, and young Stevie needed his bowels dealing with, he was dysreflexic. They thought it was his catheter causing the problem but evidently not, it was the first time he has had such a problem.

"Well, that's what they said," added Caroline while her expression cast doubt on the validity of what she had been told.

Amanda just sighed and then thought that she would have to have a word with the night staff.

"We must keep an eye on Stevie. Check his blood pressure a couple of times to make sure the problem has been dealt with, and that it's not his bladder that is really the cause. Let us not be caught out because he obviously did not recognise the symptoms." Amanda emphasised that all patients must be taught about autonomic dysreflexia at the earliest opportunity.

"How can you do it without frightening some of them?" asked Caroline.

Amanda took a simplistic and pragmatic line. "It's better that they are frightened than dead; I know everyone gets it explained to them, but it needs explaining more than once. Patients have to learn what their symptoms are likely to mean. If they get it wrong then we shouldn't criticise them. The doctors here understand the situation, well those doctors that count understand. It doesn't matter how we get the information across as long as we do in this case. With some problem areas I would take a line that did not leave anyone worried but this is different."

Caroline knew that Amanda was right and that detailed advice and explanations were necessary if patients were to survive in a reasonable manner. Amanda seemed as though she wanted to expand upon a few things at that moment.

"We have to provide support that is on going, out there it's the real world and it's not easy for our patients, in fact it can be a difficult lifestyle depending, of course, upon the individual circumstances." She was feeling angry and her heart was pounding.

"We should've put behind us the days when it's a sink or swim situation. Our patients need our support for the rest of their lives; it's as simple as that, and they should be operating from a level playing field but they aren't, but that's where our assistance is essential. We can try and improve the support we give to all of out patients."

She looked and waited for a response that was not forthcoming.

"We have to get our heads around that fact and provide the individual support we keep saying is necessary. A patient should be able to telephone here at any time and obtain sensible advice, and if they have a problem that cannot be sorted out over the 'phone, then they should come to us that day just so a Doctor can look at the problem." She did not desire to lecture anyone at that particular moment but these points were important to her and for reasons known only to herself she wanted to express these thoughts forcefully.

"We all know that there's a shortage of staff and a shortage of beds but if you are out there in the community knowing that something is wrong you require action. Or at least someone with expertise to tell you what the problem is and what is required."

"What's suddenly brought this on?" asked Caroline looking bemused.

"Are you starting on a new policy document or something? It's a little early to start taking this place serious!"

By taking a flippant attitude she was hoping to change Amanda's tone but she was not successful.

Amanda sighed and wished that she had not said anything in such an aggressive tone of voice. She was not expecting or wanting anything new or any excitement at that moment. Some days earlier she had examined her breasts and found a lump in the left one. She knew that it had not been there on the previous occasion when she had examined herself. She had tried to remember how long it was since she had examined her breasts. However, for some reason she could not remember. She tried hard to think of something, an event of some kind that would help her to fix a date, but she could not. The harder she tried the more impossible it seemed.

"It cannot be so long ago" she said to herself. She was now angry at her own stupidity. She knew that she should have checked on a regular basis, there was no excuse. She should at least have noted something down in order to aid her memory.

However, it was now too late to worry. Once she understood the urgency of the situation she had acted quickly. Finding the lump in her breast had frightened her as such problems ran in the family. She already knew that for some reason nurses and Doctors are possibly the worst offenders when it came to taking actions appertaining to them. When she had first felt the offending lump, for some inexplicable reason she remembered a scene out of the novel Cancer Unit, where a Doctor had been diagnosed with breast cancer, and she wanted someone to look at her breasts as they were, before she had them operated upon and their original form was lost forever. Amanda did not feel those emotions but she understood them. Due to her position and contacts she had arranged to see a Doctor later that day and undergo a biopsy. She could not help but feel worried although she knew that the statistics were against there being a serious problem. She also decided that until she knew what the situation was she would not mention it to anyone. If there was nothing found then it wasn't a problem. If something is found then it would be dealt with. Only then when it was unavoidable would she mention it. Common sense told her it was not necessarily the best of ideas keeping it from someone who could be trusted, but she did not find it an easy subject to discuss. It was, however, something of real importance that she could have discussed with Caroline. But her ability to think rationally seemed slightly impaired at that moment.

Caroline could be easily described as an attractive women, which means almost anything but it was hard to describe her in any other way without going into considerable detail . She was of medium build with short cut dark brown hair, and large brown eyes that appeared soft and warm. She had a generous mouth that appeared to want to smile at the least excuse, which made her endearing to the most obstreperous of patients. It seemed as though whatever was happening in the rest of the world it did not happen on the unit when she was around. The unit was a separate entity in its own time and space; a secure insular world. Here, the interactions and relationships were surprisingly symbiotic which on occasions seemed contradictory. Within this environment Caroline always seemed positive and outgoing to her colleagues, seldom miserable or complaining. No one could ever recall her complaining or moaning about the patients or her work with them. Although she often complained about the lack of standards, that in her view had declined in recent years. She went about her duties with an acceptance bordering upon pleasure. Sometimes this was difficult to comprehend by other members of staff who came into work hoping that the clock would move around as fast as possible, in order that they could escape from the establishment and do the things that offered them more pleasure or gratification. The only incentive that kept them on the unit longer was the extra money that could sometimes be earned by doing an extra shift. Overtime and extra shifts were increasingly popular, especially when it was coming up to the holidays, when extra money seemingly equated to a better time. Caroline and Amanda had noticed that there was an increasing demand for more money to spend on entertainment. Weekends had mysteriously become more expensive. Holidays were taken in places more distant. People's expectations were higher. Good times were the norm, or to be more accurate they were expected, and weekends and days off were always looked forward to, but in the cases of unit staff who were expected to work weekends in their turn, days off were always looked forward to. While this had always been the case, it was now for some reason more pronounced, or was it just imagination or one's dissatisfaction that brought about such beliefs.

Like other offices in the older part of the building the unit office was small and cramped. The bare walls had, over many years, suffered continually from numerous coats of dull off-white emulsion. The walls were very plain and only broken up by the various charts and messages stuck on numerous bits of paper, some of which went back a number of years. No-one had bothered to remove them and now they were part of the decor. Amanda lit up a cigarette and automatically offered Caroline one. She then poured herself a coffee. Somewhat reluctantly she enquired about the new male nurse who was starting later that day. She wanted someone else's opinion of him, which was not her usual practice in such circumstances. She had interviewed him and at the time she thought that he would be a useful addition to the unit. Now she was no longer sure, as was often the case, she had known little about him when she had interviewed him and she was impressed at the time. She admitted to herself that he did interview well and he was very convincing with his answers. He was on the surface a very good candidate. However, she had since found out that he wasn't quite as caring and work orientated as he first appeared. She knew from previous experience that interviews do not tell you very much about a person if they are used to being interviewed. Amanda, like everyone, realised that it's something of a game where you are told what the applicant thinks you want to hear. This new nurse had given a good impression at the time. Since then it seemed as though everyone was queuing up to tell her what a bastard he had been to his wife and children. She had told herself that his domestic affairs should be something that were separate from his work, and should have no bearing upon his ability to do the job. However, this thought did not totally reassure her. She was now concerned regarding her decision to appoint him.

Caroline thought about Amanda's question and was surprised that she had been asked. It was not like Amanda to ask her opinion after the event. She assumed that for some reason Amanda must have been having second thoughts, or she knew that she had made a mistake. She decided that as she had never worked with the man she had no real opinions, although she also had heard that he was not as open and reliable as he made himself out to be. She sensibly took a diplomatic line, although she knew that if she had a really strong opinion she could express it to Amanda without feeling compromised in anyway.

"Let's see how he fits in" she said. "If he doesn't, then it'll soon show itself and that'll be the time to do something to get him on track." She said this while looking directly at Amanda and hoping that her answer fulfilled its purpose.

Amanda just nodded signalling that she basically agreed, it was as good an answer as she had a right to expect. She knew that fitting in was the all-important requirement of any new member of staff. It was correct to say that if someone did not quickly fit in their working life would almost be that of an outcast. In this respect the unit was no different to other similar institutions that over time build up their internal culture.

People who were employed on the unit were liked, or disliked, for varying reasons. Sometimes a person was disliked because of their opinions or beliefs, and occasionally because they had no opinions or beliefs. Some individuals were just that: 'individuals'. It was often difficult for such a person to fit into an organisation which was made up of small cliques often appearing more concerned with intrigue and gossip than getting on with their work. Although most of the time the unit functioned reasonably well, considering its resources or lack of them.

"I hope that he fits in. We need another trained male nurse" said Amanda, adopting a more serious tone of voice which she sometimes used to impress a fact upon a member of staff.

"I know that he is married, but is he gay?" asked Caroline. She was surprised and suddenly wondered why she had asked that question knowing that he was married, although that would not preclude him from being gay, she thought.

She felt embarrassed as it was out of character and she would not normally have cared or even thought about anyone's sexuality.

"No," said Amanda "he isn't gay, or at least I don't think he is. But it is not something that I have actually thought about." She was about to add something regarding the rumours she had heard but she decided against it. She would have liked at that particular moment to have been able to confide in Caroline, as she knew that Caroline was not only a good nurse but a reliable and trustworthy person with common sense. It wasn't that it would be unprofessional, that did not particularly bother her in this instance. But for some reason Amanda found it hard to confide in anyone at that moment although there were times when she would really have liked to have spoken to someone. But to have done so at this time would have made her feel more vulnerable and less competent, and for the moment she thought that was something she could easily do without. She smiled to herself and briefly thought how stupid such situations were. Why couldn't she ask simple direct questions? Why couldn't she expect simple logical answers? If only life was so easy she thought.

She then thought to herself, what if the information she had been given in good faith might after all turn out to be inaccurate, as gossip sometimes was? Amanda was always fair and she prided herself on giving people the benefit of the doubt until she had information that would lead her to change her mind. She intensely disliked gossip, yet in her working environment it was impossible to escape from it. Many of the female staff seemed to thrive upon gossip, no matter how outrageous and inaccurate and the male members of staff were probably worse. It seemed to be food and drink to some staff members. She was often amused at some of the individual's imagination. One male member of staff seemed to come up with new bits of information every day about some person or other. And when he wasn't talking about other individuals he was spreading rumours of doom and gloom about closures and cutbacks. He always swore he had obtained his information from a totally reliable source. Amanda thought that he dreamt some of the things up during the night after smoking a strong joint, or imagined that he had overheard them in the dining room where information moved around faster than if it was on the internet. At that particular time she was unaware of his close relationship with someone in administration who constantly exuded misinformation knowing that it would be quickly disseminated around the hospital.

"Have you heard anymore about moving the unit when the new general hospital is built, or was it another rumour?" asked Amanda.

"There might be something to the rumours as Doctor Rand was going on about it yesterday as though the decision to move has already been decided. He was totally disillusioned with all that has been going on. Its pure politics and nothing to do with patients or care, and let's face it, we would be the last to find out about any changes. If we do actually move then I think it will be the time to move on to something very different" added Amanda, who had already had those thoughts for some time.

"I've noticed a certain level of apathy amongst the rest of the staff every time the subject is mentioned. I can remember similar rumours on a number of occasions, and in the end they came to nothing, I thought at one time it was deliberately done just to keep us on our toes. That's how paranoid you can become in this place," she yawned and stretched her arms.

"This place is a slum! We need more space."

"We need to move!" added Caroline.

Amanda said in exasperation "There are some things that need to be done now never mind about moving. We're going to be short of staff later today, I'm tired of complaining about the lack of staff. Nothing gets done. It's just a matter of muddling through from day to day. If it doesn't get any better then I'll have to have a talk with 'She who must be obeyed' about shutting some of the beds down"

"How can we do that when we have a waiting list?" asked Caroline looking confused. Amanda said "I don't like the idea but I'm not going to put the patients at risk any longer. Something has to be done."

She sat back in her chair and carefully placed the pen down on the desk.

"You know this as well as I do: the patients rely on us, they trust us to do everything in their interest. They cannot walk out of here if they are not liking it. Being spinally injured is different to breaking your leg, this condition is permanent." Caroline nodded in agreement. She knew how hard it was for most patients and their families; everything had changed for them and their world would never be the same again.

"To be honest, I'm getting tired of the situation. I have had enough of being ignored. I complain every few days and what's done? Nothing happens! So I might as well say nothing. Anyway, if there is not an improvement in the near future I will be seeking employment elsewhere."

"Are you serious?" asked Caroline.

"I have just had enough. I feel that without some serious changes we're not providing the care our patients deserve, and I'm not willing to accept it. So the only solution for me is to leave if there are no improvements."

Amanda took a deep breath, "Perhaps I am reacting a little. I'm not on my best form and I'm getting pissed off with everything at the moment. Just ignore what I have said," she looked both exasperated and disappointed.

"I could do with a long, quiet and peaceful break in the sun. I feel totally drained" said Amanda, "Nothing exciting, but pure relaxation away from everything before winter sets in."

"You find it and I'll go with you," said Caroline.

"If you are really serious, I could arrange it," said Amanda with some surprise. Amanda then paused, and thought that it might not be the most appropriate time to make any arrangements. On the other hand it could be the ideal time she concluded.

"Is there anywhere in particular you want to go?."

Caroline half closed her eyes before replying. "I want to go somewhere that's warm and quiet, a nice hotel and if possible, a bit of shopping, and even a bit of culture."

Amanda thought she must be serious if she wants culture as well as relaxation. "There are some special offers to Egypt, staying in Cairo and Luxor if you are interested. Also Visiting the Valley of the Kings, and that type of thing if you are wanting culture as well as a break."

"The pyramids by moonlight? That sounds almost romantic. I think that I can do without the romantic bit," said Caroline unconvincingly.

"Don't be so negative! You should be worth a few camels," said Amanda while laughing, then added "it would depend upon what the camels looked like of course!. Anyway, it'll be warm and sunny, probably quite hot; also there's the option of staying a few nights by the Red sea. Evidently it's good value for money at the moment. I have also read somewhere or heard that it is full of athletic Germans getting a final dose of sun before winter!"

"Find out what's on offer and if it sounds ok I will probably go for it." She stared at the wall thinking of the warm sea, blue skies, and the athletic Germans who might be ski instructors getting in a break before the winter. She liked the idea of wild romantic sex with a sun bronzed ski instructor. She then thought about the stereotype German and laughed to herself at the thought of having sex in an orderly structured Teutonic way.

"One important little point we should consider. There's always the problem of getting blown up by some militant types if we go to these places, it has to be taken into consideration. On the other hand we shouldn't let such things prevent us from doing what we want, otherwise they have won. Well, that's how I see it" she said while shrugging her shoulders.

"What about Mexico? That has sunshine, decent beaches and even some culture." Amanda shrugged her shoulders in a manner that was negative, "I've never been interested in Mexico. It seems a long way away just to relax and get some sun" and, she was about to say strange diseases.

She smiled when she considered the possibility of acquiring some unhealthy condition in Egypt. She changed the subject as though the thought of travelling to Mexico had lessened her desires and her initial enthusiasm had disappeared as quickly as it had arrived.

"If we do go away for a break don't mention it on the unit as Lucille only asked me a couple of days ago if I would be willing to take her on holiday and I did say that I would think about it. She is mainly independent but it is still work to some extent, just being there and having some responsibility for another person gives it a feeling of work. Although the last time that I went away with a patient I enjoyed it. It surprised me how he changed once out of a nursing environment. After a couple of days it was really quite good and I think that I benefited from the experience. Although I had known him for a few years and subsequently I thought that I knew him, I soon found that I did not know him at all. I had only seen a facet of his personality, actually I was pleasantly surprised. I realised that is something we tend to forget: we see people as patients in this environment, they are usually ill or awaiting treatment so we're not seeing them as they really are. Anyway I enjoyed myself, but at the moment I think that getting away totally would be a good idea so I would prefer it if Lucille was not aware of anything that we arrange."

"There was something on the internet regarding new patients. I was going to mention it last week but it slipped my mind. I cannot remember the Doctors name, but I do remember he said that skull traction was something we should introduce again. I cannot remember what reasons he gave. I have heard it mentioned in the past but I cannot say if it merits any thought or not. Fortunately we don't make those decisions."

Caroline then said, "wouldn't it be strange if it was used again?"

Amanda was lost in her thoughts and did not reply.

"They're always talking about the value of stem cells and how they might be useful once the techniques have been developed."

" We've had a large number of wonder treatments awaiting sometime in the future so don't waste your time thinking about them, it's the hear and now that's the problem."

Simon came into the office to hand over the report. "I feel really tired this morning - don't know why though, I've done bugger all really," he said while only just preventing himself from yawning. He stood to attention clicked his heels and said,

"Nothing exciting to report Commandant. The guards have changed, the dogs are unleashed, the perimeter is secure and there were no escape attempts during the night. No one throwing themselves on their swords, and some of the patients are ok as well, in fact almost sane some of them" he added while attempting a smile.

Amanda just glared at him hoping that he would not continue in that manner. I cannot do with attempts at stupid humour so early she thought. They had always got on well with one another and she knew that his report would be accurate, and if there was something that she needed to know it would be brought to her attention. Although they had not worked together very long she instinctively knew that he was reliable.

"Why didn't you make Andy more comfortable?" she asked in a manner that made Simon take notice. Simon explained that he had not been working in that part of the unit and was not aware of Andy being uncomfortable, otherwise he would have done something about it. He felt uneasy at the thought that Amanda would consider that he might not give a patient the attention they needed. Amanda just nodded and accepted what he said, knowing that Simon was not the type to neglect anyone.

It should be stated that Simon was not your usual male nurse. That is, someone who had always wanted to become a nurse. He was definitely not the stereotype of a person who wanted to look after the sick, or tend the ill and the dying. He'd had none of those more altruistic thoughts or feelings when younger. He had served in the Army for a number of years before deciding that he needed a complete change in his career. He had not fully understood at the time why he had chosen nursing. It was more or less out of the blue. He had thought that it was something totally different to what he had been doing, and that thought alone appealed to him. The one thing that did concern him was whether or not he could accept instructions from his managers, especially if he knew that they were wrong or stupid. Originally he had not found this to be a problem in the Army, which upon looking back now surprised him. It had not bothered him at all at first, that was the army and you knew what to expect, and he accepted being told to do stupid things as part of the job. After a few years he had found it more and more difficult to accept the situation. Sooner or later he had decided that he would probably find himself in trouble. He was intelligent enough to realise that it was time to get out. Although he did this with some considerable regret, as he had enjoyed the comradeship and the travel that the army had provided. He had been to some interesting places, and he had done things that he could not have hoped to have done in civilian life. But his last tour of duty which had taken him to Bosnia had lead him to believe that once he had finished his time he would leave the army.

Upon looking back there were one or two things that he now wished that he had not done, but like everyone else he had made mistakes. And the army often, by its nature, placed one in a situation that was abnormal where normal rules did not apply. And one had to live with ones mistakes. He could accept his mistakes; on occasion they kept him awake a night, but time had proved itself a good healer.

His army friends had told him that sometimes you do and see things that stay with you, but you have to accept that it is always going to happen because of the abnormal situations you are placed in. One friend had insisted that he should separate the two. There is army life and there is civilian life. Once you leave the army you have to move on mentally. Simon did not quite understand at the time but he had started to recognise the validity of the statement.

His marriage, like many others', had turned out to be something of a disaster. She was an attractive women and he had found her very desirable but things had gone badly wrong. But such things were in the past, and it was impossible to go back and change things even if he had wanted to. He had thought that in recent years the army culture along with some of the postings had brought him into close contact with too many civilians, who he automatically mistrusted as though they were the enemy when they should have been the ordinary people who, in theory, you were there to help and to protect. He was pleased to be able to think that seemingly negative aspect or part of his life was now over. However, his army life had been important to him and he had no thought of dismissing it as being of no consequence. He knew that some of his Army friendships were always going to be important to him whatever his circumstances. Such friendships formed in adversity were friendships for life, and nothing could change that.

He had changed careers and moved out of the protective environment that the forces provide. Some of his friends said that the change was too different and too radical. That he would not survive the change, that he was throwing away a good career. And that he would qualify for a pension in a few years time, etc. He knew that these arguments were sound and reasonable and that his friends were well meaning with good intentions. However, he had made the decision. He had become a nurse and to many people's surprise, but not to his own, he had soon obtained promotion. To some extent this was down to the fact that he knew how authoritarian systems tend to work. He was used to working in such an environment, therefore it was easy for him to spot the opportunities when they arose. On leaving the Army, before obtaining training as a nurse, he had really wondered if it was what he really wanted. He even had some doubts after his training, before he fully entered unit life.

To his surprise he soon found that he really enjoyed nursing, he enjoyed working with people whom he could help. He finally felt as though he was doing something useful and worthwhile. He had seen and experienced a great deal while in the Army, and some of the less pleasant incidents still came into his mind on sleepless nights. But he knew as he grew older that he wanted to help people more directly. He often thought about why he had made such a dramatic change as he did not see himself as altruistic, but nursing had opened up for him not only a new career, but a whole new approach to life. And he was now sure that he had made the correct choice, and he could hopefully rebuild his life to suit his tastes and aspirations once he had decided what they were. At the moment he was not entirely sure, but he knew that they were beginning to form.

Although some of his tastes and interests had been with him or years, recently It seemed as though it was like starting out afresh, but with the benefit of wide and varied experiences gained over a period of time. He had even thought about re-marrying. He had made the wrong choice of partner last time but he was sure that if the occasion arose he would not make the same mistake again. Youthful sex-driven enthusiasm, and a blindness to everything rational and sensible would not be part of the equation next time, he thought. He had also thought that he might just live with a partner, that it might be easier than marrying, for some reason. Less commitment or being tied down with the legalities of a situation. Whatever the situation he decided that he did not want anything that was complex, he wanted things simple without any unnecessary complications. He then thought that it might be a contradiction in terms and that most types of serious relationships tend to become complex by their nature. He dismissed the thought, knowing that if and when something arose he would deal with it at that time as logically as he could.

"Roberto was not well, but it has not been put into the report as it only happened a short while ago. The Doctor came down and gave him some antibiotics. His temperature is high and his urine smells quite strong. Roberto thought that it was a bladder infection as he is accustomed to having them occasionally. A sample has been sent to the lab. He says that he is cold at the moment." Simon proceeded to discuss with Amanda a few of the other events that she needed to be informed of.

"I'm concerned about Bernard - his condition appears to be the same, but at the same time there was something different about him." Simon searched for the right words.

"Almost something intangible. I cannot put my finger on it." Bernard was the oldest patient on the unit.

Amanda said, "Yes. I'm also concerned. I talked with Bernard the previous day and recognised things were not right."

She looked at Simon "I fully understand your feelings."

She recognised that Bernard had changed in a manner that she also could not understand. She said "Either Caroline or I will have another talk with him to see if we can establish if anything's wrong, although it's obvious that something's not right."

She told Simon that Bernard was capable of keeping his feelings to himself no matter how bad he felt, if he chose to do so. She then told him that Bernard was very special to her, but she did not elaborate. Simon thought this was unusually mysterious and out of character but he did not say anything. Suddenly the dream of Bernard talking to her returned and she shuddered at the thought. She dismissed the thoughts telling herself that it was only a dream brought about because of her own emotional state at that moment.

Deliberately changing the subject she then asked Simon what he was going to do with his days off. This was out of politeness more than anything. Simon yawned before answering.

"I'm going to bed for a few hours, and then I'm going to London for the night. I have a ticket to see Tosca at Covent Garden, then late dinner at my hotel and a good nights sleep, unless I find a women that's irresistible wealthy and willing to indulge me sexually." He stared ahead, his mind drifting along as though lost in concentration. Amanda did not disguise her surprise at his answer. She had little or no idea regarding Simon's interests, and for some reason she just could not picture him as an opera enthusiast or looking around for a women that was a stranger to him.

"Do you go regularly?" she asked.

She laughed out loud at her last remark and before he had a chance to come back with some suitable quip she added. "To the opera I mean?" she decided not to mention the women as she presumed that it was something he had just added for the sake of it.

Simon replied "I go to the opera and the ballet a few times a year," in fact he went to anything that took his fancy, except jazz. He went on "I don't understand it and I never will."

He concluded, "I often thought that it's a bit like the Emperors new clothes and no one will actually say its discordant rubbish, but then again I might be wrong as some people like it, especially the middle-aged middle-class types who first discovered it while away at University.

Caroline thought he was being very opinionated, but did not comment as she was also interested in what he was saying.

He continued to explain "Some time ago I decided that I wouldn't restrict myself to any particular type of entertainment or pleasure. I'd do just what I wanted. Given that I have to stay within the limitations of my modest income. If I wanted to see something or go somewhere in particular I do it. Perhaps for only two or three days but I'm a free agent and not willing to be constrained by artificially imposed barriers. That sounds a bit pompous!" the last bit he said while laughing.

"To be honest I just looked at my past life and became dissatisfied with things. I wanted more, much more."

He sat on the edge of the desk and started to expand upon one of his favourite subjects. "Let us face it, life is very short and it's the only life we have, therefore why not do or see the things that really interest you?." He paused hoping for some sign of agreement before continuing. He quickly continued as no-one said anything,

"Usually I go by myself, then you are not restricted by having to please someone else. I know that also sounds bloody selfish but I have not yet found anyone who always wants to do or see what I want," he shrugged his shoulders as if to indicate his indifference to what others might think. He continued, "you always tend to put things off for the future, promising that you will do them when the children are older, etc, and then it can be too late – you're too old or dead! So 'do it now', that's my policy" he said while smiling upon realising he had surprised her.

"It might have taken me a long time to realise it but, like I have just said, time is too short, so just get on with it. Call me selfish if you want, but this is it, this is our life" he said with a degree of passion that surprised the others. He leaned back in his chair and looked thoughtful before he spoke again.

Amanda wanted to say that she understood and agreed with him but refrained as some of her present thoughts were contradictory.

He continued. "There is still so much I want to see and to experience. I was brought up in a family that did not have any particular interest in music or travel, or anything other than going to work and getting through life as best as one could. As a family we did not do or see much like most other families of a similar background; I suppose we were bereft of any cultural pursuits."

He was thinking carefully now before he spoke as though recalling specific moments. "It soon dawned upon me that many of the things that I did not experience while at home or in the army were probably very enjoyable, as common sense suggested that other people were enjoying this and that, therefore some of the things I had not thought about or considered must be good, which did seem logical."

Amanda was about to say something when he stopped her. She was glad that he had stopped her as she knew that she was only going to say something about life and death that would sound totally negative.

"Everyone is different. We all have different tastes and preferences" he said,

"but I'm not satisfied by living a narrow sheltered life that revolves around work and sleep. I want more out of life than that. It is an interesting place out there," he gestured by pointing to the door. He was expecting someone to question him but no one did which was unusual.

He said "I visited the Hermitage in St Petersburg three weeks ago. It was just a two night stay," he added.

Amanda stared at him for a moment as if slightly shocked.

Simon asked her if anything was wrong.

"No! Nothing's wrong. It's just that you have surprised me; actually, I think that I'm almost impressed." She stared at him in a strange manner realising that she knew nothing about the person sat in front of her.

"I am impressed" she said again, "very impressed, well let us say reasonably impressed, just to be on the safe side." She smiled at him. Simon did not know if his impression was a good one or not, but he could see that he had surprised Amanda. He would have liked to have given a good impression as he liked Amanda. From first meeting her he had quickly obtained a high opinion of her both as a person and as a nurse, she worked in a pattern similar to him, she liked a structure, and the option to use common sense. It was also a fact that he found her physically attractive. He had often thought that it was a pity that she was married. Unlike some men this put him off from asking her out, or even attempting to get to know her better socially. His own marriage had failed, and he did not want to be the cause of someone else's failing. He knew that his attitude was not only old fashioned but possibly lacking in sense and logic, but that was how he felt about such things. He liked to think that he had good standards, and that some day the world would regain its senses, and some of his standards would once again become the accepted norm. He knew that he had not better hold his breath. Trying to retain standards was always going to be difficult. What's more if you were not careful you could be out on a limb, living in a time warp, pretending that there was once a golden age where every one acted in the best of interests, and did the decent thing. Fortunately he had not travelled that far along a branch line, and he smiled to himself when such thoughts crossed his mind. He did promise himself that if Amanda's circumstances changed he would be willing to compromise. Not much of a compromise he thought. In fact he would be the first to knock on her door. Caroline who was astute had observed this and had decided that at the appropriate time she would mention it to Amanda, but for the moment she would keep it to herself.

He stood up and adjusted his posture. "In fact, you are right to be impressed! I'm an impressive person," he said this while trying to retain a serious expression. "Shall I now give you my impression of Marlon Brando?."

"Not if it's a scene from 'Last Tango in Paris'," added Amanda.

Simon winced in an effected manner pretending to be hurt. "No, it's from 'On the Water Front' when he's in the car with his brother. Oh forget it! You're not ready for such sophistication yet" he said while smiling. "What about Bogart? I do a good Bogart!."

"We're too young, we've hardly heard of these people" said Caroline.

"Did you see the impressionists?" asked Amanda while laughing. He did not react to her question in the manner she expected, but replied

"I saw some and would've liked to have stayed longer, time was the problem - or to be more accurate the lack of it and The Hermitage is very large. There's so much to see in there, it's incredible!" he added.

"I saw some of them a couple of years back when they put on the large exhibition in London. We had to queue for what seemed a very long time but it was worth it." She then continued, "I like the impressionists, but I like a lot of other artists as well. I suppose that it's not the artist but more the specific painting or paintings that attracts me," she said while looking at Simon expecting him to respond.

He just looked ahead lost in thought, so she continued. "You'll have to talk to Andy and Harry sometime," she added, "they're interested in art, and what they don't know they will still argue over, and if you can get Bernard to talk you'll definitely learn something." He smiled and nodded as if to say he would do that sometime.

"Well I never! I did not know that you were interested in art. I've known you for years and cannot ever remember you mentioning anything about paintings," said Caroline in a surprised tone of voice.

Amanda deliberately looked surprised before answering. "I have a lot of hidden facets to my nature that you don't know about," she said with a hint of sarcasm which she then concealed by laughing. Caroline started to say something but stopped herself.

There was a brief pause in the conversation. "Art is something that's very worthwhile, it makes life and things in general look better. It takes us above all that is ordinary and mundane," said Caroline thoughtfully.

Amanda just gazed at her in surprise. "That is also a bit profound for this time of the morning. What is happening to everyone? Where did you read that?" she said while smiling.

Caroline said, "I just like good pictures. It doesn't mean that I know anything about them technically, and to be honest, the technical side doesn't interest me. That's the whole point," she said with a degree of urgency wanting to explain her train of thought while it was still relatively clear, "well, not the whole point I realise. But you don't have to know anything in great depth, you just need to look and enjoy them for what they are." Caroline was suddenly quite animated. "Actually, and this will surprise you, but I've met a few artists in my time. My father was very interested in art and we used to visit exhibitions whenever we could. Everyone tends to become too arty when looking at pictures, it tends to be off-putting for some people. No one wants to show their ignorance so they just avoid such encounters and subsequently they loose so much. I like paintings, not the artists," she added, "a good painting is evocative."

Simon and Amanda looked at each other in surprise. Caroline just smiled at them enigmatically. She continued, "A friend who happened to be an art teacher showed me what he thought was the first abstract painting, he could hardly contain his excitement. Personally I couldn't see anything in it at all."

"As long as that was all he wanted to show you!" said Amanda, "I have read of artists and impressionable girls!"

"What was it called? asked Simon.

Caroline thought for a moment. "Something to do with a black square?"

"Oh yes. I know it," added Simon, "by a Russian painter, Malevich or some similar name." He wanted to hold forth on the subject. "Russia was an interesting place art wise just before and after the revolution. The was some rubbish created but the constructivists were different, and you can still obtain some of their original posters." He realised that they were not familiar with the subject. "That was the period before everyone had to suffer Stalinist realism, and the ugly didactic rubbish that he insisted upon," he then sighed, "but the artists did as they were told or they tried to get to the west where they had the freedom to paint whatever they wanted." He continued, "It's amazing how dictators always seem to go for the similar type of art, if you can call it art, large hybrid classical with bits added on for good measure. Buildings like wedding cakes, workers shown labouring away as though they are enjoying themselves." Simon suddenly remembered where he was and he started to laugh.

"You must stop me as it can get so boring unless you're interested in the subject, and I tend to forget for the moment that I'm still at work."

They both thought it sounded unbelievably boring and they appeared to nod as if in sympathy.

"I cannot cope with Stalinist realism at the moment - whatever it is," said Amanda, she was pleased that he had decided to leave that aspect of art alone for the time being as it sounded incredibly boring.

"Anyway, I'm going off for a day next week – painting," he added with a gesture that gave the impression he was gaining a level of freedom. "It's just a short trip up to North Yorkshire. I made the usual mistake, I promised someone a painting of the moors and I need to do it soon. It's not like riding a bike - despite what some people might say or think, you need to keep your eye in and the only way is to go out and paint, and if the result is not to your satisfaction then you paint it again. Besides, it's extra money and I need it if I'm to continue living or trying to live what could be described as a decent lifestyle." He continued happily as he was talking about paintings which were a favourite subject. "It's not relaxing as some people say either, it is quite the opposite. It's sometimes hard work getting a painting right but usually the effort is worth it. At the end of the day it's my little bit towards creativity and immortality," he laughed at that point.

"You mean it's like sex," added Caroline. She continued, "just keep doing it until you are doing it right. Is that what you mean?"

Simon looked at her quizzically wondering if she was teasing him, he was tempted to say something but he ignored the remark, knowing if he said anything it would lead him away from what he wanted to say. "I used to paint quite a lot when I was younger but like a lot of things it's something you just give up, promising that you'll start again when you have more time. In the end I made time and I haven't regretted it." He suddenly stopped then added, "It's not like sex at all," he looked bemused.

She interjected. "I bet that you are good at it, in fact I bet that when you set your mind to something that you're good at most things."

Simon was now almost sure that she was winding him up but he could not think why as she had not attempted to do it before when she had the opportunity so he thought it safest to ignore her remarks.

"I always promised myself that I would take up photography," said Caroline "but I've never found time."

"It's easier now if you have a computer, you can use a digital camera and print your own, download them direct - it is so much easier," added Simon.

She sighed. "I might get around to it - someday. Besides, I'm not much good with computers, they tend to do strange things once they know it's me who has switched them on. In fact I would go as far as to say they're vindictive bastards, they're always crashing as soon as they know it's me."

Simon scratched his head in mock disbelief. He had recognised years earlier that some people treat computers as the enemy who one had an eternal struggle with, but it still left him slightly bewildered

"We should all become more computer literate," said Amanda while adding that she could not personally stand the things. She continued "somehow things seemed to work better when they didn't exist. Anyway one thing is easier, if anything goes wrong just blame it on the computer. Say something technical," she paused while trying to think of something. "Say that the hard drive, when being de-fragged, has accidentally moved some files from the registry and there is a difficulty running the recovery software."

"That sounds impressive," said Caroline. She then asked what it actually meant. Amanda replied that she hadn't a clue but it sounded appropriate, and she was sure that the last so called expert on computers had said something similar when repairing her husband's. All agreed that computers were useful in case an excuse was required, but also a curse.

"We could easily rely on the damned things and forget to use common sense," added Amanda. "In fact, I think some of us already have. Present company excluded of course!. I must point out to you before I forget, that courses are available and they will be paid for if you want to learn more about computers. In fact, I think everyone is expected to go on some of the courses, and it will look good on your CV. The way things are going we might be needing a good CV."

"What have you heard?" asked Caroline who thought that Amanda was throwing out a hint that required someone to respond.

"It's just a general comment," said Amanda, "nothing specific, so don't worry, you still have a job, well you have for the next week or two."

There was a silence before Caroline realised that Amanda was not being serious.

Simon interjected, "Before I forget, rumour has it that we will be having a new patient later today."

Both looked at Simon but did not dispute his statement as past experience had taught them that he seemed to obtain information before anyone else. And on enquiring, he had refused to names his sources.

"It's a girl," he added, "well, to be accurate, a young woman I suppose, a quad, but I'm not aware of her level of lesion. That's all I know," he held up his hands as if to indicate he was telling the whole truth.

"Well, we can get the basic equipment ready and move the beds around then no one can complain that we're not on top of things. It's very good of you to tell us," said Amanda who was annoyed. She knew that such information should have come to her first as it was her responsibility. Simon said it was not his fault that he had been given the information, and besides, he was going home as he was ready for breakfast.

'Unless you think that you cannot manage without me?" he added.

"We managed quite well before you arrived here" said Amanda.

"Let's be honest - you must have struggled until I came along and organised things!" he said while quickly making an exit.

He put his head around the door, "one last thing I've just remembered. The suppositories seemed a bit delayed in their action so we have left a few of the patients for the day staff to deal with."

"Oh thank you for such generosity! That's just the right way to start the day off," said Amanda.

"Thought that I should mention it," said Simon who was now laughing as he walked away, thinking about getting home as soon as possible to shower and change. He decided that on principle he should have the last word.

"And you will no doubt have benefited from our little chat just now, it raises the tone somehow don't you think? It's more important than bladders and bowel actions and suchlike - we must do it again tomorrow. I will call my lecture 'The Surrealists. Are they real?'. It has a nice ring to it don't you think?" he said while laughing.

"It all sounds like a load of bullshit to me! I think he's not got past painting by numbers and is just trying to impress us. Has anyone seen his paintings? Has he ever mentioned them before?" said Caroline while smiling.

Simon was about to defend himself when he thought better of it, "think what you like, but if necessary I can show you my work. But due to your doubts I will now take some persuading. It would be like casting pearls before swine showing you lot my masterpieces. I'm late now - I need to get some food in before I get home."

He hurried away down the corridor singing something that they could not recognise. "He has an appalling voice! I hope that he paints better than he sings. Perhaps we should tell him," said Amanda.

"I once went to Covent Garden" said Caroline, "I was young and it was a school trip. It was during the daytime. We then walked down to Trafalgar Square and looked in the National Gallery. At the time I didn't particularly enjoy the paintings - it seemed as though they were just too big and remote. For most of the time the subject matter seemed boring. I remember all the religious paintings, and while obviously good they did nothing for me. Years later I could appreciate them better and place them in their historical context, which always helps."

Amanda sighed, "I seem to have entered the wrong office this morning. What's happening to everyone? We're actually talking about art. It's unnatural. This is not real. Has something happened that I'm unaware of?. What about the price of washing powder, or beans or something? I'm not sure if I'm ready for this," said Amanda while pretending to look bemused.

"We'll have to seek counselling if this continues as we'll be listening to Gregorian chants next."

"That is a good idea actually, doing patients bowels to Gregorian chants! That will add to the existing surrealism of this place" These thoughts made her laugh.

"Something more triumphant is required," added Caroline, "perhaps the 'Post Horn Gallop'." She then expanded upon appropriate pieces of music for differing physical conditions. "That's not politically correct - we should be more sensitive." Caroline distorted her face as if to emphasise that some thought was going into her next sentence. "I think it's acceptable if we could say that it's musical therapy."

Amanda spoke without responding or prolonging that line of conversation. "There's a new rep calling this morning with some new dressings, evidently they have been tried in a couple of countries and they are supposed to assist the healing process. It's more than likely that they are similar to those we're already using, but we might give them a try. If I'm not available you'll have to deal with it," said Amanda while looking at Caroline. "Also, we'll be having three or four visitors from eastern Europe coming round during the afternoon. I cannot tell you who they are because I haven't been informed, after all I am only in charge of nursing here," she said scathingly.

"So, let us go out and face that brave new world and start the day with a smile." Caroline started singing "Hi ho! Hi ho! It's off to work we go!."

"With a voice like that you should be in the theatre."

Caroline waited for the following line that she knew was coming.

"Pole dancing or selling peanuts!"

CHAPTER THREE

The ambulance had arrived quickly on the scene, and it was obvious that the young couple were trapped in such a manner that the fire brigade would be required to get them out of the tangled mass of metal that was once a car. The whole process had taken longer than expected and everyone was worried about the young women. It had been quickly ascertained that the young man was already dead from his injuries.

They finally removed her from the wreckage and the ambulance sped away with its siren warning everyone in its path. Fortunately, at that time there was hardly any traffic on the road. The two paramedics quickly took her through the doors into A and E where staff were already waiting. The ambulance crew had already contacted the hospital informing them of what they perceived to be the situation.

The young doctor worked quickly with the nurse; soon the young women was being carefully examined, she was talking, but little of it made any sense. The senior doctor arrived just as the X-rays were being scrutinised. He had a short discussion with the junior doctor before examining the young women. After his examination, he asked the doctor to telephone the spinal unit to see if they had a bed available. The unit was some miles away and the senior doctor was sure that they needed to get her there as soon as possible.

"Do we know anything about her?" he asked, while looking around hoping for a response.

"On her driving licence it states her name is 'Kimberly', Kim, for short I think. The police are waiting outside - evidently one of them knows her, his son was at the same school a couple of years ago."

The doctor sighed deeply, "you'd better get them to inform the parents. And it might be better that they come here now as we have not yet obtained a time when we can transfer her. That is, if there's an available bed." He turned to the young doctor. "I don't want to keep her here, the sooner she's on a spinal unit the better. We could look after her for a short while if necessary, but it's not in her interest, and we don't have the expertise or the bed, and things can quickly take a turn for the worse, in my experience. Let's get her parents here, and as soon as possible let's get her out of here."

The young doctor was pleased to be able to confirm that a bed would be available on the spinal unit and they would like her there as soon as they could arrange suitable transport. He added that if there were any unforeseen delays they must telephone the unit again, as spare beds were in demand. He paused briefly and looked at the young women. She's in for a difficult time, he thought. He then concluded that it was fortunate that we did not know what the future had in store for us.

Amanda had dealt with all that had needed to be done, and she was ready to ensure that the rest of the staff were motivated. There was the sound of a number of voices coming from along the corridor.

"I'll round up the shock troops and we'll make a start by marching into Poland," said Caroline before draining her cup of the last mouthful of coffee. She winced and said "sooner or later we must invest in some decent coffee."

Amanda agreed that what they had been drinking recently was disgusting but it was cheap.

"We're better paying that bit more, than drinking this stuff any longer, it makes you feel as though hairs are growing on your teeth" said Caroline.

"I agree, but tell the others, they're too tight to buy decent stuff," added Amanda, "they voted for cheaper coffee."

"It's just a pity that they cannot tell the difference - this stuff makes my tongue feel as though it's growing mushrooms," said Caroline while leaving the office.

"If we bought the best quality Columbian it would be casting pearls before swine," added Amanda laughing.

"I suppose if it were Columbian, they'd be more enthusiastic if it was coke they were snorting!" She then hoped that no one had heard her last comment. Only a week before a senior nurse had been suspended and the police had been brought in to investigate how a considerable quantity of drugs had gone missing. It created the most unpleasant atmosphere throughout the hospital, rumours abounded. In the end one could have been forgiven if they had believed that the establishment was the centre of an international drugs syndicate with a direct line to Columbia. Surprisingly, a few members of staff put a little effort into trying to find the potential source of cheap drugs in the belief that various concoctions might be on offer, but this was a fruitless search.

Luna and Spike at that moment had no need or interest in drugs or hospitals. It was cold outside, and the bed was not only warm and comforting but a haven for two people who were in love. Romantics would say that it had been the same throughout history, bed was a wonderful creation for a young couple that allowed them to defy some of the boundaries imposed by the rest of the world; it was their space in their special time zone. Luna was breathing heavy and her cheeks were flushed, her lips were pressed tightly to his. He felt her open mouth with his tongue as she gasped for a deep breath. She took a few more breathes before responding. She wanted to climb all over him, to press her body tightly against his, but she knew that she could not do this as it might affect his ability to breathe. They made love again, hungrily, with a passion that left their senses reeling. He loved the taste of her and the touch of her. He wanted to run his mouth and lips over every part of her soft tender body. Their excitement at each other's touch was unrestrained.

They made love until they were exhausted and they could momentarily just lay beside each other, smiling a smile of contentment. She felt the need to speak at that moment of contentment but she did not know why.

"I used to read about such things in schoolgirl magazines and I thought that it couldn't really be like that, that the feelings they spoke of were only available for some hypothetical group who lived in an unreal world." She laughed a quiet, sensitive, warm laugh.

"It's the finest of all surprises that such feelings do really exist! I must have been so sheltered, so naïve," she said.

But even in the best of anyone's world reality has to be faced, even if it's with great reluctance, she thought.

"It's time to get up you sexy beast! Come on! Open your eyes and make love to me again while there's still time. I'm tired of you shirking your responsibilities - you promised to satisfy all my sexual needs and now you're falling down on the job."

She poked him hard on his shoulder. "You've quickly tired of me and you faithfully promised that you never would."

She continued, while shaking him. "Come on then, I'm yours, I'm giving you my body, the body of a young innocent girl, don't hide under the bed clothes," she said while poking him on his shoulder again, this time demanding a response.

He groaned very loudly but did not attempt to move.

"Come on move yourself! Open both eyes, I've told you for the very last time that I'm offering you my body, this untainted, wonderful creation. There are some men who would give a lot for a night with me."

The muffled words, "go and find one, and leave me alone! Make sure that he gives you your bus fare home," came from underneath the bed clothes.

She was persistent and added, "This is my final offer! You can do whatever disgusting things you want to me for free, and with no commitment," said the attractive elfin faced young women, while at the same time feeling with her feet for the slippers that were an essential protection against the cold floor. The man whom she had been lying next to in a warm bed just grunted something again, that sounded like, 'bugger off you slut.'

He then added, "on second thoughts, if you were on offer, you wouldn't earn your bus fare home." He then added that she would only age quicker if she did not stop abusing her body. This was one of his more polite responses. She just ignored him and methodically went into the same routine that she had done for the past two years. She would first of all have a shower and then get herself dressed. She would then fill a large washing bowl and take it to the side of the bed. Her partner, who would be lying very comfortably, would open one eye, grunt again in the certainty that his comfort was about to be disturbed.

"The water's hot," he said, as the young women washed his face for him.

"Are you certain that you want to go through with it?" he asked while trying to remove some residue of soap from the corner of his mouth.

"Of course I want to go through with it!" she said quickly, adding, "didn't we agree last night that we were certain, that there was nothing to stop us. We're adults who know our own minds." He stopped her from saying anything else.

"You said it after your fourth orgasm and that can distort one's intellectual capacity. It is well known that it can make your hair fall out. In fact, I think that I'm going a bit thin on top. You are sexually abusing me," he added while trying to smile in a cynical manner. "It'll look really good in the Sunday papers if I sell my story. 'Nymphomaniac Nurse sexually abuses refined and helpless disabled man'."

"You! Refined! You are not refined," she said loudly "you're an uncouth bit of rough who I have sympathy for."

He was laughing now, "it will say: 'Man claims compensation for loss of hair.' I wonder if I can sue anyone for loss of hair?" This remark was ignored. He wanted the last word as usual and she accepted that situation.

"You also promised me that you would make sure I could get an erection, but you've had no real success have you? Perhaps you're not doing it right? Perhaps someone else might obtain more success?"

She let the comment go as she wanted to move the conversation on to an important subject.

"Who do we tell first?" he said this in the form of a question although he already knew the answer.

"We must tell Caroline," said the young women, eagerly, like a child discussing her forthcoming birthday party.

"It must be Caroline," she said quietly while at the same time clapping her hands together with excitement. She thought of Caroline's likely expression when she told her that they had decided to get married. In fact they had decided to get married some weeks ago, and the wedding would be at the registry office on the coming Saturday just before noon. There would be little time left for their plans to go wrong.

Spike and Luna had shared a ground floor flat for the past two years. They had thought long and hard about living together as they both came from families who were, by nature, conservative. And the idea of a couple living together, while appearing to be the norm for possibly the vast majority of couples, for Spike and Luna it was quite different - almost daring. Like their respective families both of them enjoyed tradition, and the promise of stability that tradition was supposed to bring with it. They thought that if their ideas and attitudes were out of step with those of the rest of people of their age group, so what. They no longer cared about what other people thought of them. They had realised that not everyone was going to be helpful or understanding, and therefore they had concluded that the decent ordinary people who were their friends, counted, and the rest of society did not count, as far as opinions were concerned. They had quickly learned a lot about people and their attitudes over the past couple of years, and most of the time they were disappointed in the way people thought, and the way the world was going in general.

They were both romantics and believed in a society that was basically good and progressive, a society that was caring about everyone and their basic needs. And a society where the elderly were still respected and the vulnerable were protected or cared for. These were simple and old fashioned values. Both of them sometimes found it hard to understand why they felt that way as most of their peers did not, but these things were important to them and they could not remember how they had arrived at these conclusions. They talked about it on numerous occasions and after some considerable arguments and thought, they realised that they neither knew nor remembered. They put it down to one of those inexplicable happenings. But they did recognise that by sharing these ideas and principals it had brought them closer together. They were happy to believe in something; it made life better if one had beliefs, they thought, even if those beliefs were not always accepted by those around them.

They had first met on the unit some three or four years earlier. Spike had been disabled for some years due to an accident he had sustained whilst swimming. Luna was already a nurse on the unit when Spike had spent a few days on the unit with a difficult bladder infection. She had nursed him through a very difficult few days. And although at the time he was running a high temperature he made it obvious that he was enjoying her care and attention. He remembered the first time that he saw her. He thought that she was simply wonderful and beautiful. He could not find appropriate words. He did, however, try very hard. She told him that he was running a very high temperature, and that he was not seeing things properly. When his temperature had started to decline, Spike had looked at her slowly and carefully at every possible opportunity, and he thought that he had not done her justice. There were no adequate words to describe her, he thought. He had never seen anyone who looked so good, so flawless, so perfect. How could this wonderful person be looking after him? What had he done to deserve this? he constantly asked himself. He had never been a person who sought good luck or expected it. But here he was, being carefully looked after by what he thought was the most divine creature that had walked the planet. He was instantly in love, he felt stupid and almost crazy, and he knew it, but he didn't care. He had never been in love before, and for just an instance he was uncertain.

'How did he know that he was in love?' he asked himself. He was equally as quick to tell himself once again that he had never felt that way before, he felt out of control, and he did not give a toss, therefore it must be love; what else could it be? He wanted to breathe the same breath that she took; he wanted to taste the same drink, to pick her up in his arms and carry her. He enjoyed those feelings, which only a short time ago he would have thought of as being rather silly, or stupid, to say the least. He accepted that he had been infected and contaminated with this obsession. He smiled to himself a contented smile.

In the real world where cynicism is prevalent one might expect Spike to somehow find his way back to what one might call reality, and for Luna to politely and kindly let him down as gently as possible while she moved on. While at the same time reassuring him, that he knew as well as she did, that patients often fall for the nurse who has shown them some small kindness, and given them a lot of attention while they have been ill. But this was not the case, quite the opposite. Luna, who everyone agreed was an excellent nurse and very level headed, had suddenly changed. She was acting in a similar fashion to Spike. Within days they had fallen in love. Some staff members said that it was an infatuation, that for some unknown reason the pair of them were acting totally out of character, they obviously had been smoking some funny stuff, which everyone knew was Spike's favoured medicine. However, in the light of day nothing had changed; their feelings for each other only gained in intensity. There was a discussion amongst some members of staff who thought that events had gone far enough, and it might be time to move Luna off of the unit for her own good. This annoyed the nurse in charge, who, in no uncertain terms, told two members of her staff that it was more likely that they would be sent to another unit rather than Luna. She told them clearly that she expected a more sensible attitude from them, as she did from all of the staff who had worked on the unit for some time, who knew both of the individuals quite well. She carried on angrily. Telling them that their attitude would have been different if one of the individuals had not been disabled. Her outburst had the correct effect. For once, everyone seemed not only to listen, but to think about the situation.

Both Spike and Luna were popular with everyone. There wasn't anyone who had anything bad to say about them. Everything seemed as though the whirlwind romance was heading for a very popular wedding, but fate took a hand and it did not happen. On three separate occasions they had planned a quick wedding, but something always went wrong preventing it from taking place. After some prolonged discussion, which was at times very tense and upsetting, they decided to live together. Rightly or wrongly, they felt that time was short and much too precious to waste. They wanted to be together and that was all there was to it. They were disappointed when they first started to look at the practicalities, surprisingly, for some reason they had not given them much thought. It finally dawned upon them that some serious thought was required, and no matter how much they loved one another, the so called real world was waiting.

The first and most important question being, where are we going to live? In their excitement or passion, call it what you will, they had forgotten that they needed a roof over their heads, and preferably their own. The council was, to their surprise, very cooperative, and quickly offered them a small bungalow that had been built, along with a number of others, for disabled people some years earlier. They leaped at this opportunity and quickly moved in, promising each other that they would get married when they thought that the time was right. They talked this through with their friends, who all said what they did was their business, and why get married anyway? Better just to live together. Both Spike and Luna felt the same on this subject: they definitely wanted to get married one day. The strange thing about it was that their friends knew that whatever they did it would be the right choice. Spike and Luna were something quite special, everyone wanted them to be happy. There was a moment shortly after they were living together that Spike was concerned about the situation. He had started to feel, rightly or wrongly, that they were being held up to be the token disabled couple, although Luna wasn't disabled. For once Spike had got it wrong, which was something that he was pleased to admit to himself later. Nature had come together in one of those rare instances and managed to get it right.

Spike and Luna were genuinely liked, they were popular, people liked to be in their company. It was as though their love for one another might be infectious. Everyone wanted to share in something that was different and far removed from the daily tedium that affected most people's lives.

"So be it," said Spike to himself in a dramatic manner while psyching himself up as though he was about to enter the boxing ring or fight a battle.

"This is the big one! Let's go for it," he shouted.

"What do you want for breakfast?" asked Luna in a voice that was deliberately controlled in order that it might bring Spike back to reality. She was running late for work, and she was now used to Spike psyching himself up now and then, and allowing himself the odd manic outburst that to those who did not know him would seem totally out of character.

Washing and dressing Spike had taken her longer than usual for some reason.

"I'll tell Caroline, and I'll ring Shirley. She'd never forgive me if we got married without telling her. She had a soft spot for you when you first arrived on the unit. She told me that you were an opinionated young man, who enjoyed arguing with everyone, but for some strange reason she still liked you."

"She was a first rate nurse, although she had a few strange habits that surprised even me."

Luna looked at Spike and asked him to expand.

"Not just now - there isn't the time."

She paused for a moment then spoke quickly.

"And you must tell Little John that he's your best man. Try and remember or he'll have no idea, will he?" she added still smiling.

Spike thought about little John and he was not quite sure if little John was up to being at a wedding, let alone theirs. Luna guessed what he was thinking and told him that John would be fine if he remembers to take his medication. Spike grunted, but accepted what she had said. He had known John for most of his life and at times even he could not understand how John's mind worked. Everyone who knew him always said the same. They just could not decide whether he was incredibly intelligent or totally stupid; with John it was a very fine line. He was the type of person whom you would not want as a close member of your family. He came and went without notice. It was almost impossible to know where he was ,or what he was doing; he managed to get through life in a manner that was unique to him. He had never worked for anyone but himself. Although no one actually knew what it was he worked at, but occasionally it must have been successful and at other times the opposite, because John's fortunes fluctuated from week to week. One week he would be driving an expensive sports car, a little later he would be riding a small motor bike that he had stored away for such occasions when things were not easy regarding his cash flow situation. But things like that never worried him as he knew that in a very short time the good times would soon be with him again. Spike remembered one incident that had made him laugh. John, for some strange reason, had bought ten thousand old gas masks which he then could not sell; the demand for old gas masks being somewhat limited. When asked why he had paid good money for such an item he informed the person that it was only a matter of time before there would be a suitable war somewhere. In this he was correct, and he managed to rid himself of the gas masks to a small African state for a large amount of tropical fruit, as the small state did not have any hard currency. Finally, when it arrived it was over-ripe and not in a condition to sell on the open market. This did not faze John for one moment. He sold the fruit the same day to a small food manufacturer who used it in their sauces. John was quite proud of that particular deal and on occasion, when out, he would take particular notice to see if he could recognise any of the sauces that might contain the fruit he had sold. The more unkind individuals said he took notice in order to avoid food poisoning.

Spike chuckled to himself on recalling the incident. Luna reached over him and kissed him. He pulled her close to him.

"Sorry, but we haven't got the time now. You had your chance earlier and you blew it! You might be lucky tonight, though, if I feel in the mood," she added while smiling.

"You just cannot stand the pace," he said, also smiling,

"A few minutes ago you were demanding that I satisfy your carnal desires, obviously you were bluffing."

"The car has arrived for you," she said, "and it looks as though you have a new driver, a young women, in fact, a very young women."

There was a brief pause before Luna added, "And she has good legs, just the type you like. You'll really like her she's definitely the type you go for on the days when your taste is impaired."

He tried to think of a quick response but could not.

"She might get you in the right mood for tonight!"

Spike was not going to be drawn. He just grunted. He was not at his best at this time in the morning. Anytime before 10.00am was not seen as a suitable time for conversation or even polite interaction of any kind, except sex and coffee.

Spike worked as a part time lecturer at the local technical collage. He enjoyed the work and the challenge, but some days he did have to admit he would have preferred to stay at home working on one of his passions that Luna did not share. Archaeology, or to be more precise, the study of British and European Military history with his specialist subject study of Roman Britain. They both finally got off to work while looking forward to telling their friends that their wedding was all systems go, that this time they would make it. Just as he was leaving Luna stopped him. He protested that he would be late if delayed.

She leaned forward and kissed him tenderly, she looked deep into his eyes, "About last night…"

"What about last night?" said Spike wondering what was coming next.

"If anything happens to you, I'm going to have that tongue of yours embalmed," "And," she paused while looking into his eyes, "the wonderful mind blowing orgasms…"

"Yes?" said Spike, smiling in anticipation of a boost to his ego.

"I'm sorry to have to tell you this, but I was faking some of them. I moaned quite a bit simply because I had really bad indigestion!" shouted Luna while quickly pushing him out of the door.

" Which ones were you faking?" he shouted, she just laughed.!

She decided that she would then rush off and do some shopping before going to work. And she could hardly wait to tell her friends about the forthcoming marriage. She sighed, hoping that this time everything would go as planned, with no last minute problems. She could not think of anything that might suddenly appear to throw their plans into disarray, but experience had taught her that while everything had been thought out carefully, suddenly something cropped up to spoil things. It almost seemed as though they were fated not to marry. She knew that such thoughts were not sensible, but she could not stop thinking that in their case, fate had brought them together, while at the same time had thrown into the equation this problem with getting married. With most couples it would not have been important, but to them it was. Luna had asked herself on a number of occasions why it seemed so important as they were not particularly religious. Was it that they were just wanting to get married to make a statement of some kind? These thoughts confused her because she knew that they did not have to show the world anything. They owed the world nothing. Yet they both wanted to be officially married in the eyes of the law. She had mentioned this to Spike, whom was usually very sensible, but he could not explain it either. Once, he had said that perhaps they should not get married on principle, as though it might appear we're trying to conform to some norm set by society. Luna had told him that was a stupid way to look at it, as they both wanted to get married, and it had nothing to do with what anyone else thought. Spike admitted that was true. But he was still unsure. This did cause a heated conversation until they realised what it was they were arguing over, then they laughed at the absurdity of the situation. I think we would not be discussing this twenty years ago; it's a form of scrutinising ourselves for some form of political correctness, he thought.

Spike declared: "We'll be married if, and when, we want, simply because it's what we want and sod the rest! We have conformed for the greater part of our lives and it's done us little good."

They agreed that was the right conclusion. Luna smiled, she was content with Spike taking that line of action. Spike, she thought, was a wonderful man, better than any person she had ever met. But then again, I am prejudiced. She said to herself: 'I love him'. Luna loved Spike more than any words could describe, she wanted to be with him day and night, she could not explain her love or her feelings. They were larger and more expansive than anything she had ever felt. She thought that those words were not accurate, for they did not describe her feelings. She searched her mind for something more precise, but there was nothing forthcoming. Then she realised that nothing would, simply because her love was larger than whatever else she could think of to describe it. Her thoughts were so simple and innocent, her love was truly something to be wondered at, and she felt a level of happiness that transcended anything she could have imagined. Occasionally she would pause, and think to herself that being with someone is not supposed to be like this. Where are the violent arguments, the bitter disagreements, and always the lack of money, the desire for expensive things? Perhaps I have seen too many soaps on television where life is a constant battle over trivia she thought.

Spike thought that he should draw up a list of people they wanted at the reception. Luna had forgotten that there is usually some sort of reception after the event and although it did not particularly concern him, he thought that they should have one, and enjoy it with their friends. He also thought about going away for a honeymoon; then he thought it seemed a little bit odd as they had been living together for some time. He then concluded that it was not odd at all, but a good reason to go off somewhere different. He decided that he would make the arrangements and keep it as a surprise. It occurred to him that Luna might not like something of that nature forced upon her at the last minute. He reassured himself with the thought that if he found somewhere really nice, she would love it.

'That's settled', he said to himself, then added 'it's got to be special, nice and romantic; something that we will always look back upon with pleasure'. He then tried to think of suitable hotels that were romantic and still accessible for his wheelchair. We need a place where they will help me into bed as well, that requires suitable staff on duty at night, therefore, it cannot be a small undiscovered place in the back woods. He felt annoyed at having to think about such practicalities. He knew from experience that on arriving at a hotel, even though you have explained your situation in detail, you can still find that the person to whom you were talking forgot to mention that the dining room is down three steps and the bathroom doors are not wide enough. But he was determined to find somewhere that was special. He did not enjoy flying anymore, years ago it all seemed something of an adventure, but now it was hassle. Airports were larger and busier than ever, and while the number of disabled passengers had increased, the service to them had hardly improved.

He knew of some wonderful hotels abroad that had tempted him. He decided in the end that he would try and find something within a few hours' drive, but time was short and he would have to get on with it. 'Thank god for the internet', he thought. He was still not sure that he had done the right thing, now he felt strangely nervous. He looked at the telephone wondering if he should ring back and cancel the arrangements. He finally decided against it. He had found a small fisherman's cottage on the coast overlooking the beach and the rocks in Northumbria, that was stated in the brochure as being fully accessible. He had been to the area in the past, and he had always enjoyed the wild seclusion that he had felt when he was there. Whether it be for a day or for longer, there was something special about that stretch of coastline. It seemed somehow that it was steeped in mystery, and what he could only describe as a feeling of spirituality, while at the same time it remained unspoiled or depressing in anyway. You can still dream in that place, he said to himself. He also knew that he could visit a Roman fort if the opportunity arose. He laughed to himself and told himself that he had better not do that as Luna would not like his insensitivity, and would think he had chosen the cottage simply because of its proximity to the Roman remains. He pondered on the matter and thought that he could not easily let such an opportunity pass though. Given the right moment he was sure that he could get her to have a look around with him, after all, she would be in a good, carefree mood. ' It is our honeymoon and everything should be as good as we can make it, she just might go for it,' he thought.

"There are the new carers waiting for you," said Spike's boss.

"Bloody hell!" said Spike, "I'd forgotten all about them! I'm supposed to give them a brief talk on spinal injuries, so they can have a basic idea of the realities of the situation before they meet the students to whom they are going to be personal assistants."

He smiled the best he could to reassure his boss that everything would get done. "Don't worry!" he said exuding confidence, "I'll have to give them the basics after, which it might make them look for another job," he said while laughing.

His manager smiled without any real conviction, but he also knew Spike would not let him down.

The new care assistants were sat down expectantly, awaiting enlightenment. Spike told them that he was only going to inform them of the basics about spinal injuries and related conditions, and that they would obtain most of their important information when working with their disabled employers.

He continued: "If what I'm about to say gives you some concern for whatever reason, then this is the time to address the problem. Don't be shy and remain ignorant, just ask me now before you work with your clients." He paused for a moment while thinking. "I'm not sure that they are clients, or your employer, or what, as they keep changing the terminology. The point is that you are employed to provide your client with personal assistance without which they cannot undertake the courses they've signed up for, it is as simple as that. That's your role, to assist and to make sure your client can undertake the course - successfully we hope," he said, while looking at each of them in turn. This could be hard work, he decided, as the faces in front of him showed no glimmer of acceptance or any sign of life.

He had delivered a similar talk on a number of occasions, with appropriate variations, depending upon the function of the individuals he was lecturing.

He began. "First of all, have a good look at me and you can then decide what bits work and what don't; satisfy your curiosity now and then we can begin." They smiled in embarrassment. "If you're ready now, we can get on with it," he said in a controlled voice that expressed authority. "The most important point that a carer can take on board is to try and fully understand the person they are providing care for. It sounds simple enough doesn't it?" he looked around, but no one said anything so he continued. "It's not sufficient just to pay lip service to a holistic approach. You are aware of the word 'holistic', I presume?" he said, while looking at them hoping that they had. There was some nodding which he took to be affirmative and he found reassuring.

"First of all," ('I think that I've already said that,' he said to himself.)

"What I'm about to tell you is simplistic, and only a small part of what you'll learn once you're with your clients, so, don't worry, I'll just keep to the basics. A spinal injury of the type I'm referring to is usually caused by an accident. Although a spinally injured person may look somewhat fit and healthy compared with other disabled individuals, however," he paused for a moment, "outward appearances can be deceptive. So do not go on appearances alone when making a decision or arriving at a conclusion. One important fact is that the level of the lesion, which means the level where the person has damaged their spinal cord, will dictate, to a large extent, a person's physical capabilities, and this is even more the case with higher level lesions. i.e. tetraplegics or quadriplegics. But to presume a person's capabilities without having met or known them can often lead to wrong conclusions. A spinally injured person has a number of complex problems to deal, with regarding body management. This might surprise you: the paralysis, or not being able to walk, is relatively unimportant to most spinally injured individuals when they have been disabled for a number of years."

He could see by their expressions that they were not in agreement with his last statement. "This is a fact that many non-disabled like yourselves find difficult to grasp. You might always find it difficult to grasp, but that can be discussed later. For the moment just take my word for it. The main areas that constantly require attention and are of real concern are bladder control, and preventing bladder infections; bowel control and management, and the prevention of pressure sores. This is probably a new phrase to you but don't let that concern you at this moment. 'Autonomic dysreflexia' - this can be a problem for many high lesions, and this manifests itself in sweating, shivering, feeling clammy, and very bad headaches with high blood pressure. This is brought about by stimulus such as a blocked catheter etc., but almost any physical stimulus might bring it on. The disabled individual will, over the years, have a good understanding of this problem, but it is important to recognise that the high blood pressure that is brought about is dangerous and needs attention right away. i.e. you may need to change the catheter, or call Doctor etc." He gazed at them hoping they were taking this in.

"Something else that must be considered is the fact that on any particular day a spinally injured person might feel fit and well, yet two or three hours later they might not feel very well. Particularly with higher lesions the situation can change very quickly. A spinally injured person's body does not always respond to stimulus or circumstances in the manner that would be expected of a non spinally injured person. Changes can occur rapidly, but each individual becomes aware of their own body and its capabilities. Even individuals with the same level of injury often have different physical capabilities, these can seem small to outsiders but to the individual they can make a tremendous difference. The difference between feeding or washing oneself, or not ,is an example. It is important when caring for spinally injured individuals, to be capable of undertaking basic tasks that are essential for the everyday existence of the individual. Dealing with such items as the bladder, drainage bags, bowels, toileting, washing, dressing, putting to bed, turning in bed, feeding etc. Also, it is of considerable benefit if a carer can assist with what I will call secondary tasks, such as providing information, and, where appropriate, stimulation and assistance with motivation. These tasks are not always simple, but are, in my opinion, essential. It might be that you will not be called upon to assist with some of the above but it is worthwhile knowing what is involved.

"If these tasks are not undertaken by a trained personal carer the tasks would have to be undertaken by some agency, whose continuity and reliability might be in doubt, and this would impose unnecessary stress and constraints upon the disabled person to the extent that their lifestyle might possibly be adversely affected. Having a regular carer, or carers, who understand the individuals specific needs is therefore essential - it makes life a great deal easier. I can only emphasise that being spinally injured can be very stressful, having to worry about the type and quality of care that you might receive only adds to the stress, and can inhibit the person from participating in other activities. It is important that carers can deal with all everyday eventualities with a minimum of effort for themselves and the disabled person, thus not creating a situation that is medically dominated, remember your client is not sick or ill. The service should adhere to the essential elements of The Social Model of Disability, and not a medical model. Carers must be capable of a flexible response to the individuals changing needs, the carer must see themselves as facilitators, providers of essential, and perceived essential, assistance that enhances the individuals choice of lifestyles."

Spike paused for a moment and looked at his audience, they appeared to be interested, so he continued, hoping that they were understanding this basic information. "Things can and do go wrong. Therefore going back to basic elements that were mentioned earlier, i.e. bladder maintenance. AA spinally injured person can be vulnerable to acquiring a bladder infection. Usually this is the case when the individual has an indwelling catheter, although anyone can obtain such an infection, and remember hospitals are places of infection. The usual reasons for having an indwelling catheter are that the person cannot pass urine without one, or it's convenient, preventing incontinence etc. Good hygienic practices are subsequently required in assisting to prevent infections. Albeit it is impossible to avoid all infections as long as a person users an indwelling catheter. It is not unusual for a spinally injured person to feel reasonable and have a normal temperature in the morning and later that same day have a temperature of 104°F due to a dormant infection flaring up. I still work on the old thermometer, but one day I will get around to centigrade!" he said while laughing. The group looked at him with blank expressions. "In these circumstances action is required to bring the temperature down, whilst obtaining appropriate antibiotics as soon as possible. "

A youthful looking man indicated that he wanted to say something. Spike had not wanted any interruptions at that point but decided that the carer might have something useful to say. "Would we be expected to change catheters as we have not been shown how to go about it?" the others nodded in agreement.

"Good point," said Spike, "we'll arrange it for those of you who feel that they would be happy doing this after receiving training. You must accept that your client might not want you to change their catheter, but in my experience most individuals would feel more secure knowing that their carer can do that if required. I will, with your agreement, now continue although I'm glad that point was introduced as it is important." He continued, "While it is recognised that it is probable that an individual can become immune to antibiotics if they take them frequently, it should be recognised that this concern should be secondary when dealing with a spinally injured person who has a bladder infection that is causing major problems. Some spinally injured individuals use a condom that is attached to a drainage bag, these individuals can pass urine freely, but still lack bladder control. But not having an indwelling catheter usually means that one can expect fewer infections; of course, there are always exceptions to this rule. These condoms are specifically manufactured and must be put in-situ correctly, avoiding any leakage. Peeing oneself in public is not amusing. Especially when it's you who's doing it!" added Spike.

"This is a simple task that a paraplegic would do for himself but a tetraplegic would require assistance."

A young women whispered something to the women sitting next to her.

Spike was irritated by the distraction and said to the women: "I'm sure that you can demonstrate to your colleagues here, the most effective way of putting a condom in-situ." She looked at him directly and said, "Don't worry I have had a lot of practice with all shapes and sizes."

"I'm sure you have !"said Spike under his breath. Everyone was amused but Spike. Spike was very tempted to say something disparaging but decided against it as it would only serve as a further distraction.

He continued: " A minority of spinally injured use an intermittent catheter method. This requires self catheterisation every few hours, in these circumstances it is normal that the individual has the ability to do this themselves, but that is not always the case. There are an increasing number of spinally injured women who use the lavatory and drain their bladders by compression every few hours, these individuals usually require little assistance unless they are tetraplegics. One major problem seems to be that female's have urethras that break down over the years and leakage can occur while a catheter is in-situ, this is obviously a problem and must be dealt with in a sensitive manner.

"Bowels: every disabled person's second favourite subject. A spinally injured person's bowels are usually paralysed, which means that they do not usually work by themselves. Although accidents do sometimes happen because the individual usually has no sensation and no control. Because the bowel is paralysed it often requires the use of suppositories, manual evacuations etc. The individual will be aware of what process works for them. It is important that a system is organised, one that the individual knows will work effectively and reliably. Carers must not impose their system upon the disabled individual. It is both physically and psychologically important that the disabled individual is happy with any arrangements and structures. Bowels and any incontinence can be both physically and psychological difficult to cope with for the disabled individual, thus the need for common sense and sensitivity. To get a good bowel regime can prove difficult, any problems should not dominate the individual's lifestyle but be seen as a normal procedure that is part of the body's maintenance programme.

"Once again, it should be pointed out that all spinally injured people are individuals, and what works for one person might not work for another person, even though their disability seems to be the same. Carers must not presume.

"Pressure sores. These are dangerous and can occur wherever

there is pressure, such as on the hip bones, base of the spine etc. Because of the lack of sensation a spinally injured person can be at risk to pressure sores. Therefore the vulnerable parts of the body must be examined when undressed every morning and evening. Subsequently a pink patch of skin on a bony area must be watched carefully; pink patches should disappear within thirty minutes. The individual should be either turned in bed every three hours or less, if required in order to avoid pressure sores. He paused at this point as if to emphasise what he was going to say next.

"Once the skin has broken down you have a major problem, expert advice is required before this happens. The aim is to totally avoid sores, avoid bruising etc. Never rub the skin of a spinally injured person in the belief that you might be preventing a pressure sore, or apply any creams to vulnerable areas without seeking advice, as you would probably be doing serious damage, likewise when turning a client in bed, do not ever drag a paralysed person up the bed as the skin is capable of shearing very easily. Care must also be taken when putting on shoes that toes are not damaged etc. A bad pressure sore can mean twelve months in bed, or longer, for a spinally injured person. It is often worth considering special cushions and special mattresses in order to prevent sores. i.e. the ROHO or the Jay cushion. Someone might suggest a cheap ripple type mattress, but these seldom provide any benefit, and experience has told me that you cannot do things on the cheap as the disabled person will pay for that mistake at a later date. The onus must be on prevention and carers must be alert to what can easily turn into a major problem.

"Sometimes it is desirable that a trained nurse who is familiar with the problems that spinally injured people come across provides care, or is part of the care package. Or you might already have an employer who has a good relationship with a spinal unit where they can quickly obtain advice if the think something is going wrong. There are times when some medical expertise or experience comes in useful, and dealing with the prevention of pressure sores is one of those times. Especially if there has been a change in skin colour, or in texture on and around vulnerable pressure points."

Spike recognised that what he had said was almost lacking in anything positive. He paused for a while. His students were quiet also.

"This all sounds depressing but it is reality and you have to know about these problem areas, and the sooner you understand the easier it will be for both you and your client.

"Which brings me to chest infections! These can be killers. Tetraplegics are prone to chest infections, and they can experience a rapid change from breathing easily, to breathing with great difficulty, a matter of a few hours. Where there is any doubt you must call a doctor. You can also learn the value of helping to drain the lungs by raising the bottom of the bed. Obtain some guidance from a physiotherapist on how to beat the persons chest and back with cupped hands to loosen any mucus. Obviously, then, colds, the flu, etc., are major problem areas that must be dealt with carefully. When dealing with a chest infection the disabled person can easily become exhausted.

"Another problem area is one of temperature control; higher lesions cannot control their body temperatures and getting too hot, or too cold must be avoided. Sunbathing can present problems. Likewise going outside in the cold. The disabled person will feel the effects of heat and cold usually when it is too late and their core temperature is adversely affected. Well, it all sounds like good fun doesn't it?" he said, while attempting to smile for the benefit of those present.

"Before you are all tired or bored, there are some conclusions you should consider. It is important to remember that spinally injured people have good days and bad days, they are not paragons of virtue bravely suffering their personal tragedy. They are people from all walks of life with different attitudes and experiences. Their aims and desires will differ from one another and it is essential that carers see the person and not the impairment, that they recognise the value of the individual and act accordingly. Always remembering that carers "do not always know best." Someone who has been disabled for a number of years will have a reasonable understanding of their body, especially if something is not functioning correctly.

"Carers must listen carefully to what individuals say, especially if something appears to be going wrong. A competent carer will build up a good relationship with the disabled individual, learning what is required over a period of time, and hopefully will act as a trusted friend, thus sometimes being in a position to increasing the disabled individual's choice of lifestyle with all of its subtleties and nuances. For this to work successfully it must be a partnership, a disabled person must have confidence and trust in the person providing care. The carer should also expect a civil and reasonable attitude towards themselves. It is a partnership that we aim to achieve. Being physically disabled should not, by itself, provide an excuse for unreasonable behaviour, although what constitutes unreasonable behaviour can be very subjective. Only time, effort, sensitivity, and some thought will bring about the appropriate situation that makes for good care practices. Remember that this is your employment, you are being paid for your time and assistance, you are not doing your client or employee a favour by just being there."

Spike looked around to see if they were still showing signs that they were paying attention. "I hope that the above is simple and easy to follow. If it isn't, then you must ask me about the parts you do not understand; but don't worry too much at this stage," he smiled before continuing, "your employers will be only too ready to put you right. And there are printouts available covering the items I have mentioned in more detail. I hope that my little talk has not put you off being a carer. It might sound as though I have described a life that is full of misery and difficulties. And you'd be bloody right - it is!" He quickly added that he was only joking.

"I was going to deal with questions at this time, but I think we should have a coffee first. When we return, we'll discuss the social model of disability. You'll all enjoy that as it's a laugh a minute, full of humour and frivolity, but to be serious it is something you need to understand. As opposed to the compost model which states 'pile it high, leave it to rot away then expect it to provide good results.' One other small point, many of your clients will not like you to use the term carer. They will not like the thought of being cared for. The term 'personal assistant' is likely to be more acceptable." With that Spike headed for the door.

A man who had been paying particular attention to what Spike had been saying coughed to draw Spike's attention. Spike looked at him expectantly. "I thought that this was the first aid class. I'm sorry."

"Don't worry about it," said Spike who was not unused to such a situation. "There won't be any extra charge." The man smiled and apologised once more and made his way to the door. Spike sighed loudly. "Before I say anything else, are you all sure that you are in the right class? Does anyone want woodwork, aromatherapy or hair dressing?"

He had not enjoyed rushing through those basic details as he knew it could easily give a distorted picture of reality, and it could be off putting. He decided that after the break he would lighten the discussion and add a bit of humour when possible. He knew from past experience though, that there was little point in trying to hide reality, as it would be doing no one any favours. He had other things on his mind too, which were more important, he was still unsure about the cottage he had booked without mentioning it to Luna. He then thought 'bugger it', we'll be away by ourselves and that's what really counts. He then wondered if he needed some new clothes. Buying clothes was not one of his stronger points, in fact he hated shopping unless it was for something specific and once it was obtained they could get away from the shops without a delay before he became irritated with shop assistants who nowadays seemed unhelpful. Or as he usually put it, idle sods who think they are doing you a favour taking your money. I think I'll take her home some flowers tonight, he thought, just to prove how sensitive I can be, she will be suspicious, wondering what I have done wrong, this amused him.

CHAPTER FOUR

The unit was similar in its layout to some of the other older units in the hospital. It consisted of two main sections, each section having fourteen beds, and two smaller sections, each with eight beds. There was also a six bedded unit, which was used mainly by patients who were ready for going home. At the end of each section there was a storeroom and a sluice room, which also contained toilet cubicles. It was fair to say that the unit areas had seen better days, and were badly in need of renovation. The whole place had a distinctive smell which was a mixture of age disinfectant and urine. Some members of staff referred to it as a Victorian slum, some were less polite.

Along the corridor past the unit office there was the main gym, and what might be described in the modern fashion as a fitness area. The gym was relatively well equipped by hospital standards.

There had always been the temptation, when possible, to try and obtain some equipment that was state-of-the-art. It looked impressive to the management and to outsiders alike. It was also very costly, and in truth, often of little value. Experience had taught some of those who were employed there that simple regular exercises were more important than playing around on expensive gadgetry. But for many years it had become the gospel that sport was of benefit to all those who could be persuaded, by whatever means, to participate in such activities. Whether, it was table tennis, or racing around a track seated in a peculiar position in an expensive customised wheelchair, or throwing a spear. All was deemed good, and character building for the patients. It should be added that the new patients had little choice due to the fact that they knew no better and their involvement appeared mandatory. Many of the nursing staff thought it was seemingly the unwritten duty of some of the trained perpetrators of such physical demanding activities, to unwittingly extract patients further and further away from the real world. And to lead them down what seemed to be the tangential path of sporting activities for the disabled. But to say this publicly was deemed heresy, so no one said it. And with more television coverage of sport for disabled people, it was going to be even more difficult at a future date to question its real importance. Subsequently even in difficult times money and enthusiasm could usually be generated for such activities by those entrusted with improving the physical ability of the patients. And it was also something that the public could easily relate to, which is seemingly important from a public relations point of view when money needs to be both raised and justified, for some activities.

Some cynical types observed that the old or the too severely disabled tended not to be included in the ministrations of this enthusiastic group. It might have been only gossip, or envy, but it was said on occasion by even non-malicious types that those who were excluded or seemingly excluded was due only because the raw material could not be easily moulded into something that could win kudos for those concerned. Such uncharitable thoughts were probably not justified. And it is fair to say that many patients benefited from some sporting activity. However, It might surprise those who are unfamiliar with disabled people, but many are reasonably content to not work, or put in a regular amount of physical energy into non-social or recreational activities. In other words, the disabled are as active or lazy as the rest of society, whose main aim is to get through life in comfort, which after all does seem sensible. But to be fair, some benefited and gained self-esteem and status. A few pushed themselves around exuding an air of superiority due to their sporting achievements, not realising that they were not recognised by society as sporting super stars, and that society could only cope with two or three disabled celebrities at one time. Society did not want to appear discriminatory, and paid lip service to equality, but did not really find disabled people all that attractive - with the odd exception. But until something better comes along, sport will be promoted as something of a panacea for many wheelchair users whose physical ability allows their participation.

Many of the nursing staff could never come to terms with the status or the role of physiotherapists, occupational therapists, and any other form of therapists. However, due to them, on some occasions, being logical beings, they knew that such professions had their own place in the greater scheme of things. It was often hard for them to accept that anything other than nursing was secondary to the needs of the patient. It might be argued by the various therapists that it wasn't the patient's needs' which was particularly foremost in their minds, but their own status in the greater scheme of things. They could usually agree that patients had to be taught new skills before they were cast out into the world as born-again individuals. And they could see that a gym was as good a place as any where these important skills could be taught. But it was difficult not to recognise a division of interests on occasion. Who was really in charge of rehabilitation, and what did it encompass? Was it a simplistic physical thing concerning one's bodily care, or a more holistic approach that was required? It seemed that no one was willing to write a definitive programme, or if they had, it was hidden away from the patients. Subsequently the responsibility for day to day rehabilitation was an area that might be described as amorphous. And to a large extent depended upon the patient's physical condition and understanding of their own possible future situation. Saying this could be heresy, but it should not be forgotten that the external pressures upon the system generated within it, a selective approach as to who received what resources, both within the hospital setting, and in the community. Subsequently it created a situation where consistency was not always the norm. And this made the situation difficult for both staff and patients at times who wanted a better system that was structured properly with everyone's interest in mind.

Further along the corridor there was a kitchen and a staff room, next to which there was a suite of offices; these were utilised by other hospital staff. One room was shared with the representatives of the various religious groups. Although in recent years it was recognised that fewer and fewer priests and ministers were seen in and around the hospital. No one knew why this was the case, as there existed a captive group waiting to know why they had become disabled, and not someone else more deserving. For the devout few who found themselves on the unit, the lack of spiritual comfort was a cause for concern. No one had brought the subject up in recent times. Years earlier, it was normal for those who were of the Catholic persuasion to go to Lourdes for a miracle cure, although no one could remember anyone returning with their impairment radically improved. Although it was fair to say that quite a few had returned with additional problems.

For some reason in recent times miracle cures had been taken off the agenda, which seemed unfair to some patients who had thought that a free trip to France seemed quite acceptable and worth them rediscovering their faith.

The unit corridor opened out onto a main corridor, which led to the newer part of the hospital. Basically the hospital was in two parts. There were four units in the old section, which had once been a workhouse. The new section was completed in the mid-seventies. This part had some twenty units, and a number of areas of excellence, as they were now sometimes called. This terminology amused the staff as it was like being awarded an AA star, but without anything having changed, and they did not think a great deal about it, as the star ratings and the hospital status was changed on a regular basis. Although by some standards, the hospital could be considered as good as most in the area, and possibly better than a few. It was always difficult to make such an assessment. Seminars and training days were held on a regular basis, self-scrutiny was the order of the day, and everyone pondered upon the question. Is it just some kind of a simple numbers game? Or do you judge the quality of such an establishment by its standard of nursing, and the quality of the doctors who work there? Or do you take into account the quality of the facilities and the equipment? Do you look for some spurious success rate in a number of treatments? Is it possible to find out about failure rates in surgical procedures? Is the important factor of waiting lists and getting a large throughput in a minimum amount of time the be all and end all? And does anyone who is employed in such establishments really care about such statistics that tend to be meaningless, except to the politicians who could make capital out of any situation? Unfortunately, the administration did care about the numbers game, and their concerns filtered down to all employees. Get the patients in and out in as short a time as possible, get the waiting lists down and the number of treatments up.

There are, of course, the well-publicised league tables, and no hospital wants to see itself at the bottom of the table. Although if they do, the mental agility of the administrators can usually come up with some wonderful reasons why the circumstance were such, that any league tables could not disclose the true picture of the situation. In recent times the administrators had tried hard to impress upon everyone that they were all now closely observed. Everyone had to perform to their maximum. Many nurses thought that this was insulting coming from whom they thought were highly paid individuals, who had never seen a patient, who it appeared seldom left their offices, except to go on a junket somewhere at the least possible excuse. Who had well equipped and well furnished offices while many of the units were in a bad state of repair? It seemed to administrators upon hearing this, felt that nurses had always felt that way, and that nothing was new. Such attitudes regarding administrators seemed to prevail in all large organisations, and are continuously fed by misinformation and discontentment. It could be argued logically that some doctors and nursing staff need someone or something to blame, that it's good to focus one's discontent upon someone or something: it's a release, a safety valve. And it is therefore necessary for the functioning of such establishments.

All in all the hospital was no different to many others, except it contained a spinal injuries unit. This facility had, over the years, caused some concern to the powers that be, as extra staff had to be provided for the unit. And the extra costs were not welcome in the economic climate that had prevailed in recent years. It was difficult for some administrators to understand why such units required more staff no matter how often it was explained to them. They seemingly failed to grasp the subtitles and nuances of the situation. Or it was thought that they more than likely just resented the extra cost? To most outsiders it appeared that administrators grew in numbers in direct proportion to any proposed cutbacks. And that their main purpose in life was finding more ways to make life difficult for those members of staff who had direct physical contact with the patients. While this appeared to be the case, in reality it wasn't necessarily true. Administrators were often frustrated at the funds they had been allocated, and knew that they were inadequate for the running of the hospital trust. And if one of the budgets meant that there was a potential under-spend, then what was wrong in providing new carpets desks and chairs for the office section? The money had to be spent. The senior managers could not understand why anyone should complain about such events. Were not these tools and equipment? Wasn't their contribution to the running of the system as important as anyone else's? Managers seemingly felt a threatened species who could never do anything right. The staff at the sharp end of the process, which was seen by the public to mean the nursing staff, did tend to think of management as being not only remote, but sometimes lacking in care. There was the belief that the only concern that managers had was to balance the books, and stay within the allocated budget. That nothing else really mattered, and the quality of care meant nothing, which was not really logical, but those thoughts and feelings existed.

Managers nearly always felt misunderstood and under appreciated. But some nurses said that it was to some extent of their own making, they seldom rocked the boat and demanded of their political paymasters a larger cake. Better to keep within budget and let the system sort these things out in the fullness of time. Some, who were waiting for their MBE or if more fortunate their OBE, would never question or find a means of challenging the Ministry. They had always realised that making waves would not further anyone's career and demanding increased finances was definitely something one should not attempt, whatever the justification. That is how non-administrators viewed things without realising that administrators are necessary, and without them the organisation would not function.

But as Caroline started her day's work she had little interest in such problems. She had originally involved herself in the internal arguments some years ago when it was obvious to everyone that the cutbacks and the lack of modernisation were destroying what remained of the once proud health service. But, after a year or two of involvement on committees, it had suddenly dawned upon her that she was wasting both her time and her energy. She realised that changes were decided upon at a higher, remote level, and her input would make no difference whatsoever.

Others had told her, before her involvement, that all the meetings were just for show, that decisions had already been made, and going to the meeting just legitimised them. She finally realised that this was true, it hurt her seeing this because she really believed in the health service. And she cared about the people whom she nursed and the quality of the service they received..

Caroline had always wanted to become a nurse, the thought of doing any other job had never occurred to her. This had disappointed her father who had wanted her to follow in his footsteps and become a lawyer. While the law definitely interested Caroline because of her political leanings, she had become cynical towards the profession due to the prolonged discussions she had held with her father over numerous issues. It was correct to state that Caroline thought that the profession was morally corrupt, and had little or no concern with justice or change, but with just making money out of other peoples' misery. She was now convinced that the whole legal system was in need of drastic changes. Her father had disagreed, saying with some conviction that the system works. That when it is seen not to work it will regulate itself accordingly. Caroline thought this was stupid and always argued that the system was not working, and those involved were quite happy with the situation. Where is there justice in the system, where do ordinary people go for affordable justice? If it is justice you require then, you will have to wait for God. We only deal with the law, were his comments. There could be no agreement between her and her father on this point. What had caused her more concern in recent years was the thought that some of her colleagues were in the nursing profession not because they wanted to nurse. They just wanted a respectable job that provided them with some security. And at the time some of them were leaving school, unemployment was very high and nursing seemed a respectable profession with suitable status. Even if the money was inadequate. On some occasions Caroline thought that a few of her colleagues did not even earn the money they were paid. Although she was nearly always short of money, it was not something that dominated her thoughts. However, recently she had thought more about the money, especially when there appeared to be quite a lot of support from the public for an increase in pay for nurses. It had made her smile to herself on occasion when she had listened into phone-in programmes on the radio. And quite a lot of the members of the public usually recounted tales of their hospital experiences, and wonderful caring nurses who could not have looked after them any better. Strangely a good time seemed to be had by almost everyone. She laughed to herself when hearing such sentiments coming from members of the public who were usually just grateful to get out alive. "I want to thank all the staff, they were wonderful, could not do enough for me." "It's a pity they took my legs off by mistake, but it wasn't their fault they are over worked." She realised that her last thought was something of an exaggeration and cynical, owing to her present mood. She then concluded that it wasn't, as she knew such stupid, but unfortunate things actually happened. She hoped that she could avoid having to come into hospital with anything serious. She shuddered at the thought. Her mind drifted on to whom out of her colleagues could she really trust to care for her. She asked herself the question again. How many of her colleagues would she really trust if she was dependent? She decided not to think about it as she knew the conclusion would seem depressing. She was not going to disagree about the need for more money though, sometimes the work could be hard. And if you actually cared for what you were doing it could have some effect upon you physically and emotionally, irrespective of what you were taught. You did occasionally take your work home with you. Simply due to the fact that you were dealing with real people who, over a period of time, you had got to know quite well. And if they were ill, or not improving, then you felt concerned. Although she admitted to herself that this was only true with a percentage of patients. With some patients it was difficult to form any feelings, which was not a thought that really pleased Caroline. But she came to terms with this by realising that patients were, after all, members of the general public: good, bad, and indifferent. It was impossible to like them all as some were really difficult, and occasionally a minority were obnoxious. Caroline contented herself in the belief that she was fair to all her patients, whether she liked them or not, and always did whatever she could to improve their condition. She did not put this down to professionalism, but to her simple belief that she had come into nursing to help people, in her mind it was as simple as that.

"I'll be with you in a second," shouted a small slim blond woman as she hurried towards Caroline. Wendy Brett was a bubbly type, and in general a pleasant young woman who looked very young, although she was thirty-four years old with a 10 year old boy. Wendy had recently become divorced and was for the moment living with her mother in her mother's home. Her father had died some months earlier and it seemed for the time being that to move in with her mother was a sensible thing to do. Some friends had told her that she was foolish leaving her own home when she could have stayed there. But Wendy thought it best to rid herself of the place where she had been unhappy for the past few years. For some years she thought that her marriage was as near perfect as she had a right to expect. She had first met her husband-to-be at high school, and later at University. He had seemed the perfect man, but Wendy soon learned that perfection did not exist in the real world, or not in her particular world. That now seemed a long time ago. And after all, at that time, she was young and in love. She soon found out that "he needed other women." That was the phrase he used. It had stuck in her mind as though it was a knife being pushed into her chest and left there. She tried to rationalise what he had said. After some prolonged thought she knew that there was no reason to be rational, he was wrong, and if he could not change, then he had to go. After numerous trials and failures he left, admittedly with some reluctance and all the while muttering how women could never understand a man's needs. She had even argued at the time that if the situation was reversed, he would not be able to accept it. Without hesitation he agreed, saying that it was different; that men look upon these things differently. That a woman is usually content with one man, while most men want other women, not to love he said, but just for sex. He told her that he would always love her and couldn't she understand his needs, and live with them? Was it so important if he had another woman now and again? It was only sex - not love. She found it difficult to understand how the man she thought she knew had become so bloody stupid. She tried but she could not seem to reason with him, so in the end she had given up trying. Occasionally when looking back she wondered why she had not recognised these aspects of his personality a long time ago. The man is a moral imbecile, she concluded. But now she was rid of him and she had not regretted it for one moment. She, like Caroline, enjoyed her work but she realised that there was much more to life than work, and she also needed something more. She was unsure as to what she really wanted and had decided that something would turn up; until then just see what happens she thought. But one thing had changed, she admitted to herself that she liked sex and would take whatever came her way that she found acceptable. Spending a life going without something so pleasurable was not an option for her.

"We had better wait a few minutes for the others," said Caroline with some reluctance, as she did not enjoy waiting around once she had left the office. It always seemed to her as though some members of staff dragged themselves to work, hating every minute until it was time for them to leave. She often wondered why they bothered, asking herself, why didn't they get another job that did not bring them into contact with people who were ill or disabled, get a job shelf filling or something.

"Lets get on with it," said Wendy impatiently, "you know that once we get started the others will appear out of the woodwork. They hide away until we're seen to start, they are frightened that they might do a few minutes more work than the rest of us." She laughed at her last statement knowing what she had said was true. "We are in need of some team building" added Wendy.

Caroline laughed, "remember the last team building exercise we nearly finished up fighting? That was because little Cedric said that he was carrying the rest of us, and he could outwork anyone half his age. He just pretended to work and because he had been here so long he thought that he owned the place. He was a nasty spiteful little..."

Caroline stopped her, "do not speak ill of the dead."

"He was not the nicest of persons," said Wendy, smiling. "Half the patients would have hit him if they could; he took advantage of the situation. When you think of it, we've had some strange people working on the unit this past few years, some of them were definitely not normal. They are the ones who moved on and obtained promotion, you could see right away with some of them that they did not intend being around very long which was a blessing. I hate that phrase!" she said with some venom.

More often than not Wendy agreed with Caroline, they were quite close regarding some of their attitudes, yet they were very different individuals. Both enjoyed working with people. They were what was often described as hands-on-nurses by some of their colleagues. For some the word had almost taken on a derogatory meaning. But for most involved, what this had come to mean in recent years was that there seemed to be an increasing number of nurses who had an aversion to doing simple basic nursing. Both Caroline and Wendy agreed that ideas and attitudes to care were changing fast, and in their opinion, not for the better. More of their colleagues were more interested in going on nursing related courses, and working upon detailed care plans that were seldom adhered to. When such items were discussed or better to say argued over, it was seen that to cover one's back, adequate care plans were there if needed. Good, detailed evidence that would show that the correct practices were, in theory, being applied. And, as some staff pointed out, that is what really matters nowadays, getting things right in order to satisfy the government's needs.

Wendy and Caroline could not agree with this and always put up a good defence for what was deemed old fashioned hands on nursing. Where you could apply care with some good, but once again 'old fashioned' care and compassion. They often thought that in these arguments they were now in a minority. It was as though words like 'compassion' were from some distant era. An era or time that could no longer be looked upon as having anything worthwhile to say. This worried them both, because it meant in practical terms that some of their colleagues, who they would be closely working with, differed considerably in their approach to nursing patients. And this would sometimes display itself when undertaking some of the simplest of nursing tasks.

They believed, rightly or wrongly, that one day someone would recognise that there was something basically wrong, and patients were suffering. They hoped that someone would see common sense, and do something about it. They thought of how often in recent years the health service, and the hospital system, had had changes imposed upon it. Changes that were supposed to improve practices, but seldom did. They agreed that simply increasing staff numbers by itself was not the answer. Improved training was also required that understood the individuals' expectations. Nurses had to be allowed to nurse and not to be tied to desks, being bogged down with paper work, or the need to improve their computer skills. They had come to the conclusion that the aim of the politicians in charge of the health service was for an American model of nursing, where qualified nurses are also supervisors in many instances, and lower paid staff do most of the physical work that involves patients. What they could not work out was, who was it who had decided that this approach was the correct one? What expertise and empirical evidence had been utilised to suggest the direction things were taking, and what evidence was there to show that this was beneficial for the patients? Sometimes they thought that they might be looking too deeply, that there was not any particular model. Just a muddling through from day to day, and hoping the cracks would not get any larger. They were disillusioned with the occasional directive from their nursing body instructing them on not what to do, but upon what they should not do, as though reverting to industrial demarcation lines that no longer served the public's interest. Whatever the causes, they knew that drastic changes were required if any reasonable vestiges of quality was to be retained. And their nursing body had to look at the real needs of all patients, and take a sensible and practical approach that was less negative regarding some aspects of care provision, especially when it came to providing care and treatment for the spinally injured. Everyone who worked on the unit knew that you had to be both flexible and pragmatic in your approach to the job, which might sound at times like a partial contradiction, if such a thing exists. It was different to ordinary nursing where it was easier to apply rules that were applicable to most patients. But some of the directives that had been put into practice in recent years made life very difficult for some patients. And unfortunately there was an impression amongst some patients that nurses carried with them a notebook containing all the things that they could not do anymore. And common sense, which had proved successful in the past, was no longer applicable. One patient, who had been a nurse years earlier, said that she was so disappointed in the direction that nursing had taken, and she blamed her own association. She just could not understand the reasoning in the move to getting nurses further away from hands on care. She then decided that the degree in nursing was not beneficial but a hindrance, and while it sounded very good, it did not do anything for those nurses who wanted close contact with the patients. It was geared to care plans and hypothetical expectations that often lacked flexibility and common sense, where in the past a nurse soon understood the patient and provided care with a degree of warmth and understanding. That was now in the past and, if mentioned, almost frowned upon as though one was reverting to a primitive practice. One nurse, during a heated debate, stated that she felt as though she was a mechanic, or an electrician, a keeper of machinery. She no longer felt as though she was allowed to really nurse. Machines do not listen, machines show no compassion or care, they are just machines and it is time that we looked at our role. Surely as nurses our role is something more than watching equipment? I want my patients to know that I do care about their condition and that they are not just a statistic. Her colleagues clapped and agreed with her.

"I'm going out tonight," stated Wendy, in a manner that seemed to suggest that she wanted someone to disagree with her proposed action. No one did, so she continued: "I'm going to have a few drinks, have a meal and then possibly, I might go to a club." She held up her hands and started to sing a popular song, "That's just a warm up!" she said, while laughing. "Before anyone asks, I will find a friend to go with me before the day is over. I cannot stay in any longer! I'm tired of staring at four walls or watching television, I just need a change, even if it's for only a few hours. And who knows? I might be lucky! I might find a wealthy young man who cannot resist me," at that point she waited for a response that she knew would be forthcoming.

"I'm sure that someone out there is desperate and needs a bit of rough," said Caroline while laughing. No one said anything, they just waited. They didn't have to wait long.

"I might not be in the full flush of youth, but I'm definitely not in the category of a bit of rough. In fact, I was once told that I was a sophisticated lover."

"That's only because you asked for a finger bowl after giving him a quick hand job!" said Caroline.

Wendy was never slow in responding. "Actually, I wore latex gloves and a pair of Wellington boots. H he was into that sort of thing," added Wendy.

"It must have been chilly if that's all you were wearing!" replied Caroline who then added, "why the Wellington boots?"

Wendy thought for a while before answering. "Actually, I think they were on special offer. He bought them for me. "Everyone looked at one another but did not say anything. "It might be fine for you lot with a lower sex drive, but I'm bloody desperate at the moment, I would take on a gorilla if necessary."

"The last fellow you picked up was a gorilla," said Caroline while looking serious, "in fact he was not so handsome and he definitely did not look house trained."

Wendy replied "I got rid of him before he could do any real damage. On having a good look at him in a clear light, I realised that I wasn't that desperate, but unfortunately he'd spent the night with me. The good point was that I'd drunk so much I couldn't remember what we'd done." She paused for thought. "Obviously by that time I must've sampled his potential, but I will admit, I wasn't mentally in full command."

"That's the first time that I have heard it called potential," added Caroline.

Wendy sighed, "Do you think you lose sensation if you don't use it?" she asked. She then went on to say that she had worn her last vibrator out, somehow it didn't seem to vibrate at an appropriate rate for a maximum effect "Or am I getting numb down there? Losing sensation? My G spot could have disappeared! Is that possible?"

Caroline ignored Wendy's last remark as she was enjoying herself. "Come to think of it, that last fellow I saw you with wasn't as handsome as most gorillas. In fact you were lucky he didn't scrape his knuckles on the ground as he walked, and those were his better features. In fact, you couldn't call him ugly as he was past that point."

Wendy interrupted, "Funny you should mention it, but he did have a liking for bananas. And I will admit, he was a bit rough" said Wendy, "it was when he shouted out 'Me Tarzan, you Jane', that I thought it was going to be a long hard night, and it cost me a lot of money having the chandelier repaired after he had swung on it. Another strange thing about him," she added. "He wore long tartan socks and he didn't take them off, that seemed weird." She quickly added that he wasn't even Scottish. They both laughed at that point.

Caroline's voice changed. "To be serious for a moment, you aren't really going to pick some scruffy degenerate up again and take him back home are you? What about your mother, what'll she say??

Wendy thought about it for a few seconds before replying. ?I don't want to sound like a sex-starved depraved slut, but you might not have noticed it but there?s not a line of attractive men waiting to climb into my pants, and as for my mother, she?ll have to find her own fellow. I don't think my mother's had it for years! It's probably healed up, she doesn't like men, could not stand the sight of my father if the truth's known, I think he went without sex for a long time. In fact, I think that both of them decided without discussing it, that sex with each other wasn't something they desired, so they did without. They drew stumps, end of game and they only related to each other over Sunday lunch when he would congratulate her on her Yorkshire puddings. It's not much is it, after years of living together, the only nice thing that you can say is that you make good puddings. What a waste of a life!" They both burst out laughing at that point.

Caroline said, "You, and your mother and father are not by yourself in that respect, I'm living like a nun." Wendy looked at her as though she was unsure of the veracity of what Caroline had said. Caroline picked up on Wendy's thoughts: "Seriously though, it's just not such a good idea, to be honest, you know the risks. You could finish up with the dregs of society."

Wendy shrugged before saying. "If they have the necessary equipment, and I'm talking big here," she held out her arms at that point to indicate an acceptable size. "It's got to make my eyes water, and if they don't ask for their bus fare home or expect a cooked breakfast I'll risk it."

Caroline groaned, "You must be joking! Please tell me you are joking? You wouldn't, really, would you?" asked Caroline, now seemingly concerned.

Wendy laughed and then smiled ambiguously before adding, "How long is it since you experienced the full range of the carnal delights available, considering that we're not talking about the sophisticated Latin lover types? You must also have worn out the vibrator you treat yourself to last Christmas.:

"It's hardly been used," said Caroline with some pretence of indignation. "Besides, you can't get the batteries for it, they only make them in China or some similar place."

"There was no wonder it was cheap! In fact, there is something about it that is off-putting. Brightly coloured lumpy ones with stripes never work right," added Wendy, "they were specially made for some obscure sect, I saw it on television."

Caroline burst out laughing, "You lying sod!"

"I'm going through a sexual crisis!" said Wendy. "I need what they call in technical terms, a bloody good seeing to."

"Fine!" said Caroline, who was starting to loose her patience, "it's your responsibility."

"Bring on the gorilla house - trained or not." Wendy said in a loud voice. "It's not the same for you, you don't have my healthy appetite!" added Wendy once again, who tried to give the impression that she was slightly offended.

"That's the nicest thing you have said to me in a long time" said Caroline, who at the same time admitted to herself that she would not be adverse to a good sexual encounter.

She was equally quick to think that, given the situation, she would probably say no. At a time like this, which were sexually lean times for her, she still thought that at the end of the day you have to respect yourself and protect oneself. Then, as if to contradict herself, she thought that she would enjoy a good healthy sexual relationship, a relationship sounded much more acceptable, somehow a little more refined. She knew that the refinements would be a bonus, but she also knew that to expect something sensitive or subtle nowadays was asking a lot. She did not want a relationship just for the sake of being with a man now and again, she wanted something more, not the roll on roll off types who do not care who they are with, but something lasting that served a deeper need, she sighed at these thoughts. She had once experienced love and she had felt that the world was hers, but that was sometime ago and since then she had not had a regular male friend whom she could say had really meant anything to her. She had gone out and she had been away for the odd weekend with a friend, but those encounters, as she liked to think of them, had no real lasting value. They served and assisted in briefly satisfying a sexual desire, they had a simple purpose but they were transitory, they were definitely not what she wanted. She had experienced something far better and she knew that such thoughts and feelings were still there within her. She just hoped that she might meet the right person, but that is what everyone hopes she thought. Who is the right person, what do I really want out of life. She found that these questions were not easy to answer when she considered them seriously. She thought that her attitude was old fashioned and not in keeping with present day attitudes which meant that she would possibly have to change her attitude or go without sex or the possibility of a relationship. She thought about it for a while and decided that if the opportunity arose she would take it. She was annoyed at herself for allowing these contradictory thoughts to enter her mind. It was as though she clearly wanted something but then gave seemingly sound reasons why she should be careful and selective, which would preclude her from obtaining the thing she desired. Oh bugger it she said to herself its bloody complicated.

CHAPTER FIVE

The sounds on the unit grew progressively louder as the minutes ticked by. Ronny Bonds opened his eyes wide and peered at Wendy.

"Oh! I see. It's only you is it?" he muttered disappointedly.

Wendy looked at him and was about to say something then thought better of it.

"Where's that young, good looking blond nurse who was on duty yesterday, the good looking one, she did a really good job? It's too bloody early to have a wash, and I didn't have a shave yesterday," he grunted out in a voice that he knew would annoy Wendy.

"Ronny darling," said Wendy in a soft tone of voice. Ronny was suspicious but replied out of curiosity. He knew she was going to rebuke him but, he was interested in what exactly she was going to come up with. If it was not adequate as a riposte he decided that he would come back with something crisp, succinct, and witty.

"Yes my dearest," he replied ensuring that his voice would not disclose to her that he was aware of what was coming.

Wendy drew in a large breath and smiled at him. "You're a miserable sod who cannot recognise good quality care when they get it. And, regarding a shave, there's nothing wrong with your hands, so why haven't you shaved yourself?"

She moved nearer to him and leaned forward so no one else could hear.

"You're also an idle sod, laying there in bed watching the world go round, criticizing everybody and everything. Why don't you get off your arse and do something? You're quite capable." She smiled at him and was pleased with what she had said. She looked around carefully to see if anyone had heard her last comments but no one had.

She hasn't done too bad, thought Ronny, for a neophyte in insulting, but it still lacked any real clout, it wasn't anything that was likely to incense him or anyone else. The reply was hardly scathing or wounding to someone like himself who did not really care who he offended or upset.

"Are you supposed to talk to patients like that? But you do have a good point there, but you haven't grasped the fundamental point, presumably due to your inadequate education." She interrupted him as her curiosity had been aroused, which is what he had intended.

"What point exactly?" She had quickly taken the bait, and Ronny was now in the driving seat.

"It's like this, so please concentrate and try and understand if you can. Why should I do what you suggest when you're paid to do it? Admittedly you don't do it too well, but I make allowances for your lack of ability. How can I, being a reasonable person and a good socialist, undertake any activity that might undermine your employment, no matter how lacking in skills and sensitivity you might be?. You desperately need the job, my dearest, so be honest and a realist, recognise your situation: you're basically unemployable with limited skills, or have you somehow learned how to live without money?"

I cannot believe he has the audacity to say such crap, she thought to herself. But Ronny never let a fish get off the hook easily and he continued.

"The problem is one of standards and quality control, plus consistency." He was by now really enjoying himself. "We must aim for these things every day, just try and keep those thoughts with you throughout your day." He was smiling now, or to be accurate, grinning. He was into his stride now and added. "There's always room for improvement you know, especially in your case." He continued while smiling in an irritating manner, "and just going back to my original enquiry. The young nurse on duty yesterday was of a standard..." He paused while searching for the right phrase.

"A standard we would like to become accustomed to on a regular basis. I think that sums it up," he said, while trying to duck as a wet facecloth landed across his face.

"She's just an ambitious arse-licking little know-it-all, who didn't give you a shave or have you forgotten?." Wendy put her hand across her mouth. I should not have said that she said quietly to herself while genuinely concerned at her outburst.

Ronny smiled, "Don't worry; I won't tell her what you've just said. I'll phrase it better," said Ronny continuing smiling.

"Leave him alone! He's just trying to stir it - as usual" said Caroline. She moved a little closer, "You are still the most irritating self-centred man I know," she said, with an expression that showed exasperation.

"Rubbish! Absolute rubbish!" said Ronny in a loud voice. "Just be honest - you really like me, you've always liked me. Don't fight it, accept it."

She sighed before turning to confront him. "You're never satisfied, always complaining, ungrateful, dissatisfied, you are so inconsiderate!" She added that they were his good points. Ronny looked at her with a doleful expression. "You never said those things about me when you were a student on the unit, it was different then," he added in a loud voice. "She was in love with me then, used to come on the unit without any pants just for me."

"You lying sod! How dare you say such a thing?" said Caroline, angry and frustrated. "OK, to be accurate you allowed me to choose the colour. You were a sweet and obliging girl then, unspoilt and uncorrupted."

"If you don't shut up, I'll make a complaint against you. I do not have to put up with such things," she said feeling embarrassed.

"Oh you will, will you," said Ronny enjoying himself. "And at the hearing, when questioned, do I tell everything or should it be the shortened version of events?"

"There weren't any events," said Caroline, who could feel herself starting to blush.

"Obviously this is something I need to know about" said Wendy with genuine curiosity.

"There's nothing to know about," said Caroline angrily, "and he should know better than to say such things. That's how rumours start!" Caroline walked away and moved further down the room.

"Go on - tell me everything," said Wendy, "I want all the dirt; every grubby little detail." She said this just loud enough for Caroline to hear. Ronny looked her directly in the eyes and told her that she was still too young and innocent to hear such things. And if he told just a minute part of what had happened she would view Caroline in a different light, in fact you could be traumatised, he continued by saying that it might even spoil their working relationship.

He could see that he had really annoyed Caroline by the way she was dragging the sheets over the bed and uttering something of a violent nature under her breath. He lay back in contentment thinking that the day had not started out too badly.

Ronny had been disabled for over thirty years and he understood how the system worked better than many of the staff. Over the years he had fought numerous battles with different individuals both in the hospital and the Local Authority. He usually enjoyed the confrontation as it stimulated him. He needed the banter; it kept him going or, as he succinctly put it, it kept him match fit. He was feeling in a strange mood and he had almost decided that he was going to get up and do a bit of work in the gym, which was usually an anathema to him. He then quickly decided against the idea on the grounds that it was the most foolish idea that had come into his head, he wondered why he had thought of it in the first place.

He hated the sight of the keep fit types who rode around driving their wheelchairs as though they were grand prix machines. He also hated exercise in any form unless it was with a woman or lifting a glass. Ronny believed that he had got his priorities correct after years of practice. "Bring me my chair after ten as I'm getting up and going out for they day."

Wendy looked at him with disbelief. She could not remember anyone mentioning that he was going out. "When did you arrange this?" she asked.

"It has nothing to do with you; it's arranged and that is it." snapped Ronny. Wendy said that she would check to make sure he had permission. "I don't need anyone's permission to go out. All I do is call for a cab and I'm away from here."

This was not true, and he realised that. Wendy knew that he could not leave without the permission of his consultant, unless he wished to sign himself out, although it was not unusual for patients to go into town, or out for a drink. Wendy asked him again if he had permission, but he refused to answer.

"Don't argue with me, just make sure my chair is here at the side of the bed, and if you're a good little girl, daddy will bring you back something nice. How about a bag of pork scratchings?" He said this in a voice one might use while talking to a four year old. Wendy said something that Ronny could not quite hear, but he recognised the word 'bastard', which gave him some satisfaction. Happy days are here again, he thought. He lay back and tried to obtain a few minutes sleep.

The noise around Ronny's bed had awoken everyone. Harry was awake early, much too early for his liking as he had not slept well. And therefore he tried to doze off into that comfortable state between sleeping and being awake which can be very comfortable. He had heard Ronnie's voice and he thought it too early to talk to Ronny as once they started talking it tended to go on for what could appear to be an interminable period of time.

It had been a cold night. For some reason Harry had found it difficult to go to sleep for what would be considered a normal period; it seemed as though he was always half awake, or nearly awake and initially it had concerned him. He was now used to it. He realised that lengthy periods of sleep were not as important as most people thought which included himself. Doing without a bit of sleep was something that you should not be really concerned about, he had decided. In fact, he had long ago started to enjoy dozing, he found that he had some control over his dreams, which in one sense were not so much dreams but a meandering of the mind. That was how Harry tended to see them. He could almost let his mind wonder at will carefully observing most subjects and places. Unfortunately the places, the people, and the subject matter were not always in the correct place, a sort of 'Alice in Wonderland' without Alice. What this really meant was that while Harry might have been trying to get his mind to think about his last trip to London, he kept meeting people whom he knew had not been there with him. He usually met some very strange people in his meandering. But he was now used to it, and if the now departed Queen Mother had been sat next to him in Hyde Park licking an ice cream it no longer worried him. He would enter into a general conversation, probably ask her if she was eligible for the extra winter heating allowance, or something of that nature. Sometimes the characters replied, other times they did not. It did not usually matter as far as Harry was concerned. He accepted these surrealistic events as being relatively normal but still different to the ordinary, and he had found that he quite liked it. He believed that he had obtained insights into many events and happenings by his meetings with people, famous and infamous, while dozing. What did frustrate him was that sometimes he had obtained some really interesting information. But he could never usually find a way of verifying it. His favourite dream which he had to admit was surreal was when he was on stage at Las Vegas with Elvis. He was staying in the hotel where Elvis was playing and had decided to go and watch him as he had nothing better to do. Halfway through his act Elvis raised his arm and the music stopped. He peered down at the audience. He spotted Harry and he shouted to him. "Come on up here Harry and join me in a song." Harry joined Elvis for a few numbers then took his bow. The audience went wild, clapping and cheering.

"We have just got to do this again sometime," said Elvis while clapping Harry enthusiastically. He is a decent sort thought Harry, pity about the suit though, perhaps I should mention it the next time. But there wasn't a next time; he never met Elvis again which was unfortunate as Harry had given some thought as to how Elvis might improve his performance with a few small changes.

He also remembered talking to Stalin while they were reviewing the army from the wall of the Kremlin as it marched through Red Square. It's bloody cold up here, thought Harry, there's no wonder they nearly all wear fur hats. He wanted to know about all the political prisoners in the Soviet Union, and the deliberate starvation of the peasants in the thirties. Stalin, who it must be said seemed a reasonable sort after a few drinks, had told him that was the only way that he could get anything done. He explained that if you do not use fear everyone wants to debate every issue, and he knew what needed to be done, therefore instead of talking about problems just remove the problem, he said. At the time Harry thought that this seemed a reasonable answer, in fact it was one of the most sensible answers he had heard. What more can one say? he thought. He also wanted to point out to Stalin what a homicidal bastard he was. And that he was responsible for more Russian deaths than Hitler. Both of whom should have been killed at birth. But, even when dreaming, he had thought better of it. He clearly remembered that Stalin was not noted for his humour, unless it was concerned with having someone shot by mistake. This usually caused a bit of merriment amongst the politburo. Possibly because they were relieved that it wasn't them who had been shot. Harry decided that he must be careful with Stalin. He wondered if he should join the communist party as they seemed to have a few perks. He decided against the idea as paying his subscription in roubles might be complicated, and he wanted his dreams to remain simple. He mentioned this to Stalin who suggested a Swiss bank where he could get a good exchange rate if he mentioned his name. Harry thanked him profusely just to be on the safe side. Stalin reminded him that the next time they met he would appreciate it if Harry could get him a few bottles of HP sauce as it was difficult to get in the Soviet Union as he had banned it. Try vodka with a dash of HP sauce, it's the perfect drink he added. Harry promised that he would. He then wished that he had not promised as he knew that disappointing Stalin was not a good thing to do but after all, it's only a dream, he said to himself.

Harry could, on most occasion, reason in the middle of his dreams or meanderings. Sometimes if they started to get nasty he had the ability to decide that he had had enough of that particular dream, and then he would decide to move on to something more pleasant. It was a useful way of avoiding unpleasantness but it did not always work, in such difficult meanderings or complex cases he would wake up. If possible he would try and slip back into another dream that was less offensive and threatening, but it wasn't always possible. It concerned him once when, in a dream, he was just escaping from a mob that wanted to lynch him, so he pulled out of the dream. On re-entering the dream-like state he found that the mob had got hold of him. It seemed as though the dream had continued to run its course while he had opted out for a few minutes. This occurrence caused him to treat his dreams with a little more caution and to have a healthy distrust of them. Which was not difficult as they were so convoluted they rarely made any real sense. But they were his dreams from within his mind, and he sometimes thought that one day he might understand if there was any meaning to dreams. Or was it just the mind re-shuffling the pack of cards during the night? Getting the memory and cognitive systems ready for what the coming day brought with it. He knew that many tribes and cultures placed considerable importance upon the interpretation of dreams, and had even acted on the interpretation of their dreams. Their dreams must be more sensible than mine, Harry had thought. Or it could be that is the reason why they are still eating grubs and scratching around for water whenever the rains fail. He wondered for the moment if that was a racist remark, but decided that it wasn't as it appeared factual, well partially factual, give or take a bit, which in Harry's eyes was sound enough to base an argument upon.

Years ago he had tried to read Freud and Jung's work on the meaning of dreams but he found it hard going. He was not sure now if it was Freud's or Jung's work, and it no longer really mattered, he thought. Harry came to the conclusion that such texts were deliberately difficult to read or fully understand in order to give anyone who attempted to read them the impression that the writer must be a clever sod, possibly brilliant, and ahead of their time. When it was possible that they were the scribbling of a disturbed mind, trying to conceal the fact that they were not quite so clever as they would like people to think. Harry had often thought that there seemed to be any number of people in society going around pretending to be clever and making a good living at it. This then caused him to wonder why he wasn't one of them. He satisfied himself by putting it down to integrity on his part, although he did not really believe that. It was just a bit better than the truth which was, Harry just could not be bothered to make the effort anymore, the reward was not enough. A bit of instant gratification was what he needed on occasion with a minimum of effort. He could never understand why someone had not combined salt and pepper, or salty vinegar, why bother with two when one would suffice. He often allowed such useless thoughts to pervade his mind. But every now and then he came up with a winner. His latest thought was to use a laser similar to a linear motor, direct the laser in a particular direction and wrap the objects around the beam and dispatch them off to a receiving station. He then wondered if it would be difficult in slowing things down and concluded that it would not be a problem, they would just lessen the current. He wondered why no one had already done this, but decided it was too obvious, or could it be that the idea was rubbish due to the fact that it defied the laws of physics.

He then thought that someone in the future will receive a Noble prize for inventing it and it would be unfair as it was his idea. Which was not quite as good as the one he had regarding the clear sticky tape where it's almost impossible to find the end. He had thought that the obvious thing to do was coat the tape with a substance that changed colour when cut or torn, then anyone could easily find the end . He thought that over the course of a year it would save tens of thousands of hours.

But his best idea was running thin tubes through a bed sheet which were attached to a pump, water of a chosen temperature could be run around the sheet assisting someone who had a high temperature, or someone whose temperature was low. He had though of this years ago when he had his first bladder infection and high temperature. He had mentioned the idea to a few people, and even written to some about the idea but no one seemed interested. Later he thought someone had told him that they used a similar idea in space suits. This annoyed him as he knew the idea had been his. Not only that, but he had developed the idea so it was not just tubes running around cooling the person, but the inner material had a capillary type action that spread the hot or cold liquid throughout the material evenly.

He finally fully opened his eyes in a disgruntled mood not having benefited from any dreams or thoughts, bloody waste of time that night was, he thought, remembering how he had awoken when feeling cold. He had been asked what he wanted for breakfast and had settled for toast, experience had told him that it was best to leave the sausages alone, as it was difficult to discern their content. It felt, upon biting into a sausage, that they wanted to bite back. He liked bacon with mushrooms and egg in a morning, but these items were never available. He had asked why there were no eggs for breakfast and someone said that it was to do with salmonella. That some time ago patients had gone down with salmonella. Harry enquired at which naval battle had this sinking happened and did the crew take to the life boats? But such humour was lost on the clerk, who said it was nothing to do with her, she was only temporary and she did not eat eggs. That being the case, Harry could not understand why omelettes were sometimes available for the evening meal. He concluded that salmonella must only strike down people before teatime, and that the hospital cook should know what he was doing. Rumour had it that the cook had done a three month job experience course for British rail, he had worked in the buffet car on the London to Plymouth run and this had given him the experience he needed to be in charge of the kitchens in a general hospital. Harry had eaten his toast and laid back in bed stretching out his arms, how can they bugger up toast? he thought. There must be some specialised training for that. He could visualise hundreds of potential cooks being taught how to damage toast. It's the same with tea and coffee, he thought, how is it possible, with the same ingredients, that someone makes a decent drink and others don't. It defies all logic, he thought. He then decided that it must be a special tea, a cheaper brand that is not available to normal retail outlets.

He felt stiff but that was not unusual as he felt stiff most mornings. He thought that it must be a sign of ageing. Toast was not an adequate breakfast, just a cheap, simple bite which was of little value to anyone; it did not taste good and it lacked any real nutritional value. All in all, he thought it was a false economy. He was still hungry and thought about some of his past good breakfasts. Harry had the ability to recall in detail most of the things or events in his life that he had enjoyed. His mind went back to a hotel in Portugal where the buffet breakfast was superb. The bit he liked the most was that chefs were available to cook you anything you wanted if you could not find it on the buffet. He had found to his delight that a similar situation existed at The Hilton, on Park Lane, except the chef seemed restricted to omelettes, or eggs in various guises. It is high time that I had a trip off somewhere, he said to himself. Harry liked to suddenly take a few days off now and again. He usually only decided at the last minute where he was going but he was organised and he always had his necessary clothes and bits and pieces ready for a quick departure.

One of his interests was photography, and suddenly the desire to photograph something would seize him and he would be away. There was nothing particularly consistent about his photography except mood and atmosphere. It did not matter if it was an old church or a person, he had to recreate the atmosphere. Trying to obtain the composition he wanted had, on occasion, placed him in danger. Harry's favourite photographs were storms at sea, water rushing over rocks, or lonely places isolated by time and geography. Some years earlier he had found himself stranded on the moors in the middle of a snowstorm. It was a normal spring day, not very warm, but warm enough to be out in. Harry had decided to go onto the moors to photograph a Roman road that had been recently exposed. It was off the beaten track but he had managed to get himself there. To his surprise it started to snow and being at a high altitude the snow came down thick and fast. Harry quickly realised that he was stuck in his car. He did not panic, he looked around him wondering what resources he had with him as he had seen similar situations on television. After a short while his resources added up to a cheap imitation Swiss army knife, two cans of beer, a pack of fig biscuits, and half a Mars bar. And, most important, six cigarettes.

On looking at his resources he thought fortune was with him - he would not have to resort to chewing his leather shoes or drinking his own urine. After a few hours the snow stopped as quickly as it had started and Harry's car stuck out like a sore thumb. Within an hour a park ranger had made his way to the car wondering what idiot had left it there. He was surprised to find Harry still in the car, until Harry explained the circumstances and the park ranger exuded a degree or two of sympathy. He explained that it was impossible to get the car out but they would use a four-wheel drive ambulance to get as near as possible. But Harry would have to be carried the rest of the way. The thought of being carried on a stretcher did not appeal to Harry at all. He had visions of people saying: 'They should have left the fool there instead of wasting tax payers money.' It taught Harry a lesson, and on his forays he always tried to make suitable provision. He had quickly recognised the value of the mobile phone with regard to his personal safety, and adequate rations that also included a number of heating devices used by climbers and such like.

Unlike with his meanderings, Harry was given to occasionally seriously thinking and pondering on some subjects. Some years ago he had arrived at the conclusion that a spinally injured person aged more slowly socially than the average person. He did not know exactly why this was the case, but he assumed that it was to do with the length of time a person was disabled. Or the passage of time and any related events, upon which Harry had worked out a plausible theory as only Harry could. Although in his mid forties he often felt physically as though he was in his sixties, especially during the winter months when his body tended not to co-operate. Or seemingly decided to do what it wanted. Which it should be said was not always what Harry wanted. Other times he felt mentally that he was in his late twenties. For some years Harry had thought about his theory, that time for him seemed to go slowly for most of the time, and subsequently he mentally felt around the age of twenty-eight or thirty. This did not mean that he actually felt physically thirty. What he concluded was that the daily events and interactions in his lifestyle were much less than his none disabled peers. And it was the number and variety of events that a person was party to that gave them their personal feeling of time and age. Harry had decided that while he had plenty of notable events in his life, many of them unpleasant, he had, however, less events and interactions on a day-to-day basis than others who were not disabled. Therefore the variety and the sum of the events totalled up to thirty years normal living. That was Harry's theory, and although it needed some refining he was sure that he was onto something as he had mentioned this to one or two other disabled individuals. He asked about their feeling of age, and what age did they feel mentally. He knew that it was no use asking how they felt physically as most of them would state that they were fine, or go into considerable detail about all of their problems, which would have bored him.

One day someone will come up with a suitable equation that will sum up my theory, thought Harry. The number of social interactions and their variations over a given period dictates the perceived time lapsed related to one's life. That sounds nearly correct, he thought. He wondered if there were grants available or something from the Arts Council for developing such theories. He might even get lottery funding if he put in a complicated bid that confused everyone. He then thought that perhaps he should live a little more dangerously and have a sausage with his toast at breakfast next time.

Harry had been on the unit for a few weeks, he had to come in reluctantly to have surgery on his foot which had been causing him some problems for a year or two. But like many older patients Harry tried very hard to avoid returning to the unit. Only a certain level of desperation would finally make his mind up for him. Harry had been disabled for around sixteen years and was experienced in dealing with his condition, for want of a better expression. He disliked the word 'condition' as being too glib and simplistic, but he continued to use it. When he had been placed in the space next to Andy he was quite pleased as they soon got to know one another. They quickly recognised when one or the other wished to talk and when they wanted to be left to their own thoughts. From the beginning Harry had often wanted to discuss Andy's situation with him. He was curious to know what Andy thought about his personal situation, and what, if anything, he had planned or thought of for the future. It had been difficult for Harry from pursuing some lines of conversation due to the possibility that they might at that time be unhelpful to Andy. He had to constantly remind himself that everything was still relatively new to Andy. Although he already knew that Andy had few illusions regarding the severity of his condition. It was the subtleties and nuances that he could not possibly understand. Harry really wanted to tell him about these, but he had resisted. This really frustrated him and went against his natural instinct. He thought that it was like being in a secret society where you were not allowed to disclose the inner rites. Why, he had asked himself, didn't he just start from the beginning and say:

"Look here, Andy, you keep mentioning a few things about your disability and you keep hinting about your future, and some of the things you've done in the past. Do you really want to know what its like out there? how your body can treat you like shit, how the rest of society can treat you like shit if you allow them. But, also there are still a few good times to be had if you can appreciate them. Do you want to know these things so that you have time to plan your future?"

Harry knew that he could not easily do that, some aspects of what Andy might have to face were difficult, too difficult to inflict upon him at that moment. Still Harry was not happy about the situation, the unwritten conspiracy of silence that he felt part of did not seem right. On the other hand, the blunt truth as he saw it, was not necessarily the whole truth. It was based upon his observations and experiences he had to admit although this was done with some reservations. He prided himself upon being as honest and as logical as he could, also fairness was important to him, so all in all he thought that he had obtained a good overall picture over the years of what the realities were concerning his disability. He did not want Andy to waste precious time. Like many who were in hospital at the same time as Harry they did not realise that time was the most precious of all commodities. You only had so much quality time available before your body turned on you and made physical demands that would take up a large amount of time and energy.

He tried hard to think back to the first few months when he was in hospital. This was always something of an effort for him. He did not usually enjoy looking back at this period as more often than not it left him feeling somewhat miserable. This was partially due to the fact that nearly all of his original friends who had been on the unit were already dead and that was an unavoidable fact he did not like facing. He often thought how he would have liked to have met some of them before their accidents. They were real people, interesting, with interesting lives. He often tried to conjure up pictures of what they might have looked like but he found it difficult. It was similar with old school friends, he had seen very few since his accident and he always visualised them as they were when he had last seen them, which in many cases was when they were teenagers. If they were still alive they were now in their forties he thought and would possibly be unrecognisable. He realised that some of them would be grandparents. He wondered if he would recognise them after all, and more important would they recognise him? Where has time gone? Where has life gone? he gasped in exasperation. What the hell have I done with the time? he asked himself angrily.

He continued to think along those lines. I have not done anything notable or worthwhile in my life, been nowhere exciting or different, and I have seen very little compared to many men of my age. He knew that such thoughts were at the root of his desire to talk with Andy. He did not want Andy to fall into the same obvious traps he had done. Yet there remained a contradiction, he also knew that Andy was a different person. And times had changed. What right had he to proffer advice that might on the surface appear to be didactic and insensitive? And Harry felt strongly that it was not his intention to say anything to Andy that might be detrimental in any way whatsoever. There are pro's and con's for everything, Harry had thought, but this still left him perplexed. Why couldn't he just get on and tell it like it was? He kept saying this to himself yet he knew that he could not do it. He tried hard to look at his life logically and use it as some form of guide. Unfortunately he had come to the conclusion that the bad parts outweighed the good. That it had been too hard most of the time, too bloody hard with too little help of the right kind, thought Harry. Especially during those first years when everything is an unwanted challenge, those early years were the time when he really could have done with some positive assistance, not just advice but sound practical help. But times had changed he thought once again, as if to reassure himself. Some things had moved on, and he reasoned that Andy was a young man and the existing opportunities for a reasonable lifestyle were much better now. He retained the thought that basically the physical condition and many of the problems you encounter once you were living in the community remained the same. There were too many advisors and not enough practical help. Forums, meetings and workshops organised by Local Authorities disguised the Authorities' unwillingness to commit finance to the provision of good quality care. Everyone talked at length about choices and quality care but at the end of the day little was done. Authorities always said that they could not recruit suitable staff and retain them This angered Harry, who always said that if carer and personal assistants were paid properly and their role respected and valued there would be less of a problem. We need direct action, a few riots to stir society up he thought. He laughed to himself at this point.

They would have an enquiry, look at the problems and recommend bringing out quickly an act on euthanasia in order to solve the problem. That will cut the costs of care, he thought.

And the private sector would make a fortune. He remembered an old friend of his who drove a mini cab in London when people were flocking in from abroad for abortions in the private clinics that seemed to appear over night; he was picking women up at the airport four and five times a day. It would be just the same with euthanasia he thought, package deals would be worked out, fully inclusive three nights' stay, including hotel and crematorium of ones own choice. There is a gap there for professional mourners he said to himself while smiling. And as for residential care, he shuddered at the thought; on two occasions he had experienced short stays in private residential and nursing homes. The experience had both disappointed and angered him. He was appalled at the treatment of the residents. Everything looks so nice on the surface, smiling senior staff, well decorated buildings, but the care standards were criminal, he could not think of a more appropriate word. He had contacted Social Services and made a complaint but very little happened. He was then informed by a friend that nothing would change as the system could not deal with such problems, it was only interested in containment and not in improvements. He said that if prisoners of war had been treat as bad as some elderly residents are treat the perpetrators would be prosecuted.

It is hard to believe that such things are almost the norm, he added but it is a fact, and when people visit or inspect such places they tend only to see what they want to see, relatives feel guilty leaving the poor sods in such circumstances but they pretend everything is fine and for the best.

Harry had decided long ago that even with some existing social and financial improvements he would not want to start out again as a young disabled person. He realised that he was generalising, and that for others it might have been different. From his experience of knowing those who had been disabled at a similar time he had no reason to think that many of them had done any better than he had. He had seen some obvious differences that had made some aspects of life easier for some. An award of compensation, or a good disability income made a tremendous difference to some individuals and their families. Having plenty of money removed from the equation the problem of financial insecurity. He shuddered at this thought, knowing that to struggle with such a disability was hard enough for most families but to be financially impoverished on top of that was very difficult, 'that is an understatement' he thought.

He then finally decided that if Andy suggested an appropriate line of conversation that he should not hold back anymore, but expand upon it in considerable detail. He also knew that within a few minutes he might change his mind, which to Harry was not a problem.

After some soul searching he had arrived at the conclusion that it had shaped his outlook on life to some extent, that it had caused him to shield himself against disappointment and being let down by people. He would also agree that he was a little cynical in his expectations. It had made him harder with himself. He knew that this attitude had made him fight. He did not accept his lot willingly yet at the same time he did not expect any good luck to come his way. He knew that life was not kind or generous, and that natural justice was not a reality. That the shit seemingly tends to always fall on the same people, although that flies in the face of the laws of probability he had thought, nevertheless it seemed to be the case.

Yet at the same time by recognising this perceived reality he was able to look at life in a more rounded sense. He understood his prejudices and was able to take them into account when formulating an opinion. When pushing forward his views he had, on occasion, heard the comment: "He is only saying that because he is disabled." Harry would round on the person and discuss in detail the persons lack of ability to recognise that a disabled person's thinking tends to be the same as anyone else's in most circumstances. And where it might differ was simply due to the disabled persons expertise and not their ignorance. Having to explain this irritated Harry and confirmed his opinion that the non disabled would never really understand, not because it was too difficult but because they were not particularly interested which was on the surface quite sensible and realistic, although not very desirable. That is how it is, thought Harry, it's no good pretending it's any different.

It would be a nice world if society cared, but they don't and they never will do, no one will give you anything that they really value when you need it, he concluded. There were times when I would have given a great deal for someone to have knocked upon my door and offered me something that I needed, he thought. That was a major problem - loneliness, trapped by ones body and forced into a subculture. That more or less sums it up, he thought. We are forced into being aliens in our own land, we can never be the same as the majority, he sighed, thinking that was a negative thought but it was realistic.

Harry had washed and turned and he was feeling more relaxed while contemplating the day ahead. He had clearly overheard the conversation between Andy and the nurses, especially the bit relating to the red skin on Andy's rear end.

"When are you thinking of getting up?" asked Harry in a non-committal tone.

"In about an hour, when I've come round," replied Andy. He went on, "my rear end was a bit red last night, but they've only just told me. In fact, they probably wouldn't have said anything except Tony happened to mention it."

He would drop anybody in the shit, thought Harry. Although somewhat unwittingly he had done Andy a good turn by ensuring that he was aware of the situation. Harry tried to reassure Andy by telling him that if there had been a real problem either Caroline or Wendy would have been careful. And their experience would not have let him get up if he had still shown signs of there being a problem.

Harry added, "you're right to be concerned though as most pressure sores are a real bastard to deal with. And once you have one you've always got to watch the area. They take a few hours to obtain and God knows how long to get rid of. That is if you don't get gangrene first!. They can keep you in bed forever," continued Harry.

Cheerful sod, thought Andy. Andy was already aware of Harry's opinions on pressure sores from previous conversations and decided to change the subject before Harry totally depressed him. Harry was about to hold forth at length upon pressure sores and the various concoctions that had been used over the years to try and heal them, but decided that at that moment he could not be bothered.

CHAPTER SIX

"I think Caroline fancies me a bit," said Andy sounding serious. Harry looked at him carefully, unsure as to whether or not he was being serious, or just attempting to wind him up, knowing that Harry had himself expressed at some length a liking for Caroline only a few days earlier.

"What makes you think that?" asked Harry cautiously.

"It's difficult to say really, it's more of a feeling" said Andy. "Call it intuition if you want or a gut feeling, but believe me I can always tell when a women is interested in me." Andy was now on one of his favourite subjects, 'women and him'.

"They'll always confuse you in the end, just when you think you understand them," added Harry somewhat philosophically. He went on. "You never know what they're thinking, no matter how well you think you know them. And what's more they do not think like us. They'll let you down and kick you, while at the same time telling you that you are the only person they could ever care about, they are cleverer than us, not particularly intellectually, but just cleverer, they outthink us." He paused for a moment, he was about to say something when he stopped himself on realising that his own experience was at that moment clouding his judgement.

Andy said that women tended to like him because he knew what they wanted from him. Harry laughed out loud at Andy's confidence. "What is it you think they want?" said Harry looking forward to Andy's answer.

"They want an uninhibited, easy going, but," Andy paused at this point in order to emphasize the point he was about to make, "a sensitive understanding person."

Harry burst out laughing. "You! Understanding! Be serious for a moment, and sensitive? I do not believe this, surely you're talking about someone else?" He was laughing out loud. "You are joking? You cannot expect me to accept that crap," said Harry still laughing.

Andy tried hard to look hurt, "it's true!" he said with some conviction. "I'm a modern, sensitive man and most young women like that sort of thing. I'll listen to their problems with

PMT, and nod at the appropriate time, change my underpants daily and wear good quality aftershave - not the cheap stuff that smells disgusting - and I'm house trained." Harry smiled a knowing smile before telling Andy that a dog is house trained, and it was the best line in bullshit he had heard that week.

Andy said that he worked on a pure results basis and his approach was scientific and never failed. Whatever obtained the desired results was what he would do. He continued at some length enjoying himself. "I cannot take a moralistic approach to these things. I know what I want and I go after it. Why be hypocritical?" he added.

"You're a real hypocrite if you tell them a load of bullshit just to get their pants off," said Harry sounding really disappointed. Andy continued apparently unconcerned. "Times have changed since you were chasing around, Harry. Most of the time you don't have to say anything at all, most women are up front gagging for it nowadays, you don't have to try and get their pants off anymore, those days have gone. Haven't you heard women are emancipated, free and on the pull? They have their hand on your dick while they are getting into the taxi. Either that, or they're feeling for your wallet. It's sometimes difficult to know which is most important to some of them."

Harry groaned out loud in dismay at that point, hoping it wasn't true, while at the same time telling Andy that he was a sexist pig who must only go out with the real dross of the female world. Andy did not take any notice and continued. "Women have power now and they know how to use it, they are out looking for sex, and a good time and they go after it, there's no buggering about nowadays. It's just with those few, those precious few, who require nurturing carefully. And then I'm in there, like a ferret up a drainpipe. I just cannot get enough of it, first the chase and then in for the final act." Andy said this with relish, visualising some past success akin to a panzer movement on the Russian front.

"Well, one thing is certainly correct," said Harry "that is definitely not a moralistic approach. Anyone hearing that would conclude that morality and you are total strangers," added Harry.

"Like most men of my age who are not gay, I like and appreciate women a lot, I cherish them, even worship the ground they walk on and can't wait to get at them, in the nicest possible and sensitive way," said Andy pretending to look really sincere. "Admittedly my appetite is considerable, possibly unquenchable, if that's the word, well, perhaps that's not the correct word." He closed his eyes as though searching for the correct phrase. "I think that it's fair to say I like to fill my boots, get my fill," he added while smiling at the thought. Andy smiled to himself again before closing his eyes as he was sure that the last phrase summed things up accurately and with a touch of colour.

Harry sighed loudly which seemed to be some sort of sign of disapproval. This was not really the case, for like Andy, Harry had always had a large appetite when it came to sexual activity and attractive women. And it was possible that his tastes and attitudes were more liberal than those of Andy's. However, he was just unwilling to use the same terminology which dragged down to a low level something he liked to think of as being finer or slightly more refined, or of an aesthetic value over and above just 'having it off' with anything that still drew breath and did not look like they had been put together in a backroom on a bad day.

"What you really need is a good honest women to keep you on the right path," said Harry. He then quickly added, "but I can't think where you might find one nowadays that would be suited to your needs."

Andy looked at Harry with some suspicion for a moment expecting some form of rebuke. "Anybody under the age of thirty seems to be obsessed with thinking about forthcoming holidays and clubbing at the weekends, and then telling everyone at length with a distorted sort of pride about how stupid they had acted. This psychological fix of degradation gets them through for the rest of the week." Harry was starting to get on his high horse. He recognised this but he did not stop himself as he had a captive audience with Andy. "All you have to do is listen to some of the younger bunch in here. After the pubs close, it's around the clubs with the odd interval for chucking up." Harry paused, then continued, "'chucking up', what a bloody expression!" he said with disdain. "I loathe it, but sad to say, that's the expression they use around here for being sick nowadays. Just so they can force a bit more drink down. Then it's a quick look around to grab hold of somebody to shag, as the night would not be complete without a bit of rough. That's our society today," said Harry his voice getting louder, "no bloody taste! No fucking finesse! They are like a bunch of animals. Except that most animals tend to have more taste." Harry was expanding very loudly at this point, he really did feel strongly about the lowering of certain standards but he had tried to be honest with himself and he was sometimes unsure about his reasons.

He continued, "some of them are so bloody rough, some of the women," he paused to regain his thoughts. "Well, it's very hard to call them women really. Anyway, I wouldn't touch some of them with yours." Harry briefly shuddered at the thought. He then quickly gave an unconvincing laugh which seemed totally out of context.

Andy had heard all of this before from Harry and sometimes responded in defence of the present day's norms. Sometimes though, he agreed with Harry, it depended upon his mood at the time. Today he felt that he could disagree with Harry and put forward a reasoned argument if necessary. He thought about it for a while and decided that he would approach the subject direct. He started quietly and in a controlled voice. "If you were coming out of a club after drinking most of the evening or night, and you noticed an attractive women who was smiling at you, well not necessarily attractive in your case but bordering upon the acceptable. And she obviously fancied you - you wouldn't say, 'go away my dear and sober up'. You'd be in there like a shot, just like the rest of us, thinking all your birthdays had come at once." Andy was sure that his reasoning was sound. "What do you automatically think of when you've just had that right amount to drink, and the world almost seems yours, except you need sex to round it all off?" asked Andy.

"Fish and chips or a good curry," replied Harry without hesitation.

"Bollocks!" exclaimed Andy, knowing that Harry was playing him along and not being honest, recognising Andy's particular line of questioning. "Fish and fucking chips!" snorted Andy. "A good shagging is what you are looking for, and the more pissed you are the better she will look, after enough to drink they all tend to look as desirable as Miss World." Harry groaned loudly at that point. "After enough to drink she **will** look like Miss World. Be honest, we've all been there." He continued, "Anything that still breathes will do when you have had enough to drink," he said while retaining a serious expression. Harry sighed again and shook his head in despair at Andy's attitude.

Harry then retorted, "that might be good enough for you degenerate little deviants who are devoid of any finesse, but I expect something a bit better than a quick shag with someone you wouldn't want to wake up next to."

"You can't beat a bit of rough trade - it's sex, not love, just simple sex," said Andy with some relish knowing that he was really irritating Harry. "Wonderfully unpredictable, you can find yourself winning the jackpot! Anything goes with some of them - , you just wouldn't believe it!" He sighed a deep meaningful sigh at that point.

"Only because they are so pissed, or doped up, they hardly know what they're doing, otherwise why would they take the risk of going with you and your perverted mates?" said Harry his arms thrashing about with some indignation, now knowing that he wasn't making much progress with the argument. Andy laughed loudly, which really irritated Harry.

"It's like doing the lottery, but with more winners than losers," he said. "I've had some great times, I'll never forget some of them, I've woken up sometimes having no idea where I was. Started in London one Friday and finished up in Sunderland with the wife of a guy who worked on the oil-rigs. I had both her and her eldest daughter before I left, and a full English breakfast," added Andy who was now laughing loudly, "and could they both go!" he added with enthusiasm. "They were like express trains - no holds barred! It was fantastic!" Harry thought that Andy was exaggerating but wasn't definitely sure, so he said nothing. He was tempted to say something about the quality of the breakfast but he decided not to bother as it would only encourage Andy. Unfortunately for Harry he could not resist saying something. "You mean you were in bed with the mother and daughter?.."

"Of course not! I'm more sensitive than to expect that situation automatically on first meeting someone. I had the daughter when her mother had set off for work." Harry could have hit himself for asking a stupid question. At this point Andy tried to introduce a serious tone to his voice. "By the way, don't think that my desire for Caroline is superficial and just lust," said Andy while still smiling, "the other day I wrote a poem for her. Admittedly I haven't given it to her yet as she might not be into poetry, and I would feel a total idiot ."

"Well, let's have a read of it then," said Harry.

"Not a bloody chance," said Andy who expected Harry to pull it to pieces given the opportunity.

"Come on! Let me read it, unless you are somehow ashamed of it. Let me listen to it then."

"Are you sure that you want me to read it?" asked Andy, unsure as to whether Harry was winding him up or not.

"I want to read it!" insisted Harry, now sounding irritated. Andy looked at Harry with suspicion, but he wasn't laughing, so Andy thought that he would give it a go on the basis that if Harry then laughed he would soon find the opportunity of getting back at him.

"Are you really sure about this?" said Andy thinking that Harry could not wait to get back at him.

"Bloody positive!" said Harry in exasperation.

"Right, here goes!" said Andy wishing he had never mentioned poetry.

"It's about a woman," he added.

"Well I never! You do surprise me," said Harry impatiently.

"You'll have to be patient, as I have to do this from memory and I might get it wrong.

'In deepest dreams I taste the fresh sprung dew,
Gossamer silk, like sheen of sensual delight
Mist like cream, out of infinite heaven
Shrouded in the heady aroma of wanton despair.
Thy inner substance drowning lesser tastes,
Sweet nectar pours forth, that smiles a defiant smile
It teasingly lingers, it dwells but a moment. Alas, it is gone.
The body and soul search again for such a prize.
A prize that invades reason and makes fools of us all.'

"That's not too bad," said Harry wistfully, "in fact, it's quite good, in a simplistic, earthy sort of way. I like it. It's sensual, yet tasteful, well almost tasteful by your standards. It definitely sums up the attractive part of a women's sensuality and inner being. And still shows her perfidiousness, and our weakness, or inability to resist something that is seemingly so important."

Andy smiled with satisfaction at Harry's comments as he was expecting some form of ridicule.

"No, to be honest, it's not bad at all," continued Harry. "Obviously it's not Keats or Milton, or about the raging sea or the glorious countryside. You've chosen your subject matter carefully in keeping with your personality," said Harry while staring into space. One sarcastic dig was not usually enough for Harry. Andy awaited the forthcoming sarcasm but surprisingly Harry did not say anything else.

Harry sighed, "a few years ago I wrote a short article on what it felt like being disabled, or to be more accurate during the first few days, but it was bloody difficult. It was difficult to get across to people what it really felt like so I used a prose-like format. I used to meet people and they would all say the same thing, well those who actually spoke to you. It went something like, 'how do you keep yourself busy?' followed by 'do you sleep well?' I could never associate the two items but those morons could, it seemed. Oh, and the favourite one was, 'how do you pass the time?' Whatever the reply was they always said, 'well, it'll keep you occupied then.' While slapping you on the back the individual would probably say: 'I couldn't do it, y'know.' That was my usual conversation upon meeting strangers over the years. They were deaf, they did not recognise or even hear what you had said. What they really wanted was just an opening so they could tell you how, if you really put your mind to it, you could get up and walk. 'The disability bit is all in the mind,' they would say. I say 'they' because they tend to come in pairs for some unknown reason. They tell you this crap with authority and conviction because he really knew. Note we are singular now!. 'He' had suffered something similar years ago when a stone fell on his head and he couldn't move properly for a couple of days. But by persevering it all came back. At that point they always smile which is followed by a look of vague optimism, that's the only way that I can describe it really. They then bugger off to tell the nearest person how good or bad the company they're working for is doing and redundancies are being talked about." Harry grunted in anger. "It's not a real world for us out there, sometimes it really is not, the relationships and interactions are different, we inhabit a different planet at times" said Harry.

"Can I hear it?" asked Andy, "the poem or prose whatever you call it."

Harry looked as though his mind was drifting about in some far flung place away from everyday reality. He shook his head and he seemed to get his thoughts together. Harry then quickly reached into the drawer of his locker and brought out a few stained pages.

"I thought you were never going to ask. I was going to re-type them while I was in here," he said, offering an excuse for there scruffy state. "I suppose that I'll have to read it to you," muttered Harry. "Are you sure you want to hear it?" asked Harry. Andy nodded.

"Remember it was written some time ago, after the events. It might not seem quite as relevant now and it was an attempt to, well, just see what you think."

"Get on with it," said Andy, "don't keep make excuses for it, if it's, crap it's crap!"

"It's not crap!" retorted Harry it has a good use of metaphor, OK, it might be just a bit crap, but they were a mixture of thoughts and feelings which were hard to define after the event, and I certainly wasn't in a position to describe them until some time later. So I wrote it hoping it would make sense of experiences that were impossible to describe accurately shortly after the event. If you start taking the piss out of me, I'll throw my water jug at you!" he added.

"The beginning."

Andy sighed, "You've actually called it the beginning? Don't you think that's a bit pretentious, like this is genesis or something similar?" said Andy. That remark instantly annoyed Harry who was quite proud of his efforts.

"I'm putting it away if you are going to take issue with every sentence. Just listen and try and think what your first few days were like. It's bloody hard to hit the right tone or feeling; it's complicated, but perhaps in your case it might be easier because you've had me here to guide you." Harry gave a wry smile at that point.

He tried to explain as best as he could in order that Andy might understand. To turn one's inner thoughts and feelings of any given moment into words that accurately describe those feelings is always difficult. It is always hard, it appears, to get across to the reader what it was really like, how it really felt; therefore it is always seemingly inadequate even with the best usage of metaphor and analogy "but I've tried, so don't bloody knock it. I'm not a writer, and I don't pretend to be and at the time it was the best I could come up with so take account of that fact.

"'The Beginning', that's what it's called although you might be correct, it could sound a bit crap. I can always find a better title. Anyway are you laying comfortable?" Harry cleared his throat and started read aloud. "Remember that these were my thoughts and I'm not pretending that they are clever or sophisticated, it's the best that I could do at the time."

"'Time is not a good companion and it always plays tricks with our thoughts and feelings, and after so many years it is now difficult to remember all the details, and the subtleties. But if I close my eyes and carefully cast my mind back I do remember that the seemingly endless nights turned into sleepless days, and with the coming of dawn I still felt no better.

"'Lying in bed during this strange surreal time I was trying hard to think clearly, yet I was knowingly confused, and for some reason also relentlessly being driven on, being pushed and harried for no discernible reason towards an invisible winning line where there was no line. By people who remained invisible.

"'While in a soporific state of mind I still concentrated as hard as I could on the scene that I was part of. I was there participating and I moved slowly forward, my knees bending under an unseen burden, it appeared as though I was pushing painfully through the impenetrable mass of greenery that surrounded me.

"'Sadistic tree roots that were short and knurled reached out grasping my ankles, pulling me back down towards the dank cloying earth that gave off the sickly smell of decaying vegetation.

"'I scrambled forward in desperation while reaching out trying to get a better grip on the hard stone that protruded out above me.

I took a deep breath trying to fill my lungs with precious energy tensing all the sinews in my body ready to put in one last effort.

"'I lunged forward but my foot slipped back, while my forearm dragged painfully against a rock, taking off a jagged layer of skin. I ignored the pain, fearing to stop.

"'I looked up wondering if I should try and force my way forward once again. But I was now doubting my strength.

"'Time had bled from me the energy that I needed to keep moving forward. I finally rested, although not fully conscious, falling in and out of sleep through many long days and night's, time had lost its meeting. I was waiting for a sign of renewed strength, but it failed to appear. I started to have doubts. 'Was it better to turn back?', but where was back? It made no sense, my mind asked for an explanation, but while I knew they understood my thoughts, no explanation was forthcoming. They were the timeless ones that are always with us. They have no body or mind, they reside within us, untouchable, unreachable, devoid of reason, but there awaiting the moment to pervade our being.

"'Slowly I moved forward not really feeling my body. I drifted like a straw on a gently moving stream that meandered between high river banks. It was not possible to see over the banks, I had no knowledge of where I was going,

"'I drifted along anxious at any change in current or breath of air. I had no knowledge of where I was being taken. I wasn't sure that I cared.

"'I looked ahead of me trying to penetrate the threatening darkness that was looming towards me, its speed changing constantly as if to warn me of some unseen potential threat. Yet I cared not for threats anymore.

"'How many days and months I drifted along this river I can't tell you but it seemed an eternity. The scenery was constant, never changing. Only the occasional discordant sound in the distance that attracted my attention

"'When I do not know, but I felt movement around me, I was lifted somehow up above the water, but still being carried forward.

"'Around me the sky had taken on a different colour, not lighter or darker but a shade that was beyond description. A shade that signified nothing, I was now afraid this nothingness created despair: "this was worse than the darkness," there it seemed I could lay awhile secure in its depth and morbidity. I asked myself to move, to walk slowly forward, but my legs were heavy, sticking in some unforeseen morass. For a brief moment I saw light, indistinct but real, the light was some way off but I found that by concentrating very hard I could move towards it although my progress was slow and painful.'"

I had briefly forgotten about pain; for some time I had not needed pain or any such stimulus that served to distract me. I could not, nor would not, afford myself the supposed luxury of dwelling upon unused and discarded emotions. They were a potential burden that I was not yet equipped to carry.

"'The light surrounded me slowly but surely. I needed to muster the strength to make a desperate effort. This was the time, I reached out to grasp what was there before me, and then I awoke. Yet I knew that I had not really been asleep. I had moved from one reality to another, or so I perceived; I lay there analysing my situation but to no effect. The cold sweat clung to my body, my breathing was easier, I slowly looked around the familiar room noting slight changes.

"'How long had I slept? The remnants of my dreams started to return, at first they were fragmented like a jigsaw puzzle, but slowly the pieces started to fall into place making connections that I could gaze upon but could not yet understand.

"'I looked back and I once again saw my image in a strange land, in a distant time conversing with wraiths. They carried me away laughing silently at some unknown amusement. I tried to talk to them, asking them why they were treating me in this way, but they simply laughed.

"'Then I recalled my fate, I shuddered at my mortality, my inability to shape my destiny. I felt warm, bitter tears running down my cheeks. I cried in desperation but no one heard my pleas. Was I to be lost forever, never seeing, never really knowing or understanding; would there be no reason forthcoming that would lighten my load and ignorance?

"'My heart was beating faster, fear gripped me once again having to look upon the pitiful wretch before me, seemingly in limbo, awaiting a judgement that was not forthcoming for some unknown and forgotten reason.

"'My thoughts turned to anger at the plight of the miserable soul who in desperation thought of begging for forgiveness for some unknown sin.

"'I shouted and pleaded that he desist, "that he should stand up and fight," fearing not for his life or soul as they were already taken. But fight for what remained, what small glimmer of existence that he still owned, what semblance of sanity he possessed.

"'The figure at last heard my voice and carefully stood up casting away the drab cloud of despair, and walked forward, slowly at first, but quickly gaining in confidence. He gazed around him and offered a faint smile of relief. He remembered where he had recently been, and it was a land he vowed that he would not cross again, the pain was still with him but it was a load he could learn to carry. He had found another path and he would tread this pathway observing and learning, while hoping that he might yet understand. But if he failed to understand he knew that it did not really matter, in the end nothing really mattered, what had been, had been, and what was to come, would come.

"'Could he exert any control over these coming events, he did not know, but he thought not, although time might tell him; but time had not yet showed itself to be his friend.

"'He would tread softly through the land observing the changes and listening to the sounds that filled the air. He would gaze with regret on many of the sights that lay before him, his eyes would moisten with tears at the suffering going on around him. He would feel helpless and frustrated at his inability to prevent these happenings, this is where the pain would strike hard.

"'He was destined to slowly but surely understand, the picture would unravel before him, but he could never make the changes to the design that he knew were needed. That was his fate: to see, to hear, to understand, and to be constrained with the strongest of chains that would prevent an intervention. He knew that a life of dissatisfaction and frustration was to be fate; he brushed away a tear and thought of the time that lay ahead.'"

Andy drew in a large breath while thinking. He was not sure as to how he should respond to Harry's piece of work, if he said too little he knew Harry would think he was being dismissive, but if he said too much then Harry would think that he was being patronised.

"That is interesting and thought provoking, you could say it's surrealistic to a certain extent without going over the top. I like it, I think its quite good in its own strange way," said Andy, alert to the fact that he must not sound patronising. "It's just that little bit different, well to be honest jumbled up. I would have to read it again to get the subtleties."

"Shall I read it again?" asked Harry.

"Yes, go on," said Andy regretting already he had said that he would like to hear it again. "I'll try to take it in, so don't go too fast."

Harry appeared pleased. He read it again, this time slowly.

"I think I understand," said Andy, whose tone of voice suggested that he was trying hard to maximise the meaning of what had just been said. This pleased Harry for the moment. Andy then asked the question which he knew that he should not have asked.

"But where are the wine and the women, where are the good times, the music and laughter. Where's the optimism and the desire for the good life?" asked Andy.

"There wasn't any optimism or the good life," said Harry loudly, "that's the whole bloody point! You've missed the point of those few days of confusion and conflict. How could there be any good times? The thought of good times would be idiotic!."

Andy frowned at that point. "I want and need some of the good times included!" shouted Andy almost irrationally. He held up his arm the best he could to indicate that he had more to say.

"It's good in a negative sense, or so it appears, and to me it seems quite imaginative, and I must presume it is honest. But let's be fair - it is bloody depressing without some lighter moments or women, or if I dare use the expression 'love and affection'. It's so cold and negative."

He then spoke more quietly. "Something else has to be included; you can't leave it like that. I would personally require it to have large, attractive, vulgar women with no inhibitions, corrupt and decadent if necessary, they would be your harpies."

"They would be a negative element," added Harry, "and you've just said it needs the opposite or something of that nature."

"They would've made a good contrast to the grey hopelessness."

Harry looked at him carefully, unsure as to whether or not he was being serious. I will kill the little bastard if he comes out with a snide remark, he thought. He started to say something, thinking he had better expand a little while he had the opportunity.

"You've missed the point, so listen carefully. There are some things which we call 'art' whether it is written in that particular manner or in the form of a photograph or painting or poetry without involving women," said Harry seriously. "I'm going off at a slight tangent here. But it is a fact there are only a few good women artists throughout history and that's not being sexist." He continued, "And before you say anything I didn't go as far as to say it was art. It's not art! Let's be honest, I never pretended it was anything but a few thoughts."

"But it is descriptive and imaginative," said Andy quickly. "And further more it's not relevant that there might be only a few good women artists in history. That has absolutely nothing to do with it so don't go off at a tangent."

Harry masked his disappointment. "I agree it's not art," he said reluctantly, "but it's my feelings displayed in a particular style at a particular time. You must remember I was trying to look back and put down in writing what it felt like. Can you remember the first two weeks in detail?" he asked, aggressively.

Andy ignored the question. "I liked it, I've already said that. All I said was it could probably do with some women."

"Where could you put the women, what would they signify? If anything they were not part of my interpretation." With that Harry gave a snort of frustration and poured himself a glass of water. "You and women! You're obsessed with women, it's time you thought of something more useful to you. When you get a little older you might start to appreciate things other than women, because let's be honest, you just want women for sex; you do not value them."

"You could be right, but I don't think you are," said Andy,

"besides, there are some wonderful attractive women around."
Harry groaned loudly.

Andy was not to be discouraged. "I should point out to you there are a lot of women throughout history who have made their mark in the arts," said Andy.

"Name one!" said Harry quickly in the belief he was going to put Andy under pressure, "just one who was in the top hundred."

"You can't treat art as though it is similar to the top twenty pop records, there's much more to art than that." Harry with some reluctance had to agree.

"I don't suppose you've heard of Angelica Kaufman or Dame Laura Knight, or Barbara Hepworth?"

"Don't go on! I get the point," said Harry. He continued digging himself in deeper. "Let's be realistic - they more or less had the personalities of men." Andy burst out laughing.

He looked at Harry, "is that the best you can come up with? That's pure sexist!."

"They were not indicative of their sex," said Harry sounding very serious.

"The social and economic factors prevented women from participating," said Andy quickly. Harry could do little but agree with the last point. Andy added, "I can't believe you have just said what you have. Presumably they were all lesbians as well?"

"Some of them were," added Harry. Andy burst out into hysterical laughter that really irritated Harry.

Harry was going to fight a defensive action now. He was keen on getting across the idea that irrespective of what Andy had said the women who appeared to be successful in the past acted more like men than their own sex. Although given time to consider he also knew that his argument was relatively weak if taken to its conclusion. In fact, if it was taken to its conclusion, he did not have an argument, but that had never inhibited Harry from trying to tease out of a morass some semblance of a logical conclusion even if the premises were more than suspect.

He was interrupted. "Is that the only subject that you men can ever talk about?" said Elisabeth, who was already up in her wheelchair. "If you could direct your energy and thoughts into something more useful, you'd be a great deal happier."

"Does she know anything about artistic women?" said Andy

rhetorically. Both Harry and Andy just grunted.

Then Harry shouted across towards her. "Fucking is the lyricism of the masses!

C H Baudelaire said that and he was no fool, although he was French. By the way - Andy was just wondering if you were a lesbian/'

"Take no notice of him!" shouted Andy "he's going through a funny time - it must be something to do with his age."

Elisabeth then said "It was nothing to do with his age; it was a denial of reality."

"What the hell does that mean?" shouted Harry. "I'm the most realistic person I know, I can't think of anyone more realistic."

"That's when you are talking about something other than women. I've never known you get on with a women yet. Remember Tamara, the student nurse?"

"That's my private business!" said Harry angrily. Elisabeth just laughed.

"Who's this Tamara?" asked Andy.

"She has nothing to do with this, and in future I'll make sure that you see or hear nothing," he said in a loud voice towards Elisabeth, who just smiled a knowing smile.

"Who is Tamara?" asked Andy in a voice that required an answer. Elisabeth was only too happy to tell him: She was a large girl, a South African, very attractive and obviously desirable, because our friend Harry could not resist her; in his eyes she could do no wrong. He asked her out, and wined and dined her.

"Isn't that correct, Harry?" said Elisabeth, enjoying Harry's discomfort. "Harry wanted his wicked way with her but he was the only person around who didn't know that she was a lesbian."

Andy burst out laughing at that point. "I like it! I like it a lot! That's wonderful, Harry spending money trying to seduce a lesbian."

"She was bloody attractive - everyone said so, and you have to admit that although I was on a futile pursuit, at least I put the effort in."

"It still sounds good to me!" laughed Andy.

Harry grunted in a manner that indicated that he was unwilling to discuss the incident. Elisabeth was in the bed directly across from Andy. She had been on the unit some weeks after having a problem with a difficult bladder infection. This had been cleared with appropriate antibiotics, but she had acquired a small pressure sore on her left hip which she did not have when she had been admitted to the unit. The staff wanted to clear the sore up in order that she could go home in the same, or a better condition than on her admittance to the unit, although due to the lack of beds it was not unusual for patients to be sent home earlier than they should have.

"How's the sore?" enquired Harry.

"It's doing quite well," replied Elisabeth, seemingly pleased with the situation. She added that she was only going to stay up for a few hours as the skin was delicate but was holding up. She was annoyed at getting a pressure sore but she knew that it was par for the course.

"Try Manuca honey on your next sore," said Harry. "It's from New Zealand, it contains a healing agent that other honey does not have. Andy has promised to massage some into his head in order to get nutrients to his brain." They both laughed.

"I'll try and remember that," she replied "and I'll observe Andy closely for a day or two, in order to see if there is a discernable improvement."

For some reason she felt stiff and uncomfortable. She was used to her physical condition; she had been disabled for over sixteen years and had a daughter and a husband. Elisabeth had always thought that she was a very lucky woman. Like most of her peers she did not like her condition and the problems that came with it. She had always thought that was more or less common sense. Although she had once heard some individual who thought himself a superior being, stating that his disability was the best thing that had happened to him. At the time she thought that his previous situation must have been bad, or that he was just plain stupid trying to create an impression of some kind. Later on she understood that his disability had not destroyed his life but had steered him in a direction that he had found acceptable and fulfilling. Although his statement regarding that his disability was the best thing that had ever happened to him would never seem sensible in her mind.

Elisabeth was an interesting person and had been physically very attractive when younger, and while her disability had taken its toll in some areas she was still attractive. Like many disabled people she had put on weight over the past two or three years, and she had acquired a more mature figure. Almost everyone who met her said that she had something about her that was different, and it made her more than just attractive. It was an intangible element that very few are fortunate enough to possess. And what was unusual in such a situation was she was genuinely liked by both men and women. Both found her attractive. And to her constant surprise her company was always being sought after by the other patients. She was the sort of person who seemed to have time for everyone. And if asked would proffer an opinion without being overtly judgemental. Due to her having been disabled for some considerable years she also had a good knowledge of her condition and many of the related problems. Her sensible advice upon how to deal with Social Services or a housing department had proved useful to many. And on the important issue of benefits she was seen as something of an expert. Although she would never claim such a title knowing how difficult and complex the area of benefits could be. All in all, Elisabeth was a nice person in the best meaning of the word.

"Is there anybody coming to see you today?" enquired Harry.

"My sister should be coming this afternoon, if her husband allows her to have the car, or my husband will be coming - they'll have sorted something out."

"It's his car then is it?" asked Harry. "It's their car really, I suppose," said Elisabeth "it's just that he uses it for his work some days."

"His needs take precedence then" said Harry in a serious tone of voice.

Elisabeth thought for a while. "I haven't given it any thought but perhaps it does, my sister only works in the mornings."

Harry went on, "but what if she needs it to come and see you? There isn't a bus route where your sister lives."

"If she needed to see me, I'm sure that she would get use of the car," said Elisabeth without any real conviction.

"If she's working she should have a car of her own. What about equality?" added Harry, trying hard to stir Elisabeth up. But Elisabeth was familiar with Harry and she did not allow herself to be drawn on the subject.

"I'm sure that if my sister wanted a car she would get one," said Elisabeth unconcerned. Harry muttered something that she didn't quite catch but she didn't bother to ask him to repeat what he had said. She knew that he had not really meant her to hear it. It must be something nasty or critical, thought Elisabeth. She had known Harry for some years and they had always got on well together although she knew that Harry could be provocative if you did not know him. On occasions like Christmas they had telephoned each other over the years, but rarely had they met except on visits to hospital when attending an out patients clinic or visiting a friend. In different circumstances she would have liked to spend more time with Harry. He amused her and occasionally made her angry, but she knew that he liked her although he kept it to himself. She really liked Harry a lot; deep down he was basically a good man, interesting and attractive, also a bit of a bastard at times. One thing she was sure of was that she should not let Harry know how she felt, as he would take advantage of it given any slight opportunity.

Elisabeth was realistic regarding her situation but she still desperately wanted to go home as soon as possible. Just waiting for sores to heal seemed such a waste of valuable time. But there was no other route, they took time and that was it. She really missed her husband and daughter during such times. Her daughter had recently taken her mock exams and was awaiting the results. Elisabeth hoped that she had done well and had gained good grades. It was important to her that her daughter did well academically and had the same opportunities as her friends. Over the years this had caused Elisabeth some concern. The main concern that had always been with her and that had caused her many sleepless nights was the thought of her daughter being disadvantaged in any way because her mother was disabled. She had done everything possible to make sure that that was not the case. If it had been the case it would have made her feel very guilty, and that was something she would have had great difficulty in dealing with. Everything would have come back to haunt her, her doubts and her fears, and her original feelings of inadequacy.

Elisabeth, like many disabled women and men, felt very

vulnerable at times, especially in those early years when they are trying to adjust to society's perceptions and attitudes towards them as a disabled person.

Elisabeth winced and thought about the trouble her pregnancy had caused at the time they announced it. Neither her parents nor her husbands parents were in favour of her having a child. She could still clearly visualise the awful scene when she told them the news as though it was only yesterday.

Elisabeth and her husband had thought about having children for a long time, and had discussed the pros and cons. They knew that there could be some medical problems, but other couples had gone through the process before and had overcome any problems that had arisen. They decided that they would discuss the situation with the nursing sister who was their community nurse, and having known one another for a long time they hoped for some moral support. Upon being informed she was delighted at the prospect, and was quick to tell them that they would have her full support. This reassured them both as they realised that not everyone would be so supportive. Although they were not naïve it still was something of a shock when their GP told them that she did not think that it was a very good idea. She then went on at great length explaining some of the medical problems that might occur. She then started to expand upon the social aspects. Who was physically going to be looking after the baby, who was going to get up in the night? Elisabeth stopped her at that point and told her that was not what they had come to see her about. That the bringing up of the baby was something they had considered at length, and they knew what was required, and they were prepared to do it. Their GP seemed more than unhappy at this point realising that her advice was gong to be unheeded. She told them in no uncertain terms that they were asking for trouble and that when something went wrong someone else would have to pick up the pieces. This made Elisabeth angry and before she could say anymore, Elisabeth told her that she was a foolish and stupid person who should know better, and it was none of her business who would be doing what. She finally said that they obviously were not going to get any help from her so they might as well leave. With that they both left the health centre vowing that they would change their doctor as soon as possible. Outside the surgery they looked at one another, they burst out laughing, and then Elisabeth cried. She wanted to be logical and in control of her emotions but it was not as easy as she had imagined. She was hurting and she could not dismiss the emotional pain as being of no consequence.

Elisabeth had told Kay, her community nurse, about the events with the GP, and Kay had told her that she was not surprised as that particular GP was generally unsupportive to anyone who wanted or needed something that might require a modicum of thought. She also had to admit that quite a few doctors have little or no understanding of disability. They think that you are sick, or ill, and that you are different to other couples. Elisabeth looked at her with what could only be described as a blank expression. Kay put her arms around her and gave her a hug. She explained that there was still a great deal of prejudice when it came to dealing with disability. She went on, you would think that after all the publicity in recent years people would be not only understanding, but supportive,

"But I'm afraid that's not the case," she said, her eyes were moist with tears. They hugged each other and both shed tears. "But don't worry about it," said Kay suddenly, "Bugger them all. We'll sort out what needs to be done, if and when necessary." They hugged each other again, and Elisabeth started to feel better. She felt as though someone whom she could trust was on their side and that was so important to her.

It still came as something of a surprise when Elisabeth found herself pregnant, although they had been trying for some months to conceive. Both of them were happy with the situation. They constantly looked at each other and smiled; they felt a strange level of pleasure and inner contentment, they could only describe the feeling as being satisfied, and it was an unusual feeling thought Elisabeth, something different to how she had ever felt before. In the past when she had not become pregnant as quickly as she had wanted and expected Bob had made a joke about having a lot of sex, saying if they could not manage to have a baby just think of all the pleasure they were having while trying. She knew that he was joking and trying to make light of the situation in order that it might help minimise the hurt she might feel. She was happy about their sex life, or as she preferred to call it, their love life. She loved to look closely at her husband. It was so pleasurable to see him on top of her pressing himself against her. She knew that he liked sex with her; although she was paralysed, it did not seem to make any difference in his desire for her. She also liked to reach down and place her hand on him, to feel his erection and knowing that his desire for her had created it. She could not feel it inside her but she could feel that he was there, joining them together in something special. And when he was achieving an orgasm, she was there sharing it with him - it was theirs.

Elisabeth had decided, with her husband Bob, that they should tell both sets of parents at the same time. Otherwise one set of in laws would feel put out if the other had been told later. And it had always been something of a balancing act as neither families liked one another. There was no particular reason for this, so both of them accepted that their families were strange, but not unlike many other families they were familiar with. It almost seemed that if things were simple and running smoothly, it was lacking something. Disruption and arguments plus problems were more normal, and in a perverse sort of way more desirable. Bob had said that he thought it was part sociological or psychological, their parents were not struggling anymore and it had left such a gap in their lives, they had not learned how to not struggle and subsequently they were always pessimistic, thriving on potential doom and gloom and the acquisition of various ailments.

When the time came, both Bob's mother and her mother looked at each other, and both shook their heads in dismay. Her mother then seemed to lose any semblance of self- control and could not stop herself from almost shouting. "Do you realise what you've done? Have you any idea? You must be wrong in your heads!" She stopped and turned to Bob. "It's you, isn't it?" she said accusingly and with some venom, "you've done this! How could you? How could you do this?" She could not continue; she was seemingly lost for words for the moment. Her husband, who was a quiet little man, tried to put his arm around her, only to have it brushed aside.

"It takes two to make a bargain!" interjected Bob's mother in his defence, although she agreed with most of what had been said. She continued, "I don't believe Bob had to hold her down to do it to her," she added. Elisabeth's mother almost choked, she tried to visualise her disabled daughter having sex.

"It's disgusting!" she shouted, "It's absolutely disgusting, it's unnatural, the whole thing is just beyond words. Oh my God just what will they think at the Chapel?" She turned to her husband for support, "he's nothing but a pervert, an animal. How could you do that to our daughter, our little girl?" she said this while turning away from her husband who dare not interject and glared at Bob. By this time both Bob and Elisabeth had heard enough. They had discussed the various ways the conversation might go once they had made the situation known but they had not expected a reaction of this kind. They were shocked and astonished at the reaction at what they thought was good news. They had expected a few gasps of surprise, followed by mutterings of support, but not this theatrical outburst that was abusive and almost threatening.

"And have you thought who is going to look after the baby? They don't look after themselves you know" said Elisabeth's mother getting her breath back.

"We'll manage," said Elisabeth defensively.

"Manage! Manage! How do you think you are going to manage?" said Bob's mother getting in on the act, she continued. "Don't expect me to be around every day will you."

"The same goes for me," said Elisabeth's mother glancing across to show that the in- laws were at last united.

Bob could not contain himself any longer. He told Elisabeth's mother and his mother to shut up, that at the end of the day it was nothing to do with them. To his surprise they did. He went on and told them that they were looking forward to having a baby, and all that they had done as potential grandparents upon being told the news was to act almost hysterical, and shout out loud about who is going to look after the baby. Bob was in full stride now.

"Well, I'll make it clear to you, so just listen carefully and take in what I'm saying," he said while glaring at them. "We'll do everything ourselves, your help will not be required. We'll ask you for nothing, bugger all, do you understand me? Have you grasped it? We want nothing from either of you, now nor in the future. What have you done for us in the past? Sod all! That's what! So why should we expect anything now?" he added whilst putting an arm around Elisabeth. "This is my wife," he said this with considerable emotion, he then placed a hand upon Elisabeth's abdomen, "and in here is our child, your grandchild. A child you have already rejected. A child I will make bloody sure you will never see unless you have a quick change of mind."

He continued. "You sanctimonious buggers! Laying down the law in our house! Who the hell do you think you are? What right have you to come here and talk to us as though we're school children? Where have you been when we have needed help in the past? You've kept well away from us, frightened that we might ask you to do something. Well, you don't have to worry on that account." Bobs voice had quietened, he felt anger and hurt. He pointed to the door and suggested that they leave. They moved towards the door and Elisabeth's mother turned looked at Elisabeth and said in a controlled voice that tried to muster a little empathy. "Elisabeth dear, before we go, can I ask you. Do think about an abortion will you? We'll pay for it, won't? we," she said this while looking at her husband, who just nodded, as he had been trained to do over the years.

"We'll be happy to contribute," said Bob's mother quickly, once again getting in on the act, "We're happy to share any costs. No one is going to say we were unwilling to pay our share."

"That's agreed then," said Elisabeth's mother forcing a smile, "I'll ring the doctor for you and arrange everything. You'll have nothing to worry about and we can then all get back to normal."

Elisabeth was now in tears. "Get out, now, before I throw you out!" said Bob moving forward menacingly.

"That's gratitude for you," shouted Elisabeth's mother unable, to believe that their generosity had been rejected, "you'll regret this my girl, mark my words, you'll live to regret it!" she shouted. "And there's another thing you obviously have not thought about, your condition, let's be honest, it's not the usual run of events is it? How do you know the child will be normal?"

Before she could say anymore Bob pushed her outside and closed the door. He looked at Elisabeth and smiled. "It's up to us," he said. "In fact, it was always up to us! We should've realised it; we were foolish not to have realised it," Bob sounded angry.

"I just don't understand," said Elisabeth looking bemused, "we have a house, you have a good job, we're not destitute. Why are they so angry?" She was crying again, she could not stop herself; she felt so unhappy, she had never felt as bad as she felt at that moment. She could not understand their reasoning. She looked at her husband and asked him. "Am I so different to other women? Is that how people really see me?"

He pulled her close to him as she sobbed. "You're not like other women," he said. "You're better than any other women I have ever known."

"hat sounds as though it's right out of a romantic novel! You've read that somewhere," she said, trying to make light of the situation, although she knew that the past couple of hours would stay with her for the rest of her life. She would never forget what had been said, and at that time she was sure that she would never forgive. He held her close to him until her tears had dried.

Things had not been easy from the start but they had managed, and Elisabeth's daughter had grown up no different to other girls of her age. But the thought had always remained with Elisabeth that she must bring her daughter up successfully. She did not know what that measure of success would be. She did not know why it constantly played upon her mind after all these years but it did. She had often thought, rightly or wrongly, that everyone was waiting for something to go wrong, and for her to fail or to display some inadequacy. Then they could all turn and say 'we told you so, it was only a matter of time.' But she had not failed yet, her daughter was the same as the rest, she felt pleased at this thought as though she had accomplished something worthwhile. Bob had recognised early on that Elisabeth was more concerned than she needed to have been in ensuring that everything was right. And that their daughter would not be different or neglected. But this was so very important to Elisabeth that it had started to dominate her thoughts. Fortunately over the first few years a few good friends did rally round and while not getting too involved did provide some moral support which helped in the long run.

Elisabeth's thoughts returned to the present. "I think I'll go and do a bit of exercise while I'm in the right frame of mind," she said to Harry. Harry just nodded as exercise was not something that he was particularly fond of. Before his accident he had enjoyed sport, although not particularly athletic, and he still enjoyed watching sport, especially football. But as far as participation went he had decided that it wasn't for him anymore. He had tried to participate at a few things but he found them lacking in pleasure. What is the point in putting in more than you can get out of something that you are supposed to enjoy, he rationalised; if in doubt, give up.

CHAPTER SEVEN

Elisabeth had left the room and was making her way to the gym. "Nice woman, decent body for her age," said Andy perusing her carefully.

"Not bad, is she?" said Harry. He continued. "When I first met her, just after her accident, she looked fantastic, and with a great figure! Everyone fancied her, and she happens to be the real thing, not false or two-faced. A genuine, honest person," he added "she's a very nice woman, and there aren't many of them about like her, I'm sorry to say."

It was obvious to Andy that Harry thought quite a bit about Elisabeth, and this gave him the opportunity to wind Harry up.

"What's she like when you get her going? Presumably you've had a go with her then? Tried it on?" enquired Andy.

Harry stared hard at him before replying. "Tried it on? Had a go? You don't 'have a go' with someone like Elisabeth," he said in a tone of incredulity, "she's a friend, and she has morals." He almost gasped out the last word. "She's married, with a daughter," he paused for a moment before saying, "she's respectable and decent."

Andy kept a serious expression on his face before pursuing the matter. "I do realise that she's respectable and a saint, but you're evading giving me a proper answer, which makes me just a little bit suspicious, knowing you for these past few months. So I'll ask you once again, have you had a go at her? Have you tried it on?" he repeated, while smiling. He continued enjoying himself with this line of questioning. "I can tell that you fancy her, or at least you did when she was in a bit better condition, with still plenty of tread on the tyres."

"You're talking about her as though she's a used car," said Harry, sounding really annoyed although he knew that Andy was deliberately winding him up. Andy persisted along the same lines. "Well, I wouldn't' have minded giving her one when she was a bit younger," said Andy, while at the same time trying to make a suitable gesture of his intent. This was just too much for Harry, he was getting angry. He knew that he should not have allowed himself to be drawn on the subject, and it irritated him as such banter was the norm. But this was Elisabeth and he did really care about her. He looked across at Andy and said in a very controlled voice.

"Andy, my dear, young but deluded friend, let me tell you this important bit of information which you should consider very carefully." In a deliberate increasingly strong tone of voice Harry announced. "Your shagging days are over, or more or less over, so put it out of your mind. All that young, female flesh you see around you is not going to be yours. And it's never going to be yours, someone else will be 'giving them one', as you so eloquently put it. The plug has been pulled on your equipment – you're no longer wired up.

"Haven't you noticed yet? It doesn't bloody work! And, wherever you are in the future while you are thinking about her, whoever she might be, someone else will be seeing to her sexual needs, someone whose equipment works properly. It's kaput! Finished! You might as well have it chopped off and put on display for all the use it is to you. Now, just think carefully about giving someone 'one' and tell me how you're going to manage it, because I'm really interested to know. So, let's hear it: How are you going to manage this feat?" said Harry angrily.

Harry regretted saying this almost before he had got the words out of his mouth.

He had tried hard over the weeks to contain himself, but it was not to be. He knew what was coming next.

"What the hell do you mean it doesn't work?" said Andy with some indignation. He quickly added in support of his question that he had an erection every time he was placed upon his back. "It's there, pointing at me as stiff as a board," he said confidently, "like a flag pole. It's like that for an hour, sometimes it just will not go down. I can't get rid of it," he said, feeling pleased as he contemplated the situation.

Harry thought for the moment on how he should reply. It was only a short time ago that he had decided that if the occasion arose he would tell the truth as he saw it. Now the situation had arisen he was no longer so sure. After a few moments he thought, bugger it, why not tell it as it is.

"It's like this," said Harry, in an almost fatherly tone of voice, having quickly lost his irritation with Andy. "Nearly everyone who gets spasms in their legs or body can obtain an erection, I think the term's 'reflexogenic', or something like that." Andy looked at him waiting for Harry to continue. "It means that it's a reflex action, similar to when something hits you below your knee and your leg jumps. What happens is bugger all to do with you and any thoughts you might have. It's a simple reflex action, do you understand?"

Andy thought for a few seconds and said. "But if I give it a few shakes I can get a hard on."

"That's exactly what I mean - it's just a reflex," said Harry, knowing that this was not going to be easy. "It's just a reflex action and you're providing the stimulation. Can you feel your favourite organ when you're playing with it?" said Harry, "can you actually feel it?"

"Sometimes I can!" answered Andy defensively. Harry pressed him upon the matter. "Can you really feel it, or do you think that you can feel it just a bit?" He was getting a bit exasperated but continued knowing that once he had started, he had to explain as best he could. "Can you feel it as good as you could before your accident?"

Andy thought about it for a moment and then replied that he could not. But then quickly added, "that was surely due to the shock of the accident. I'm sure that as long as I can get an erection it'll come back soon. It's only a matter of time," he said with some confidence. Harry felt just a bit sorry for Andy at that moment. He knew that Andy was intelligent and he realised that, like the rest of the patients, his sexual ability was something that he had considered in an optimistic sense, due to the fact that no one had explained the reality of the situation. There was an unwillingness to put two and two together and make four. Why wasn't it obvious to the patients that after a time when the rest of one's body was not functioning, there were not going to be any special exceptions.

Harry asked Andy, almost in desperation, to think about it carefully. He asked Andy, "Try and take this in, although I realise that you didn't go to one of the better Universities. How can it work properly? How can you expect to feel it if you can't feel anything else?" Andy interjected that young Jimmy in the bed around the corner could get an erection anytime he wanted, and he could feel it.

"He's not a complete lesion like you," said Harry. "Jimmy is in here for a series of tests; he can walk with crutches. He's not like you, there's bugger all wrong with him really in comparison to you."

"He has three children," said Andy.

"Only one of them is his, the other two are one of his mates." Harry wished that he had not added the last few words, as it was only a malicious rumour that two of Jimmy's children were fathered by a friend. Sadly it was a rumour that had been started by a nurse who lived near to Jimmy, and who was friendly with Jimmy's wife. It was also rumoured that it was done at Jimmy's instigation before he was aware that he could have children.

"Anyway, forget Jimmy!" said Harry somewhat exasperated, "your condition is not the same. Surely that's been obvious to you?" asked Harry in a voice that suggested he was enquiring from Andy what Andy actually knew about his impairment. Harry realised that Andy probably knew less than he had thought. It's too late now thought Harry, I just hope the poor bugger does not expect to walk out of here. He could not possibly think that he might, thought Harry, but he was unsure as to what Andy did know or understand. He is washed every morning, and sometimes dressed, he is fed by someone, his limbs not only don't work but he can't feel them except part of his arms and hands. Surely it must be obvious that he is paralysed, and by talking to others in here he must know it's not going to change in the future. Harry now wished that he had said nothing.

Andy did not reply, he just looked into space, his mind turning over rapidly. He suddenly realised he had not thought it through properly. He had really hoped that he would get most sensation back, but he wasn't totally sure that he would, he just hoped. What Harry had said had shocked and surprised him. He knew that Harry was not lying or even trying to wind him up. He felt bitter and angry for a moment and he asked why the hell could he get an erection that looked so good, so bloody hard and that was it. No sensation to go with it. It seemed totally senseless. He thought that it must be bloody awful having to go through life without being able to have an orgasm, a really good shag made life so much better, and normal, everyone shagged, he thought.

He was confused and unhappy. That can't be right he thought, it does not sound right, it can't be permanent, 'not forever!' He spoke the last two words out loud in desperation. It was finally dawning upon him that it might be forever. There was no reprieve, nor time off for good behaviour.

"How can I go through life without fucking? It's just not natural! It's…" He stopped himself as a wave of despair flooded over him. His thoughts turned to his present girl friend, he had been promising her the fucking of a lifetime when he left hospital. How could he face her and tell her that he was no longer capable of doing it properly. She liked sex so much she revelled in all aspects of it. These thoughts made him feel even more miserable. He briefly tried to comfort himself by telling himself that a good relationship wasn't built only on sex. But he could not convince himself, his experiences had taught him the importance of sex to his female friends. He tried to think of their reaction upon being told that they might have to restrict themselves. No bloody chance he thought. Mention that to them and they might sympathise and then kick me into touch. Even murderer's and rapists can still shag. It's all bloody wrong, it isn't fair. He felt worse than he had felt before, and somehow he felt very childish as though some powerful entity had deprived him of something that belonged to him. Part of him wanted to put on a brave face, and say and do the right things, which meant not allowing anyone to see a weakness or anything that might suggest he was not handling the situation in a proper manner. One thing that Andy was certain of was, at that particular moment, he did not give a damn what anyone else thought or said. It was he who was stuck for the rest of his life with this problem, and it was hurting him.

Harry had overheard him. "Look, Andy, fairness doesn't come into it," said Harry quietly, "it's no good me pretending to you that it's fine, and everything will work out to your satisfaction. It's not going to happen. I just can't say it in a way that makes it easier, most of us are in the same boat; it's not just you who is in that situation."

Andy grunted and sighed but said nothing. Harry knew that it was the time to keep quiet, and he turned to face away from Andy. He was angry with himself. He switched on the television in the hope that Andy would not ask him any more questions; he knew that what he had said would have such an effect on Andy. What he had not realised was, that in discussing it, the effect that it had upon himself. His mind reluctantly drifted back in time.

It was a summers day, a very pleasant day, until his wife left him and made him aware that she had been having an affair for a few months, and that she was leaving him that day, and taking their young daughter with her. In fact, it was not quite like that; she had left him a letter but he chose to recall the event in a way that suited him. To say that it was a shock to Harry was an understatement. He had not suspected a thing. He believed that his marriage was sound and good. He thought that he and his wife were partners, a good couple who really loved one another. They had decided to get married when she had become pregnant, but this wasn't a problem as they would have married anyway. Shortly after their daughter was born Harry had his accident. Later he bought a small bungalow. At least we will have a roof over our heads, he thought.

It had not been an easy time after his accident but they had supported one another, his wife had been there every day while he was in hospital. She told him how much she loved him, how they would always be together. Harry had told her that she should seriously consider their situation even though they had a baby. She might be better if she went home to her mother. He remembered the words as if it was yesterday. He did not really mean them, he wanted the opposite, but he felt compelled to say them. It just seemed like the right thing to say at that time. Looking back he realised that it was all very noble, but totally stupid, he thought. He then clearly remembered, she smiled at him and told him that she would never leave him. She loved him more than anything in the world and that they would always be together, no matter how difficult things might get, it would not matter, they would be together.

Harry tried hard to be a good father. He was something of a modern man, that was before the concept was promulgated by the media. He enjoyed looking after their daughter. He enjoyed cooking and even going shopping. He was surprised at his domesticity. And he was, to all intents and purposes, very happy despite his disability.

What a fool, he thought to himself what a bloody fool! Harry had looked back with bitterness many times over the years. To some extent this had dissipated in recent times. He had finally realised that there was no point or benefit in him feeling so bitter and angry. He tried hard to rationalise the situation, and over a period of time he came to realise that he just could not forget or forgive, irrespective of what society thought he should do. It was not in his nature; he had been hurt too much. But he recognised that he could place the events and the pain further back in his mind, and that had helped him survive.

The other matter that was more important as the years moved on was his daughter. He wondered if he would ever see his daughter again. He retained the hope that when she was a little older she might want to find him. To find out what he was like. He hoped that she would understand that he had always wanted her and loved her, and that she had been taken away from him. He often thought about their first meeting, wondering what it might be like. Would they find it difficult, what would they say to one another? Or would she do as he really wished, as he really hoped, would she simply throw her arms around him? He shook his head as if to clear away his thoughts. He had thought these same thoughts a thousand times. He was now feeling sorry for himself as he knew that he would. Long ago he had decided that occasionally he had the right to feel sorry. He had lost more than those who had told him to keep looking on the bright side. Harry, at times, could not envisage a bright side. Such feelings and emotions did not last and he did move on. He thought to himself that life is harder for some than for others. And if there is a great design to these happenings, he would like to meet the bastard who had dealt him his hand.

Anyway that's my miserable period over for the day, he said to himself. He decided to try and make light of anything Andy might say in the next hour or so, otherwise he knew that Andy would only feel worse. There was no easy solution to this little problem said Harry quietly to himself. And it's only the start. Suddenly Harry decided that what was said could not be changed and that they should be able to talk in a sensible manner. He then thought how he had felt just a few minutes earlier when recalling the time when he had been badly hurt. "It's not bloody easy! I still fucking hate this form of lifestyle!" he said out loud. "I don't suppose that I'll ever get used to it." He wondered if anyone totally accepted such a situation.

"I think that its time for you to get up," said Caroline pulling the curtains around Andy's bed. He did not reply, he had not heard her approach the bed. She did not wait for a reply but started to take his clothes out of his locker. When she had done this she turned around and started to pull back the bedclothes. At this point it was usual for Andy to tell who ever it was who was performing this act to sod off if they knew what was good for them. Appropriate banter would follow for the next two minutes with other residents on the unit joining in. To Caroline's surprise, no response was forth coming which lead her to believe that in the past few minutes something of a detrimental nature had occurred which was effecting Andy's mood. When she had previously left him he had seemed his normal self, now he was obviously not willingly going to communicate.

"Anything wrong?" she enquired in a low -key manner as though not wanting to show any undue concern. There was no reply. Andy just stared ahead with his eyes half closed lost in his thoughts. Caroline decided it best to simply continue and proceeded to start to dress him.

"What's wrong with him?" said Caroline leaning out of the curtains and looking at Harry.

"He's got a problem with an organ, can't get a tune out of it. In fact, he can't play it at all," said Harry trying to be humorous for Andy's sake, but with little success. That did not sound very sympathetic or understanding. Why can't you just keep your mouth shut, he thought to himself. Caroline looked bemused but did not ask for an explanation.

"Have you been upsetting our little Andy? Has the nasty old man said bad things to you?" she said mockingly. She expected Andy to say something but he didn't. She realised that she had walked into something that had created an atmosphere, but she did not have a clue what had happened or what might have been said. She could not bother finding out if she had been interested as she had not the time at that moment.

Andy opened his eyes and nudged her, gaining her attention. "Is it true?" he asked. Caroline's suspicion was aroused. "Is what true?" asked Caroline, while pulling a stocking over Andy's toes. "Is it true he repeated?."

"It's like something out of the film 'Marathon Man'," said Caroline in exasperation, "Is what true? What are you talking about? Either explain or shut up, as it's just confusing and I'm already confused enough. Is it some kind of game that you and Harry have thought up between you to wind me up? Because if it is, you've failed."

Andy faltered for the moment; he found it hard to ask the question knowing that the answer might not be to his liking. Caroline looked at him and asked him again what it was that he was going on about. Andy did not know if he should ask her, normally he would have asked her anything without hesitation. She was one of the few members of staff that he thought that he could trust. But a simple question now seemed difficult. He finally managed to ask her the question as blunt as possible in order that there could not be any misunderstanding, Or any possibility of an evasive answer that would only add to his existing confusion.

"It's like this," he said in a faltering manner that was unusual for him. He continued. "I get a hard-on most mornings." Caroline sighed, expecting some joke at her expense was about to be delivered. She was determined that she would not show any change of her facial expression whatever she was about to be made aware of.

"An erection you mean? It's impossible to miss! Actually it's a shame to waste it, but I've seen better," said Caroline injecting some light relief upon recognising that Andy was having some difficulty in asking her whatever it was he wanted to ask her. Andy ignored her remarks and hoped that she would take him seriously. For a moment he thought that it might be better if he did not ask her. He did not relish the idea of sounding stupid. He had a picture of the staff sat together having a coffee and a smoke when Caroline suddenly said. 'You'll not believe what Andy said to me today.' The thought of this possible betrayal made him shudder. And then for a few seconds angry. He decided that he must put the question.

"Like I said, I can easily get an erection. What about an orgasm?"

"What d'you mean?" said Caroline, knowing exactly what he meant. She retained a facial expression that conveyed the type of vagueness that comes into existence when someone does not want to answer a particular question, in the certain knowledge that the answer will not be the desired nor the acceptable one.

"Who gets orgasms these days?" she said laughingly, while knowing that Andy would not allow her to get away with a flippant response of that nature. "I'm bloody serious!" he said, and as if to emphasise the point somehow hooked his wrist around her arm and pulled her nearer. Caroline knew that he was serious and thought that she might suggest that he talk with a certain member of the staff, someone who had been trained to deal with such matters. She realised that would not be sensible as she knew that Andy could not stand the sight of the man.

"It's difficult to say in all honesty," said Caroline looking at Andy in a way that she hoped conveyed some sincerity. She continued, "everyone is different, and relatively shortly after an injury it's very difficult to tell. There are so many subtleties related to both movement and sensation. You only have to look around the unit, everyone is different, even those with the same lesion."

Andy quickly jumped in and retorted, "how come we're all treated as though we're the same? A bunch of clones, everything depending upon the level of injury. We're not treat as though we're different, until it's convenient for the bloody system!" he retorted with anger. Caroline did not want Andy to feel any angrier than he was and she tried to explain, hoping that he would, for the time being, accept her reply. At that moment she felt sorry for Andy although she had been asked similar questions by many young men in recent years. And her answer always upset her. She would have liked to be able to have said something useful. She would have liked to have said, 'don't worry, everything will be fine and back to normal if you just give it time.' But she knew that for the majority of patients this would be a lie.

She did not want to appear insensitive in any way as she liked Andy, and she did not want to add to his obviously miserable mood, which she now had a good idea had been caused to some extent by Harry. She thought carefully for a short while then said, "All I can say, and I'm saying this in all honesty so you don't misunderstand. That at this moment it's impossible to say what your sexual capabilities are, although going on past patients who are similar to you," she paused briefly at this point before continuing. "I would think that it might not be easy for you to gain an orgasm without some difficulty." She looked carefully at Andy trying to judge his likely response. She did not have long to wait.

"Why?" asked Andy looking bemused, "for what reason?" Andy was unsure of what to ask next and he posed a question which he knew required a technical response. At that moment Caroline could not give him the technical reason. There was not the time, she told him, although they both knew that she was stalling and feeling uncomfortable. Andy was feeling very unhappy and did not really know what else to say at that moment. He looked at Caroline scrutinising her features carefully. His eyes fell on hers and she could see the pain he was in. And then suddenly as though his mind had lost control he said in desperation that he would really liked to have fucked her. Caroline took in a deep breath and was about to respond in a vigorous manner that would leave Andy in little doubt that their existing interaction would suffer if he were to continue bringing that specific desire of his into the equation on a regular basis. She then thought better of it, realising that it was an outburst in desperation and was intended to be something of a compliment. She wondered what he must be feeling at that moment. It must be very difficult to accept, she thought, although she had heard both men and women saying almost similar things over the years. If he had been left with sex it would probably have made it easier somehow, she thought, but she was not sure. What she did recognise was the importance to the individual of any loss that the rest of society accepts as a norm. She felt that her answers had been inadequate. How can you soften it, how can you say 'don't worry?" It would be a useless lie doing no one any favours she thought, but the situation left her feeling less than happy.

She then decided to tell him that one day, if he was both very good and very rich, he might get the opportunity. Caroline had chosen her words cleverly in order to allow Andy the opportunity of retrieving the situation. "That's it, is it?" said Andy sounding a

191

little more confident yet knowing she was deliberately helping him, "you'll do it for a large amount of money? What if I take a collection around the unit?" he said.

"You wouldn't get enough!" laughed Caroline. "I would if we allowed them to watch, and we had it on video," added Andy, now sounding better. "Doing it for a large amount of money," he said again, then he added in a serious tone of voice, "you wouldn't really do that, would you?" Caroline smiled at him and said nothing for a moment, then said, "how much money are we talking about?" she smiled at that point. While they were talking, and without him realising it, Caroline had dressed him. She left him to get the hoist. Andy realised that life had suddenly become worse when he thought that nothing else was waiting to surprise him. He could not think of how he was going to deal with a life without feeling sexually good. And he then realised what had already crossed his mind earlier. What would any woman think, once they realised his limitations?

They would not give me the time of day, he thought. Andy thought at that moment he did not want anything to do with women anymore, he saw no point in even thinking about them, he really felt miserable as though any expectation that he might have had, suddenly had been taken from him.

CHAPTER EIGHT

Elisabeth had made her way to the gym having decided that it was in her interest to strengthen her arms, knowing that any time spent in a hospital bed tended to weaken you. Unlike some patients Elisabeth had kept herself relatively fit, she had been concerned when she had started to put on weight, so she then made a concerted effort in making sure that it did not increase. Some of her friends had put on a large amount of weight and despite their efforts they could not get rid of it. Subsequently Elisabeth had a strict regime when it came to looking after herself. She knew that the effort would be worthwhile although she did not go over the top and train everyday. After some basic exercises she looked around her and observed the new patients struggling to increase their physical potential. She could clearly remember her first few times in the gym. She believed that if she put in the effort that there would be an improvement in her condition, little realising that he condition was permanent, and that no amount of exercise or effort would provide her with any more movement than she already had. It did not take her long to realise this truth with the help of older patients who enjoyed passing onto her the doom and gloom of disabled life. At first she thought that such things did not apply to her, but she then realised that she was no different to everyone else, she was one of the team irrespective of whether she wanted to be or not. Being pragmatic, she accepted the situation and thought about getting on with her life. Looking around at the new patients she wondered how they were feeling, did they feel the same as she had, or had they more of an understanding than she had. She thought that they were in for a difficult time whatever they thought or understood. Like many disabled people she would not have wanted to relive those first few years of disability, it was too complex and most of the time she did not understand what was happening to her when things were going wrong. She decided that she had exercised enough and she made her way back to the unit.

"What's for lunch? asked Elisabeth. "I think it's some kind of curry, yesterday's leftovers probably, now that we're really into cost cutting in a big way."

"Don't start again! I just asked you what's for lunch. I don't want a lecture on the economic state of the nation or the problems with the health service."

"Go on then, just bury your head," said Harry, "pretend that everything is fine." He pulled himself up in bed in order to give greater emphasis to his statement. "Look at these," he said while holding up a recycled paper receptacle. "This is what we now pee in, a bloody cardboard bottle. We did have glass bottles at one time, not bloody cardboard!"

"Obviously it's more hygienic," said Elisabeth tired of listening to Harry. "I wouldn't mind if that was the reason, but I don't think it is. Cardboard is cheaper – it's as simple as that. Anyway, we can't do anything about it. And to be honest, I don't really care." Harry grunted loudly and eased himself down in bed. "We'll not be getting lunch until the politburo has finished having their meeting" added Harry. "The union rep is attending so it must be one of three things. The union is putting it's subscription up. There is a disagreement over what wage increase they will be asking for. Or, more important, they are getting rid of the staff's smoking room. One thing you can be sure they will not be talking about is improving the service they provide, or improving our c o n d i t i o n s . Harry was once again animated. "The only thing they're concerned about is themselves, and what they want, sod the rest of us, we're just patients! They should remember that without us they'd be without work, they should think of that sometimes."

Someone in the room groaned loudly as they had heard Harry many times before on this subject. For once Harry took the not too subtle hint and with some reluctance shut up, but not before looking around to see if he could spot the dissenter for future reference.

The small room was full of cigarette smoke. The smokers had taken their coffee break first. Brenda Cross, a nurse of diminutive stature, was holding forth about a particular patient. Stating that it was time she was going home, that she was as fit as she ever would be and she was taking up a bed that someone else could be using. She reminded those present that there was a waiting list for beds on the unit. Wendy had heard enough and told her that she only wanted her out because she did not like her.

"Perhaps it was due to the fact that she called you a stupid religious bigot, or was it a stupid religious hypocrite? I can't remember which," added Wendy while smiling.

"That has nothing at all to do with it," replied Brenda in indignation. "Besides, she was wrong, she just wanted to have a go at me."

"Of course she wanted to have a go at you," said Wendy in a loud voice that contained an angry tone, "you'd left her in the bath and forgotten about her, poor bugger nearly drowned, and you've let her slip out of the hoist, and you've spilled coffee all over her, she's bloody lucky to survive your help."

"They were all simple accidents that any of us here could make," said Brenda in defence. "Agreed," said Wendy in mock humility before adding in a stronger tone of voice. "In your case accidents only seem to happen when you're left alone with her."

"What do you mean by that?" said Brenda, her voice getting louder and indicating her raising anger. Wendy thought that she might have just said a little bit too much and could have kicked herself. She did not like Brenda, in fact no one really liked Brenda once they knew her. On the surface she appeared a normal reasonable person going about her job effectively, not particularly bothering anyone. But underneath the veneer there existed a mean and bitter woman. Not only had she a mean personality, she was insensitive and sometimes vindictive. She was a very devout, religious person, due to the fact that she could only get on with God, and this was only because he never told her that she might be wrong. She did not like or trust anyone else. It had always seemed that throughout her life everyone was against her, even her parents who had desperately wanted a boy, but Brenda arrived to everyone's obvious disappointment. Her parents were just as insensitive as she had become, they told her, while still in her formative years, how they had longed for a boy, and how disappointed they were to produce a girl. The irony of it was that when Brenda was a young girl and this subject was broached she automatically felt sorry for her parents. It was only years later that she became angry at the thought of not really being wanted by her family, which also included her aunts and uncles.

She had found some solace at school by sucking up to the teachers. The praise she received was some compensation for the lack of support and the warmth she received from home, although in material terms she wanted for nothing.

But her pattern of life was set at a relatively young age. She learned very quickly that to appear to be good had advantages with adults and teachers, and any people in authority. She carried on this practice while at work, sucking up to whoever was in charge of the unit while always appearing to work hard and efficiently. Talking to the patients when appropriate, and seemingly caring and compassionate, if compassion seemed to be the sensible option for maximising her standing. Fortunately for the rest of the staff and the patients, many of her peers had soon recognised these personality traits. And they always took account of them when having to work with her, or in their daily interactions. The unfortunate part was that some of her superiors had not recognised what a scheming person she really was, and subsequently allowed her to create problems and mischief at every opportunity. But Brenda was a particular type of malevolent person. In her mind she was not doing anyone any harm. This being due to the belief that her actions were always sanctioned by God. She knew that she was doing the best she could for everyone, because she went to church and prayed to God. She knew that she was on the right track and the others were not. She also realised that she was disliked but she no longer cared, she was superior to her colleagues and she could find solace in God who she knew loved her above the philistines that surrounded her. He must have loved her, she had reasoned, because he had provided her with a husband and three good children. And by most standards they were comfortable, quite well off really. These thoughts comforted her when the odd doubt came into her mind regarding a particular act or action she had taken during the day. Was Wendy right? Had she been hard on the patient? And she did really care, she wanted to care for everyone, but she knew that in this area she was a failure. But that did not matter because God would forgive her if she always was honest and true to him. These thoughts always comforted her, especially when most of the rest of the staff seemed to be criticising her or avoiding her company. She did not worry about the latter anymore, she could not care less about the rest of the staff, she had her thoughts and beliefs and she knew deep down within her that she was right. That was all that really mattered to her. She believed in predestination and she could attempt to reach out for the moral high ground. And besides, she was a nurse working with the disabled. She could have chosen some other form of employment, therefore she must care deep down whatever doubts she might have at the odd moment.

"What about the restructuring?" asked Caroline changing the subject, "has anyone heard anything new, or are we to stay the same?" Eric, who was the union representative, spoke with some reluctance, as he could not tell them anything that they did not already know. He reluctantly started to speak. "It seems that there'll be the opportunity for some re-grading, on the same terms as the last re-grading exercise" he said.

"That was a wonderful exercise!" said Wendy contemptuously, she had applied for a higher grade but had not received one, while two of her colleagues who she knew were no better skilled than she was, obtained the higher grading.

Noreen, who was a nursing auxiliary, who, to put it crudely, could only be described as being somewhat rough in her manner, and from a less affluent part of town where they were not always used to choosing their words carefully, interjected at that point.

"This re-grading exercise is always the bloody same, because we're untrained, we're not part of the great scheme - whatever that might be." She continued, her voice getting louder. "And I, for one, am fed up at been left on the side like a fucking peasant who is expected to work alongside you trained staff." She emphasised the last phrase. She said this while glaring around; she then continued. "We're doing most of the things you do, but we're getting no recognition for it." She was in full stride now and was not going to stop until she had said what had been boiling up inside her for a long time.

"And while I'm talking, I might as well tell you that there is the odd nurse here who treats us like shit, as though she is some kind of a superior being, and I do not mean superior in her position on the unit." Noreen paused for a moment before continuing. "She thinks she's above the rest of us, she talks down to all of us. But if she carries on I'm likely to swipe her one; she's a clever little cow," added Noreen before sitting back and lighting another cigarette.

"Can I take it that the person you're referring to is not present?" said Wendy.

"No you bloody well can't" said Noreen quickly. "I've said what I intended to say and that's it, but if she keeps on shouting across the unit for me to come running like a pet dog, then she's in for a fucking surprise!" Everyone looked at one another and said nothing, but they knew that Noreen had a case. As there were times when the auxiliary nurses were seemingly talked down to by some individuals who, for whatever reason, thought themselves superior. This was usually through their arrogance, or ignorance, it was difficult to tell. Of course that was no excuse; they should have been a bit more sensitive thought most of the staff. It was sometimes difficult for trained staff to appreciate that their pay and prospects were far better than the so-called non-qualified staff. And that their attitude and interaction could exacerbate a difficult working relationship. On the other hand, some non trained staff thought it their right to obtain the same remuneration as the other staff due to working alongside them, which was, in reality, an unreasonable expectation. Such feelings exist in all places of employment, it's just that on occasion some problem will rise to the surface and become disproportionate in relation to the nature of the problem. It then requires time and energy that could be better spent on other things to sort the situation out, and to get the ship once again steering the correct course.

"It's something we're looking into again," said Eric, "in fact, we're proposing to have an half day workshop on working in teams. Nothing has been finalised yet, but it's something that we know needs to be done."

"What you've just said is basically meaningless, just more union bullshit," said Noreen. She was angry once again at being fobbed off, knowing that a workshop or a training day or anything that lacked a real offer of change was a waste of time.

She spoke in a raised voice. "Be honest, the union hasn't thought of doing anything other than collecting our money. The union has done nothing for us whatsoever, but just watch television and all you hear is "the wonderful nurses" and the wonderful job they are doing, we're not included in this, we don't exist, our contribution isn't recognised by anyone. And as for working in teams, we all work in teams! You can't work in any other way on this unit. It just feels bloody unfair, I'm pissed off with the whole situation," said Noreen almost in desperation.

"It's not us," said Eric, trying hard to appeal to her sense of justice "it's administration. They spend half their time holding meetings with other administrators about what," he gestured with his hands, "no one knows! It's one of life's great mysteries." Almost everyone murmured in agreement. "What do administrators do with their time he asked? If you have chance to visit headquarters, they're always wining and dining some group or other, if not each other. The money that's wasted is unbelievable." Everyone nodded again in agreement. Eric felt content that he had successfully changed the subject and redirected any venom towards the administration. He smiled to himself, if in doubt blame the administration, it works every time.

"I'm on my break," said Caroline "and I can't be bothered to either talk or listen about administration and such things." She quickly held her hand up to stop anyone interrupting her. "We have a new patient due in about two hours, a quad. Where are we moving the other beds.?"

"Its Amanda's responsibility. Hasn't she decided?" asked Wendy who thought that it was something of a minor problem shuffling the beds around.

"I've not had much of a chance to talk to her yet, and she's off the unit after lunch," said Caroline while looking around hoping for suggestions. None were forthcoming. "Thank you one and all for your helpful contribution! Anyway don't forget, we'll need some assistance from members of other teams." She then continued on a lighter note which she knew would be received with some enthusiasm.

"By the way," she paused for effect, "there is some really good news! At the end of the week, Spike and Luna are getting married and we're arranging their stag do. I only heard a short time ago, but give it some thought as to what we should arrange. I'm going round to see them tonight. We have to do something special, something a bit better than the usual." Everyone seemed to agree. Wendy added that there was not a great deal of time left so they had better think of something quickly. Caroline added that anyone who is off duty, or can make it, is invited to the wedding and the 'do' afterwards. Noreen had calmed down upon hearing about the forthcoming wedding. She had always thought Spike and Luna were special people, almost unique. She would enjoy the wedding and the party the night before or whenever it was. That was what she needed, a really good night out with the girls away from the unit, "I'm going to get legless!" she said. "You're always legless after pay-day!" said someone, but Noreen ignored the comment. "A few drinks inside me and I'll be fit for anything."

"Don't you mean 'anyone'?" laughed Wendy.

"My men are always tasty, not your soft floppy types who don't know who, or what they want. They know what they want, and believe me, I give it to them," said Noreen.

"Fish and chips are tasty, but you wouldn't want them in bed with you."

"I like them in bed!" said Noreen looking surprised, "you should try it, when finished, just roll the papers up and toss them on the floor until morning."

"That's disgusting!" said Caroline.

"When you pick them up and throw them out, you can throw out whoever you came home with the previous night." Noreen burst out laughing, "I usually give them a continental breakfast if I can stand the sight of them in the daylight."

"God knows what they'd have to do to earn an English breakfast," said Wendy shuddering at the thought.

"You're just jealous because you're going without!" laughed Noreen.

"Who's said that?" snapped Wendy, while looking around at Caroline. Caroline ignored her and turned away. "Everyone knows," said Noreen "but I'll fix you up with someone if you want."

"It's very considerate of you, but no thanks. Some of the dross you've been with makes mine look sophisticated."

"Please yourself, but beggars can't be choosers, and you've your begging bowl out for all to see," said Noreen as her parting shot.

"That's bloody nasty, and it's untrue," said Wendy, looking hurt and wondering if it would be worthwhile expanding once again on her situation, or would it end with her feeling dejected. She decided that she would say nothing as it would only provide the rest of them with entertainment at her expense. One thing she had made up her mind over was that the next opportunity would not be lost, and she would give the lucky man the best fucking he had ever had.

CHAPTER NINE

Harry had noticed the activity. He had seen it all before and although curious as to who the new patient would be, he felt a wave of sadness envelope him. His thoughts momentarily drifted back, he thought of the family involved. He knew what they were going to go through in the coming months and he felt sorry for them. There wasn't going to be miracle cures or a bright light descending from heaven, only a long hard period of confusion and distress, where lives would never be the same again.

Beds were being moved around like musical chairs in order to place the new patient near to the nurse's station. The nurses were around the bed when the paramedics arrived with the new patient. Andy stopped a young nurse and asked her about the new arrival. Not being discreet she told him that she thought it was a nineteen year-old female who had been injured in a road accident, and that was all she knew. Andy wondered what she looked like, and then passed the information on to Harry who could only say in a quiet voice, "the poor sod."

"We'll get her comfortable and then the doctor would like to have a word with you," said Caroline to the women who was sat by herself in the room next to the office.

The women was tall and slim with auburn hair, her eyes were red from crying. "She'll be well, she will get better ,won't she?" Her voice trailed away; she couldn't speak clearly as her emotions welled up inside of her. No answer was forthcoming. It was her daughter lying there unable to move. Her thoughts made her tearful once more. She was their only child, Nineteen years old and just starting at University. They had bought her a car for obtaining her A-levels, only a small second hand car. But it was something she really wanted. "And now this has happened,: she said out loud. Her father was now flying back from a business trip. He could not grasp what had happened, he did not seem to take in what she was saying. And she knew that she could not explain it properly over the telephone, if only she could have explained it better. She hoped that he would soon arrive, his plane was due within the next few hours. She thought that she would not know what to say to him but she needed him there with her, with them both. She looked around the bare room; there was no comfort or solace in her surroundings. Her mind was racing almost out of control, she could not remove or negate the feeling of desperation that was controlling her. She wondered what they were doing to her daughter, why was it taking so long.

"I've made you a cup of tea, do you take sugar?" asked a young women.

"I don't have sugar," replied the woman, automatically. Just at that moment Caroline came into the room and told her that she could sit with her daughter and she would inform her when the doctor arrived.

The doctor almost casually asked her, "what's your daughter's first name?" The women looked puzzled, and then seemingly remembered what was happening.

"My daughter…" she said out loud. She started once again but with difficulty. "My daughter's called Kim, short for Kimberley," she added, as though it was of some special significance. Just at that moment she cried harder than she had ever cried before.

Kim's mother tried hard to stop her tears. For some strange reason she felt as though tears were not an appropriate reaction in front of a young doctor. She should try hard to appear calm and logical, and listen carefully to what the doctor had to say, it might not be as bad as it seems she thought. She knew that she was clutching at straws. Everything she had seen and heard told her that it was serious, that her daughter was very ill.

Twenty-four hours earlier everything had been normal, now everything had changed, and all the other events that had recently occurred were of no importance.

The man in front of her seemed at that moment too young to be a doctor. She thought that she needed to talk to someone more senior, someone who could tell her exactly what the situation was. She could almost hear her husband telling her 'Make sure that you ask the right questions, and that you obtain complete answers.' She felt helpless at that moment, as she had no idea what were or were not, the right questions.

She looked at the young man once again. He had an honest open face she thought, he will tell me everything I need to know. If anything was forgotten it could be asked later.

"There's quite a lot you'll want to know," said the young man.

"First of all, my name is Khan, Doctor Khan. I'm the registrar on the unit."

He looked directly at her. "Your daughter's name you said, was Kim." Cynthia Stackman nodded in response. "What's going to happen to her?" she said, while at the same time holding back her tears. Doctor Khan carefully cleared his throat, this was a part of the job that he did not like. "To be honest, it's not easy to be precise at this moment." He knew when he was saying this, that the words would not really mean anything. They would provide little or no comfort. And they were unlikely to be accurate. His examination had supported the original examination in the casualty department of the hospital that had received Kim. In his mind there was little doubt that the spinal cord had received considerable damage around the fifth and sixth cervical, and that Kim would most likely be paralysed from just below her shoulders. Her hands and arms would also be partially affected. And she would not, in the foreseeable future, walk again.

Cynthia Stackman was not the type of women that one could brush aside with simplistic platitudes, or generalities. The initial shock had been considerable and momentarily had disabled Cynthia. Her ability to think as clearly as usual had been snatched from her. But a few hours had passed, and although she knew she was not functioning to the best of her ability, she also knew that she was at least thinking in a reasonably logical manner. She had told herself that this was a necessity. Her daughter's life, or condition, might somehow depend upon her trying to keep a calm and logical frame of mind. Tears started to form in the corner of her eyes again, but she tried to suppress them. She thought that it was impossible to stay calm and logical in such a situation, no matter how hard she tried.

Cynthia had in normal circumstances few doubts regarding her ability to deal with things logically, she had been doing it for years. Her husband was a successful businessman commuting between the London office, New York, and Berlin. Since the political fall of Eastern Europe his trips to Germany and the former communist states had become quite frequent. Seemingly it was important to get established in Eastern Europe with good quality staff, before everyone moved in desperately trying to cut their operating costs. Although she possessed a good business brain Cynthia wasn't sure that transferring manufacturing to Eastern Europe was a good thing. It meant redundancies locally, for one thing. And this distressed her, as it had been her father, thirty years ago, who had started up the company with just a few local employees. It was a family affair where everyone knew the status of the business, and subsequently pulled together through good times and bad, in mutual interest. But that had long since gone. Her brother and her husband now ran the company. And any pretences of a paternalistic approach would be anathema to management and the unions. Cynthia was sure that it used to be better. These thoughts were then set aside by the thought of how many people were being employed and paid a good wage. The thought of this stopping and the seeking out of cheaper labour went against her feelings. She wasn't interested in the crude economics or the politics. She just felt that it was morally wrong, irrespective of the fact that her husband had carefully explained to her that it was impossible to compete if they could not gain access to cheaper labour.

She had operated her own small business for some years without having to resort to cheap labour, she had told him. He had always replied to the effect that she did not understand the real world. That life was hard, and winning was everything; there was no prize for coming second, you either won or lost. At that moment none of that meant anything to her. The only thing that mattered was that her daughter was lying in a hospital bed, wired up to an array of strange machines, and she wasn't answering or responding to her approaches. At that moment the acting unit sister, Rita Carr, came up to her and asked her if she would accompany her to a room where they might talk. Cynthia followed her to the same room that she had sat in earlier.

Rita started to explain that although she had worked on the unit she had only been sent down for the day due to staff shortages. Cynthia felt like saying, what has this got to do with me and my daughter. Rita smiled, a well practiced smile that portrayed only ambiguity.

"I'm not sure what you've been told, but I always tend to think that it's for the best, in everyone's interest, if we're as open and honest as we can be." She managed to say this while still retaining her smile. Cynthia did not like or trust the woman on sight. She somehow knew that the women in front of her was not going to tell her anything that was in her interest.

"First of all, you need to know that everything possible will be done to help Kim, she's a sick girl. Let me rephrase that," said Rita realising that her approach was heading in the wrong direction. "Kim has had a serious accident. And there's no point in pretending that she'll recover and just walk out of here." This was not a shock or surprise, Cynthia was somehow already aware of this, but she did not need it to be reinforced at that particular moment. Rita continued, "but we have to be positive and look on the bright side. We'll ensure that she gets the best treatment possible. We're equipped to provide all that she needs for her rehabilitation." Rita reached over and took a few sheets of paper from within a drawer. "It might help you if you read this; it was produced a few years ago about some of the basic things you need to know when caring for a spinally injured patient." She handed Cynthia the papers. The words 'spinally injured' stayed in her mind.

"If there's anything else that I can help you with, don't hesitate to ask," added Rita with the smile widening as if to state that the conversation was terminated.

Cynthia felt suddenly tired, she had forgotten how long she had been awake; time had lost meaning for her. She found a chair in the day room and closed her eyes. She did not want to fall asleep, but just to rest. Her body would not cooperate and soon her thoughts were moving around apparently without control. After a while she somehow managed to control them. She then found herself in that state between sleep and dreams, the area where one can still direct one's thoughts, yet have no control over them. The thoughts drift into one's mind out of time and sequence, waiting to be reconstructed in some form of order, where sense can be made of them. Cynthia tried to make some sense of her thoughts. She drifted into this strange sleep unable to help herself.

She had not slept since being informed of the accident and tiredness was starting to play tricks with her ability to think clearly. Her mind drifted into a disturbed form of sleep that feeds voraciously in such situations. Cynthia was unsure if it was her, or someone she once knew, whom she was observing. The young women raised herself to her knees and then slowly stood upright, her legs for the moment seemingly infirm as though they were unable to bare the weight of her slim body. She tried to take a step forward but stopped as though realising that for the moment it was not possible to move. She looked around slowly, taking in the strange landscape that confronted her. She could not see into the far distance as a soft grey mist obscured any detail.

She looked closely around her trying to take in her surroundings. She appeared to be standing in open fields; she felt grass beneath her feet, not fresh young grass, but the pale, yellowing grass of early autumn. There was no wall or fences that marked any boundary, only a small stream that slowly ran over stones and gravel into small deeper pools that had been created by the erosion of the banking every few yards.

Past the stream in the distance the young women could see the edge of a wood. Inexplicable she decided to walk in the direction of the wood. The grass was soft beneath her feet and somehow felt comforting. She reached the stream and as she could clearly see the bottom she started to wade across; the water was colder than she had expected, this made her move quickly up the shallow banking onto the warm dry grass.

Surprisingly the wood was suddenly in front of her. Trees of every age and size confronted her with an enigmatic charm that was both disarming and enticing. The wind started to sing as it rustled through the leaves. The sounds were familiar, like a long forgotten tune, and she paused to listen. She knew the tune but could not remember where she had heard it before, although she knew that it was a long time ago in some other time and place. She came across an overgrown path which and had not seemingly been used recently. The singing of the wind in the trees told her to go on and follow the path. She stepped forward and the branches that had grown over the path parted upon her approach as though they were welcoming her into their midst.

Cynthia knew that she was dreaming, it was not real, but her senses insisted that she continued to watch the unfolding events.

The path wound its way carefully following the slight

undulations of the ground. It was difficult to tell exactly where you were as the trees were dense, and the path had taken many turns. The young women was getting tired; she had little idea of how far she had travelled or where she was heading, but she was compelled by some unseen force to proceed forward as though there was logic and sense to her wanderings. Suddenly the trees opened out into a large glade, here the grass was soft again, and welcoming to the touch. Towards the far end of the glade, near where the wood started again, there was a pile of stones. It was apparent that the stones had not been left there by nature, but had been placed in such a manner as to form a place for someone to sit while retaining the ability to look all around them. It was not a surprise to find a figure sat perched upon the largest stone as though waiting for someone. The figure was that of an old man, his face was aged by time. Only his eyes betrayed his awareness. Cynthia, on observing this, thought that such a scene was so unreal, so child-like in its simplicity. She was not a simplistic person and could not understand the situation, even in her dreaming she was aware of herself.

He turned towards the young women as though he was expecting her. She moved towards him. He was a stranger but she felt no fear, or apprehension. He started to speak to her, but his lips did not move, this did not worry her as she clearly understood what he was saying. His eyes told her everything. She looked into his eyes and saw herself drifting in the mists of time. She allowed herself to look deeper and she could see herself surrounded by people. She was in what looked like a market place but no one was trying to sell anything. Everyone was speaking at once, they were all talking to her. She could not clearly make out what it was they were saying. She wanted to hear but she couldn't. She looked at the man and was about to ask him what it meant, what was it she should glean from what she had seen in his eyes. He placed a finger upon her lips as though to suppress any forthcoming sound. He turned and pointed to the trees and the pathway. He suddenly held out his hand which contained a cloak of the finest silk. The cloak shimmered in the light, unlike anything she had ever seen before. She heard the man's voice in her head telling her that the cloak would always provide her with warmth and comfort if she draped it around herself. She thanked him, and took the cloak from him. He smiled at her. For an instance she thought that she knew the man, and she smiled back at him with affection.

The trees quickly surrounded her again and she felt comforted by the thought that the cloak she was carrying would help her. She suddenly was concerned about the cloak, was it a gift or should she return it? For some reason it seemed important that she knew.

The trees thinned out and before her there was a great plain reaching out into the distance, further than the eye could see.

The plain was barren, almost without colour or a sign of life. Unexpectedly towards the centre of this plain there stood an ancient and great city. The walls of the city towered upwards as though reaching out to touch the clouds. Above these massive structures it was possible to see the rooftops of buildings and the spires and domes of larger buildings. She knew that the city was her destination, and it was there she hoped she would find the reason for her unhappy condition. And the reason for her presence in that mysterious non-world where she was herself, and at the same time, the young women whom she recognised yet did not, but she felt her thoughts, but only fleetingly, and she could not understand anything as she was confused..

She needed to know and to understand what was happening to her, where she had been before. She could not remember any beginning but she knew that she was not from this place, that she was from elsewhere. She walked towards the city gates, she had walked for a long time yet the city did not appear to be getting any nearer. Night-time quickly came upon her and she lay down and covered herself with the cloak. The night held many dreams for her, strange lands and people whom she had never met, yet they seemed to know her. They tried to talk to her; they were telling her something that was important but she could not understand them. There were moments when she wanted to cry, drowning in her loneliness. She would then hold her cloak and her fear would leave her. A man appeared in her dreams who knelt down beside her and held her hand, she felt comforted, but only for a few moments as she felt that she must think clearly and to not place her trust in anyone. She knew that she was in a strange land without friends or any understanding.

She awoke to find that she was outside the city walls looking at the large bronze doors which were gleaming in the early morning sunlight. A sound came from within the city, as though life had suddenly begun. The doors opened on their own accord. The young women was drawn forward though the doors into the city. Before her, there were a thousand sights and sounds intermingled, bombarding her senses. She could not deal with the intensity of the moment; her head was reeling yet she wanted more. She could not stop herself from wanting to feel and to taste and touch all that was around her, intoxicating her. She was drunk with the passion of her being and her understanding of herself. She wanted this moment to last forever. For the first time she knew who she was. She was alive, and really living a person who had dreams and feelings, someone who could reach out and touch the far corners of the universe. All was within her reach. But her touch and senses were starting to leave her, she knew that they were quickly draining away. She tried to stop them but to no avail. She needed to retain what she had seen. She felt fear and promised herself that she would remember everything, but she also knew that she could not. In desperation, she begged to remain there a little longer, she needed to know more, just to understand. She felt as though someone was empathising with her but she awoke. Her feelings were contradictory. While she needed to understand, she was pleased to be awake, she was afraid and she attempted to control her feelings as she had always done, but no matter how hard she tried she still felt apprehensive, but she did not know why.

"Are you asleep? I'm sorry for wakening you, here's a cup of coffee," said the nurse placing the cup on a small table. Cynthia thanked her and took a sip of the hot coffee. The coffee was too hot to drink but once again she was glad that she was awake, her dreams had not comforted her. She remembered very little of what she had dreamt, although she knew that she had promised herself she would remember as much as she could. She could not understand why she had made such a promise, she had often thought that dreams were only there to confuse, and definitely not to inform. But she felt that there was something more to this particular dream although she had no idea what it was. She then rationalised the situation and came to the conclusion that her thoughts were so confused due to the obvious stress, knowing that her daughter was lying around the corner, struggling to exist.

She sat back in the chair not knowing how long she had been asleep. Her head now seemed inexplicably clear. What were they going to do, what needed to be done, was this the best place for Kim, or was there another hospital that offered something better? She had realised the implications of what she had been told, and reading between the lines she recognised the seriousness of the situation. But she also knew that there were ways around most situations, money could buy expertise and better care. And her husband and herself were not short of money. For a fleeting moment she felt a surge of optimism. Suddenly she realised that if this was the case then the wealthy individuals who had become paralysed through accidents would already have sought out such care and treatment. She could not remember seeing anyone who had been cured or helped. She saw the papers on the table that Rita had given her. The thought of the woman made Cynthia shudder. She started to read the papers. After about ten minutes she put the papers down upon the table. There were tears in her eyes. She could not decide whether or not what she had read allowed her a degree of optimism or totally depressed her, her emotions were confusing. She presumed that what she had read was probably the truth as someone saw it. It seemed matter of fact, almost brutal in its acceptance. She could not accept that this was how it was going to be for her daughter, she would be better off dead, she quietly said to herself. She quickly dismissed the thought, thinking that was a weak and stupid thing to think, even under stress, after all it was her daughter, her only child. She was determined to find a way of making it better than it appeared but she had no idea how. She wanted desperately to cry, but she did not want to be seen to cry, she had not been brought up to display her feelings in such a situation, tears were private, something not to be shared. She did not know how to share her feelings, her desperate fear, but she wanted to.

Her thoughts were suddenly interrupted by a woman of similar age to herself. The women smiled at her and intended to speak.

She was not sure if she wanted to talk to anyone, she was unsure of everything. "My name is Jenny," said the women, and before anything else could be said she continued: "I believe that it's your daughter they have brought in. My daughter was in here two years ago, a car accident. It takes time you know," said Jenny nodding in a controlled manner as if to emphasise the point. "Time is everything, you'll soon find that out." Cynthia felt like telling her to go away but for some reason she didn't. "My girl has done well, really well. We didn't expect her to live." Suddenly Jenny bethought herself. She raised her hand to her mouth and said that she was sorry, that she had somehow forgot that Kim's mother had little or no time to understand what was happening. She remembered how confusing it had been for her when they tried to explain the situation. "I'm sorry," she said again, this time with more conviction. Cynthia tried to smile to show her that it was of no importance. Jenny started to talk again after quickly gaining her composure. "How old is your daughter?" she tentatively enquired.

"Kim's nineteen, and she's a good girl." She added the last phrase without thinking. She wondered why she had said it. She did not have to justify Kim to anyone. "She's going to University, reading History. She did very well with her A-Levels. She always wanted to be a historian for some reason. Her father and I couldn't understand it. He wanted her to do business studies. I was hoping she'd become involved with music. She's a good musician - has a natural aptitude for music. But she chose history and there's no point in trying to make them do something they don't want to do." Jenny nodded in agreement.

"It was the car really," said Cynthia while staring ahead of her focusing upon some unseen object. She repeated herself. "It was the car really." She looked across at Jenny. "We promised her a car if she did well in her exams. She had worked hard and we bought her the car. It wasn't a brand new car, but it was in good condition. She'd passed her test a few months earlier and she used to borrow my car occasionally, but only if I knew where she was going, and who she was going with. We never let her have the car to go out in at night." Cynthia was now talking fast and in an agitated manner.

"She wanted to borrow it, of course, but we were strict about that. At their age there are so many temptations, so much peer group pressure. And no matter what they say, it's a lot to expect them not to drink when all of their friends are drinking." Cynthia briefly smiled, "Of course we trusted her, she's a good girl. She's never given us any real trouble. She's so obliging. She's our only daughter." At that point she burst into tears. She could not, nor did she try to. stop herself, her pent up emotions poured out like the bursting of a dam wall. Jenny moved closer to her and put her arm around her as if it was the obvious thing to do.

"I don't know what to tell her father, I don't know what he'll say," she cried. "There, there," said Jenny not knowing what else to say.

"He'll go mad; he'll never accept it. It'll be my fault, it will all be my fault."

"Isn't your husband with you?" asked Jenny hoping that her question would illicit an answer and the tears might be minimised.

"He's abroad, but he's on his way back. He'll be here later, it depends upon whether he can get on a flight or not. I tried to explain over the telephone but it was impossible, he wouldn't listen, he didn't give me a chance to explain." She started crying again. Jenny was unsure what to do but it did not matter, very soon the crying stopped. A handkerchief was produced. After some clearing of the eyes she was able to continue.

"My husband's not an understanding man." Before Jenny could interject she repeated the sentence as if to really impress the message upon Jenny.

"Don't worry," said Jenny trying to sound optimistic, "he'll understand; he's bound to be worried." She looked carefully at Jenny before speaking. "Believe me, he'll never understand this. This has happened to him and his daughter, our daughter. It's not within his capabilities to comprehend how it could happen to us. We're so bloody successful," she said in an angry tone of voice. "We're on the right track, know the right people. Believe me this could not happen to us, this happens to other people, but not us." She looked long and hard at Jenny, desperately desiring that Jenny might understand.

"You can't expect too much from husbands," said Jenny with some conviction, "after all, they're only men." Cynthia smiled at the thought. "It's hard at first," said Jenny, "very hard. All your plans for their future are gone in a second. It's as though life has stood still and it'll never be the same again. We had our thoughts and dreams, we looked to the future like everyone else, but then it happens when you are least expecting it. It's a good job we don't know what lays around the corner," she said quietly. "I know that this will not mean anything to you at this moment, but it does get better; perhaps better is the wrong word. Whatever happens, they're our children and we have to do our best for them." A tear started to form in Jenny's eye upon remembering how difficult it had been. How all the family were effected by the events. How everyone had an opinion on why it had happened and who was to blame. She shuddered at the thought of the arguments that went on hour after hour regarding who was responsible, who was at fault. She had already decided it was of no importance, her daughter was laying there in bed. Who cared about who was responsible? All she cared about was she wanted her to live. She was not a regular churchgoer but she promised God that she would do anything if He would only let her daughter live. But that time had passed. She had tried to keep her promise, but her time had been taken up looking after her daughter. If only her family had helped, things might have been easier, she thought. But she could not make them cooperate, it was up to them. They had managed up to now and they would continue to manage. Her thoughts suddenly returned to Cynthia.

"You were saying something about managing?" said Cynthia. Jenny smiled and pondered a moment in order to give the impression that she was trying to recall her thoughts. "Oh yes! You'll manage; you'll not fail or let your daughter down, don't worry." She pressed Cynthia's hand in a reassuring grasp.

The sounds were distant, yet the figures were near. "Try getting it into her left arm," someone said. "Hold her head still." Kim could hear them speaking but she was confused, something had happened to her, she wasn't sure what it was. She wanted to tell them to stop whatever they were doing to her. She tried hard to shout but nothing happened, no one was taking any notice of her, she tried again but to no avail. Just get on with it she thought, I can't do anything about it. She shouted once again but they still ignored her. "Fuck off will you!," she shouted. It had no effect, she was still being man-handled against her will.

Suddenly she started to relax. She instinctively knew that they had done something to her. She thought that she could hear her mother in the distance but she wasn't sure. She thought that she did not want to see her mother. She felt afraid, she had done something dreadfully wrong; something terrible had happened but she did not know what it was. Her mother was there again, it was definitely her mother's voice. She tried to answer. She thought that she could see her mother leaning over her saying something. She tried to think rationally but there was no compulsion to do so, she was tired, she wanted to sleep. She would deal with everything in the morning if only they would leave her alone. The words 'Doctor Khan' were ringing in her ear. Someone was asking her questions, and she tried hard to answer. But they were not listening, no one was listening she thought. She knew she was confused and she tried hard to look at things logically, and to try and think what had happened. But she was too tired and fell into a disturbed sleep. Her sleep was unreal. She thought she remembered an accident, she could hear herself screaming and shouting. James was with her but he said nothing, he just smiled as he always did. She could hear screaming once again, and there was a tearing noise, the sound of tearing metal. There was the sound of an object being dragged along the floor. She did not understand, but she was frightened. Wherever she was, she thought that she should not be there. She struggled to remove herself from whatever it was that was holding her down, preventing her from moving. It was dark, incredibly dark, and suddenly lights were shining directly at her. She could not see due to the glaring lights that shone directly into her eyes. She did not know who was shining the lights, or why they were doing this to her. She silently pleaded with them to go away, to leave her alone, to stop tormenting her. Couldn't they understand what they were doing to her? She could not understand why no one was listening, she finally drifted off into a deeper sleep, but it was only temporarily, her dreams were to come back to her. And James was not helping her. He had always helped her before, but now he just smiled at her, he did not even say her name. She could still hear her mother, the words 'Kim! Kim!' were from some distant place, they receded even further away. Kim felt frightened at the disappearance of the sound of her name. She tried to regain her thoughts to get some order out of the chaos. She was capable of rational thinking and problem solving and now she had a problem. I don't know where I am or what is happening, she thought. I could be dreaming, but it does not feel like a dream. She knew that some dreams felt very real. She tried to control her thoughts. What was I doing, where was I going? she asked herself. Then the pain took over and she could not stop herself from shouting. There were people around her talking. I'm not really here, she thought. Then she drifted away, not feeling nor caring, just so very tired. The voices around her receded and finally disappeared.

"Let's all lift her across together," said Wendy. On the word three, everyone lifted Kim from the trolley onto the bed. "Check that all of the lines are intact and running properly" someone said, "the doctor's here to examine her." The paramedics moved away and asked a young nurse if they could get something to eat and drink and she explained to them that the dining room was open and pointed them in the right direction.

"I don't know what to say to James's mother," said Cynthia. Jenny could hardly make out what Cynthia had said but it did not matter as Cynthia repeated it. "Who's James?" asked Jenny in a quiet voice not wanting to appear as though she was prying at an inappropriate time. Cynthia raised her head. "James," she said in almost a whisper. She turned to face Jenny. "He was Kim's boyfriend." She paused before continuing. "He died in the accident. His family are away on holiday touring Southern Italy. I have no address for them. I have no idea how to contact them." She seemed to be in a state of total desperation. She said once again. "I just don't know what to do." Her tears seemed to scold her cheeks, she had never experienced the pain and loneliness that she felt at that moment. Jenny knew that she could say or do little at that time that would help Cynthia, so she said nothing.

Kim lay there knowing that something was going on around her, people were moving around her and touching her. She no longer cared, the lights were still there moving back and forth, the voices were also still there, but not the same voices, they were new and sounded different. She tried to lick her lips as they felt dry, for some reason she found it difficult. She thought that if she could remove the dryness then she could talk better and then the people around her might listen. There are not listening to anything I say she thought. She had no longer the energy to bother or resist, she drifted into a state that was neither sleep or awake. Her mind teased her with convoluted thoughts that were not recognisable, or capable of any meaningful interpretation. This would be the first of many such experiences, which seemingly serve no purpose.

CHAPTER TEN

That must be the mother, said Harry talking to himself. It's going to be a miserable time in that household, he thought. He continued to think how hard it was for the relatives, upon hearing that your son or daughter is spinally injured, and will probably not walk again. It is never going to be easy, thought Harry, while sighing. If it was only the inability to walk this business would not be so bad. He then thought that it wasn't really true, whichever way he looked at it, it was still bad, he assumed that such a thought had drifted into his mind simply because he was used to the situation. He had recognised his own ignorance relatively quickly when he realised that not walking was a minor problem in reality. Walking was getting from one point to another, and that was it. What you did not realise was the other bits, your bladder and bowels did not work, you were liable to get infections of the chest, bladder and kidneys, then there was the problem of bed sores. These are the real physical problems, thought Harry. But that was just part of it. At sometime you had to re-enter society and to interact with the non-disabled. Then you had a whole new set of problems to contend with. How the rest of society saw you, how it dealt with you and your needs. He was pleased that he had recognised these problems, as it was less disappointing to him when he was later confronted by the many social, and physical barriers that had been constructed by society.

"How do you feel now that you're up?" Harry asked. Andy looked at Harry and grimaced, "not brilliant," he replied "in fact just a bit off, light headed and short of breath. Evidently one's blood pressure falls when first getting up, I've been told." Harry grunted in reply fully understanding that 'a bit off' meant that Andy was not feeling good at all. It seemed strange, thought Harry that most patients, when asked by another patient under-played their present state. 'A bit off,' or 'not so good,' these usually signified that the person might be better off in bed, but everyone was different and dealt with each situation differently. One thing that Harry was certain about was the fact that if you were feeling reasonably well at the beginning of the day it was unlikely to continue throughout the day. "You'd better see how it goes, and if I were you I'd go back to bed after lunch," he said looking at Andy in order to see if it had registered. Andy muttered something that Harry could not quite hear, but he picked up on the word 'shagging.' Harry looked at Andy and said. "Look, don't blame me. I just told you the truth as I know it, you might be different, God might have smiled upon you, and said, 'behold he is a prince amongst men' and therefore he has been awarded the grand prize - Andy's dick still works." Andy snorted something in anger.

Harry tried to be as reasonable as he knew how. "We're all different, to some extent. For all I know, you might leave here and father a football team, although I doubt it. They might even give you a bionic, digital dick. Everything's going digital nowadays," mused Harry. "If they ask you, make sure of the size and colour, you could have it made to your own specification." Harry could not help himself and chuckled at that point. "Look how many of the para's are having children by whatever means." Harry wished he had not added the last phrase and hoped that Andy would not pick up on it. Andy was, for the moment, lost in his thoughts. His thoughts were then interrupted by Brenda, who took pleasure in telling him that his girlfriend had just telephoned to say that she would not be visiting in the afternoon.

"She's heard about your flaccid appendage. She's found someone else already!" laughed Harry insensitively. "Bloody hell! I've done it again," he thought, but being Harry he could not be angry with himself for too long, he thought better of himself to bother about the odd slip of the tongue. Andy did not appear to be amused at the quip. Harry had observed Andy and his girlfriend, and Harry was of the opinion that the relationship was not going to last. She seemed a pleasant young woman, who was attractive and very sexy, thought Harry. And while she played a great deal of attention to Andy, and said all of the right things, Harry was not convinced by her ministrations at all, and this saddened him for Andy's sake. She will not be around for him once she gets the picture, he was sure of that. At least I had a few years happiness he thought to himself. He then wondered which was best. A few good years, and then to be let down by someone you really believed loved you, or to be let down quickly before the relationship had developed. He was devastated when he had been let down. But on reflection, he would not have wanted to miss the chance to have felt and experienced love, although he had never experienced such emotional pain when his wife had left him. It is an impossible question to answer, he thought, and it is a bloody stupid question, he felt angry with himself for once again allowing it to enter his mind.

"Had enough exercise?" asked Harry sarcastically as Elisabeth pushed her way into the room, "managed to keep Tristan off of you did you?"

"A little bit at a time is enough for me," she replied smiling, Harry just smiled back and added that they could all do with a bit. Elisabeth gave him a scathing glance. Harry smiled at her and continued. "Exercise is for those that need it, and others who think that they need it," he added. He was pleased with himself at delivering such a minor pearl of wisdom. Harry had never been impressed with the sports ethic that had dominated the unit for years. And he wasn't going to change his opinion now. He could not understand the motivation of the many young women who took up the profession in the earlier days. Why had they to be remedial gymnasts, why not physiotherapists? They worked in a hospital setting, not in a sports centre. He presumed that the gymnast bit must have appealed to them when looking around for a career. He had to admit to himself that most of them looked physically fit. Then he reasoned, that in comparison with the patients, nearly anyone looked fit. Most of them have nice arses, he thought, rarely flabby or drifting out sideways, but that might be because of their age. Anyway times had changed and they were all physiotherapists now, doing the same courses, he had been informed. His thoughts were suddenly interrupted by an elderly man in the bed at the end of the room. He rarely spoke, and subsequently nobody bothered to take the trouble to speak to him. This included some of the staff who seemed set in the belief that time spent with the younger patients is time better spent. Some members of staff disagreed with this point of view, and while it was not something that was openly discussed, the reality was there to be observed. One cynical older quad had said that to get any attention around here you either have to be young, a sporting potential or wealthy. If you were not in any of these categories life could be more difficult. Whether or not this was true it was hard to say, but it was thought by some staff and patients to be true, which for those interested in such interactions was indicative of a potential problem, or an existing problem. But no one seemed over interested as sport was accepted as being automatically beneficial, and true or false, nothing was done about the situation.

The old man in the bottom bed, who it turned out was called Bernard, politely asked if he was getting up. Caroline said that she and Amanda were going to get him up for a short time, in a few minutes. Andy looked at Harry with an expression of surprise on his face, neither of them had seen Bernard out of bed. In fact, over the weeks they had rarely spoken to him, except out of politeness.

"Getting up are you?" asked Harry turning to face the end of the room.

"Just for a short while" said Bernard, "a few minutes at most."

"Hardly worth the effort," added Andy. He looked across at Harry. "Why does he want to get up for a few minutes? He hasn't been out of bed since I have been here."

"How the hell should I know? I don't even know why he's here," added Harry. "He's been here for months. I can't understand why they haven't sent him home, or to a nursing home. Sometimes they're in and out of here before they're ready; others, they seem to keep them here forever." Then Harry came up with another gem. "I think it's the doctors who occasionally drop on to an interesting case and they want to keep them here to experiment on, or to just observe them. I think they do swaps with them, competing with other doctors, a bit of one-upmanship. They vie with one another for rarities. If someone came on here today with laughing sickness, the hospital would be at war, everyone would want him."

"What on earth is laughing sickness?" asked Elisabeth. Harry was about to tell her when the old man said. "It's a very rare condition that seemingly effects a particular Amazonian tribe, and it's always fatal."

"How the hell does he know that?" said Harry in a hushed tone. Elisabeth looked slightly bemused and shrugged her shoulders, "he must have heard everything that you've said." Harry was both impressed and disappointed as he thought that he would be the only person present who had heard of laughing sickness. He must be a bloody know-all, thought Harry. He then wondered if he should have had a conversation with the old man before. Harry reasoned that if he knew about laughing sickness he could be worth talking to. He then presumed that the old man must have a wide general knowledge and wondered what else might he know something about. For all we know he could have worked for MI6, or played first violin in the LSO. Harry then thought that Bernard was obviously polite and well spoken, with a good education, he must have been a teacher he concluded, he looks the teaching type, a bit studious without any signs of affluence. Harry was annoyed with himself for neglecting to speak at length with Bernard. He quickly tried to remedy the situation.

"When did you first come in here?" said Harry loudly, in the belief that Bernard must be deaf as he had not contributed to any of the conversations. "A long time ago, before you were thought of, and you do not have to shout, my hearing is fine," said Bernard. He continued before Harry could say anything. "I listened to the bit you had written about being disabled. 'The beginning' wasn't it called?." Harry was pleasantly surprised.

"That's right, just a few lines."

"Yes, I see," said Bernard showing no sign of approval.

"Did you like it?" asked Harry optimistically. Bernard replied with just a hint of sarcasm that Harry would never replace Byron, Milton, or Andy, which caused Andy to laugh . Harry totally ignored the remark while feeling just a little bruised by the comment. He expected such banter from Andy, but coming from an old man wasn't quite as acceptable. He is probably a bit senile, the clever bugger, thought Harry. "What sort of things do you like?" asked Harry with genuine interest. He replied quickly and in a firm distinct voice that he used to enjoy most of the arts and most types of music, but his real love was the visual arts, photography and the cinema. This surprised Harry who had expected something classical and obscure. He can't be all that bad if he likes photography and the cinema, thought Harry.

"I still enjoy a decent film," added Harry quickly. He thought that he had allowed Bernard quite a bit of leeway by not responding to his sarcasm, but it was now the time to put him under a little bit of pressure in order to get him back into line. He continued.

"Did you ever see 'Ballad of a soldier,' a Russian film?"

"Yes, years ago," said Bernard who looked as though he was trying hard to recall the detail. He had not expected Bernard to have seen the film and the response perplexed Harry. He decided that he was going to hold forth at some length but now he could not do that.

"Well, what did you think of it?."

"Sentimental propaganda," said Bernard, "but a decent story and a decent film for all that."

"It's a depressing film, leaves you quite emotional," added Harry.

"That's its intention," said Bernard seemingly unwilling to expand on the attributes or lack of them of the film. Bernard then continued. "If you really want something in a depressing style you must see 'Kanal', a Polish film, it's a very good, honest, propaganda film, if you can ever equate propaganda with honesty. However, it shows that right does not always triumph, it's about the Warsaw uprising. If you want something depressing, what about Bergman's 'Seventh Seal'?."

"We've all seen that," said Andy who had been listening with interest. "Anything with that Swedish actor in it, Max whatever his name is, seems depressing."

"Ideal for such parts," added Bernard. He continued, "it's the visual images that interest me, that's what the cinema is all about, or should be about. There have been too many plays that have been turned into poor films. They should have remained plays. The cinema does things on a different scale, whether it's an epic with a cast of thousands or a small budget film like 'Kes'."

"Shakespeare has been turned into film successfully," said Harry defending a particular position for some unknown reason. Bernard was quick to respond.

"How many of the films were actually good? You tended to finish up with Lawrence Olivia over acting and rolling his eyes."

That is true thought Harry. "He was good in 'Spartacus' though."

"That's not Shakespeare," added Andy. Harry did not bother to answer.

"So was Kirk Douglas. He's often underrated as an actor simply because of his tough guy roles. He also played Vincent Van Gogh reasonably well. And of course the film based on the French army in the First World War, which was banned in France for years. I think it was called 'Paths of Glory' or something like that."

"I'd almost forgotten about that film," said Bernard seemingly pleased to have remembered it.

"You don't mean 'Tunes of Glory' do you?" said Harry, who then remembered that 'Tunes of Glory' was about a Scottish regiment, he felt stupid. Bernard did not bother replying which was a relief to him.

"What do you consider the best film of all time?" asked Andy, who then expected Bernard to mention 'Citizen Kane' or some other notable film. He thought about it for a short while before replying.

"I think Eisenstein's 'Ivan the Terrible' is in my top ten. So is 'The Seven Samurai' but it's difficult to decide upon the criteria that you judge them by as they can be so different. If it's purely entertainment value, what about 'Lawrence of Arabia', or 'El Cid'?. What about some of the great musicals like 'Showboat,' 'Westside Story', and that type of thing?"

Harry agreed that it was difficult. "I always thought 'The Longest Day' was good, and entertaining, he then quickly added, "although it does come across as something of a compilation, with everyone having a mention as though it would be a major calamity if anyone was left out.

"What about something more modern? Something that anyone under the age of forty might have seen," added Andy.

"Name something worthwhile," said Harry quickly passing the buck.

"Some say that the best comedy of all time was 'Some Like It Hot'."

"I thought it was totally over-rated," said Bernard barely disguising his disliking of the film, "could not stand that film, and Monroe was definitely devoid of any real talent when it came to acting. Over the years, people in the entertainment business whom you would consider sensible types, have done everything to give the impression that she was under appreciated. I may sound cynical but as far as I'm concerned she just slept with famous people and died tragically."

"Before my time!" added Andy.

Bernard ignored him, "just consider some of John Ford's westerns, like 'She Wore A Yellow Ribbon.' Good settings, very visual, a simple story and even a social document."

"How can a film with John Wayne in it become a social document? He was just a red-necked fascist!."

"Where in that film is the social document?" asked Harry, who was genuinely interested in what Bernard's answer would be.

"It's a social document in the context of how Americans saw the west, and portrayed it, and delivered it to the white public at that particular time. The Indians were usually seen as mindless savages, with a few noble exceptions, and their suppression and humiliation was therefore very acceptable."

"You're reading too much into it," suggested Andy.

"Possibly I am, but I don't think so," said Bernard. "If you look at how we treat Africans in films around the same time. They were either carrying some delicate white women on safari, or they might be loyal house servants, or chasing around with spears uttering some incomprehensible gibberish. They were never intelligent, sophisticated or cultured. We treat the Africans and the Indians similarly to how the Americans treat their Indians, or native Americans as they now call them. We had Paul Robson playing a native in 'Sanders of the River.' Which was absolute rubbish, Paul Robson was a good actor, and a great singer and a really decent human being, so we dressed him up, gave him a spear and all the rest of the trappings. It makes me cringe when I think of such films. But there was another difference with the films, we tended to get better scenery from American films," he said this with a touch or sarcasm.

He then added. "You can look upon films in the same way as anything else, they can be a primary source, read into them whatever you want, and if they have a message at all you have to determine its value. But personally, I just like being entertained. I want enjoyment from films, nothing pretentious, anything else has to be a bonus," he said with some emphasis.

"Well, everyone likes to be entertained," said Harry, relieved that the conversation wasn't going to drift into the outer reaches of some obscure philosophical tract. "I think that in some films there are just a few minutes, or a particular scene, that lingers in your memory, those are the important bits, and often they mean something special to you personally. I think that's why the generation who lived through the war thought that 'A Brief Encounter' was a good film. They could relate to it."

"I saw it once," added Andy, "it wasn't my type of film, although Trevor Howard was a good actor. He played a bastard in the re-make of 'The Charge of the Light Brigade'," he added.

"Who's your favourite actor?" asked Harry. Bernard grunted to signify he was thinking. "Spencer Tracey was very good, he didn't look anything exceptional but he was convincing, he always seemed to be such an ordinary looking man. The same applied to Henry Fonda. Ingrid Bergman was possibly my favourite female. She was an exceptionally attractive woman," he added. Harry grunted in approval.

"They are all before my time," said Andy, "but I'll take your word for it." He was quickly losing interest in the conversation, he could not remember ever seeing Spencer Tracey. And the only time he had seen Ingrid Bergman was in 'Casablanca', which he thought was another over-rated film. He had come to the conclusion that tastes change quickly when it comes to physical attraction. He decided that was another area where some research might prove interesting. He thought back to when he had watched quite a lot of old films, or classics, as they were sometimes called just to disguise how bad they were. He could hardly remember seeing a woman whom he thought really attractive. And most of the leading men were well into middle age, yet still playing the role of someone in their twenties. Everyone appeared squeaky clean he thought, just as though they had been well scrubbed a few minutes earlier. Bernard seemed to know what Andy was thinking.

"We're all products of our time, and we live with those values, but we have the ability to see things differently if we choose to exercise our discretion. I personally find quite a number of the young actresses attractive, and one realises that they are more overtly sexually attractive by their willingness to be more explicit. To some extent the same applies to some of the old films, some look good, while others do not. I think we were led to believe by the publicity who was supposed to be attractive, and we accepted those values. The same is true of most things in life, we accept values without really questioning them."

Harry had to respond to such a statement. "I think you're probably correct regarding films and such like, but in general, we all make choices if we want to."

Bernard laughed a controlled cynical laugh which really annoyed Harry.

"Do you honestly believe that you are in a position to make a choice of importance? I mean of real importance? Something that profoundly effects many others?" asked Bernard.

Harry said that in recent years he had made decisions with some considerable thought, and he believed that those decisions had turned out more or less the way he had wanted them to. Harry was annoyed with himself as he knew what he had just said was not entirely correct. He also knew that Bernard was right but he was not going to admit it without a struggle. Bernard laughed again and then said that he was not wanting to insult anyone, but he believed that most decisions of any real importance were, in reality, made by an elite; not an elite who had a very clear picture of what they wanted, just the direction of how they wanted things to go and remain.

Bernard continued. "If you look at society, and ask yourself what bits don't you like, what would you really like to change, then you'll see how difficult it is. Changing a few items that effect you personally can be relatively easy, but when you affect others who might not share your perception of events, then they will take decisions that are in opposition to yours. And you will find there is no mechanism for debating the issues. Your ideas or needs will be lost. You have little or no power to shape events in our society. Unfortunately that also applies to most societies. We're only individuals exercising choice if the choices are insignificant."

Harry thought that Bernard was an argumentative old sod, but he was wary as to how he was going to construct an argument. He said that he could not totally agree with that point of view, as it seemed that we were just like sheep being directed against our will. Harry told Bernard that he was exaggerating the power of an elite nowadays, it might have been like that until the end of the second world war but afterwards things changed, society became more pluralistic.. Bernard said that was the impression you had occasionally until you observed things more carefully, but the reality was very different. He said that he would give a simple example. "What percentage of the population wants an end to what we would call unacceptable crime? What percent wants an end to real poverty? What percent wants an end to warfare?."

"Everyone wants those things," interjected Andy.

"That being the case, why have we not obtained such a situation?" asked Bernard. "You must ask yourself: is it because we're alone as a society in wanting those things? Of course not!" he added almost contemptuously. "Then who really wants them, why does this situation continue to exist?."

"It's got to be more complicated than that," said Harry while scratching his head, knowing that Bernard's argument, while over-simple, seemed a good one.

Bernard continued, "It is made more complicated by those who hold and retain power, we're led to believe that utilising power is complicated in order that we don't demand changes that just might make things worse, we give them the benefit of the doubt, we accept all too easy because it takes very little effort. Only when the social and economic pain becomes so uncomfortable will we be motivated enough to put in any effort to make changes. But then again, I'm an old man now, and my views might be coloured by my personal experiences. But one thing is certain- your participation in the great scheme of things is almost non-existent. I'm not saying it's some kind of complex, well-organised conspiracy from generation to generation, or anything like that, it's much more simplistic, but it takes one almost a lifetime to recognise it." And with that, Bernard closed his eyes as if to say he had said enough, knowing that he had not the inclination to waste time on explanations that were likely to be dismissed as the ramblings of an old man who knew no better. He had been down that road before and he knew he would be misunderstood.

Andy had been listening carefully and was mulling over what had been said. "If what you say is correct, then what is the purpose of anything if we're just pawns, or less, in the great scheme of things?."

Bernard was reluctant to answer but he felt compelled to do so. "There is no purpose." He paused before continuing, knowing that what he was about to say would not sound agreeable. "That's the only thing that you need to know really, that there is no purpose."

Andy was not sure what Bernard had meant and wanted a better explanation. Before he could say anything Harry chipped in, presuming he was onto a winning line once the argument developed. "There must be purpose, everything has a purpose of some kind."

Bernard now regretted getting involved as he knew that this could take a considerable amount of time, time which he thought could spend better.

"You're assuming that the world is an orderly place, and we're individuals who are in control of the running of this enterprise which we call 'Earth'. We have existed for a very limited time compared to most living organisms, we're new creations that have come into being over a period of time that has left us at the top of the food chain, with the bonus of being able to destroy ourselves, while in theory, still capable of reason. But as for a purpose, there is no purpose; we exist and we attempt to survive. We're not sophisticated creatures who can do a great deal, we're almost ant-like, living and existing with not any sense of direction. Where do we want to go? What do we want to achieve?."

"Happiness," said Harry with little hesitation.

"What is happiness?" asked Bernard rhetorically, "a state of mind brought about by the belief that one is not in a state that causes undue concern for anything spiritual or material. So that's our purpose, our destiny, to obtain such a state. It seems somewhat trivial, don't you think?" he said while smiling.

"What else should we aim for?" said Harry, whose curiosity was aroused simply because he had not considered Bernard's points previously.

"I have no idea! That's my point. We have this desire to exist, which most organic things seem to have to a greater or lesser degree, but there is no purpose to it."

"Existence for existence's sake? Surely we're seeking some form of enlightenment?" said Andy who was getting interested in the conversation. "I've never seen enlightenment in the sense you're suggesting, and I can't see any reason to suspect it exists. We're here, and we live and die, and we make it difficult, we can't learn to live in a reasonable state. So I've concluded that there is no master plan, and no real purpose. We're just very insignificant creatures in a very large universe and we should recognise it."

"It's not easy," added Bernard, he then continued. "Everything in our society suggests that we should be heading in a suitable direction, where we will find whatever it is we're supposed to find, but we don't know what we're really looking for; it's therefore meaningless. We manage to survive and that's it. We drift along because we know no better, because there is no better. We are what we are, we're basically very primitive, we will, no doubt, be replaced sometime, and who knows," he laughed at that point, "nature will come up with something better, but that doesn't mean it will have a purpose. And you must ask yourself, does it really matter?."

Harry was not at all sure what Bernard was really saying; he assumed that there must be more to life than that, but he could tell that Bernard was not going to say anything else on the subject. He's a miserable bugger, thought Harry, who had decided that it would be sensible if he said nothing more at that moment, but he would consider what Bernard had said, but for there to be no purpose was something that he had not seriously considered, not even in his mental meanderings.

"What do you think?" asked Andy.

"Something has effected his vision of the world," said Harry almost sarcastically. "Everything has a purpose, even if it's only to provide food for some other life form."

"He wasn't meaning that," said Andy.

"I know that!" said Harry who was frustrated in not being able to come up with a suitable response without giving the concept more thought.

"If life has no meaning, then why do we exist?" said Andy quietly. "Are we an accident of nature, whose beliefs are primitive and based upon our desires, when reality is something totally different? Are we so insular that we can't see anything with clarity other than what our ego dictates?."

Harry looked at Andy and said that he could not answer such questions at that moment as he had not really given enough thought to the matter.

"They are interesting points, though," said Andy while wondering if they were worth giving any time and thought to.

Bernard interjected, "one thing you know already is the difference between being disabled and non-disabled; such a small item really, but how do you perceive the consequences?" he asked awaiting a response.

"We're small and meaningless, and our lack of intelligence is so restrictive. But we don't like the situation we find ourselves in. We're so vulnerable, so powerless in reality. Step aside if you can, and think about it for a while."

Caroline appeared and spoke up. "Before any of you disappear, I want your money."

"Always collecting for something," said Harry, who resented giving but knew that he would not allow himself to appear greedy in front of Caroline.

"What's this for, destitute civil servants or such like?" he added.

"A sports event for quads in Holland," added Elisabeth.

"Sod that!" said Harry, "if they want a trip abroad, then let them pay for it. And if they are fit enough to play at games or whatever, then it's time they looked for work, the idle sods. And why Holland? Probably after cheap dope, and smoking and drinking them selves silly" added Harry.

"You get more miserable the older you get," said Elisabeth.

"Just hold on a minute! Let's consider this," he said loudly, "these people have the same income as you and I, yet they want subsidising for their trips off, well not by me their not," said Harry sounding angry. "Would they contribute to a trip to Tenerife for me? Like hell they would! And I suppose that they're taking a few nurses along to assist. I'll also make a little bet that there'll not be any quads going over the age of forty."

"I don't know in detail who's going, except that you would not be welcome as you would make everyone as cynical as yourself."

"That's telling you!" added Andy.

"How much do you want?" asked Andy.

"It's only for a few raffle tickets," said Elisabeth.

"If it's a raffle, that's different! I presume there's something worth winning?" said Harry quickly getting himself out of Elisabeth's bad books, "I thought you were shaking a tin, or something."

"Come on, dig deep and spend something! You can't take it with you" added Andy. Harry grunted and bought a few tickets. He wished that he had retained the courage to have said no, and that he was totally against such collecting, as he was opposed to providing anything for disabled people out of charity. Harry had always believed that if something was required by disabled people it should be provided out of taxation. Disabled people should not have to go cap in hand to charities in order to obtain those things that society takes for granted.

But he did not want to appear mean when everyone else appeared willing to give something, and this annoyed him. If it had been someone else collecting he would have probably told them where to go, but that moment of weakness was something he would remember, and the next time something similar occurred he promised himself that he would not allow himself to be embarrassed, whoever it was, or whatever it was they were collecting for.

CHAPTER ELEVEN

"Now then Bernard, how are we today?." Bernard looked at Amanda and scrutinised her carefully before answering, wondering if she was being humorous. He realised that her question was serious.

"We're not too bad really, I suppose," he said while smiling, "I must admit though we feel a bit weary." He smiled broadly at that point.

"You might feel a bit better once you're sat up, and you might feel like something to eat," added Caroline, trying hard to project a positive atmosphere for Bernard's sake. "Besides, I overheard the earlier conversation and you made the mistake of expecting reason, imagination, and common sense from this bunch of degenerates." She deliberately laughed out loud in order that Harry would want to catch the conversation.

"If you've been trying to talk sense to this lot, that would tire anyone. Their inability to act normal is definitely genetic, some of them, I suspect, are just a little inbred," she said. "Therefore all that free education was just wasted on them." She left him to continue thinking. Bernard smiled at her again and said that there was some hope for them, but not a great deal, unless they started thinking more clearly as individuals and not like sheep. He had quite enjoyed himself but he decided that he would not let anyone see that he had. It is surprising how one's mind works, and a long lost thought came into his mind, something he had come across after the war. He had listened to Germans who could not understand why the Jews had not rebelled when they were being confronted by certain death, what had they to lose and why did they accept what was happening. He did not know the answer, and it disappointed him at the time, realising that the human condition is so complex and often contradictory. "Like lambs to the slaughter, all of us," he said quietly. "We're so primitive, we can't solve even the simplest of problems because it effects someone else's interest, " he sighed at that point.

Bernard was soon dressed and into his wheelchair. "Where do you want to be?" asked Amanda.

"I wouldn't mind spending a few minutes by the trees at the

edge of the garden, the smell of the trees and plants might rejuvenate me." Amanda said that if she had the opportunity she would talk with him later, as they had not talked at any length for some time. Bernard said that he would really like that but then added, "I think you might have a busy day today, and it will keep a while," he smiled at her. She beckoned a young male auxiliary nurse towards her and told him to take Bernard wherever he wanted to go, and to stay with him. She wondered what Bernard had meant by her having a busy day, At that moment her dream, or to be precise, fragments of her dream, from the previous night came back to her. She shrugged her shoulders and went along the to the office. Harry and Andy looked at one another with a knowing expression on their faces.

"He must be worth some money," said Harry cynically, "take him where he wants to go!" he said in a mocking tone of voice, just loud enough for Amanda and Caroline to hear. Amanda turned and gave him a scathing look that indicated he had best not say another word until she was out of earshot.

"You've just lost any chance there," said Andy smiling.

"No chance there anyway!" said Harry, who quickly added, "I tried years ago, and before you ask, I failed, perhaps it was for the best. Who knows? According to Bernard it would have been of little importance anyway, because we've no idea why we're here or what we're doing."

"He didn't exactly say that," added Andy, smiling at Harry's irritable state of mind. Harry grunted and then thought that he would not waste his time thinking about what Bernard had said.

"He looks old and tired," said Elisabeth, quietly, but with some concern.

"He doesn't look fit enough to be out of bed. Looks like some old dosser that has been brought in from the streets," said Andy. Elisabeth was quick to rebuke him for being unkind and stupid. "You don't know anything about him," she added, although she had to admit to herself that she had rarely spoken to him.

"He must have something," said Harry "they're always nice and polite to him. They never give him a hard time. He must have money as that usually brings resentment or better treatment. I've never seen him have a visitor, except for the other old fellow who comes twice a week. I think it's probably his brother he looks similar."

"Or it might be his partner," added Andy. "He never says much does he? Doesn't watch television either, he reads quite a bit though."

"I think that I'll have a word with him when he comes back in, I'll see what he has to say," said Harry, whose curiosity had been aroused. "He seems to have some strong views on films and literature. And he was not slow in putting forward his opinion, he did not seem so tired then, quite the opposite, he looked as though he was enjoying giving us a bollocking disguised as a set of principles. But not to worry, comrades, I'll be ready for him next time."

Caroline stood at the bottom of Harry's bed. "I must tell you before I forget to mention it. Spike and Luna are getting married," said Caroline.

"This will be about the third time that they have tried," added Harry. "Before you forget to mention it!" he said sarcastically, "how would you, in all honesty, forget something like that?." Andy wanted to know who they were, so Elisabeth started to tell him. Harry kept adding bits to the story, due to the fact that he and Spike had been together on the unit in the past.

"Superb guy," said Harry.

"That's a real compliment, coming from Harry," laughed Elisabeth. "He must owe Spike some money, or something."

"I always give credit where it's deserved, and Spike is a decent type, won't let you down, salt of the earth."

"Do you owe him something?" said Elisabeth, who could not remember such praise coming from Harry with regard to anyone other than himself.

"I like Spike and Luna as they are different, and if you doubt that there is a purpose in life, then talk to those two. They were made for one another." Harry was relieved that he had found an example that, in his mind, gave a purpose to life, although in truth he could not work out the details, but for some reason Spike and Luna fitted his need at that moment.

"The purpose must be the uniting of two people in love and harmony. How's that for the meaning of life?" he said, while looking around for agreement.

"Doesn't sound like enlightenment to me," added Andy. Harry

just grunted.

"How does that feel?" said the young man who had carefully pushed Bernard into the position he wanted. "That feels good, really good, just to smell and taste the fresh air. It's like a good wine, full of subtleties and nuances that titillate one's palette." The young man laughed he liked Bernard quite a lot, although he had only worked on the unit for a few months it seemed as though he and Bernard had an affinity of some kind, although it was impossible to clarify. Bernard seemed little interested in talking at any length to most of the staff, except Amanda and Caroline. And it was fair to say that none of the other staff had made any effort to talk to Bernard. It was as if Bernard's age precluded him from the normal conversations and banter that was the everyday norm on the unit. This had upset and disappointed him a little at first, but he had become used to the situation. The staff, who were many years younger than he was, could not relate to him it seemed, or they had no interest in what he might have to say as he was old, and what did he know of their problems or aspirations. No one was intentionally unkind to Bernard, it was just that he no longer mattered as a person; he was just there awaiting whatever fate had in store for him. He felt that in the eyes of others he was no longer a person with anything more to contribute, he had no particular role in life, and there was definitely no future for him. He had seen and experienced much more than they had, but he recognised that it counted for nothing and that was a sad reality. If only they would listen and try and understand, he thought, there was so much he could teach them. The poet said something about going screaming into that long dark night. Bernard used to care about leaving his mark, proclaiming that his existence had been worthwhile, and he had tried hard to leave the world just that little bit better. That was how he thought, even in his darkest moments. But he no longer thought like that anymore. Time had cheated him of everything he valued. And because no one really valued him, he no longer valued himself, in the sense that he had anything left within him to provide himself with a modicum of gratification. He felt hurt, a deep hurt, born out of disappointment and loss and he felt the pain of loneliness, but there was nothing left that he could do. He had experienced life in its extremes; there had been tremendous joy and happiness, which was often followed by pain and misery. Bernard knew that fate was cruel and without compassion, he had witnessed fate's darker side during his earlier years. He had interjected earlier for a few minutes on films and this had momentarily cheered him up. It was his first conversation for some time, albeit it was only for a few minutes. He decided that he would join in more conversations from now on as it might amuse him, and who knows, it could be enjoyable as his fellow patients were not a bad bunch, and quite interesting compared to some people he had the misfortune to be incarcerated with in the past.

He thought for a while about his present situation which was not new to him, and he tried to smile to himself as a form of acceptance. He sat under the tree feeling the breeze upon his face. "Pass me a cigarette," he said to the young man, who then delved into his pocket and then placed the cigarette in Bernard's mouth. "I can put them in my own mouth," said Bernard without any malice in his voice. The young man laughed as he had only seen Bernard in bed, which somehow had given him the impression that Bernard was more disabled than he was. The smoke filled his lungs, the taste brought back memories, and he thought it one of the best smokes that he had ever had. "I could now sip a glass of Châteaux Lafite 1961, a really good year that was," he concluded.

"I used to smoke Havana cigars all of the time," he said, "but they didn't taste any better than this tastes. I enjoyed Bolivar's while everyone grabbed the Monte Christo's," he added, "can't afford to buy a couple of the things today," he suddenly laughed surprisingly loudly and the young man waited to hear what had made him laugh. "Think of this for common sense, we pay a fortune for a Havana cigar, which is after all only a plant leaf. We then set fire to it, and years later it kills us. Is there any wonder we only make progress so slowly?" he laughed. "You're definitely better off with a good cigar than a woman though, if you want to indulge yourself. They're less dangerous. Having said that, there's a lot to be said for women. Wonderfully attractive, and desirable, and irresistible at their best. They're a constant source of pleasure and pain to we lesser mortals," said Bernard while laughing.

The young man coughed the type of cough when you want to draw someone's attention to something. "Ask me, if you want," said Bernard predicting the young man's thoughts. The young man was surprised at Bernard's perception. The young man took the opportunity. "How did you loose your legs and then acquire a spinal injury?" he asked.

"I appreciate the subtle approach," laughed Bernard. "It does seem careless of me," he said. "There just isn't the time to tell you it all," he said while attempting to smile. "So you'll have to make do with the shorter version."

"Only if you really want to tell me, I wasn't prying," said the young man who was now unsure as to whether or not he should have spoken.

Bernard turned to look at him. "Just a piece of advice, if you want to know something, then always ask, life is too short to harbour ignorance when..." He stopped himself, recognising that he was about to enter into what would only seem to be a lecture.

Bernard began, "it was during the war, that is the second world war. I'm not old enough for the first one." The humour was lost on the young man who was listening carefully. Bernard continued. "I was basically an ordinary, working-class young man, but I was at university through hard work, the sacrifice by my family, and my own ambition. You have to realise, few working class people had the opportunity to go to University before the war. We were oddities and I suppose we stuck out like sore thumbs. We were very different, we didn't really fit in and I suppose we knew it. We didn't even know which knife or fork to use at the compulsory dinners; we were fish out of water. We had one advantage though, we were more intelligent than many of the better off types who were there with us. I use the word 'we', but there were only a few of us.

"Anyway, as luck would have it, a fellow called Hitler marched into Poland and we declared war on Germany. Presumably you have heard of him?" quipped Bernard who did not wait for a response. "And I was called up like everyone else. I was young, fit and strong, admittedly relatively stupid and also partially educated, prime cannon fodder in time of war. I was in the flying corps at the university, so it was natural that I finished up in the army. This didn't surprise me or anyone else at the time, because that's how the military system works, it's totally incompetent. It's an old British tradition that has become almost an art form. It was a similar situation with many of the generals who were around at the beginning of the war. They were allowed a couple of massive blunders through their incompetence. And then we sack the stupid bastards. Then they chase around in the hope of finding someone with a few brain cells, whose aim isn't to destroy the male population by having them charge with bayonets against tanks, or similar stupid actions." Bernard's tone of voice indicated that he had strong feelings about the subject. He continued, "I was made an officer, which worried me at the time, as I didn't have the accent or the background, so I presumed that I must be exceptionally good or they were really desperate. It didn't matter as I did nothing about it, I thought that it must be better than being an ordinary soldier, and you have to get your priorities right. The uniform looked better to start with, and it was easier to get a girl friend when on leave. That's where one's ego pushes out one's common sense and values." He smiled and looked towards the young man to see if his point had been taken. He was gratified to see that it had.

"After a bit of training I flew out to North Africa. I was put in charge of a group of men who, fortunately, knew what it was all about, as they'd been out there for some time, which was very helpful to me as I knew bugger all! Having said that, they'd only been in the army for a few months themselves. They seemed to know more than I did but I don't know why, as most of them had come from a similar background to myself.

"Anyway, The fighting had been going back and forth for God knows how long. Few of us had any idea why we were fighting over thousands of square miles of desert, miles and miles of rock and sand. There was nothing there worth fighting over, well, not at that time anyway, as the oil was found later in that area. Can you imagine? Mile after mile of sand and a coastal road. Now, you don't have to be very bright to quickly recognise that in order to push the Germans out we had to use that road. The enemy was in the same position; it was the only real way that you could move things about in that area.

"I remember that this half-witted major gave us what you might loosely call a pep talk. We were informed that we must protect the Suez Canal at all costs, and ensure that the Germans could not push through the Middle East, and join up with their armies in Russia, everything depended upon us holding the line, etc. It seemed plausible at the time, I suppose, but if you look at a map it would leave you wondering. How were they going to do it? - the Germans that is - due to the distances involved, and the simple logistics, but we questioned nothing. We honestly thought that if a superior officer comes along gives you a pep talk, and tells you what he wants, then he must know what he is doing - otherwise he wouldn't say anything. The military mind seldom functions in a way that we would consider as being normal." He moved on quickly before he had a chance to move off at a tangent by discussing the logistics involved.

"We pushed the Germans back and lost some men, and then surprisingly we won. This was a surprise, because the normal pattern had been to push the Germans back a thousand miles, lose thousands of men. Then the Germans would push us back; we were fighting for the same sand dunes month after month." He laughed at that point when he thought of the futility of it all, "but surprisingly, we won, or they said we'd won, but what exactly had we won? I wasn't sure, but I didn't question it. That is, we pushed them back and captured North Africa," he added, realising that the young man was not over-familiar with history.

"Next thing of importance, we had landed in Italy and we moved inland, and we were then stuck at a place called Monte Casino, the founding monastery of the Benedictines. It was a wonderful building, perched right on top of the mountain. Naturally we bombed it, and levelled it to the ground, and then tried to take the place. My company was almost wiped out by this action, most of them were under your age with the whole of their lives before them. I was their officer, and I was supposed to look after them and try to keep them from getting killed, or that's how I saw things." His voice was saddened and a tear formed in his eyes upon remembering the events. He carried on talking, but it was difficult for him to control his emotions. He continued slowly. "When we took the place, the Germans had gone, it was a total waste of time, but being the army, they couldn't just go around things like sensible people, they had to take them. You can never over-estimate the stupidity of the military mind," he added.

"I, for my sins, shortly afterwards, and unfortunately I might add, got caught by the Germans. I was wounded in both legs and with Teutonic logic they kindly cut my legs off. I have to give them credit though, as they did a decent job," he smiled at that point. "I was then sent to a hospital in northern Italy for a short time. And then I was shipped out to a prison camp in southern Germany." His voice softened, "it was my stay in hospital in Italy that really saved my life, and to a certain extent has effected my life. It was a very strange experience." As he said this, his eyes seemed to stare deep into space as though trying to visualise those past events. "I was being looked after so well, yet we were at war with these people. One of the Italian nurses who spoke some English had lost two brothers in North Africa. Yet she didn't hate me at all; on the contrary, she went out of her way to be kind, bringing me extra food and cigarettes whenever she could. She was also incredibly beautiful. I've been around this world of ours and I've never met anyone like her." Bernard still looked ahead as if he was trying to remember more clearly. "There was still some kindness and compassion in the middle of the war," he pondered upon this thought. "If I were to evaluate things properly, from a personal point of view, I think her kindness was the most important event in my life." He looked at the young man, hoping that he might understand. "She loved me," he said, "she loved me because I was a human being who needed her. It was as simple as that. I had nothing to give or offer her. But she gave me everything, that makes humans, on rare occasion, superior to other creatures. The rest of the time we're barbaric to one another."

He sighed, "I should have tried to find her after the war, if I'd retained any sense. I briefly thought about it and then dismissed the idea. What on earth would I say to her? A legless man, with no job at that time, looking to find an attractive young woman who, only a couple of years earlier, had been the enemy. It was ludicrous, utterly stupid. That was the thought that passed through my mind. I still wish I knew what had happened to her though." He looked perplexed for a moment, "after all these years and I still think of her." He paused a short while and changed his line of thought as though it was too painful for him to continue.

"After a short while, and obviously due to my condition, the Red Cross did an exchange deal and I was sent home. I was allowed to regain my weight and I suppose I could have sat out the rest of the war, but my mind was active and I needed a challenge. Something where it was possible to lose oneself. I don't know how it came about, but one day I was told to report to a building off such and such a road, on the outskirts of Manchester. To my surprise there was a few of us there, not really knowing what we were doing. But the conditions were better than I was used to, and the work wasn't difficult, people from some ministry would dump a large parcel of documents on a desk a couple of times a week, and we would sift through them, adding out comments. We became used to it, and it seemed so normal none of us even bothered to ask what it was we were supposed to be doing. During a war strange things happen all the time, and you just do not question them, it seems stupid now, but that's how it was then. It was a different time, with different attitudes and values. I should mention to you that not all of the existing attitudes were bad. There was loyalty, and comradeship that no longer exists, and at times you did believe in doing what was right, although it was an area of confusion at times." He smiled as though he could remember an incident.

He continued, "at the end of the war I went back to my old university for a short time to see if any of my friends had survived, surprisingly quite a few had.. I then obtained a job and settled down to civilian life. To be accurate, I was offered a job." It appeared for a moment that Bernard was not going to say anymore. But the young man prompted him and Bernard continued. "I got a job at Aldermaston working on atomic weapons. It was all very exciting at the time. It was state-of-the-art killing, and all that stupidity. I was sent to the US for a couple of years, to Oak Ridge." The young man had never heard of the place but he did not interrupt Bernard. "It was at that time that I…" He paused for a moment as if he was trying to find the right words. He continued, "I fell out with the whole system." He looked hurt for a moment, and paused again before he could continue. "I fell out with almost everyone, and everything, in fact. I was soon sent home, and more or less told to seek employment elsewhere, but I was not allowed to use the knowledge I had obtained. I had signed the Official Secrets Act." Bernard stopped talking and asked for another smoke.

"I forgot to mention it, but I was married just before I went out to the US. It seemed a good idea at the time, she was quite attractive, very sexy in an aggressive sort of way, and we worked together, and therefore she was allowed to go with me. That was one of the problems, she enjoyed her work, she actually believed that what she was doing was worthwhile."

"What was it you were actually doing?" asked the young man.

"We were making atomic weapons. I thought I'd just mentioned it? These were good ones though, much bigger, wonderful devices that could destroy the world." Bernard looked at the young man intently before saying anything else. He then continued, "think about it carefully and logically. We were scientists, and we knew what we were creating. Does it seem sensible to create something that, in some lunatic politician's hands, such a thing could actually be used?. The worst scenario was simply the end of the world, and there I was, helping them to achieve it." Bernard said this with considerable passion. "Anyway, I told them that I disagreed with the whole idea as I had just been in a war that had killed millions, my wife didn't agree with me and we parted disliking one another, the divorce soon followed. I left her feeling happy, in a new country with a good job and a new husband. I saw her at a conference some years later and her opinions had not changed, on the contrary they had hardened, It was sad, really, as we had nothing to say to each other. I joined CND and tried to make a living teaching physics. The system was against me, and saw me as some kind of threat, but I got by. My friends who remained sympathetic helped me when they could. It was a strange time during the late fifties as spy scandals were rife. Anything at all to do with nuclear weapons, or defence, was sensitive. I believe that I was followed around by the Special Branch for years. That was due to my support of CND I think, but I don't know if I was or not, they might have thought I was a potential traitor, there was enough of them around at the time. But they should have realised most traitors were the products of public schools." The last few words seemed to amuse Bernard. He continued as though it was of some importance that the young man clearly understood what he was saying.

"Looking back, if I'm honest, I'm not sure that we achieved anything. They still built the bombs without me, and those who thought like me. The system portrayed us as loony, left-wing cranks, who were somehow unpatriotic. I suppose it doesn't matter anymore what they said and did at the time. Whoever writes the history of the period will finally decide if the effort was worthwhile. Just one last point," he said grasping the young man's sleeve, "never trust any government to tell you the truth or to do what is noble or decent. They will always do what they consider expedient and commensurate with their own survival. And I don't mean survival of the government. I mean that there are individuals within government who will sacrifice any ideals they might have had to retain the power and status that we bestow upon them. They forget that power does not come from them, but from the people. They hold power only as long as we allow them to. That sounds like a line from Marx, but it's true. It contradicts what I said earlier, but power does exist with the people, it's just that we've lost the desire or ability to do something about it." He looked at the young man hoping he would remember that particular point.

"Are you sure that you want to hear all of this as it's before your time? And it's my time, not yours, so you might find it difficult to relate to. Or perhaps I'm doing you an injustice?" added Bernard The young man assured Bernard that he was not unaware of recent history, and the interrelated aspects that had created what we have today. Bernard was pleased to hear this as it was quite a long time since he had been allowed to hold forth at some length.

He leaned back in his wheelchair and inhaled deeply. His voice was strong and for a moment it startled the young man. "But it all started long ago, we could see it happening, and we did nothing," he paused as though he was arranging his thoughts into a form of order. The young man waited for him to add something to his statement. Bernard looked at him and he started to speak slowly.

"We have to constantly relive our mistakes. Generation after generation, we never seem to learn, and those who do, seem powerless." Bernard had a look of desperation on his face and tears were forming in the corner of his eyes. He sighed deeply and wiped his eyes. "This is going to sound like a crude quick history lesson, so just bear with me if you can, but if you get tired of listening, just say so. It started in the twenties after the First World War, 'the war to end all wars' it was called. We had not moved on, we were fools, we tried to make the Germans pay for the war. The world was entering a recession and Germany was impoverished, the rest of Europe was no better." He leaned forward as though he needed to make the next point clear. "There was no sound economic or political structure in Germany, at the time it was chaos. The left and the right were fighting for power in their meandering way, which meant stalemate. In such situations the opportunists move, in which is either the far right or the far left. Both try and promise the same thing. 'Give us power and everything will be fine.' And the people did give them power. Unfortunately it was to Adolf Hitler. But the point I'm making is that we assisted in creating the situation where the Hitler's of this world could flourish. He told the masses exactly what they wanted to hear. He told them that they, the German people, were the finest people on this planet, that they deserved better than their present status. He then told them that the mess they were in was nothing at all to do with them. Naturally that sounded good to them, removed any guilt, or responsibility, for the state Germany was in."

The young man was about to say something when Bernard stopped him. "I know what you are going to ask. How did he convince them that they had nothing to do with their condition? It was easy just blame someone else. And Hitler blamed the Jews and the communists."

The young man interjected. "But surely the Germans were not so stupid as to believe that the Jews or the communists were responsible for everything that had gone wrong?"

Bernard smiled, "they loved to blame the Jews mainly, they were perfect, ideal scapegoats. They blamed losing the first world war onto the Jews, they said that the international Jewish bankers had got together and undermined Germany. This made them feel so much better, within a short time they believed that they had not really lost the war. Once everyone recognised that all the problems stemmed from the Jews, or the Communists, then everyone could feel better. But once you go down that road there comes a time when you have got to do something about the source of the problem, and of course, Hitler did. The resulting war we all know about. And at the end we had made progress. We dropped two atomic bombs on Japan, and allowed the political division between the east and the west."

"Those bombs must have saved lives, the lives of those on our side," said the young man.

"It's difficult to estimate," said Bernard looking very serious. "They weren't dropped just for that purpose."

The young man, who had a reasonable understanding of history, looked at Bernard with some expectancy. He was not going to be disappointed.

"The bombs were dropped to impress the Russians, and to actually see what the results would be. Japan had been trying to find a way to negotiate some form of surrender for weeks. They knew they were beaten. The problem was that the fanatics would have killed anyone they thought might be considering surrender. The powers that-be knew of the situation, the war was coming to a close and everyone was thinking of what was going to be the world order once the war was over. And just look at what happened; we have lived in fear ever since. Russia has finally collapsed, of course, but that hasn't changed anything, the thinking is still the same. The arms manufacturers are still there creating situations."

He sighed again before continuing. "It'll be China's turn next. They'll want a piece of the action, they'll want to take their place at the top table, irrespective of the fact that half the nation still lives in poverty. They will, of course, be the world's leading manufacturer within a short time and everyone will then complain about unfair practices and such like, we'll all have more consumer goods than we can handle. And so it will continue, all of the effort will be wasted when we could feed the world, eliminate poverty and many diseases. The so called third-world will still be the third-world. No one has any interest in changing the situation. The World Bank and the IMF weren't created to solve their economic problems; they were created in order that the west can control the situation, and keeping them relatively poor is the policy. Everyone pretends it isn't, but reality shows you otherwise, it's very sad, very sad," he said quietly. "Years ago they were growing various things in east Africa and getting a very modest amount for their efforts. They're not getting anymore today - just look at the percentage of the income that goes on food; it has changed very little in some countries, and you also have to look at the community and how it functioned in support of the individual. They are losing what communities they once had, we've not done them a service at all, they're left in a state of confusion . There is little political stability, which usually means a dictatorship, or being controlled by the army, this often means total poverty and misery for ordinary people. The one thing we do not value in this world is ordinary people, people who wonder where their next meal is coming from; they're of little value to anyone, just a drain on inadequate resources and we treat them accordingly. "

He looked carefully at the young man. "It's not a good picture is it? I'd like to offer you some words of advice that might serve you well, but I don't think that I can add much to what I've said." He was almost thinking out loud, the thoughts were coming into his mind without him having to put in any intellectual effort, as though they were imprinted forever.

"Times have changed and we haven't learned anything. And your generation seems to have settled for the easy option, a lifestyle demanding instant gratification or some form of oblivion. Even in the sixties there was a chance, students throughout Europe were protesting and demanding a better world to live in. What has happened?. You've been bought off by the system. Follow the rules' and you have some form of prize dangled in front of you. Your generation has lost direction, it's not your fault though," he sighed out loud when he thought about the situation. "We failed and you're left without any worthwhile aims, other than to get on in life, whatever that means. Bring out the brass bands, wave the flag now and again and you'll just follow the same path like sheep." Bernard sounded angry at having to say the last phrase.

"And look at this situation! This place and what goes on in the community once patients have left here. Have we progressed? Is life so much better for disabled people? Except for a few minor changes, which I'm not disagreeing with, very little has improved. Disabled people are stigmatised the same as before. The only difference now is that most disabled are not aware of it. Disabled people are still at the bottom of the social and economic pile and that is how it's likely to stay. Society will sound sympathetic and toss you a few crumbs now and then, but at the end of the day a disabled person, if not working or is lacking in status, which most are, then they are also just a drain upon resources. I wouldn't want to be a young person coming into here severely disabled with all those years ahead, it's too bloody difficult. It should be relatively easy! We know what's needed and we have the means. This is why, in that sense, disabled people are in the same position as most people in the less developed world. We can solve most of the problems but there is no real incentive to do so."

He looked at the young man before continuing. "There are many disabilities in this world: social, physical, mental, economic, etc., and they effect individuals differently, but one thing is more or less certain, and that is, you are disadvantaged if you have a disability. If you have a serious impairment then it's likely that life will be difficult, and will continue to be difficult. The important point is that most disabled people know that life is unlikely to get better once they've thought about their situation. I'm talking about serious impairments of course, not just a slight limp or a twitch." Bernard paused for a few seconds. "Even those impairments can have a serious effect upon a person's life," he added. "Once you know that life is not going to be easy, a strange thing tends to happen with some people. Some accept their lot and do the best they can, seemingly content to outsiders, but it's a front - they usually loathe their situation, well, most of them do. And they will rarely tell you how they really feel, because they know that whatever they say is unlikely to make any difference. The reason being they know that you do not really understand how they feel, because you can't share their experiences. You can't understand what it's like, the psychological and the physical melange that exists. If you talk in depth to the patients on this unit, and you believe that you have some idea of what it feels like to have their disability, I can assure you that you do not know. It's so much more complex than that.

It's such a mixture of emotions and feelings that are driven by the circumstances that it makes any understanding difficult. Obviously, you have some idea of what it feels like to have some of the problems i.e. bladder infections, chest infections and such like. But remember, these are in addition to the existing difficult situation. It's the lack of understanding, or the inability to empathise that is part of the larger problem. I might not have explained this correctly, but it's the best that I can do at the moment. Anyway, just try and understand, listen carefully and read between the lines; patients are still people even on spinal units.

"Leaving the patients for a moment let me expand upon another subject. If we look at what's happening throughout the world - we have globalisation, what a wonderful word." His voice did not disguise his contempt of the word. "What does it mean? It means that real trade and real competition no longer exists, giant organisations that are above the law roam the world like sharks, money follows cheap labour. Which in theory should help these countries out of poverty, but we've refined the system to enable us to keep them in poverty. We don't manufacture anymore, we provide services. We live on the provision of services, which really means playing around with money which makes money."

He smiled, "these are old fashioned arguments, but still valid I think, although I realise they're not very fashionable. And nowadays fashion is everything, it controls us; we all want what we're told is fashionable, whether it's clothes, or a car, or a house, even our drinking and eating habits." He wanted to say that the system does nothing but ensure that the bastards climb to the positions of power but he refrained.

He shivered as though he had become cold. "Actually, I think that I'm feeling a bit tired now and it's become chilly. I'll go back inside, if you don't mind." He smiled at the young man and told him not to worry, he was an old man and that times might get better if he was lucky .

Bernard was pushed inside and put into bed. He had enjoyed being out in the fresh air, even for such a short time it had felt strangely very good. Cleaner and fresher than he thought it would be. He was tired, tired of almost everything, and he knew that the world, or any small part of it was no longer his, he was an old man who could not hope to pass on his experiences and understanding. And it hurt him to realise that was always going to be the problem, no one was willing to listen and to learn.

Once again his thoughts drifted back to the time in Italy, and the nurse who had looked after him. He could see the faces of his friends who had died at his side, we were all so young, he thought. They were young men who were very ordinary, who wanted to live and enjoy life. Yet they had to die, because fools who controlled events had allowed the world to slip once again into war. What might they have achieved if they had lived? He still felt guilty and his eyes filled with tears. He closed his eyes hoping to shut out the painful memories. He tried to think of the young women who had helped him so long ago. If only he had returned to look for her. He knew her for only a matter of weeks, but he had loved her for the rest of his life. He could only dream about what he might have lost, and he felt the pain, the deep pain of such a love that was lost to him. He thought that there were few things in life that were really valuable. And of these, love was the most valuable in all its complexity and its ability to inflict pain. He had enjoyed the smell of the trees and the fresh air. He thought that the young man must have thought that the past few minutes, or whatever time had elapsed, had allowed an old man to ramble on talking about times, places and ideas that no longer had any meaning. Bernard asked himself. How many times did I criticise the military and the politicians? He must have thought that I was paranoid, or that's how old people tend to act, always devoid of any happiness or joy, while looking back on days that might have been better. He briefly thought that he might have sounded just plain foolish, which he did not want to do, but he had found it difficult controlling his emotions, which was unlike him really, as he understood the world. He recognised the value of what history could and could not teach, but for reasons unknown to him today he felt very emotional. At times he wanted to shout, to rant and rave, to demand better lifestyles and opportunities, but he could not do that anymore, they were just other items amongst many others that were now out of his reach. He enjoyed the smoke, but now he was tired and he quickly fell asleep on being helped back to bed. He dreamed of a love that was lost forever, but clearly and painfully remembered through the mists of time. And he felt lonely, the loneliness of being alone, trapped with one's thoughts and experiences that would never be seen or heard by others. A book of life that would remain closed. He was isolated by time and events, walking endlessly in a barren land without a companion or friend. He wept within his dreams until his dreams stood still. What happened to our world? he said to himself. We could do so much, yet we do so little.

Lunch passed and visitors started to enter the unit. Some of the visitors had known the unit for years, and nothing had really changed. They were familiar with the layout of the beds and many of the occupants. Visiting time was one of those items that can seem to be contradictory in its intent and outcomes. It is assumed that everyone wants visitors the whole of the time, that visitors have a positive effect upon patients. Harry had thought about this, having been in hospital for some time. He had concluded that if you were a new patient you needed regular visitors. But if you were an older patient returning to the unit, then you needed visitors for the first couple of weeks on a regular basis. But after that time, you only needed visitors when you actually felt like them. There was nothing worse, thought Harry, than someone sitting at the side of the bed not knowing what to talk about, all of the conversation having dried up weeks earlier. Harry thought that it sounded a bit anti-social, but he had learned that there were visitors and visitors. Some you could relax with and talk about anything, others took a formal approach and made small talk that was of no consequence. Totally bloody boring, he thought. I suppose they mean well and they have taken the trouble to visit, thought Harry.

CHAPTER TWELVE

Amanda decided to tell Caroline about the lumps in her breast. Caroline replied in a predictable manner, stating what Amanda was already aware of, that statistically the lumps would, more than likely, be of little consequence. Amanda confided in Caroline that for some reason she did not think that would be the case. Before Caroline could interrupt her Amanda said. "Don't ask me how I know, it's irrational, I keep telling myself, but that's how I feel. There's something wrong, and I know it." Caroline listened and understood the anxiety that Amanda was feeling as she had gone through the same problem only a few months earlier. She tried to explain to Amanda that she felt the same. until she was told that everything was fine. She continued. "You're bound to think of the worst scenario, you're a nurse, and you've worked on the units where most of the patients were there due to breast cancer or some other form of cancer. That has got to colour your judgement, you know it has."

Amanda looked at Caroline and half smiled, "you're probably right. But it still sounds as though you're trying to reassure a patient, knowing that what you're saying might not be true."

"I'm just being logical, and you know that. I can't pretend that everything is wonderful until you get your results. You know these things as well as I do and you also know that you're likely to be OK," added Caroline. Amanda was not convinced and now wished that she had not mentioned it. Earlier, she had decided not to say anything, but for some reason had changed her mind. She knew that sharing was often a good idea, that sometimes it gave you some relief, She also knew that at the end of the day the problem was hers, and hers alone. She then thought about her failing relationship and this did not help her mood. She just thought that her life appeared to be going from bad to worse, there was nothing to look forward to but difficulties and stress. I hate that word she suddenly thought, but it was appropriate at that moment.

Caroline asked when her appointment was. Amanda surprised her by saying that it was in thirty minutes, and that is why she had not had anything to eat or drink since early morning. "I'm lucky I suppose, they're fitting me in at short notice." She went on in a deliberately calm controlled voice, "If there's a problem, they'll undertake the necessary surgery." Although she said this in a deliberate, matter of fact way, it could not disguise her true feelings.

"Well, best of luck. I'm sure it'll be fine," said Caroline, "I'll call in and see you when I go off duty." Amanda told her that she did not want the other staff to know any details as they would find out soon enough. Caroline promised faithfully that she would not say anything, but knew that everyone would find out every detail within hours at the latest.

The young auxiliary nurse who had taken Bernard outside by the trees a little earlier entered the office and poured himself a coffee. "Did Bernard enjoy being out in the fresh air?" asked Amanda. "He seemed to enjoy it quite a lot." The young man paused for a short while and then added. "Do you know what Bernard's done? He's had an amazing life, bloody amazing!," he continued. "In fact, I don't think that I've ever met anyone quite like him."

"I'm sure that you haven't, few of us have met anyone like Bernard," said Caroline.

"Do you know much about him, then?" queried the young man, "do you know what he's been involved in?." Both Amanda and Caroline nodded indicating that they knew.

"You don't know the half of it," said Amanda. "He was a friend of my grandfather." She continued, "he's lived in the area since he finished work at the University. Actually, he originally came from this area and he was at school with my grandfather. I first met him years ago with my grandfather, when I was researching a project on CND while I was at school." She leaned back, half closed her eyes as though she was trying hard to recall the details. "He was a brilliant speaker. He seemed to know something about everything. And he always had the time to explain things in such a way that they were easily understood. Bernard is a very special man," said Amanda, "if you listen to him, you'll possibly learn something worthwhile about life, we could all learn from Bernard."

Caroline could not resist adding to the conversation. "He won the military cross during the war, he saved some of the soldiers in his platoon. That's when he was wounded and lost both his legs." Amanda stopped her from saying anymore by telling her that she was about to leave and that she wanted Caroline to keep an eye on Bernard.

The young man interrupted, "wouldn't it be worthwhile if Bernard could talk to more staff and patients? He knows so much, he understands so much." They both looked at him as though he was asking the most stupid of questions.

"No one wants to listen, or learn," said Caroline, "or haven't you noticed that yet?" She put a hand upon his shoulder and in a quiet controlled voice told him, "to be old is not to be respected, but to be looked upon as someone who has past their usefulness."

"People don't want to learn and understand anymore," added Amanda. "They want every night to be Saturday night. To be old is not automatically seen as something good or wise, it doesn't confer any respect in our society. Actually I don't know if there was a time when it was good," she said with some disappointment. She continued, "although, when I was young, I was taught to respect people who were older. I just accepted older people were there, and we sometimes listened, possibly more often than not we didn't, but at least we showed respect."

"I suppose it's how one is brought up," said Caroline in agreement. The young man said that he was interested and that in a short time he had learned a great deal. This pleased Amanda who said. "In that case, why don't you ask him if he'd like to go out for a smoke some other time? If he enjoyed your company he'll talk to you at length, and if you have the time to listen, you'll enjoy it a great deal. As I've already said, the problem you might have is that you'll have to keep any such pearls of wisdom to yourself, as I doubt if anyone here will listen to what you might have to say, so don't be over concerned as there is nothing that you can do about it, as it's a sign of the times we live in," she shrugged her shoulders as she spoke. Amanda then smiled at him as though to compensate him for any disappointment. She placed her hand upon his shoulder again, "go and talk to him whenever you can, he'll enjoy talking to you, I'm sure," she smiled as she spoke. "I wish that I'd spent more time with him myself, this past few weeks, he was so kind and understanding when I was young, he would listen when no one else in our household had the time. He seemed to know what I was thinking, or wanted to say," she sighed and smiled at the young man who nodded as though he understood.

Caroline said that she needed to have a talk about Andy when it was convenient. She thought that he was finding things just a bit difficult. Amanda said that it was a stage that he would have to pass through like all of the others, there was no escape from reality for him, but they would talk about it later.

Andy had not stayed on the unit to watch the news, but had made his way along the corridor and out towards the car park where he could sit by himself and think. He could also, at the same time, have a smoke. He had stopped a passer by who had helped him take a cigarette out and lit it for him.

He had been thinking seriously and trying to adjust his thoughts. He had carefully considered what Harry had said, and it had upset him at the time, and now some hours later he was still upset and angry. The thought of having a reduced sex life did not appeal to him. Sex was important. The whole of society was highly geared towards sex. It was on advertisements, on television and in every novel, it made up a large part of male conversation. And what was more, he really enjoyed it, everything about it made him feel good. He could not think of anything better, except perhaps his football team getting the wining goal in the European cup final in the last minute. He agreed that would be worth the odd orgasm, but anything less than that just did not enter the picture. He thought to himself that it would be an insult to try and convince himself that it was not important. Just ask others to go without, he thought, then you will see how important it becomes. He was not sure that he should have mentioned it to Caroline as he now felt vulnerable. Although he believed that he trusted her, yet somehow it had still made him feel vulnerable disclosing his feelings in that manner, without giving them some detailed thought. He then thought that she would keep their conversation confidential, but he wasn't totally sure. Because he had been in close proximity to Caroline for the past few months, and she had nursed him at some length, he felt close to her, as one feels close to the nurse who provides most of that initial care. However, he realised that it was a possibly a false picture of the real situation. The reality was she was doing her job, and he was just another patient in a long line of patients. He thought that he had to recognise that fact, and not read anything else into the situation. He had told himself a number of times that he was not special, but just another patient. No matter how many times he told himself this, he did not want to really believe it, he wanted to be an individual, not just another patient in an endless line of patients, who come onto the unit get themselves as fit as possible and then move on to wherever their circumstances take them.

At that moment, for some unknown reason, his eyes were drawn to a car that had just parked in the corner of the car park near to the trees. Andy watched the couple kiss each other quite passionately, before the man got out of the car. Andy was surprised to see that it was Elisabeth's husband. The woman remained in the car. Elisabeth's husband made his way between the parked cars and headed for the entrance to the building. Andy suddenly felt a mixture of emotions due to what he had just seen, part of him smiled instantly and said "you lecherous sod," while the other part of him felt sad. He felt sorry for Elisabeth, whom he liked. He also felt anger, remembering how often Elisabeth had said what a good husband he had been, and how fortunate she was. Andy decided that he would go back onto the unit and tell Harry. He could not keep this to himself, although he realised that it was nothing to do with him really, it was other people's lives and he should mind his own business. But he also knew that he could not keep it to himself, it was just too important in a daily routine that was mundane at best, this new variable gave the day something different, almost a level of excitement.

He told Harry what he had witnessed and then sat back waiting for an appropriate response. Harry just grunted and then sighed deeply. Andy looked at him in expectation, still Harry did not say anything.

"What do you think?" asked Andy impatiently.

"About what?" asked Harry somewhat vaguely.

"Don't fuck me about, as though I'm the village idiot!" said Andy, starting to get angry. He had just imparted this interesting piece of information and it warranted a suitable response. He wondered what was Harry playing at. He usually has an answer for everything, and now, when an answer is required, he was saying nothing. Andy was now mystified.

After what seemed an eternity Harry beckoned Andy closer, "it's been going on for years," he said. "Elisabeth's aware of it, and he's aware that she knows, but they keep up the pretence."

"Why the hell doesn't she tell him to get on his bike?" said Andy.

"Simple," said Harry, "for some reason, she loves the cheating bastard! In his own way, he probably loves her just as much, but they stay together and they seem happy, so why knock it?" he looked at Andy whose expression indicated disbelief.

"Are you certain that she knows?" he asked.

"Certain," replied Harry, who indicated that it was something that he did not want to discuss any further. Andy wanted to shout something across the room to Elisabeth warning her of her husband's infidelity, but unusually for him his common sense prevailed and he resisted the temptation. What a lousy bastard, he thought. Then his thoughts moved ahead, returning once again to his own situation. He wondered if such situations were the norm. Were they to be expected? If he ever settled down with a partner, should he expect to have to share her with someone more physically able than himself? Would his partner want someone else, knowing how he would feel and how painful it would be? He decided that he would not be willing to do that, he knew that he could not do it. His personality and attitude would not permit it. How far down the line have you got to go, he thought, how much dignity and self-respect have you to give up? Integrity would no longer exist, he could not envisage being seen, or thought of, as an inferior person who could be treat with contempt by anyone and their dog. It's like the Lady Chatterley syndrome, he thought. Would a partner, who professed her love for him, do that to him? Would she inflict so much pain on him? If she was willing to do that, had she ever really loved him in the first place? He was becoming emotional and confused. He wished at that moment that he had not seen Elisabeth's husband with another woman. He was beginning to realise how easy it was for people to inflict emotional pain upon you when you are vulnerable. He also had the intelligence to know that he was always going to be vulnerable, unless he could do something about it. Just at that moment he had no idea of what he should do. He told himself that he had learned a great deal in the past few hours and he had enjoyed none of it.

Harry leaned over and said. "As far as I can tell, it's just sex. He loves Elizabeth, I'm sure, but for some reason he also wants another woman, life's often like that," he then shrugged his shoulders as if to indicate that it was not something one should be surprised at. Harry explained in a manner that he hoped would find a degree of understanding. "We aren't monogamous, we do like and desire others, it's a fact of life. And we only live once, and obviously for some reason he feels the need for someone else sexually. You can both want and love more than one person at the same time, laws surrounding morality were usually based on religion, which has bugger all to do with reality."

"So, loving only one person could be unnatural if we accept that premise?."

"I don't know why it's like that, I don't have an answer, but that's how it is, we're not perfect and such things exist to try us. I will confess that I didn't always think like this, but time and experience have educated me. It might not fit into one's ideal scenario, but that's how it is. He might enjoy sex with Elisabeth, but he might think he's missing out and needs a body that's more physically responsive. In other words, he might want to fuck someone who can feel and appreciate his efforts. It's a crude way of putting it, but that seems to sum it up. I might've got it wrong though, he might've gone with other women if Elisabeth hadn't been disabled. I don't know what it's like, having sex with a woman whose body doesn't respond in a way you would normally expect, it might not be so satisfying for some reason, I just don't know."

Andy had not expected such a response from Harry. He could not understand why Harry had taken that line as though it was normal and acceptable. What a bloody education it has been he thought, he had expected something very different and it seemed as though things were now turned upside down.

Caroline saw Amanda in the end bed, she looked as

though she was asleep, but when she moved closer Amanda opened her eyes. "I told you that something was wrong didn't I," she said while forcing a smile. Before Caroline could say anything, Amanda told her that it had required a partial mastectomy. "I'm glad that I didn't wait any longer," she added. Caroline held her hand and they said nothing, they smiled a knowing smile, words were not needed at that moment. "I'll soon be back on the unit, I might as well take the opportunity and get some rest."

"What about Athol? Is he coming to see you tonight" asked Caroline.

Amanda tried to smile as she spoke. "Athol doesn't know anything about this, anyway, he's down in the Midlands somewhere, probably with his other women, and he's not due back until the weekend."

Caroline was not sure what to say, she knew that Amanda's marriage was not exactly blooming, but whose was she thought. She had not realised that the relationship had reached such a low point, that Amanda had not bothered, or thought fit, to tell her husband about her problem. And when Amanda mentioned another women, she could not make her mind up whether or not she was being serious or flippant. Caroline felt sorry for Amanda at that moment, knowing that her own social situation needed working on. The thought of a partnership, or relationship, being a reality for herself was non-existent at that moment. She was unsure as to what to do to improve her life in the short-term. Perhaps if she just left things alone for awhile things might improve. Her thoughts then quickly returned to Amanda. She sighed and then squeezed Amanda's arm and told her that she would call in and see her in the morning. She told Amanda that it was impossible to keep anything from the staff now, as more than likely the whole of the hospital would know that she had been operated on. Amanda agreed and said that it did not matter anyway, she was just glad that it was over.

"There was something I thought that I should mention while there is no one around."

"That sounds mysterious," said Amanda her curiosity aroused.

"Well, you might like it, or you might not," said Caroline smiling.

"Please! Just come out with it!," said Amanda getting impatient.

"Well, it's Simon. I've noticed, over these past few weeks, his body language when he's with you. He really fancies you, and he's a nice. He has a really good body and he's in good shape."

Amanda stopped her from saying anything else. "That's bloody typical of your observation," said Amanda. "You've got it wrong, besides, I'm not interested. I have enough problems at the moment. Don't you remember? A few minutes ago I told you I've had a part of me cut off, and you're telling me about someone who you think fancies me!. I just can't believe you sometimes," said Amanda.

Caroline just smiled and said, "I've worked with Wendy too long. There! I knew that would cheer you up!" she laughed at that point. "But I still want you to look at the possibility of going to Egypt. It would do us both a lot of good, well, perhaps some good, just to have a change."

Once Caroline had left the room, Amanda thought about Athol and their future. It has to be over, she thought. She realised that it was time to start again, this time by herself. She did not relish the thought, but time had taught her that this was the right time to make the necessary changes in her life. To prolong the sham of appearing to be a happy couple seemed pointless. Who cares?, she thought, she no longer did.

And as for what Caroline had said regarding Simon, this was not the time to think about any involvement. However, if it was true, it was better than being disliked, she thought. She liked Simon; he was an attractive man, but she had never thought that he might like her, except as a colleague. Any other ideas had not entered her head. It is something to think about if it's true, she said to herself. She then dismissed the thought, knowing that she had more important things to deal with. Her future had to be decided, it could no longer be left to fate. She had to take some form of positive action and if this meant moving on, then she would have to move. But she was tired, and she decided that she would think about these things in the morning.

"Elvis has arranged to go for the fish and chips, or burgers, if you want some," said Harry loud enough in order that everyone could hear. Elvis was a young man who was always on night duty, or so it seemed. Elvis was not his real name. His real name was Bradshaw after his mother's side of the family. But he could not bear to be called Bradshaw or even Brad. So he answered to Elvis quite happily. He had soon acquired the name Elvis as he often walked around the hospital strumming an imaginary guitar, while singing the first few lines of 'Jailhouse Rock.' He would have liked to have known the rest of the song, but it was popular before he was born, and it had never fully registered with him. And he thought that any words were of secondary importance to the rock and roll beat that he could imagine, and on occasion he would sing the odd line from 'Peggy Sue.'

"Who wants what?" shouted Elvis. He quickly added that he was not getting any curry sauce for anyone, as the last time he got some, it ran down his coat. It was impossible to get the stain out, he said. God knows what they put in the stuff.

"I'll have some as well," said Elisabeth cheerfully.

"What's brightened you up? Have you won the lottery?" asked Harry.

"Almost!" said Elisabeth obviously excited. She continued excitedly "When I get out of here, we're going on holiday together, as a family. We're going to Dubrovnik, we went there years ago, it was wonderful, it was so romantic, the sea was so blue and the old city was just something special, so historic Richard the Lionheart landed there after the crusades."

"Very interesting," said Harry, "but he's not going to the fish and chip shop."

She did not care about Harry's sarcasm at that moment.

"Do you want bits on your fish and chips?" said Harry.

Elisabeth did not reply; she was for the moment lost in dreams of the Adriatic and small villages hugging the coast. Andy said quietly to himself that he wouldn't cross the road with that bastard of a husband of hers.

"Will you be going by yourselves, or will you be taking someone along to help out?" asked Andy. Harry glared at him in a threatening manner, but he need not have worried as Andy had decided not to mention what he had seen.

"We'll take along Bob's brother's wife, when Bob's brother died, she seemed lost, not knowing what she wanted to do, so she spends quite a bit of time with us. It helps me, because I can't keep the house as clean and tidy as I'd like, and it helps her financially to provide me with some care. And we all get on so well, we have lots of things in common," said Elisabeth.

Andy smiled to himself, while thinking that the woman in the car who he had seen with Bob. It was most likely the sister-in-law.

"Nothing like keeping it in the family," said Andy quietly.

Harry cleared his throat loudly as if to say to Andy, leave it alone.

"I bet they have threesomes," added Andy, he turned to Harry and asked him once again. 'I bet they have threesomes! What do you think?"

"How the hell do I know!" growled Harry. Andy would not let the matter go.

"He's got it made, really, when you think about it. Elisabeth is his wife, dutiful and loving. He's shagging his sister-in-law, and Elisabeth is paying her for some domestic help. He's definitely found his niche in life. He looks a greasy bastard! I didn't like him the first time that I saw him. He's typical of his type, possibly got through life without dirtying his hands, never had to struggle for anything. She's definitely too good for him. I can't understand how she finished up with him."

Harry made a noise that sounded like a motorbike starting up before he spoke. "She loves him, always has loved him, and these faults, or whatever you might call them, are of little importance to her. She's clearly decided what's important, and what's not, so don't be so judgemental, because you aren't fully aware of the facts."

Andy stared at Harry in disbelief! "You're the most judgemental person that I have ever met! So don't start telling me how to think!. There's an obvious difference, I'm being judgemental, but it's based upon experience and not just prejudice, therefore it's acceptable."

"What facts? Don't give me such a load of bullshit and expect me to accept it as though it's the gospel. He could have left her anytime if he'd wanted, he works fulltime, he doesn't live on her income, they go everywhere together and they're happy," said Harry.

"That's just on the surface in order to keep up appearances.

She can't be happy, she's probably thinking if he's having sex with my sister-in-law, when is he going to say that he's moving into a place with her permanently. She feels trapped, she has to let him do what he wants, or she'll lose him; that's her line of thinking," said Andy with some confidence.

"You're wrong, but then again, that's not unusual and it's none of our business at the end of the day." Harry yawned, and said that he was already tired as he had not slept well.

"Do you think Bernard might want some fish and chips?" asked Andy "after all, he's been up today and taken in the fresh air, it should have given him an appetite."

"I don't know," said Harry, "he looks as though he's asleep."

"He always looks as though he is asleep. Ask him!" insisted Andy. Elvis walked down to Bernard's bed and looked carefully at Bernard, he then pulled the curtains around the bed and quickly walked back to the nursing station.

"There must be something wrong with Bernard," said Harry.

"The fresh air was too much for him!" laughed Andy. The nurse and Elvis entered the curtains. Soon a doctor appeared and then left the unit.

"Does he want any fish and chips?" shouted Andy. Elvis came from behind the curtains and came up to Andy's bed. "I don't think that he'll want any, he's dead."

"He was alive this afternoon," said Andy, feeling totally stupid and embarrassed at his earlier comments. "Well, take it from me, he's bloody dead now," said Elvis in a serious tone of voice.

"Does this mean that the fish and chips will be a bit late?" enquired Harry who tried to lighten the dark mood that had descended upon the room.

"I don't think that I want any," said Elisabeth, her excitement suddenly having left her.

"I don't fancy them anymore, either," added Andy.

"Best leave it then," said Harry, not wanting to eat alone and thinking it was inconsiderate of Bernard dying when they were asking him if he wanted some fish and chips. After a few minutes Harry said. "Don't you think that it's odd? Life is so odd." He paused for his words to sink in. "He had got up for the first time in months, sat outside and had a smoke, and then he dies, without a word, or a goodbye – it's bloody strange. What kind of life is that? There's no sense or reason! That could be any of us in a few years time," added Harry.

"I think that I have a few years to go yet!" said Andy in mock indignation. "I'm a young, virile man."

"This will soon age you," said Harry. "Even if I say it myself though, and believe me it's true, you could have some interesting times ahead of you." He quickly added, "I didn't say 'good times,' I said 'interesting,' there's a big difference, don't forget it."

Andy thought about the day that had gone. What was it Bernard had said? There is no purpose to life. It had been a little bit different to recent days, he thought, and for some inexplicable reason, he looked forward to the following day, as this day had been nothing but information and events that were depressing.

Even the social worker who had come down to discuss his housing needs, had said that the authority did realise what he needed, and as authorities go, he was fortunate, as they were more cooperative and understanding than most. Andy had explained what he thought he needed, and his ideas seemed to illicit a favourable response.

It was a shame about Bernard, though, as he seemed an interesting old man, not the usual miserable old sod who has seen nothing, done nothing, and been nowhere, yet expects everyone to listen and accept what they say just because they are old. Ignorance is not confined to the young, thought Andy. Who then thought that statement was a bit profound, and that he was almost beginning to sound like Harry. I had better be careful or I could be old before my time, he thought.

He was about to try and go to sleep when a thought occurred to him.

"Are you awake Harry?" he said, in a voice that was almost a whisper. Harry grunted in the affirmative.

"I've been thinking about something," continued Andy. Harry grunted again to indicate that he was listening, but under duress.

"It's about what you said earlier, about not getting an orgasm. Are you really sure about it? Totally sure?"

"I bloody knew what you were going to say! I should've kept my mouth shut. I'm totally certain. Get to sleep, and don't try and play with yourself - it won't work, it'll only make it sore," said Harry whilst pulling the sheet up around his shoulders.

He quickly added, "you might get phantom orgasms, though some do, and some don't." Harry was about to go into some detail but decided against the idea. A

Andy's interest had been gained and he said, "what are those? They sound interesting! No one has mentioned those before."

Harry smiled to himself, "I'll tell you in the morning if you remind me, but don't get excited about them, as you might never get one."

"There's just one more thing before you go to sleep, and this is serious."

Harry pushed back the sheet. "What is it that's so serious and can't wait?"

Andy was tentative. "Please, don't take this the wrong way, will you? I don't want to sound as though I'm interfering or anything." Harry assured him that whatever it was he would not take it the wrong way.

Andy took a deep breath before speaking. "Well it's about your daughter."

Harry's full attention had been obtained at the mention of his daughter.

"Don't you think that it's about time you got in touch with her? Time moves quickly, that's all that I have to say."

He awaited Harry's reply, expecting to be told to mind his own business. Harry was about to tell him where to go, when he stopped himself. He was right, Andy was right, of course, he should make contact, life is too short, look what's just happened to Bernard. Harry knew it was his responsibility - he is her father, he reminded himself. Why has he waited so long? Why hasn't he done it before? he asked himself. He thought about it some more and could not understand his own lack of action over the years. It had taken a conversation with Andy, who was a relative stranger, to bring what had lingered at the back of his mind out into the open, where it now seemed acceptable to think about it. He quickly made his mind up that in the morning he would try and find her, he thought about it some more and he felt better.

"Are you still awake?" he asked Andy, who had his back to him. Andy grunted, awaiting a rebuke for his suggestion.

Harry continued, "if you keep practicing, you might get an half orgasm." At that point he burst out laughing. "There's no such bloody thing! Who has heard of an half orgasm.?"

Andy also laughed, but he could not understand why, it's a bloody strange life he thought, and this is a bloody strange place.

"And while we're talking seriously, there's something else that I think you should know," said Harry. He did not wait for a response before continuing. "There's more to a relationship than sexual intercourse, and take note, I'm using the correct terminology, which means I am being serious."

Andy nodded and then waited in anticipation.

Harry placed his hands at the back of his head and stared ahead while he spoke as though his thoughts were coming from deep within him.

"There's warmth and understanding that can be created over time, also the pleasure of touch and taste. An understanding of your partner to the extent that being physically close gives you a level of pleasure that is exceptional. Just touching and feeling the warmth from one another is so wonderful. You don't even have to say anything, the being together and the closeness..." He paused as if to try and find the correct words. "If you have real feelings for your partner, then over a period of time you'll find that you can share something very special, a physical and mental closeness that almost makes you one person. As though your minds and bodies have joined, a form of harmony, I suppose," he added. "It might sound strange, but that is out there awaiting you, if you can find it. It's something very special, and just because you have acquired a disability, it doesn't mean that you've lost everything."

Harry looked across at Andy. "I hope you understand what I've been saying."

Andy said that he thought he understood in order to encourage Harry to enlarge on the subject. "What you're saying, in simplistic terms, is that there's more to life than sex."

"No, I did not say that," said Harry in exasperation. "It's part sexual, the sex is important, but it's somehow much more. It's hard to explain, but if and when you feel that way about someone, you'll understand.

"You're just past desiring sex. You're older than you think," said Andy laughing.

Harry grunted to show his irritation, "I'm trying to pass onto you valuable information, and you haven't the ability to recognise it. Obviously your limited education was wasted upon you, they should have sent someone else who might have made a useful contribution to society."

Andy grinned and then laughed quietly.

"One day, I might come across a young person who has a modicum of sensitivity and intelligence," he said under his breath but loud enough for Andy to hear.

Harry had the time to let his mind wonder again. Although during this particular night he had decided to think in a more structured manner. He thought of his daughter and he thought about his future, he was still relatively young, well, young in mind and spirit, he mused. It is time I did something positive, something worthwhile, he thought. He continued with this train of thought. I can't spend the rest of my life as a member of a sub culture, a group drifting along without direction. He now knew that he wanted to participate in society again, to push aside the negative aspects that had often effected his life and to get on with living. He was a realist and he understood the existing constraints, but he had decided that with the new day he would start to try and live again, although it would not be the first time he had told himself that. He also knew that it was not going to be easy. Society and conditions had not improved for disabled people in recent years. If anything life had, for many, become more difficult, as everyone seemed to be living under a threat of having their care package removed, or their income cut. Pressures that disabled people could well do without. But as Harry saw it, he had no choice but to try and go forward the best he could, and deal with whatever life decided to throw at him. He no longer expected life to be kind or compassionate, he knew that no favours would ever come his way. He had felt the pain and the hurt that life can bring with it. But there was no way back, no waving of an imaginary wand. No one would reach down and help him. There were no guardian angels watching over you. He would attempt to shape his own future, but he knew that in reality he was still, to a large extent, under the influence of forces outside of his control. He knew that the professional talkers on disability issues would pretend otherwise, but he tried to avoid such types due to them being dangerous because of their ignorance. His experience had taught him that talking about something and doing it were often a long way apart.

But at that moment, the difference was he now felt like fighting the system again, he had not felt that way for a long time and somehow it came as a good feeling. What a difference a day can make, he thought. He then laughed remembering that it was the title of a song. And it's amazing how someone's death can motivate you and help get things in perspective. It then dawned upon him that he did not really have to fight the system anymore, or at least to the extent that he had in the past. He was reasonably secure financially, and if short of money, he knew how to earn some if the worst came to the worst. He had a good property, and there was the possibility of expansion with some of the buildings he was refurbishing, quite a few possibilities, he thought to himself.

Like Andy, Harry was disappointed at Bernard's death. He wasn't sad; he accepted the situation, and he had been looking forward to getting Bernard's view on one or two books. Or, to be more precise, arguing over aspects of particular books that Harry had already argued over a number of times in the past. I suppose Bernard would have a view on these things, it's a pity he had to die, just when we were starting to get to know him. It was a bit of bad luck, thought Harry. He then thought about his daughter. He imagined that she would be sophisticated, and intelligent; he then thought, that being the case, she might not want to know him, as she might be a snob or not very understanding. He reassured himself by thinking that she would be too bright to be insensitive, and after all, she was his daughter. Harry had never suffered from modesty.

CHAPTER THIRTEEN

Harry was restless, he had presumed wrongly that he would easily fall asleep. He turned over on his side and looked at Andy to see if he was still awake. He was now feeling almost positive, and he wanted to talk, he wanted to expand upon the bits concerning his life that he had already imparted to Andy.

"Do you still want to hear my story?" asked Harry, while hoping that Andy had not fallen asleep. Andy grunted in the affirmative.

"Are you awake? Or are you asleep? Give me a sign?" asked Harry loudly, making sure that he would be awake irrespective.

"Bloody stupid question," said Andy. "Get on with it then."

Harry coughed and cleared his throat. He paused for a moment and concentrated his thoughts wanting to ensure accuracy. Harry did not want to tell only part of his story as it would not give anything like an accurate picture. If anything, he would prefer not to discuss his life if he could not discuss it in some detail. He felt that there was little point in recounting his past only for it to be misunderstood by someone who did not know him very well, or anything about him, yet still be in a position to be capable of putting a strange and distorted interpretation on his thoughts and his life.

Why this was important to him, he did not fully understand, and he was not going to analyse the situation, but it was important. He needed to be understood.

"It's a long story," said Harry, as if to warn Andy. "But if you're sure you want to hear it, and you must consider it was a few years ago," he continued with this preamble. "And to some extent some things were a bit different then, especially peoples' attitudes."

Andy groaned in a theatrical manner and said that he was sure he wanted to hear it, as long as it wasn't too boring and wallowing in self-pity. He had only enough pity for himself at the moment.

Harry said "Bollocks! This is important. It's almost the sum total of my life, encapsulated just for you." He grunted once more and then began.

"Tell me when you've heard enough, won't you?"

"If you're going to tell me your life history, for Christ's sake, please get on with it, before you drift off into senility," said Andy with some impatience. "Is there something you are scared to tell me? Have you done something so embarrassing, or what? Get on with it, before you forget what you are supposedly going to say."

They were suddenly interrupted by noise coming from the central part of the unit. "What's going on?" asked Andy, as a young nurse ran past the bottom of his bed.

"Don't worry about it," said Harry, "Solvent, who came in yesterday, has fallen out of bed."

"Why do they call him Solvent? Or shouldn't I ask?" said Andy.

"Well, ever since anyone can remember, he's been on some stuff or other, and no one can remember what he was like before he started taking whatever it is he takes. Somehow, he gets hold of the stuff, and he'll be stoned, then he turns over and falls out of bed. He never seems to hurt himself, well, he never complains, so he mustn't feel anything. He's a nice fellow, although he never understands a bloody word you're saying, but he seems to nod in the right places. Anyway, it seems as though they've managed to get him back into bed. It seems as though they are going to get a doctor, so something must be wrong. No, I was wrong – they're not bothering with a doctor, so he must be lucid, or as lucid as he gets, which can be confusing. Have a talk with sometime, he's an interesting fellow really. He told me his wife left him and his dog died the very same day, he said he wasn't bothered about his wife, but he really missed his dog as it used to go for his wife if she raised her voice." Harry burst out laughing at that point.

"Another great line of his was that his wife only wanted him for sex, and when he refused on the grounds that he thought she was too ugly to fuck, that set the rot in, regarding their relationship." The thought of it caused Harry to chuckle. "I must admit, I saw her once, and believe me, she was bloody ugly! Normally, I can accept those types as they have interesting features, but in her case, no, she was just plain ugly.

"I've just been thinking that when I leave here, I'll have a total change, a good holiday, I'll take someone I can get along with, and we'll live in luxury for awhile. I don't need culture, or education, but something nice simple and pleasurable. One of the better hotels, somewhere in Europe, preferably with good views. I know the place, in fact I know a few places that are so bloody good, it's a pleasure to wake up and," he suddenly paused. "It was just a thought."

"You've suddenly thought how much it might cost you! Luxury hotels, taking someone with you! That doesn't sound like the Harry we all know, the greedy sod who is a legend for being tight. "

"Right! Let's get back to where I was." Harry gave another little cough and then began. "We were both around twenty, and we'd been going together off and on for nearly two years. I'd known her at school, although she was in a class below me. I hadn't really noticed her at the time, but it's one of those strange things in life. Suddenly, you see this girl, and you think she's wonderful! The most wonderful person that God created. And you can't understand why you'd not noticed her before. After all, you'd spent four or five years of your life at school with her. Anyway, I met her at a dance. I was with some friends and she was with a few friends. We were attracted to each other right away. I didn't have to say anything really, I just looked at her and right away I knew that I was going home with her that night."

Andy interrupted and asked how much he had drunk.

"If you aren't being serious, I will not continue!" snapped Harry angrily. Andy decided that he should not interrupt as Harry was taking this serious.

Harry continued, "I walked her to her home, which did not seem far at the time, but it was a few miles away from where I lived. It seemed as though we arrived at her home almost instantly. I can't remember what we talked about as it went so quickly. I kissed her a few times and I could feel that she liked me, and I mean really liked me."

Andy was about to interrupt and ask if she was gagging for it, but then thought better of it.

"I left her upon the doorstep. I felt strange, almost unreal. I didn't want it to ever end. The evening had been perfect." Harry's tone of voice had softened as he described her. "She looked so bloody good, and she tasted so good. I really

271

remember how good she tasted. Soft and sweet; subtle. She was really wonderful, something very special." His eyes momentarily glazed over at the thought of her.

"You mean that you didn't shag her then?" said Andy getting interested.

Harry did not seem to hear Andy. He continued quickly as if he had suddenly decided that he wanted to remove those thoughts from his mind. His voice now took on a more casual and relaxed tone as though he was unaware of anyone listening. He looked at Andy and added.

"Until then, as far as I was concerned, something special was if you managed to get their pants off before they were half way home." He wanted to emphasise this point. "That was the important marker those days. If you had walked them more than half way home without successfully getting anywhere, you knew you'd blown it. You had to make your moves before you reached half distance. It was all part of the strategy. It might surprise you, but not everyone had a car nearly twenty years ago, well not everyone aged twenty."

"You don't have to bother with such things nowadays as strategy," said Andy in a casual tone. "They're all desperate for a good seeing to."

Harry ignored the comment. He continued, "anyway, she must have felt the same about me, as she agreed to go out with me the following night. I left her and ran home like a schoolboy! I was so bloody excited I'd never felt like that. It's hard to explain exactly, now, how it really felt. Almost like winning the cup and scoring the winning goal, but better than that, so much better. You felt so good, you couldn't believe that anyone else could feel so good. It was impossible for anyone to feel better. I think that's as near as I can get to how it felt." Harry paused for a while, his mind trying to recollect those moments.

"Love at first sight," added Andy. "Or more likely lust at first sight."

Harry pretended not to have heard him and continued. "Anyway, we went out on a regular basis. I was happy for the first time in my life, I mean, really happy," he said this loudly, as if to emphasise the point. "And she was happy and felt the same for some reason, although I couldn't understand why she loved me.

She actually thought I was perfect, I couldn't say, or do, anything wrong. That's how we felt about one another. We just didn't need anyone or anything else, I would have willingly died for her."

"Sorry to interrupt," said Andy "but this is something I need to know in order to get a better picture of events. What did she look like this person you were willing to die for?"

Harry grunted again then sighed deeply before answering. "Her hair was just cut short of her shoulders, really well cut, nothing fancy, just well cut. It was very black; it shined because of the intense black. She had a nice oval shaped face, with a superb bone structure, very photogenic. And a wonderful, sensuous mouth. In fact, a fabulous mouth that you couldn't wait to kiss. She had large, dark eyes that you could look into for an eternity." He paused trying to visualise her accurately. "She wasn't too tall, about 5 '4, but in high heeled shoes she looked fabulous, superb legs and a delicate figure, not big and busty like those blond types."

"OK. I think I get the picture - a bit like Audrey Hepburn," said Andy, who then, while smiling, quickly added "whoever she was."

He now realised that Harry was probably going a little bit over the top in his appraisal of his ex-wife, but he thought that it was not something he should mention.

"She was everything that I wanted," said Harry seriously. "My mates really envied me, and one or two of them really fancied her, but she wasn't interested in them at all. And that made me feel even better. On the downside, and there is usually a downside, her parents didn't particularly like me. They thought I wasn't good enough for their only daughter. But parents are always protective, I thought, so it didn't bother me too much at the time, although I was realistic about the situation. If she'd been my daughter I would not have wanted her going with someone like me," added Harry, he briefly laughed at that point. "Not that there was anything wrong with me," he quickly added. "We went everywhere together, and just loved being together' we didn't want to be apart. I wanted to touch her hand, or her arm all of the time. I could have just stood still, looking into her eyes for hours. I know it now sounds like something out of a television play." Harry paused at this point as thought he was

273

reluctant to continue. He cleared his throat again and then continued. "When she became pregnant, it was a bit of a shock." Harry looked at Andy as though he expected some comment. "It wasn't like it is now. I had to think about her parents' reaction. I have to admit the thought of it terrified me. Her father was a big man, a really nasty bastard, and short tempered. I knew life had suddenly taken a turn for the worse, and we talked about the various possibilities, even emigrating or running away. We agreed that we definitely did not want an abortion. We loved one another and we knew that we wanted to get married one day, so we thought that we should go ahead and do it earlier. It was going to be our child, something special. Something that was created by us; it would be another living human being. Then the ordeal began."

Andy interrupted him. "You managed to get this paragon of virtue pregnant? She didn't decline your sexual approaches? You didn't have to hold her down, or restrain her in any way?"

"We were normal! What did you expect me to do? I was healthy, she was healthy, we wanted each other."

"Don't shout! I was only trying to get a clear picture of the situation."

"We had decided that the sooner we told her parents the better. It didn't matter telling mine, as all the women in our family had to get married; it was normal practice and once I had left it would mean more room for the others, so no one made any waves; but her parents were something different. I remember sitting in their kitchen. I was frightened I do not mind admitting it. I tried to look strong, and confident, but I was almost wetting myself. I promised myself at the time that I would not go through that again, that there must be some other way. We told her mother first, and she seemed to take it quite well, I thought, almost too well. In fact, she didn't seem surprised. I was stupid, as I was lulled into a false sense of security by the cunning bitch. I was starting to relax and think that it wasn't going to be such a trying experience after all."

"I can see you really liked your mother-in-law," added Andy while holding back a smile.

Harry grunted something but continued. "But as soon as her father came home she changed, her mother just couldn't wait to tell him. 'They have something to tell you,' she said, while at the same time expressing disapproval by her grim expression and her arms folded across her chest. I wondered why a few minutes earlier she had seemed reasonable and now in front of her husband her attitude had changed. It wasn't long before I realised she was choosing safe ground, experience had taught her that she needed to be on his side. I explained to him the situation as best I could in the circumstances, and of our desire to get married. He looked stunned for a moment, then he looked at me carefully, his eyes glinting with anger. At that moment I thought that my life was coming to an end. I was sure that he was going to grab me by the throat and kick the shit out of me, but he didn't. He just sat there glaring at me, while choking slightly but saying nothing, although his face was purple. I thought with a bit of luck he might have a stroke, it would be better if he dropped dead at that moment, but the inconsiderate bugger didn't. The tension was killing me! I dare not move or twitch. I thought at the time it would be easier if he just hit me and got it over with, then someone would collect my body later."

Andy was listening eagerly at this point expecting some violent outcome.

"He finally got up from the table. He stared hard at his wife, and then at Judith, then back at me. 'What did I bloody well tell you!' he shouted at his wife before pointing at me, 'He's no fucking good and he never will be! She has ruined her life for that fucking article there,' he said it while shaking his fist at me. He then suddenly went storming out of the room, it was like a scene from a play, it just didn't feel normal. Or it might be that I was so terrified I didn't feel that the whole experience was real. For a minute I thought I must have missed something: I'm still sitting here, and I'm alive, with nothing broken."

"What did he do then?" asked Andy.

"Nothing! Bugger all! He just didn't speak to me until the day of the wedding, which didn't bother me much, but it upset Judith. She couldn't understand why he was so upset. They'd always been very close and she thought that he would have understood." Harry paused for a moment before continuing. "That's something I never understood about her. She actually believed that her father would be understanding and welcome me into the family with open arms. As far as I was concerned, he looked upon me as the filthy little sod who had seduced his innocent daughter, and got her pregnant without her having played any part in it. And in his eyes I should have been at least castrated, with rusty blunt instruments.

"At the end of the day there was nothing that he could do really, but it didn't seem like that at the time; the bugger intimidated me. The wedding went quite well, considering, there was only one fight when her oldest brother made some comment regarding what he would have done to me if he'd known earlier about her pregnancy. At which point my oldest brother had the bad taste to mention something to the effect that Judith's brother should keep his mouth shut, as he'd got his wife and another young woman pregnant at the same time, which was shortly before he was married. A few punches were thrown and a few glasses was knocked over, but apart from that, everything went well." Harry started laughing to himself and found it difficult to continue. He finally regained his composure.

"The best bit was when her father decided to speak to me. I must admit that by that time he'd drunk quite a bit. He put his arm on my shoulder, looked me in the eye and said, 'It's no good lad. I can't pretend to like you; in fact, I would say I cannot stand the fucking sight of you. However, the deed is done, and we have to make the best of a bad job, if you ever hurt her I will shoot you where you stand,' those were his words. His grip started to tighten on my shoulder. 'We must make the best of it,' he said again. He then threatened me again and told me what he would do at me if I ever hurt her or let her down. I remember just stuttering that I loved her, and would never hurt her, he did not appear to hear what I said, and if he did, he showed no signs of it. His grip tightened on my shoulder. I thought that whatever happens, I'm not gong to give him the pleasure of thinking that he is inflicting pain on me. The bastard really hurt me. I was bruised for a month but I got through it without being hospitalised, and that seemed to me at the time a bonus. It then occurred to me that his threat to shoot me was a bluff, as he didn't own a gun. For some reason that didn't give me any feeling of security at the time.

"Anyway, the honeymoon made up for it. We had three days in

London. We didn't see much of the capital, we were too occupied. It was the first time she'd been to London, and when we got back home everyone said 'did you see this and did you see that?' It was as though no one remembered that it was our honeymoon. What do you do and see on your honeymoon?" asked Harry, "we might as well have been in Greenland for all we cared. Looking back, it was a stupid place to go really, but it sounded glamorous at the time I suppose, a big hotel in the west end. Staying in hotels tended to be either rare or non-existent in our family at that time. A week at Blackpool or Skegness was more the norm in the early years, then a few years later on, off to Benidorm with the lads. We really enjoyed ourselves though, it was our first bit of real freedom and we were man and wife, which meant to us that we now had a licence to indulge ourselves. We learned more about each other on our honeymoon than we had done in previous months. I'll admit we went over the top; we couldn't get enough of one another, we rarely left the room except for food. When I found out they had room service, we didn't bother moving, we could have still been there now.

"Then it was back to reality, back to the factory for a short time before I obtained a job driving and delivering books and such like to local bookshops and libraries. Just thinking about it makes me shudder. It was so boring, but it gave me the time to go and study at the local technical college. I was studying history and art. It sounded impressive to my friends, most of whom at that time only studied the racing pages. I'd decided that I wanted to be a teacher, looking back I can't think why I'd thought that, it still baffles me today. I needed a couple more exams before the teacher training college would accept me and it was hard work studying and working at the same time," said Harry.

"I do know that as I've done it myself," said Andy feeling annoyed that Harry had forgotten. He decided that he was not going to fall for the old routine that everything was harder a few years back. "It's harder now," said Andy "getting in first, there's too much pressure."

Harry was about to argue with him when he stopped himself and continued with his story, he was not going to allow himself to be distracted. "We arrived back and we went into our first home together. A two up and two down terrace house near her parents. It was the last place I wanted to live but it was affordable, and not in bad condition; a bit damp, but all houses seemed damp around where I lived. We weren't buying it, of course, just renting, but that's what most young couples did, as getting a council house in a decent area wasn't easy. You could have had the choice of a few hundred in some areas, but even by our standards those areas were more like the killing fields than places for people to live. And as for buying a house, it didn't really enter our minds at the time, but nowadays everyone wants their own home because it's seen as an investment. Which proves that you can fool most of the people some of the time."

"Why don't you get on with the story instead of throwing in your personal prejudices, as it causes me to lose track of where you'd got to."

Harry seemed to recognise the validity of the point. "As I was saying. The important bit was that it was ours. Our first home with nobody to bother us - it seemed too good to be true. It was like a dream come true, everything you thought you would ever want was suddenly yours. I thought at the time that life could not get any better than this."

"What did she say?" asked Andy, who now seemed genuinely interested.

"She felt the same as I," said Harry. "We were like one person; we could feel what each of us was thinking, we didn't have to say anything, we could just look at one another and feel something so good and so special it was indescribable." Harry paused for a moment before continuing. "It was the best part of my life - I'm sure that nothing could have been better.

"Then the baby came along and to my amazement it seemed as though it could get better. Both families loved the baby. Suddenly, no one could do too much for us. Even her father started to like me. Well, to say he liked me might have been an exaggeration, but he at least talked to me without seeming to threaten me, which was an improvement. And unlike some women who'd just had a baby, Judith blossomed, that's the only word that describes it, she looked even better." Harry sighed once more visualising his young wife.

"Everything seemed to be going so bloody well, I should've known that it just could not last," said Harry whose tone of voice suddenly changed.

"Go on! What happened?" asked Andy, with impatience.

"What happened?" said Harry. "This happened, just driving along, going to my job, everything right with the world and then this." He stopped for the moment while waiting for his words to have some impact. As Andy did not say anything Harry continued. "Just driving along and out of a side street a car pulled out. I swerved to miss him and hit an oncoming car. Finished up in this place. I didn't know what was happening to me."

Andy grunted as though he understood the last remarks.

"What do you remember of the first few weeks?" asked Harry.

"I can't remember my first week here, yet I remember my accident," said Andy. He continued to tell Harry that some instances were very clear in his mind, while others were not, although he had tried hard to remember as much as he could.

Harry told him that some memories might come back, but others might stay locked away for some unknown reason. "Why we're allowed to remember some things and not others doesn't seem logical. I've often heard that it's the mind that's protecting you from remembering bad and painful experiences, but I think that's bollocks. I don't think there's a sound explanation. One thing I know for certain is that I've had some painful experiences that my mind has not blocked out. It might have been better if it had blocked them out," he sighed once again a deep sigh of regret.

Andy thought that Harry probably would not continue to talk as it seemed as though he had talked himself into a mood of gloom and misery. Just as he was thinking this Harry started talking again.

"Are you sure that you want to hear this stuff?" he asked Andy. Andy grunted so Harry continued. "I remember an argument about skull traction. They couldn't decide whether or not I needed it, as I had some arm and hand movement. Anyway, they decided to do it and they wheeled me into the treatment room. I had no bloody idea what they were going to do until this doctor gave a brief explanation that they were going to attach this metal equipment to my head, which would help me. At the time I wasn't interested or felt capable of thinking, so I just listened.

Then came the shock when the doctor produced a hand drill, those old-fashioned brace and bit things. I wondered, as one would, what is he going to do with that. It then dawned upon me that he was going to drill into my head with the bloody thing. They turned my head on one side and injected me with a local anaesthetic I think, I can't remember that bit accurately because I was so terrified as to what they were about to do. I remember it so clearly drilling into my skull, the thought of it still makes me shudder," said Harry. "I could feel the grinding into the bone. I thought that they would suddenly break through my skull into my brain and that would be it. totally finished, or brain damaged. I was really shitting myself at the thought of it. Then they turned my head over and did the same to the other side, and for some reason this seemed worse. All the time a young nurse was saying 'Relax! Everything is fine. Don't worry, it's going OK.' At the time I thought you wouldn't be saying that if it was your head they were drilling into. When they were finished they added some weights, which pulled my head back once they had laid me flat on my back. I thought they were going to pull my head off, but they didn't. It was just after that when some things became vague."

Andy nodded in agreement as though he understood.

Harry continued, "I remember hearing a nurse say, 'you have some visitors, wake up, he's had a bad night, but if he sleeps through the day he won't sleep at night. Come on Harry, wake up your wife is here.' I could hear all of this, but it didn't seem to matter for some reason. I tried hard to open my eyes but they didn't want to respond. I tried hard until they partially opened. Everything seemed unclear, yet I could see her leaning over me. She kissed my cheek, but it was so soft I hardly felt it. I tried to focus better and as I did so I could see that she had been crying; her eyes were red and sore; I wondered why. At that time it didn't dawn upon me that I was the cause. I clearly remember the look of fear, mixed with sadness, on her face. I wanted to ask her what was the matter. For some reason I couldn't ask questions. To this day I don't know why the obvious questions did not come into my mind. For all intents and purposes, I appeared to be thinking normally, but it was that tiredness that seemed to control me at the time. It was as though few things really mattered just then, I was too tired to bother, or to ask. But I could see her, and hear her, and she looked so sad. Then my mother and father arrived. They must have been waiting on the corridor. 'Don't worry, you're in a really good place, they'll look after you,' said my father. His facial expression suggested that all was not well with the world, but even then I hadn't the energy or the compulsion to ask any questions. My mother told me to try and get some sleep, that I needed my strength. She looked really sad and had obviously been crying. The following days were a mixture of crystal clear reality and surrealism." Harry concentrated trying to accurately recall the events.

"Days ran into nights, it was difficult to say on what day a particular thing happened. Judith was there beside my bed for most of the time, while her mother was looking after our daughter. I kept asking about our daughter and she told me that she would bring her to see me soon. I just accepted what she said. I accepted everything I was told. She constantly told me how much she loved me and how she would help me get better. Even though it was sometimes painful for me to move my head, or have it knocked, it felt so good when her face was next to mine, she was soft and warm, and she felt so bloody good. Even though by this time I was feeling some aches and pains, the closeness of her took most of them away. In a few days time though, your head clears a little, and reasoning creeps in and you start to ask a few questions of your visitors and the staff. You accept most of the answers, you never think that there could be a reason for people to be evasive. But it's when you start talking to other patients, or overhearing conversations that you really start to think. When you learn that the fellow in the bed across has already been at home for years and has come back due to something that needs treatment, you start thinking: Why is he still using a wheelchair after all of this time? Then you mention it to someone and they imply that you're different to him, and to disregard it as you've not the same problems. You relax a little, thinking poor sod, little knowing.

The conversation was briefly interrupted. "Do you want some tea?" asked Pauline. Harry and Andy said that they did. "Can you keep your voices down as well?; it's the middle of the night and some people want to sleep."

"We're keeping you awake are we?" said Andy, with a hint of sarcasm.

"You did say you wanted some tea didn't you?" said Pauline, looking at him in a way that threatened that tea would not be forthcoming if Andy continued to be sarcastic.

"I'll have some toast, as well," said Harry while quickly adding the word "please. We haven't had any fish and chips tonight; old Bernard died and that seemed to remove everyone's appetite."

"Yes, it was sad," she said while turning away.

"I'm having a quick smoke," said Harry.

"They'll shoot you for that," said Andy "it's a capital offence in here. Is there no end to the risks you are willing to take?"

Harry grunted at the sarcasm. "They can do bugger all, in reality," said Harry feeling a little bit bolshi. "Who'll bother at this time? The non-smokers are all off duty, and those on nights don't care." He lit up and inhaled deeply. "That's good! That is so good," he was about to say better than sex when he changed his mind. "That's almost as good as sex," he said while smiling as if to emphasise the point.

"No, it bloody isn't," said Andy, who then added you must not have been doing it right. "What's that you are smoking? It smells like…" Harry stopped him, "it's purely for medicinal reasons." Harry ignored him and started to talk about the past again. To Andy's surprise he was keen to listen, it was helping him understand some of his own feelings and also too answer a few questions. "Anyway," said Harry "time passed slowly as it does when you're not feeling good. But I was lucky, as one or two of the patients had only been admitted a couple of weeks before me and their condition seemed similar. So I tended to measure my progress against theirs. In an unspoken way there was competition between us, although it didn't feel like that at the time. We became close friends, really good friends."

Andy interrupted. "Where are they now?"

"They're dead," said Harry abruptly. "They were good friends, they were also very special and you never forget them. They meant a lot to me. In fact, they were some of the closest friendships I've ever had. What would they be doing now?" he said out loud. "We were all without money, borrowed from each other and totally trusted each other. Looked after each other's interest, when we were going through the usual problems we cared for one another, and that's real friendship. And we needed to, as a few of the nurses didn't give a thought about us, some were what I can only say as being sadistic in their attitude. The enjoyed watching you in pain and discomfort."

Andy looked as though he was finding Harry's statement difficult to believe.

"It's true! Although you'll not accept it until you observe it for yourself," he added, "there were a couple of sadistic bastards working here, and everyone knew what they were like, but for some reason they were never sacked. They were evil, made new patients lives a bloody misery, I hope they suffered the…" He did not bother to finish the sentence, realising that it was difficult for Andy to accept that such individuals as described would have been allowed to work with people, let alone patients.

He then continued without further explanation. "The time came for me to have the skull traction out. And I'll admit I was not looking forward to the process. Don't get me wrong, I wanted the thing out, but I could envisage a considerable amount of pain. I clearly remember asking a member of staff about it who said: 'You'll not feel a thing. It's over in seconds.' When they had levered it out of my skull, with bits of flesh clinging to the metal, the first thing I did was to tell the member of staff what a lying bastard he was. It really hurt, felt as though they were pulling my head off.

"But what seemed more unusual was that with the weights off, my head felt as though it was disappearing into my shoulders. It was a very strange sensation. I think it was the day after they sat me up in bed for a short time, trying to acclimatise me to an upright position. Naturally my head started spinning and my breathing became more difficult. I passed out for the first time in my life! It was a lousy experience. When I came round they had lowered the bed and everything seemed back to normal. A nurse said 'it'll be better the next time.' I thought that there has got to be a better way than this, but there wasn't, of course. Getting up was just as bad the first few times, it felt as though my head was on a concrete block, devoid of any sensation. And I wouldn't move my head from side to side; I was scared that something would break. Stupid really but that's how it seemed at the time."

"I really looked forward to getting up," said Andy "I'm not sure what I expected, but it wasn't what I expected. For some reason it was a disappointment. I expected something better, something dramatic, it's hard to explain really."

"I know what you mean," said Harry sympathetically "it's not as good as you expected. I can't remember accurately exactly what I expected. I think that the whole thing was so strange any expectations I had were probably lost.

"But it got better once we started to explore the hospital. Previously we'd heard about places but had no idea where they were, so it became something of an adventure learning to use what movement you had, while trying to move the chair a bit further each day. It was a damn sight harder than working," added Harry. "But somehow exciting in a strange, trivial sort of way," he added, "but at that time, anything different seemed somehow to be an achievement, or progress in the right direction. Although no one suggested what the right direction was. Everyone seemed as clueless as one another, unless there was a secret that we were not party to. Sometimes you had a suspicion that there was something that was really important awaiting you; you couldn't place your finger upon it, but you felt it was out there. But you had no idea what it was."

"Sounds as though you were all paranoid!" said Andy.

"We might've been. We weren't feeling normal, that's a fact," said Harry seriously, "but we didn't know, so it didn't matter. There could have been some form of a holy grail but we never found it. Anyway," he continued "we explored the place, while at the same time getting used to our bodies and the lack of its compliance with our wishes. It was around this time we became friendly with a few of the nurses. This was part of the larger strategy, because if you were friendly with a nurse they could take you out, and put you back to bed. And going out to a pub or club was a desirable thing to do. A genuine part of your rehabilitation, in fact, one of the better ideas," he added. "Some of the nursing staff, who had little or no real understanding of the unit, were naturally against the idea. And they tried to have these outings stopped. Fortunately the consultant in charge had more sense and was quite happy to sanction these outings, or trips to the pub. In theory, we were supposed to arrive back on the unit in a sensible condition, but we seldom did. It was often the case that we would start arguing with some of the night staff, who resented the fact that we seemed to be enjoying ourselves.

"It was during some of these outings that relationships started between the nurses and a few of the lads. One or two ended in permanent relationships, others in unhappiness. One friend of mine started going out with a particular nurse three or four nights a week. He was keen on her and expressed his feelings to her. He arranged to meet her after he had left hospital. She turned up with her new boyfriend in tow; seemingly most of the others knew about the boyfriend, but because my friend was at home, he was unaware of the changes in the situation. She should've had the decency to tell him, but she didn't, she turned up without a blush. He felt humiliated and would have liked to have hit her there and then. Everyone could see his anger. It was years before he spoke to her again. That seemed to be one of the problems with some people," added Harry, "their insensitivity, as though it was acceptable to treat you like shit if you were disabled, and not give it another thought. As though spending time with you was a really big favour. It sounds bitter and twisted doesn't it?" asked Harry. "But it seemed as though you and your feelings were just not as important as the non-disabled. Everyone would say that you were imagining it, if you said it now, and that you're just as good as the next person, that you weren't looking at things objectively. That somehow you must have got it wrong. They say the same to black people, that they are imagining that they're being discriminated against, the patronising sods." Harry was in full flow and enjoying hearing his own voice.

He did not wait for a reply or interjection. "It was an interesting time, even if it was full of trials and tribulations," he said. "I wasn't in a great position myself at the time, but I felt sorry for those poor buggers whose wife had left them before they had a chance to go home. That seemed cruel, as though it was kicking you when you were really down, and not in a position to fight back. Sad to say, on occasion, it was quiet common. And to tell you the truth, it made you feel a bit vulnerable at the time. But then you'd think of your partner and you knew that it was different, that you had something special, something that could not really affect your relationship, or so you thought at the time.

"In truth, I don't think anyone was really rehabilitated. It was more of a matter of getting you out and home in as good a shape as possible. I was suffering from a bladder infection, but I didn't know until my GP took a urine sample. I can remember getting up every day sweating and clammy. while feeling cold; it was as though you were permanently suffering from the 'flu. Everyone said 'it's your condition, you'll just have to live with it.' There was no incentive to solve these problems, it seemed. It still confuses me when I think about it. Why didn't they give all of us a good examination before they sent us home? Why send us home with problems that we didn't understand? That's how it was at the time," he said in a more thoughtful tone of voice.

"The major problem seemed to be the accommodation. Once you were up and about you had to think about managing at home. It was obvious that I couldn't live in the existing accommodation' and money was short at that moment' but fortunately I had a court case for compensation already in the system. But the situation and everything was new to Judith and I. Neither of us had any idea how things worked, so we left it to my solicitor to get on with things. That was a mistake, a big mistake," said Harry again as if to emphasise the point. "He was totally incompetent and lost us money in the long run, or to be more precise, advised us to take what was offered, which meant that he got paid without putting much effort in, and in our ignorance, we just accepted his advice.

"At this time, I was discussing with Judith what I would need when I came home and how I would manage. It hardly occurred to me what she might be feeling. In fact I don't remember asking her anything about it, which in retrospect sounds awful and selfish. She had already told me how much she loved me, and I suppose I just accepted it without giving it any thought. There was a time when I was worried, due to my thinking about our sex life."

He then looked at Andy as though expecting him to say something, "I probably felt the way you're feeling now." Andy did not comment, although he was tempted.

"Sex was brilliant, it always had been between us, but now I realised it wasn't going to be the same. I had no sensation and could not always get an erection by stimulus. This was worrying and all sorts of ideas went through my mind, none of them were positive, I might add. I thought that she'd be dissatisfied, and that I wouldn't be able to do anything about it. Actually, the thought of it frightened me. But she was good, and she quickly reassured me, telling me that she loved me so much, nothing mattered but us being together, and that there were lots of ways to have good sex. It made me feel so good, I was looking forward to getting out of here, I could hardly wait."

"You're not exactly making me feel any better," said Andy.

"I'm being honest and open with you; if you don't want to hear this, then I'll shut up."

"I want to hear it! Go on - it's interesting," said Andy still concerned over the sexual aspects, but not wanting Harry to stop.

"Then my solicitor came to visit me, and told me that the opposition had accepted liability and made me an offer. I didn't think it was very much after listening to the stories of what others had obtained, but he insisted that in the circumstances it was a reasonable offer, and it would allow me to obtain a small, but accessible bungalow. I think that was the selling point. I could obtain suitable accommodation and quickly get out of the unit. Anyway, that's what I did. Looking back, it was a big mistake, I should have waited for a better offer, but I'd made the decision, and that was that. It's easy looking back and saying 'if only,' but life tends to be unforgiving in such situations.

"Once in the bungalow everything seemed reasonably good, or better than I had expected. Although you just can't get it out of your mind that the last time you were at home you were walking about, and that you were doing normal things. Now you're in a wheelchair, having to be helped with everything, even needing help with going to the lavatory. It felt as if I was like a large child having to be looked after, it was degrading somehow, or perhaps demeaning is a better word," said Harry. "I quickly knew that I didn't like it, but there wasn't any choice in the matter. I must confess that Judith seemed to accept things at first better than I, she never lost her patience or became angry. She always said that we were better off than many. We had our own place and it was paid for, and we had our baby and our love for each other. When she said this, it always made me feel really good, and I loved her for it. I thought that to have such a wife I was the luckiest man around. What's more, we learned to make love even better than before. It was surprisingly really good."

At this point Andy's curiosity got the better of him. "I thought that you couldn't have an orgasm?" he said. while staring intensely towards Harry.

"That's right," said Harry. "To my surprise, I found that making love to Judith felt so good, so intense, that I didn't need an orgasm for it to be pleasurable. I enjoyed giving her pleasure. And when I could feel the pleasure pulsating through her body. it gave me a lot of pleasure, I was sharing it with her."

Harry could see that Andy was unconvinced. "Believe me," said Harry "giving and sharing is good, there's a closeness that you can achieve that's wonderful. You feel closer somehow, although it's hard to explain. I tried to explain it to you earlier, but I should've realised I hadn't succeeded." Harry sounded a little disappointed at that moment, but continued.

"Of course, it would've been even better if I could have had orgasms, but they were no longer as important as I thought they were. But it does depend upon what you feel for you partner, I loved her more than you could imagine. I wanted everything for her, I was so in love with her and that was it. And we had our daughter, and she was also wonderful. Life wasn't easy though, my body tended to bugger me about like it still does, but that becomes the norm. You can't allow your body to dictate how you are going to live and what you do with your life. Sometime you need to just sit and think 'what you are going to do with your life?'. A cold, logical, approach is required." Harry was hoping that Andy was taking some of this in.

"Another good thing was that we were surviving on my income my benefits. Our income wasn't great, but we could just manage, we had no debts, we had accommodation and we acquired a small car. We both had driving lessons, we passed our test and we felt that we were doing quite well. After I'd been home about twelve months I had got into a routine, visiting the unit, going to the pub, that sort of thing. When, one day, while eating our evening meal, Judith said that she'd obtained a part-time job, and that the money would be really useful. I was surprised. I could not think for the moment. When my mind started to function I wondered how she'd obtained the job. I also wondered why she had not discussed it with me. I didn't even know that she wanted a job, I had no idea. I thought we were doing reasonably well. Looking back now. I suppose I dealt with it badly, although it probably wouldn't have made much difference. I just reacted and told her not to be stupid, that she had a baby to look after. Her reply was, do you mean you and I have a baby. That response really hurt me, she stuck the knife in, or so it seemed. I just could not understand her. She'd never said anything like that before. I was bemused with what was going on. I naturally retaliated and we had our first row. It was not a good feeling. I needed to think, and I then realised that she'd kept her frustration and fears to herself since my accident. It was an eye opener for me, it really was." Harry gently shook his head from side to side in bewilderment. "I had honestly thought that we were doing OK when we were obviously not."

"It was your baby," added Andy in a serious tone of voice.

Harry continued, "she said that she was just an unpaid servant, doing the same things day in and day out. I asked her what was it that she wanted. All she would say was she wanted a change, something else other than the same routine day after day. I remember that I asked her who was going to look after the baby. She replied that as I was the father there was no reason why I should not look after her. She quickly added, and if I couldn't manage, then her mother would assist. Her tone of voice was something that I had not experienced from her before. I then realised that she had discussed everything with her mother, everything had been carefully organised, except me. I was the last hurdle. We went to bed feeling miserable. And for the first time we didn't speak to one another. In the morning I told her that I had carefully thought about everything she had said, that it seemed sensible, and for her to go ahead if it was what she wanted. I agreed with her that the money would be useful, and that she needed a change. I didn't really mean any of it at the time. I pretended to myself that I did. In all honesty, I just could not see how I could stop her, if she'd already planned everything and made up her mind." Harry paused at this point.

"I think I could do with another cup of tea," said Harry.

Andy could see that Harry was upset. But he wasn't sure whether he was sad or angry, perhaps a bit of both, thought Andy who was enjoying listening to Harry. Andy had soon learned that by listening to the experiences of others who were on the unit it might be possible to miss some of the many hazards that were out there, waiting to make life even more difficult.

"Where was I?" said Harry, who had recovered his composure.

"You thought you could do with another cup of tea," added Andy.

"Bugger tea! Try some of this," Harry reached into his locker and produced a bottle of whiskey.

"No thanks," said Andy quickly. "It doesn't agree with me."

Harry looked at him in disbelief, and then drank out of the bottle, "that's much better!" he gasped. "I don't do this normally," he added quickly.

"No, of course not," said Andy with a touch of sarcasm.

"I bloody well don't!" said Harry loudly. Andy started to laugh, then Harry laughed. "Where was I?" said Harry. "Oh yes, it was when she had looked around for a job.

"I soon got used to the idea of looking after the baby three or four times a week, sometimes mornings, sometimes afternoons. In fact, before very long, I was enjoying it. At first, getting around the place with water and food was difficult, but once I'd planned it out, it was relatively simple."

"I just can't imagine looking after a baby!" said Andy, "it's not natural, somehow."

"Of course it's fucking natural!" he said loudly, "it's the most natural thing in the world. Men don't want to look after children, they prefer to be sat in the pub, swilling larger or whatever they drink. That's nearer the truth," said Harry.

He looked at Andy and said "I would not have missed it, one of the best experiences of my life." Tears came into his eyes. Andy briefly turned away, not wanting to embarrass him.

"I was surprised myself, I suppose," added Harry "but it was good, and besides, Judith also seemed happy, she was getting out, meeting more people and the money was useful, we were not bad off, really," said Harry with a shrug of his shoulders. "Now and again, her mother would pop round, to make sure that

I wasn't doing anything stupid. She delighted in telling me the best, or, to be more accurate, the only way, to do something. It pissed me off really, but I got her to cook the lunch on account that I was incapable of doing it properly. It wasn't long before Judith said that she'd been offered a few more hours work, that if she took them it would mean a promotion. Her mother said how good it was that she was getting on, her father said that she was a capable girl who always had a lot of potential, if she had the opportunity. What the bastard meant was she would have done well for herself if she had not met me. Anyway, she took the extra hours and everything seemed well. We were getting on together really well. I don't mind saying, but I loved her even more than the day I married her. And she looked better every day. She was exceptional, that's the only word for her. I would have done anything for her, and the best part of it, was she said how much she loved me. On the odd occasion I had mentioned my disability and the things that I could no longer do. She always stopped me before I could explain my feelings. She just used to look at me, and smile and say, 'it's of no importance I married you, your disability doesn't mean anything.' She would then sit on my knee and we would cuddle. We always finished up laughing, it felt so good, everything felt right. Those are things you can't forget," he said.

Andy just nodded. "I suppose you can look back on the good times and think positively. Forget the bad bits, and the hurt, and look at the good times."

Harry scowled at Andy before telling him he was talking rubbish. "And that if you really get hurt, you don't always feel like remembering the good bits, but want to damage the person who's hurting you." He then added everyone is different, and their circumstances are different, but I am talking about me, at a particular time.

"It was just an opinion!" said Andy, realising that he had touched a raw nerve.

He continued, "Well, things were going fine, the baby was growing, and walking about, and exploring her world, which was good to watch. My mother had also started to visit. This tended to create a bit of competition between her and my mother-in-law, which amused me. It didn't amuse Judith, who tried to complain that my mother was interfering. Obviously, her mother had put her up to it, as she was a nasty sod, like her husband, but I just ignored it. Then there came a bit of a hitch. Judith said that there was the opportunity to go to a trade fair in London, all the staff were going in turn. to assist. I forgot to mention it," said Harry "but she worked for a travel agent. It was a private company with half a dozen shops locally. The owner was a local man who had worked hard and had done quite well for himself. He was well known in the area, gave quite a bit to local charities and was always in the local paper, involved in something or other. Anyway, Judith said that if she didn't go it was unfair on the rest of the staff, and the extra money would be good. Both her mother and mine, without hesitation, agreed that she should go. I didn't like the idea, but I couldn't think of a good enough reason to say no, without looking stupid, so I agreed. I wanted to say 'your place is here at home with us,' but I couldn't. I would be denying her an opportunity and her rights, etc., although I'm not sure that 'rights' came into it. I remember we all sat around agreeing how good it would be for her. We laughed and joked, but for some reason I was apprehensive. The time came for her to be away and everything was fine, my mother slept the two nights with us while Judith was away. When she came back she looked wonderful, as though she'd been on holiday. She was attentive and kind, she seemed full of life. I thought that the change had really done her a lot of good.

"Life was very good at that time and during the next year. On occasion there were more seminars and trade fairs which she attended. From what was said at the time by her boss, she was an excellent sales women. She obtained another promotion and became the manager of a small shop that they'd just opened. She had only two assistants, but she was in charge. I was really proud of her. She was doing well and we were very happy, we were still in love. She couldn't do enough for me at times. Other times she could appear distant. She almost spoiled me by helping me become interested in a number of different things. She insisted that I needed something outside of the home, other interests and such like. Actually, it seemed like a good idea, and I joined a couple of classes at the Further Education Centre. Her mother, or my mother, looked after Petra while I was out. I forgot to mention Petra is the name of my daughter, well her middle name, but we both liked it."

Andy just nodded.

"We'd all been on holiday that year to Scotland; we could get a good holiday relatively cheap, due to her being in the trade. We were planning another one, taking the car across the North Sea. I wasn't too sure about it, but she said that we would enjoy the change and that travel was good for everyone. We seemed to have plenty of money and I thought 'why not? Let's get away.' Judith and I were still acting like teenagers in bed, enjoying each other almost every night. We even talked about the possibility of having another baby - we knew that a few couples had done it. To be honest, I didn't know how they had managed it. I assumed that it was down to artificial insemination, that somehow they had obtained sperm from the disabled fellow and managed to successfully implant it, but I had not much of an idea on the subject. I said that I'd speak to someone on the unit on my next visit. I thought about it, and having another baby seemed a good idea, we weren't well off, but neither were most people who lived around us. I think the fairest thing to say is, we were managing, and we had no debts. I loved my wife and daughter, and my wife loved me, so what more could I have hoped for.

"I enquired about having a child on the unit, and I'd arranged to see someone in a few weeks' time. I couldn't wait to tell Judith, but on arriving home from the hospital I instantly knew that something was wrong. As soon as I entered the room it hit me. 'I'll be going then,' said her mother, putting on her coat. 'Give me a ring if you need anything,' she said. She looked at me and just pushed past me without speaking. I asked Judith what was wrong with her mother. 'Oh, you know what mother's like. She's in one of her funny moods' she said. I looked at her and she wasn't looking at me, as though she didn't want to catch my eye. She wasn't telling me the whole truth, but I was used to that when her mother had been around. She never did tell me what her mother said, due to the fact that it was not likely that she'd sang my praises, but that's the norm for mother-in-laws, so it never worried me. What did worry me was Judith's attitude, she seemed so strange and distant, I'd never seen her in such a mood. Perhaps 'mood' is the wrong word, it was more of a combination of moods. I couldn't seem to say the right thing, anything I said was wrong. It was as though she wanted to pick an argument with me for no apparent reason. It was as though if we could have a row she would have felt better, but I didn't know why. Then she was nice to me, kind and considerate. But it only lasted minutes. I was as confused as hell. In bed. I cuddled up to her and she started to pull away from me, then she stopped. I can clearly remember telling her how much I loved her. That I could never imagine wanting anyone else. She smiled at me and told me how much she loved me. She kissed me and we made love until the early hours of the morning. I felt good, as good as anyone could feel. The next day I went to the further education centre. When I arrived home Judith was there, but her mother had gone home and taken Petra. I asked what was wrong, had something happened for her to be home from work early? Was she well? I asked. She looked very serious.

"'I don't really know how to tell you this,' she said. I instantly felt bad, it's something serious; someone's very ill. What is it? Who is it? I asked urgently. She looked at me in a pitying manner, or so I thought, as though wanting to save me from some pain or grief. 'It's me Harry,' she said in a toneless voice. My heart sank I felt sickened. She started to speak again and I managed to catch a few words. She was saying how sorry she was, that it would be for the best, and Petra would have a better chance. I didn't understand what it was she was saying. She must have recognised this and gave me an envelope, 'it's all in there, Harry, I'm very sorry, but I must go.' She brushed past me and hurried towards the door. What the hell's the matter? What's going on? I shouted, by then she had gone. It still hadn't dawned on me. I was still thinking that something has happened to someone. I opened the envelope and read the letter."

Harry looked at Andy, "the gist of it was that she'd left me, she was staying the night with her mother' who already had the baby at their house. Judith had fallen in love with the owner of the company she worked for, and he could offer them both a good future. She knew how I felt about her, and that I would be hurt, but she knew that in time I would get over it and that I also knew that it was in Petra's interest. I just sat there for ages staring at the letter, wondering what the hell had happened, not really believing what I'd read. I then started to cry, I'm not ashamed to say. I've never felt so bad in my life. I just could not understand it. A few hours earlier, she'd told me how much she loved me. I felt her body next to mine, and I felt her breathing. She was laying by my side, her arms around me. Then she says that she is in love with someone else. How the hell could that be? She had just told me that she loved me and I believed every word.

"I didn't know what to do, I didn't know who to talk to. I felt helpless, alone and devastated. And they'd taken my daughter, who knew nothing of what was happening. I asked myself time and time again, why had they taken her from me? I couldn't understand why they wanted to hurt me so much. I didn't know what I had done to deserve it."

Harry's voice was choking with emotion at this point. And Andy thought that it was time he interjected even if it was just to lighten the direction of what Harry had been saying. It was as though Harry had read his mind.

"Don't worry, I'm not about to throw a wobbly or anything silly. It's a long time ago. It's just remembering those events still make me feel emotional. I might be contradicting myself, but it feels like yesterday. And while you come to terms with such items in your life, you will not forget, or in my case, forgive," he added with meaning. "You learn, over time, to cope and look at things logically, but you don't feel any better when someone you love really hurts you. And what's, more it makes you cynical in your future friendships. You're half expecting people to let you down, which is a pity really. But that's how it's been for me." Harry's tone suddenly changed and he continued with his story.

"I desperately wanted my wife and daughter back, but I had no idea how to go about it. I was in a daze, unable to do anything. I seemed totally helpless, almost pathetic. What was worse, everyone gave me the impression that it was somehow bound to happen, that it was all for the best, as though my wife leaving me was in everyone's best interest. I just couldn't understand anyone thinking that way. It seemed as though there were two sets of rules in our society, a general rule for everyone else, and a separate rule for me, as though my needs and feelings were less important than other peoples. They didn't count the same or have the same value. It sounds as though I was feeling sorry for myself," said Harry. "And believe me, I was. I thought the world was laughing at me. It had quickly gone from being the best part of my life, to the worst, in a matter of months."

"Hard to get over something like that," added Andy, who thought that he could understand what Harry was saying.

"Naturally she had a solicitor working for her, paid for by the new boyfriend." Harry was sounding angry at this point. "To cut a long story short, I kept the bungalow and she had custody of our daughter. Everyone said that I stood no chance if I went to court asking for custody, although it was what I wanted to do. I then started to live by myself, almost like a recluse, I thought about her every bloody day! I just couldn't help myself. I will admit some nights I cried myself to sleep, not wanting to waken up. The nights are long, and only fill you with desperation when you feel the way I was feeling. I obtained some physical help, first of all from the district nurses, and then from social services. I could do most things for myself, and once that was established, they left me to get on with it. A woman came in twice a week to do a bit of cleaning, and washing for me. I did nothing much. I found it difficult to leave the place. I felt as though everyone was laughing at me behind my back, or they were saying 'told you it wouldn't last, you were lucky she stayed so long with you.' Then I wondered how many others there were while she was at work. I tried to think of the opportunities she had to go with other men. She could have gone with almost anyone she had wanted, and I would have been the last to know. She had cheated on me, how often had she done it, I thought. I think I was becoming paranoid at the time. But the bloody pain of it all, and the sleepless nights, wondering what I had done wrong and how could I get her back. It was pure desperation, I couldn't concentrate upon anything else. It was like a knife sticking in my chest, I honestly thought that I was going out of my mind at the time.

"My GP helped sort me out, he called in to see me one day, out of the blue. Obviously someone had told him that things were far from being right. He arranged for me to see someone, I don't think she was a psychologist, but she helped by just listening and by not criticising, or telling me to pull myself together. If she had said that to me I would've hit her. She was careful, and she seemed understanding. Somehow it started to help, although it took a few months. There was no instant fix. No flash of light, or a voice from out of the sky. It was a slow process. But I started to get my act together when I received a letter from my wife, She hadn't obtained a divorce at that time. The letter said that they were moving down south, that the business had been sold and everything was right in the world. I was told that I could keep in touch with Petra by writing to her, and that Judith would be coming up to her mother's, three or four times a year, bringing Petra with her. And if I wanted to see her, then I could.

"Surprisingly, this didn't shock me at all. It was as though I almost expected something of that nature to happen. I did by this time feel angry every time her name was mentioned. And although I am sure that I still loved my wife. I also still wanted to hurt her. I wanted her to know and feel how I'd felt. I wanted her to realise what she had done to me, at that time I really could have damaged her," admitted Harry.

"But things did slowly start to change. A social worker. who had become a good friend of mine. suggested that I might speed up my training to be a teacher. After some negative thoughts. I suddenly realised that it was a viable possibility, and I started to work towards that end.

"After a lot of hard work, I qualified and became a teacher. I thought that my life had started to take off again, but I was brought down to earth when I started applying for jobs. There was a shortage of teachers and I thought that there would be no problems. I should have had more sense by that time. But once I started applying for jobs it was obvious that most places of education were not accessible, and I would not have been able to carry out my full range of duties, etc. It was a blow, a very big disappointment at the time. I remember sitting by myself, eating my evening meal, and thinking why have I bothered making all this effort? I'm back where I started. Only this time I didn't feel sorry for myself, instead, I felt angry. I was angry at the lack of thought on the part of society. I asked why were schools not accessible, as there were plenty of disabled children around. And then when I really gave the situation some thought, I realised that the vast majority of public buildings were not accessible. What surprised me was that I had always known this, but I had never bothered before. I had somehow managed, I had accepted the status without thinking. Now I wanted to change things! I felt like a revolutionary. I would argue with anyone over any subject at that time. I was fortunate in meeting two or three likeminded disabled people at that time. And we assisted each other I think, although we constantly argued with each other. We were also constantly having a go at the council. Sometimes we had a modest success, other times it was like bashing your head against a brick wall, as we quickly realised many members of the council did not give a toss, or they were just plain stupid. But it was all part of my education and I was really learning about life. None of it was fun, none of it was a jolly jape," said Harry scathingly. "But I learned a great deal very quickly. And then, right out of the blue, a stroke of luck. I was offered a teaching job, which was quite a few miles from home, but it was a start. I went and had a look around the place, and quickly realised that it was as accessible a place as I would find. So I took the job and leaped into mainstream employment. I had arrived, I was back working. I felt better, although I wasn't sure why, as going back to work after a few years seemed daunting.

"To my surprise I enjoyed it, every day was a challenge or it appeared to be. With some classes, it was like climbing a mountain in bare feet. Needless to say, I had a few comments from the children but they weren't too bad. The school was in a decent area, not a large inner city dumping ground where the kids would probably have stolen my wheels while I sat in the chair.

"I felt that life was definitely starting to feel better. I was a busy person, involved in a number of groups and organisations. But I was still living by myself and that was, at times, physically hard. But I was out most nights at some meeting or other, plotting the revolution. The only thing I thought that I missed was my daughter. I had written to her every week when her mother took her away. And I had asked her mother if she would be good enough to read my letters to Petra. She said that she would, and it worked, or seemed to work. At birthdays and Christmas I would send toys down to her, and on the odd occasion I telephoned and managed to speak with her. She seemed pleased that I had telephoned. I was pleased that she seemed to remember me, as young children can soon forget. When she had learned to write I used to get short letters in reply to mine, or a thank you note, which made me feel that there was some contact. But this dropped off relatively suddenly. I found that I wasn't receiving any replies and so I rang Judith to find out what was going on. Her reply was she and her husband, which made them sound like royalty," added Harry in a cynical tone of voice. "They had decided that while Petra should be aware that I am her father, they considered that it was not in anyone's interest that she should correspond with me. That her future was settled, and she was a happy, well-adjusted young girl and any disruption would be to her disadvantage. I can't remember all of the claptrap in detail, but that's what it amounted to. I thought that there is no way they can stop me from communicating with my daughter. I wrote, and I telephoned but couldn't get through or receive a reply. I still sent gifts, but received no acknowledgment. I went round to see her mother and father, although it was something I didn't want to do as they loathed me. And to be fair, I detested them, and I didn't gain anything. They did say that Petra was happy, that the school was a good one, and that it would not be fair on Petra if I created problems for her just to get at her mother. I was so angry to think that that was the mentality I was dealing with, they had not the capacity to realise how much my daughter meant to me. All they could think of was that I wanted to make life difficult for their precious daughter. Stupid as it might sound, I would have had Judith back at that time. Anger and hatred and love are close partners, and I still loved her, which might seem stupid or illogical, but that's the truth.

Harry paused for a moment and then continued. "I went home and gave some serious thought to what they had said. I thought, with some reluctance, that they might have a point if Petra was settled in her environment, should I rock the boat. I was confused: would I be rocking the boat, or would I be like any other father wanting to see their child grow up? I was so bloody angry again. In the end I decided that I would write to her now and again and to continue sending her presents. I didn't expect to receive any replies, but I thought that someday she might ask about me. And I didn't want her to think that I had forgotten her.

I had this strange idea that some day she would be on my doorstep, angry with me. And demand to know why I had not been there for her. I had no idea what she was told about me. How did they explain why her mother had left me? I can't imagine what they said. But one thing is certain, it wasn't the truth and it would not paint a decent picture of me. They could not paint me in a good light, or my daughter would've been in touch with me, wouldn't she?"

Harry stared at Andy awaiting an appropriate response.

"It's difficult to say, really, their existing circumstances might be complex," said Andy. He realised that at this point he should choose his words carefully. Harry was looking sullen and this was not the time to debate the issue. He thought it appropriate to say something, as Harry had become silent.

"What do you remember of her?" asked Andy. He then wished that he had not said anything as there are times when memories are just too sensitive at a particular moment to contemplate or deal with logically. Harry gazed at him as if trying to come up with a suitable answer. He paused before saying "She was the most beautiful child you could ever wish to see. It's embarrassing to talk about your own daughter in these terms, but she was as near to perfection as you could wish for."

"She took after her mother then!" said Andy while laughing. What on earth have I said that for thought Andy, how bloody stupid can I get? The poor bugger is feeling bad enough at the moment. This is not the time for smart arsed quips. For some reason Harry did not appear to notice what Andy had said or he had just disregarded it.

Harry took another drink from the bottle of whiskey he had in his locker. He then continued. "Shortly after that time, I met a women who both looked, and was, very different to Judith. But we got on reasonably well for a period of time. She was a single parent with a son in my class. He wasn't a bad pupil really just a bit rough and ready, like his friends, but no better or no worse. Anyway his mother was keen that he did as well as possible at school, and she was on the parent teachers committee, and a couple of other committees. I came across her almost on a regular basis. One particular time she stopped me outside the supermarket to tell me she was concerned about her son's history results. She asked me if I thought he needed extra tuition. Well, it might not really benefit him at the moment, I said. He's just below average, but that can change in the next few months if he tries. That just did not seem a good enough answer for her. A week later she was knocking on my door asking if she could speak to me.

"I finished up offering to give her son some extra homework and to review his progress in a few months time. Now you must just accept what I'm going to say as the truth. It's going to be difficult for you, as it still is for me, when I think about it. Within three weeks she'd moved in with me. And I was giving her son free extra tuition nearly every night. I look back and I don't know how it happened. It was like an alien landing. She just arrived, cooked us all a meal and then looked around the place. I could see she wasn't too impressed. Then she told me I had been neglecting myself and that a busy man like me needed help with cooking and cleaning, and that sort of thing. I could only nod in agreement. After which there was no stopping her, she told me it was her duty to look after my interests, after all, wasn't I looking after her boys interest. I tried to explain that it was my job and I wanted him to do well, to achieve his full potential. Of course you do, she said. You're going to make sure that he does. I was about to say something when she sat down on my knee and put her arms around me. The wheelchair started to wobble - I thought it was about to tip over, but she adjusted her position and the chair was stable. 'Go and have a look at your new room, Justin,' she said, 'while I get to know uncle Harry a little bit better.' Who the hell's uncle Harry? I thought. I was like a lamb to the slaughter," said Harry.

"Justin did as he was told, as though he was used to such situations, and so did I. She just took over, like I said, it was like a lamb to the slaughter. Surprisingly, things went quite well for a while. To be honest, I'd almost forgotten what it was like to have someone around the house. I was used to cooking for myself and having the place to myself. Which also meant I was living in relative squalor according to Sarah, that was her name, Sarah. Sarah carefully explained to me in great detail how a house must be run, if a good impression was to be created. I told her that I wasn't out to impress anyone, at which she just smiled and carried on regardless. My late husband used to say that you can only judge a man by the pride he takes in his appearance. I told her that her husband was obviously a bigoted prick, and that you can't truly judge anyone by their appearance. You do not judge a horse by the finery of its saddle, Socrates said, that I told her. I've never heard of him, she replied, and he definitely would not have been accepted in my husband's Masonic lodge. Not with a name like Socrates, didn't accept foreign types in the lodge, very select it was, she said. I can hear her voice now," said Harry, wincing at the thought.

"The most pretentious, jumped up little bitch you could ever wish to meet. And even worse, at that time, she was all mine. I suppose, looking back, it wasn't all bad, it just felt like it was," said Harry. He laughed at this point. "She was good around the house and I ate well. She was also quite good in bed." At this point Harry burst out laughing again, and for the moment could not continue. Once he had managed to stop laughing he explained that on the first day she moved in, he had decided that at a particular time he was going to bed. And that she could make whatever arrangements she wanted.

The time came, and I told her that I was going to bed. I was in bed getting comfortable, having a last smoke, when she came into the room. I was surprised because I thought that she would have shared the room that her son was in. Or she might sleep in a chair, or something. I don't remember exactly what I said, but I can remember her assuring me that she didn't snore. She pulled back the bed clothes, undid the dressing type wrap, or whatever they call those things, and slipped quite gracefully into bed. Although it was my house, and my bed, I felt embarrassed for some reason. It felt as though the alien force had once again taken control of me. I then thought: What the hell! In for a penny, in for a pound. I thought that there was no point in being embarrassed about the situation. I sat up in bed and said to her, that for both our sakes she should try and understand the ramifications of my disability. I tried hard to explain. as clearly as possible. with regard to what I could and what I could not do. She propped herself up on one elbow and said. 'Well I never, who would have thought it.' I realised then that my condition had never entered her head. I found it hard to believe at the time, but

I realised it was true. She thought that the only thing wrong with me was that for some reason I could not walk. Her mind had not travelled any further. Nothing works down there? she said, pointing under the bedclothes. I remember clearly saying to her. 'No, it doesn't work; it's all there, but it doesn't work.' I remember her peering under the bedclothes and then saying. 'It's a damn shame,' at the same time giving it a poke with her index finger, 'who would have thought it,' she said, while tutt tutting. Then she suddenly got up out of bed."

Harry prodded Andy to make sure that he was fully awake, because he did not want him to miss this bit.

"I had no idea what was on her mind, for a moment I thought the shock must have really discouraged her. She was only gone a couple of minutes, I thought she was gone for good, a totally disappointed but wiser women. But this wasn't the case. She came back into the room carrying a cucumber and a knife. For a moment I thought she was seeking revenge for having her sexual desires thwarted. She told me to sit up in bed. I obeyed without waiting or questioning her; I didn't know what she was going to do. 'Just carefully peel the last inch of the cucumber, will you?' she said, handing me the knife and the elongated vegetable. 'We'll see what you can do, and if it's not quite good enough, we'll finish off with the cucumber,' she just smiled at me and then said 'it's a good friend in troubled times.'"

"You are joking!" said Andy, sounding surprised.

Harry looked across at him and assured him that he was not joking. He continued. "It was a night to remember, she put me through my paces! I thought that I was quite good, that is within certain physical constraints, but she tested me to the end, and then some. What an appetite that women had," said Harry.

"Well?" said Andy,

"What?" said Harry, looking bemused.

"What about the cucumber?"

"Oh! That!" said Harry, "we had it with a salad the following day."

Andy looked at him quizzically. Harry anticipated the question. "No, we didn't use it that night."

Andy grinned. "At least, I don't think we did," said Harry. "It was a bloody strange time in my life," continued Harry, "I never really knew Sarah, she was attractive in a big, expressive sort of way, which is difficult to describe accurately. And she was sometimes bordering on being intelligent, but these were occasional flashes, and not something you could expect on a daily basis. But she was easy to live with, if you always did what you were told. Any opinions other than her own were just disregarded. But she always knew what she wanted, and nothing stood in the way of her getting it. But it was difficult to be angry with her for any length of time. One year we went to Spain on holiday, and she had gone back to the bedroom after lunch for a sleep out of the sun. I went back to the room for something and caught her in bed with a waiter. He extracted himself and started to apologise in Spanish. I always assumed he was apologising. Sarah could only say that a gentleman always knocks before entering a room and then he does not get an unwelcome surprise. I was unsure as to whether I should hit her, or just burst out laughing. I did say that a gentleman does not expect the waiter, whom he had tipped the previous evening, to be shagging his partner. She told me that I made the whole thing sound rather common, when it was just a holiday romance. I remember shouting at her, how can it be a romance, this is our first full day here. She said that if I shouted at her she would not discuss it any further. I realised I was on a loser, and decided that when we returned home she would have to go.

"Fortunately, I didn't have to push her out. He unremarkable son was going into the sixth form, and she quickly found one of his teachers who was single. Within a week or two she had moved in with him, thus trying to ensure her son's education. Looking back, I must admit she was a strange women, but she was difficult to dislike. She was different; she had her own carefully controlled agenda built around her son, and that was what she basically lived for. She had few ordinary, moral scruples, but she was not malicious in anyway. She would not deliberately hurt anyone, she was too insensitive. But then again, if she had hurt anyone, she wouldn't have recognised it. She was bloody strange," said Harry with a sigh. "I don't know what happened to her. I believe her son got to University and then obtained a job in the city. Last I heard he was a prospective parliamentary candidate, what a little creep! He'll go far in politics," said Harry laughing.

"I bet his mother obtained for him his nomination!" laughed Harry. "When she left I was relieved, the place was mine again and I could return to being scruffy and untidy. I did miss her cooking and, of course, the sex. But on balance, I was glad to see the back of her.

"After that, I became involved in disability politics, which lasted a few years; it was boring, but at the time I believed that we were about to make radical changes. But like anything else, after a time I became tired of fighting the same battles over and over again. We needed a proper disability pension, suitable accommodation and care packages, good accessible buildings and an accessible transport system." Harry suddenly stopped and looked at Andy. "Sorry about that outburst, but it does piss me off how little we have progressed. But I don't want to talk to you about that at the moment, it'll take too long. Besides, it'll wait until tomorrow night. But it is something you should know about. The social model of disability could serve you well in understanding what actions need to be addressed. You're going to have to fight when you leave here, and you need to know what has gone before."

"I'm aware of the social model," said Andy. "But like most models, it has to be understood that it is a model, and further refinements are likely to be needed over a period of time." Harry just grunted. Andy recognised the validity of what Harry was saying, but at that moment he much preferred getting back to the story, the social model could wait.

"Where was I?" said Harry aloud. "Ah yes, I changed jobs and went to a larger establishment. I taught a few subjects, they were so short of staff I found myself teaching Spanish one morning. I had no idea what was going on, the only Spanish I knew was from films. In which the term 'gringo' seemed to be prominent. The students didn't give a toss, they were only there on some courses so they wouldn't show up on the unemployment register. It was at that place that I met a really nice young woman. I say young, she was in her mid twenties, so I suppose that still counts as being young. She was a very active type, a real activist in the Labour party. Or it could have been the Socialist Workers' party. If the truth was known, she was probably a member of half a dozen fringe parties. I think she probably supported the one which was most radical at the time. Anyway, for some reason we got on quite well. I think it was because I was shouting about disabled peoples rights, and I had a good working-class background, salt of the earth, all that kind of crap. She saw me as a repressed person fighting against the system. I saw her as someone I would like to fuck. She was attractive, and passionate and I fancied her. It was really good for the ego when she moved in with me as word got around quickly. And all other male members of staff and a few females were really jealous. It felt good, I will admit it. I had something that most of the others wanted, yet could not have. It might have been a childish emotion but nevertheless it felt good .It didn't last too long; she was too active in every sense. If there hadn't been a cause to fight for she would have created one. She couldn't remain in one place long enough to establish herself. There was always something beckoning her from over the horizon. It was a pity, because she did have a considerable ability, and she was passionate about her beliefs.

"After her I decided that I would be a bit more careful regarding relationships, as they often created more problems than any benefits. It might have been me at fault, it's hard to say," said Harry, while making a facial expression that suggested he did not really believe that it was him, or anything to do with him. "Perhaps I was difficult to live with? or they wanted more than I could give, although they were soon aware of my physical limitations. There was little point in pretending you were something you were not.

"So, I had the odd friendship when it occurred or was available. I didn't put much effort into seeking a longstanding relationship. By that time I realised that women didn't particularly want long-term relationships with me. I think that going with me was sometimes a novelty for some of them, or a social statement. I don't think they really cared for me as a man, but I could have been wrong. Also, they were sometimes too young to settle for simple domesticity and a quiet life. And as for the others, well, I had difficulty putting up with them, they were what I called transients, here today, gone tomorrow. So I ploughed my own furrow, so to speak, and did the best that I could. I moved location a couple of years ago, started afresh. I built a bungalow out of some farm buildings. I helped design the conversion along with an architect, it's not just a bungalow, it's rather better than that. And it turned out pretty good, in fact, it's better than good," said Harry, looking pleased with himself. I'm thinking about getting a housekeeper to live-in, once I've left here," he said.

Andy thought about it and said. "What sort of duties would she be expected to undertake?"

Harry smiled, full knowing what Andy meant. "It would be normal duties. Cooking, keeping the place clean and tidy, washing as well," said Harry. "I've never really got the hang of ironing. I bloody hate the job. I forgot to mention that when I could afford it, I bought up cheap property, had it improved over time and rented it out. When prices started to move, I sold, and invested again in better properties and they've not done too badly over the years."

"That sounds very sensible, considering you were by yourself, and what about your recreation?" asked Andy.

"You mean my house keeper? Of course," said Harry "I'd get her a season ticket for the team if she was reasonable. Before you go any further, the answer is definitely no. You have to get your priorities right, and a good reliable person who will do what they're supposed to do' without complaining' is what you need. Anything that develops is more often than not a bonus, or sometimes a bloody hindrance. It can also be a pathway to misery and problems. And I don't want any more problems of that nature, but on the other hand…"

They both laughed out loud at that point. Harry continued, "About the time I bought the new property, I had heard that my wife's, or to be accurate, my ex-wife's husband had died suddenly. Although he was twenty odd years older than she was, it was still a surprise as he seemed healthy. I thought that it could not have happened to a better man, I'm just a bit vindictive," he said while smiling. "The best part of it was that it followed that not everything was plain sailing. In his will he had left a major part of his estate to his children by his first marriage. I'm not sure how these things work," said Harry "but the gist was that Judith had to sell up and buy a smaller property. And she has had to seek a job, which would do her good," added Harry, smiling at the thought. "I know that I should be able to rise above such things, but I must say it gave me a lot of pleasure. I really felt good at the time. Bloody childish of me after all these years, but I don't mind telling you it's the truth, that's how I felt. I believe she had to give up the golf club, the tennis club and a few other things of that nature. She became downwardly mobile," laughed Harry, "'downwardly mobile!' I love the thought, and the sound of it" he said.

Andy had listened carefully, and with some patience, but he interjected at this point as his curiosity had got the better of him. "What about seeing her again, what would you say if you bumped into her?" He looked carefully at Harry trying to judge from his expression what his reply might be. He had deliberately put Harry on a spot and he was looking forward to hearing his answer. Harry thought carefully and it seemed a long time before he could answer. When he did answer he started in a thoughtful manner.

"It's hard to say really, I would like to see what she looks like now. I already told you she was exceptional, for want of a better word. I realise such things are subjective, but believe me she was so attractive, she really was. But more than anything, I'd like to take her on one side and ask her why she had prevented me from writing to my daughter. And does my daughter know of my existence?" Harry paused for a few seconds. Andy could see that a raw nerve had been touched again. "The other thing I would really like to know is," he paused for a moment as though it was difficult for him to continue. "I would like to know how could she tell me that she loved me one night, and fuck-off with someone else the following day, taking my daughter with them. What were her feelings for me, did she ever have any at all after my accident? I'd really like to know. Because I've thought about it over the years, and I still don't understand. I loved her, and she said that she loved me, and then she fucked off for pastures new, as if she had found a better social and financial deal. Off with the old and on with the new," said Harry loudly. He was almost shouting at this point and Andy told him to speak a little quieter, which he duly ignored. "The last time we were together, I asked her what did love mean to her. She paused and thought carefully. She then said, that you wanted to be with the person all of the time, wherever they were, that you needed them. She then turned, and looked at me and said 'I don't need you anymore.' I'd never felt as bad as I did at that moment. I felt discarded, like a piece of rubbish. Looking back was I so stupid, or thick at the time, to have believed everything she had previously said, or are most women mercenary in such situations? Are they always on the look out for a better set-up somewhere else? Looking for a better model, with fewer problems. Do they give a shit if they hurt you?" He paused as though he was waiting for Andy to comment. He then continued. "I think they can convince themselves that they're in the right, that it's all for the best." Harry sounded angrier than ever at this point. "The bit they tend to forget is, they really mean it's in their best interest, sod what happens to you!" He was talking loudly again. "Is faithfulness, wedding vows and loyalty just more bullshit?" he asked loudly. Harry was sounding too emotional; there were tears on his cheek. It was all too clear that he was hurting badly. Andy wished that he had not mentioned the subject. Andy was about to say that Harry had said earlier that people had different attitudes and needs, when they had been talking about Elisabeth's husband, but Andy thought this is definitely not the time to mention their previous conversation.

After a seemingly long pause Harry apologised which embarrassed Andy. "They're not all like that, there are lots of good women about. I was talking about my experience with my wife, and when she left, I honestly thought I was going insane." He looked at Andy in order to see if Andy had accepted what he had just said. "Not all women are like that," he said, trying to confer a modicum of optimism. He paused for a while before saying. "It's been good to talk, it helps one think, and it can help get things into perspective. I'll admit I lost my cool for a minute, but I haven't talked like this in years, and surprisingly, everything just flooded back as though it was yesterday. I thought that it was all tucked away in the recesses of my mind but apparently its still lurking under the surface. I've surprised myself!" he said, in a tone that illustrated his genuine surprise.

He then smiled as though some unusual form of realisation had spread over him. "In the morning, I'll make contact with my daughter, as you might say 'I'll go for it and see what happens.'

Although I did decide to do that earlier on, but now I'm sure."

"You have to think positive, and make things happen," added Andy, relieved that Harry now seemed calmer. "I hope she looks like her mother! It would be a cruel trick of fate if she looks anything like you," said Andy. Harry was going to say something but he stopped himself. "Actually," said Harry, "I've been thinking about that new nurse, the young nurse that you say fancies you, I think I might ask her out when I feel a bit fitter. I might even put a word in for you for, when you're feeling better and acting more civilized. But on second thoughts, I suppose she wouldn't look at you once she'd been out with me, a man of experience and sophistication."

"In your dreams! You're too old for her, she'd look on you as a father figure," said Andy.

"I think that might be the right approach," said Harry, while smiling, "some young women learn quickly to appreciate older men, we have experience and are generally more understanding; they don't have to pretend or compete, in fact it's a lot easier for them if only they knew it. I read an article only last week where young women want to go with older men for the experience, before settling down with someone. I think it'll help them recognise the dross and help eliminate them from the equation. Nowadays a young women should ensure that her prospective partner is not some idle sod who loathes the idea of having to earn money. I know a few young men who pretend to look for work, but never quite manage to find it, while they have their partners working all hours. I even know one fellow who used to look in the newspaper to find his wife extra jobs, just to make sure that she had no spare time." Harry suddenly realised that he was going off at a tangent.

"One last question," said Andy.

"What is it?" said Harry, now sounding both tired and a bit suspicious. Andy cleared his throat before speaking.

"What if Judith said that she would like to come back to you?."

"Are you being serious?" said Harry, his voice getting louder at the prospect of Andy being flippant. Andy said that it was a serious question, and he wanted a proper answer, having listened carefully to everything that had gone before. Harry paused awhile, then grunted a few times and then said.

"I'll admit that I've never loved anyone like I have loved her. I've never wanted anyone as much as I wanted her. For a time it was the only thing that I could think of. And some of those feelings never leave you, and I mean never," he said as if to emphasise the point. "That's all I can say; who can tell what anyone would do?." He paused, then he continued in a subdued tone of voice as though he was finding it difficult. "We think that we know what we would do. I have rehearsed it a hundred times over the years, but we don't know until it happens. And, even worse, we don't always remember the warning bells or the pain at the right time. You're only aware of these things when it's too late. Besides, there's that all important question, did she really love me after my accident or was she waiting for something or someone better to turn up? Did she want to be seen to be doing the right thing by staying with me?." At that point he stared right at Andy almost challenging him to say something. Andy had more sense and kept quiet. "But you have all these mistakes to make." He quickly added. "You'll be fortunate if you can avoid them. What made you ask such a question?" asked Harry. "You know it's impossible for anyone to come up with an instant answer. It's too complex, too difficult; it's something I would need to think about."

"It occurred to me that if you loved her so much, which definitely seems to be the case," added Andy quickly. "then given the time that has elapsed, couldn't you forgive her the hurt or pain she left you with, or whatever you might call it? I don't know if such wounds can ever heal. It's just a thought," he said while wondering what Harry would make of his last question.

"To forgive is supposed to be good," said Harry "it's a possibility, but can you forget? That is the difficult bit. In such circumstances you have to make things work, anyway the situation won't arise; it's been too long." Harry was quiet and appeared to be thinking about what had just been said. He prodded Andy and said. "I still miss her. I've not met anyone over the years that I want in the way I always wanted her," his voice quietened, "I don't think I ever will." He continued in a subdued tone of voice. "I felt that I had lost everything, I had tasted real love for the one and only time, a love so strong it's hard to imagine. Afterwards you feel empty, it's as though you don't exist as a person. And it isn't that you've done anything to lose it, it's been taken from you and given to someone else, that's the most painful blow of all." Harry closed his eyes as he felt the tears forming. "I used to dream of holding her in my arms while dancing to our favourite music, we were dancing in the clouds with no one there but the two of us. It was like a scene from an old film, but it felt so real, so bloody painful. A type of pain that you have no control over. You are left desolate. I can't find words that adequately describe the feeling. I've heard many say that you have to move on, and that there are millions of other women, etc. But if they can just move on like that, then I don't know what they felt, except it was nothing similar to what I felt."

Andy was not sure at that moment that listening to Harry had done Harry any good. The opening up of such deep wounds had been painful. Andy had listened carefully to what Harry had said. He recognised how difficult it had been and he thought of his own circumstances. He knew that the road before him was not an easy one. Andy wasn't stupid, or naive, but he knew he had a great deal to learn and understand. He supposed that the physical problems were obvious, but having listened to Harry, he also knew that the emotional issues were not as simplistic as they might have been. He thought that it seemed like a balance of risk taking. If you don't take a risk you feel half alive, on the other hand if you take risks, you stand a good chance of being hurt. He was trying hard to analyse what Harry had said.

After some thought, he came to the conclusion that, according to Harry's ideas and experience, it's hard to compete with some other men regarding relationships, or to be accurate, able-bodied men. It seemed as though he thought they might take advantage of your situation given a chance. It caused him to think about relationships, especially now he had been informed of his sexual situation. He had already witnessed Elisabeth's husband with another women, and although it was none of his business it had infuriated him. He thought about Harry's main theme. Your wife or partner can just walk away from you at anytime for someone who seems to offer them more. It really must have hurt the poor sod at the time, thought Andy. His mind tried to rationalise what he had heard. He thought they can still walk away if you are not disabled, and they do all of the time. But he knew that would never be a source of comfort to anyone.

And there were some good, long lasting relationship. He only had to look around the unit to confirm it. He smiled to himself and he told himself that Harry's situation was different, that everyone's life was different, it was just how it had worked out for Harry. He knew that it would be different for him. He would go out and live, he would take whatever came his way, and he would deal with it. He knew not to expect any favours, but he also knew that sometimes, with some effort, you can help to make your own luck. In the past, when something had needed some extra effort, he had found that he was capable of succeeding often where others had given up or failed. He told himself that he had never failed in the past, that failing was something he could not accept and would not accept. "I have a life to live, and I'm going to live it," he said out loud. He was reassured by that thought. He was surprised at what Harry had told him. Although they had talked before at length he never realised how much Harry had loved his wife and how hurt he had been. He thought that if he had been in Harry's position he would have got over her a long time ago. He then realised that he had never been in love. Probably a good thing, he said to himself, it sounds dangerous and sometimes painful. He then wondered if he would ever fall in love, would someone fall in love with him? What had he to offer someone? He told himself that they would have him, and that is it, they get me and who could want more? He smiled to himself at his last thought.

A voice from the nurse's station sounding illogically loud for that time of night said. "Will you both try and get off to sleep! You're keeping people awake, who'd like to sleep, that is if you don't mind. It's typical of you two to lack consideration for others. Harry was about to tell her where she should go, but decided he could not raise any enthusiasm for an argument.

"Better let her get some sleep, she needs all the beauty sleep she can get," said Harry just loud enough for her to hear. "It's been a funny day today," said Harry, while half asleep. "For some strange reason I believe that I've worked up an appetite, I think that I could just eat some fish and chips!" he added, while pulling the sheet up to his chin. "It's a pity about old Bernard, he would've enjoyed some fish and chips," he said, while yawning.

"Don't forget to try and get in touch with your daughter, will you?" said Andy. He then added thoughtfully, "I'm sure she'll be pleased to see you again; she's bound to be curious." The thought of that possibility made Harry smile. "She might think you're a miserable old sod, but otherwise she should get on with you; it's not too difficult if one makes allowances."

He did not rise to the bait. Harry spoke in a low voice. "I hope it'll be like you say. I must admit, it's a struggle at times to think it'll work out like that." He leaned back and smiled again. "You're lucky that you're in the next bed to me, you could learn a lot if you had half a brain," said Harry seriously. Andy knew that Harry was right but he would never tell him.

CHAPTER FOURTEEN

Caroline was not really enjoying herself at all, she could not understand why she had agreed to go out on the town with Wendy that night, especially when she already knew what Wendy was looking for. It was against almost everything she thought she believed in. But here she was contradicting herself. She thought of Amanda and how she had kept her situation to herself. She felt guilty for a moment for trying to enjoy herself when her friend had just undergone surgery that afternoon, but she realised that such thoughts were stupid, but that was her personality, she could easily feel guilty about almost anything.

She looked around her hoping that no one would recognise her. "Here, this'll help," said Wendy, thrusting a large glass of green liquid into Caroline's hand.

"I've already had more than usual," said Caroline, who was not sure if she should drink any more as she could feel the effects already.

"Do you want some of these or have you remembered to bring your own this time?" said Wendy, while handing Caroline a pack of condoms.

"What on earth are these, they don't look normal.?"

"That is a new line, I was told, the lumpy bits are different colours, and due to friction they secrete oriental juices of some kind. Great, aren't they?"

"I'm not carrying those things about with me! They're...," for a moment she could not find the appropriate words. "They should carry a health warning! They could rot away your inside with whatever they secrete."

"You'd better keep them if you've forgotten to obtain some, again, you don't know who you might meet, whom you might meet."

"Whoever," said Wendy, while looking around to see if any innocent male was ready to be seduced.

"Hello girls! Can we get you both something to drink?" The man who spoke was tall and slim, his hair was going thin, but this was hard to discern due to the remaining hair having been cut short. It was difficult to judge his age, it could have been anything between thirty-five and forty. His friend was somewhat shorter and of a stocky build, his hair was longer, but also relatively thin.

"We've just got some drinks," said Wendy who quickly added. "I bet you waited until we'd bought some drinks before you asked."

"Do we look like the type of men who would pull a cheap trick like that?" he said, while holding his hand over his heart.

"Definitely!" said Wendy. He wasn't going to be put off so easily. "If that's what you think, we insist on buying your next drinks, don't we?" he said this while looking for agreement from his companion who nodded appropriately. "By the way, my name's Dave, and this is my oppo, Wilson. And before you ask, it was his mothers doing, she liked Harold Wilson."

"Never heard of him," said Wendy.

"You must've heard of him! He was the Prime Minister." He stopped himself, realizing that she was winding him up. Wendy looked at Dave. then at Wilson. and said in a scathing tone of voice. "What's this 'oppo,'? It's not a phrase I'm familiar with. Do you possibly mean friend, or colleague, or even servant?" To her surprise Dave was not slow in coming back with a quick response. "Actually, it's derived from the Latin, I believe it was a Centurion's understudy in the Roman legions. Presumably you've heard of the Romans.?"

Caroline started laughing and while prodding Wendy said "that's pretty good! I'm almost impressed. Have you just made that up? It's bloody brilliant!"

"Actually, it is Latin," he said while smirking. "I don't know any Latin," said Wendy, "except for the waiters at Romano's Pizza place."

"I don't know Latin from Greek," Caroline said. Then she added "what about that porter who hangs around the dining room smelling of garlic?"

"Oh, him, he's from Scotland," said Wendy "is that Latin enough?" Dave quickly interjected before the conversation slipped away from him. "Do I look like the person who would make something up like that?"

"Don't let's go through all that again," said Wendy.

"What sort of business are you and your friend in? I'm

presuming that you work together?" said Wilson while shrugging his shoulders and tightening his tie "Your oppo. is as good at presuming - is he any good at anything else?" said Wendy while looking at Dave in a manner that was less than subtle. "Our ability to presume is an art form," said Dave, realising that he had his foot inside the door.

"Watch my drink, I'll be back in a minute," said Caroline. "Watch mine as well," added Wendy. "What do you think of them?."

"I'm not so bloody desperate. Come on! Tell me you're not serious, are you? Please say you're not; they're absolute crud." Caroline looked at Wendy hoping for a negative response but Wendy had already made up her mind that Dave was not too bad, and she had been out with worse. "Don't tell me you actually fancy him! He's arrogant and he's a creep."

"He has a way with him, he has something that's a bit different, looks aren't everything you know."

"In his case, you're right on that point - he looks like a used car salesmen on a bad day. And his friend, well…" Wendy quickly interrupted. "The one you're going with?." There ensued a heated discussion, the final outcome was unsettled, but the idea was that they would have a drink or two and see what materialised. Or, in other words, see if anything better turned up. "Here, take these," said Wendy, taking another pack of condoms out of her bag "you'll need them and I know you won't have any with you."

"I'm not planning to do anything with either of those two,! You must be joking! I would rather go without forever. And as for carrying condoms every time I go out, just in case I meet someone who isn't decrepit or out of some institution for the abnormal, no thank you! I have a bit more self-respect."

"Are you saying that you don't want them?"

"You've already given me a pack, or have you forgotten?." Wendy looked a bit bemused. "I've not forgotten; it occurred to me that later on, if things go OK, then you might want to swap, could be a laugh, make it a bit interesting."

"You can forget that! I don't like either of them. Look at them! They're rejects from somewhere, they're…," she was lost for words again for the moment.

"You've not touched our drinks then," said Wendy, while pretending to scrutinise her glass. "Drink that, and order anything you want," said Dave in an exaggerated manner. Wendy was awaiting such an opening. "Big spenders are we boys? Well, let me tell you, we have expensive tastes. My friend and I are used to the finer things in life, so don't say it if you don't mean it."

Wilson quickly said "of course we mean it! Choose whatever you fancy," he regretted committing himself to spending money and did not know what had come over him.

"I might surprise you!" laughed Wendy with as much subtlety as a lead weight. Caroline shuddered upon hearing this and started to wish that she had not decided to accompany Wendy on her search for whatever it was she was looking for. They had agreed that they were going out for a few drinks, a dance, and perhaps a few laughs and that was it. She had made Wendy promise her that they were not getting involved with anything in trousers that still breathed, just to satisfy her sexual cravings. Wendy agreed and replied that she was not craving anything. She then added while laughing, "I could do with a really big rough one," quickly adding it sounded like being addicted to cigarettes. Caroline was not taken in by this, and knew that once Wendy had a few drinks nothing was likely to stop her.

Wilson foolishly said that they could have a bag of nuts as well if they liked. The women both looked at each other and smiled. They did not have to say anything, the question was, which one of them was going to respond with some appropriate put down. Caroline shook her head before saying. "Best let it go. It's not even a challenge."

"I'll have a dance and then a double Champagne," said Wendy. The two men looked perplexed for the moment before one asked. "What's a double Champagne?." Wendy obliged. "Simple, it's a speciality around here, they fill a brandy glass. You don't come from round here do you?" she paused, as she was about to say you are having a rare night out away from your dreary wives, while hoping to strike lucky with a quick cheap shag. Common sense told her it would be both a foolish and pointless question. "I'm ready to dance," said Wendy while grabbing hold of Caroline and pulling her towards the dance floor. Dave and Wilson promised they would have the Champagne ready.

"What do you think?" said Wilson.

"We've cracked it, we have it - the jackpot, a couple of drinks and they'll be gagging for it,, said Dave "but let's not get them so pissed that they don't know what they are doing." Wilson looked bemused. "I thought that was the idea, get them pissed and back to the hotel."

"Of course that's the idea, but we don't want them comatose, I'm not paying out good money and trying to shag someone who is incapable of responding in a reasonable manner."

"What's with this 'responding' bit? I thought we were just going to give them a seeing to." He looked at Wilson before continuing. "How long is it, exactly, since you have been away from your wife for a night? I don't mean away with relatives or in hospital. I mean really away, free, no restrictions, that kind of away."

Wilson stuttered something. "I couldn't quite catch - it what did you say?."

Wilson said that he had never been in such a position before and he wanted his money's worth. Dave groaned "you must listen carefully, and do not screw up, don't be too eager. These two girls are not the usual dross that you can easily pick up around any club bar, they're better than that take my word for it, I've been with some dross. I realise that they're attractive, possibly very attractive, but they're not nineteen year olds with pouting lips and nice cute arses." Dave groaned again, "where are you going to find anyone like that without it costing you a fortune? One of the good points about these two is that they are not going to be particularly expensive. And they know what to expect, they won't bugger us about."

"Where's the Champagne?" asked Wendy. She looked around the bar and could not see any, which disappointed her. She was sure that it would be waiting, that they would not leave themselves open to more jibes about them being slow to buy a drink. "It's on ice awaiting your pleasure," said Dave in his smarmy salesman voice.

After a few more drinks all four were dancing and enjoying themselves. "I must stop for minute," said Caroline, "I'm out of breath; I haven't danced much recently."

"You look fit enough for me!" said Wilson while attempting to give her a nudge with his elbow. Caroline smiled then laughed out loud. She could not stop herself. What a little tosser, she thought. But he is trying so bloody hard. I will be nice to him, he's not a bad guy. And we're enjoying ourselves. She was really feeling the effects of the drink and she liked it. "I've not enjoyed myself for what seems ages" she said out loud. Wendy agreed that she was enjoying herself as well. The two men looked at each other and smiled.

"My legs are weak," said Wendy "Champagne tends to do that to me, as well as making me want to pee a lot, if you'll excuse my technical terminology."

"You said earlier that you were nurses, do you have your own place, or share, or what?" asked Dave. "It's classified," said Caroline "we're not allowed to disclose any information leading to us getting shagged." She burst out laughing, she then felt cold, then hot, upon realising what she had said. My god I must be pissed she thought. Then she realised she did not particularly care. Upon hearing her Wendy said "I hope you boys can handle us when we really get going." She laughed while reaching down and giving Dave a squeeze. "Hello, big boy!" laughed Wendy "who's your friend?." The two men realised that this was definitely their lucky night.

"That 'big boy' remark, that was Mae West wasn't it?" said Wilson. "Who the hell's Mae West?" said Dave. Caroline and Wendy looked at one another and just shrugged their shoulders, "I've never heard it called 'Mae West' before," laughed Wendy. "That's her,: said Wilson, "she shrugs her shoulders like that."

"What have you been feeding him?" asked Wendy, "buy him some nuts or throw him a fish."

"Don't be so bloody clever just because you don't know these people," he said while looking hurt.

"I want a Chinese," said Wendy.

"Good idea," agreed Caroline, "although I could prefer an Italian, bit small for my taste those Chinese, but nicely formed. They taste sweet and sour, I can suck on those ribs all night" said Wendy. "So everyone says!" added Caroline sniggering, they both laughed out loud, the drinking had taken hold of them and common sense was quickly departing and drifting into that level of stupidity that only comes with drinking too much. . Dave and Wilson looked at each other, the same thoughts going through their heads. If they went for a meal, the girls might sober up a little and lose some of the existing enthusiasm. On the other hand, if they did not agree to the girls wishes it might piss them off and the whole of the night's efforts would have been wasted.

They both said, "where's the nearest Chinese then?"

"It's the 'Flying Sampan' on Canal Street," said Wendy, "a place of oriental culinary delight, and salmonella."

"She's talking crap," said Wilson, "she's just fine! Just keep her topped up and you'll have a night to remember."

"I must start with ribs in a sweet and sour sauce."

"The same for me," said Caroline, who then added, "make them big, Wendy's in a sucking mood," they all laughed. "Then the duck, and we must have some crab claws or king prawns. Then we'll take it from there. How's that for starters, boys?" said Caroline. "And, to make it simple, we'll have some of your best champagne."

"I thought you said it wasn't going to be expensive," said Wilson, looking gloomy at forking out more money without seeing a return on his investment.

"Stop whining and order something. Just think, you might be stuck at home with that miserable wife and your screaming kids." Wilson looked at him trying to focus. "My wife's not miserable, she's just a bit…" He could not think of a word so he agreed. "You're right! She is miserable, in fact she's the most miserable women on the fucking planet."

"Let's be fair, she's not as miserable as mine. Mine is a real, one hundred percent vindictive cow. God alone knows why I married her," he said. Wilson looked at him. "Her father threatened to fucking kill you, that's why, have you forgotten?." Then they both burst out laughing.

"I enjoyed that," said Caroline, "that was good, and those ribs were really good."

"Could you eat a pudding, or anything else? Perhaps a pig, or half an elephant?" said Wilson sarcastically. "I can't remember anyone eating so much - that's about seven courses!"

"I told you we were expensive," laughed Wendy, "but we're worth every penny of it my little cuddly friend." With that she leaned over and kissed Wilson on his forehead, "you're a bit small, but not to worry, the climb will be worth the effort," everyone laughed at that remark.

Wilson and Dave were typical of their type. Once in a blue moon they escaped from their wives looking for recreation. They desperately wanted the excitement of such encounters. The flow in the equation was that they hated spending money, but they were realistic enough to know that at their age, seldom were the good things in life freely available.

The night had turned cold and it hit them as soon as they stepped outside.

"I can't see things properly," said Caroline, "my legs seem to want to go in different directions," she burst out laughing at her ridiculous situation. They walked down the street not knowing or thinking where they were going. Dave could not wait any longer, he wanted a return on his investment. He stopped and pressed Wendy against the wall, she did not resist, she wondered why he had waited so long. He pressed his mouth against her while his hand clasped her breast. Her hand went down to his zip and she was soon inside, she took hold of him and soon found that he had already obtained a decent erection. Wendy tried to say something but his mouth prevented it. She tried to move her mouth away for a moment in order to get some air. Her hand was now outside his flies, clutching his erect appendage; she still had a good hold on him, but she was not feeling as good as she should have been and her head was starting to spin. Wilson was also wanting also return on his investment and was climbing all over Caroline, she wanted to stop him and to tell him to slow down a little as she was not feeling too good. Suddenly she heard Dave shout out. She looked at Wendy, who was leaning over and vomiting profuse amounts of sweet and sour. "She's thrown up! Down my best suit!," he said in a voice that lacked any restrain. "It's my best suit, and I need the bloody thing in the morning and she's done this!." The front of his suit was covered in a mixture of Chinese food in a semi-solid state. Wendy stared at him with a glazed expression. "Your dick's hanging out," she said while laughing. Caroline also started laughing, she could not stop, then she too started feeling ill. "Oh god," she said, while she pushed Wilson aside and started vomiting. She thought she was dying, it was as if her stomach belonged to some other world. She could hear Dave and Wilson shouting and arguing but she could not have cared less. She heard Wendy shouting, the voices were angry. She looked around, she could clearly make out Dave holding Wendy and threatening her. Wilson was trying to hold him back but he let go of Dave's arm. Dave's arm went forward and his clenched fist passed Wendy's head and hit the wall. He screamed out that he had broken his hand. Wendy pushed him aside. Suddenly a taxi pulled up and a voice shouted for them to get in. Without any hesitation they got in the cab.

"You're still up to your old tricks again, soliciting on street corners," said the man in the back seat, "are you trying to earn a bit on the side?" Caroline looked at him and groaned loudly, then she laughed. Wendy was almost falling off the seat onto the floor. She looked at the man and she also groaned. "We will never ever hear the end of this, will we?" she said, while looking at Ronny. "How did you know it was us?" she said. "I was in the Chinese with a friend; you two were so pissed you didn't notice me, you never even saw the wheelchair. It was obvious what might happen and as I had ordered a taxi I just followed you knowing that I would have to offer you a lift. Caroline put her arm around him, she was unsteady but she tried to focus in on his eyes. "Ronny, you are a wonderful man, a prince amongst a sea of riff raff. And to show my appreciation I'm going to give you a big kiss." She rolled forward. "Bloody hell you smell a bit!" said Ronny, "your eau de toilette isn't working."

"Don't worry about it," said Caroline "it's only vomit." Ronny pushed her away. Wendy tried to lean across to touch him and say something, but the words would not form correctly. "Ronny you are the best and," she was slurring her words to such an extent it was difficult to comprehend what she was trying to say. He could make out the word bastard and rotten but that was all.

The taxi pulled up outside a bungalow and Ronny got out into his chair with the help of the driver. "Help me get these two inside will you?" he asked the driver. Fortunately the driver had known Ronny for years and he obliged. "Where's your wife?" he asked as he manhandled Wendy and Caroline into a bedroom. Ronny could read his thoughts and before he could say anymore, gave the driver some money and told him that he could manage. The driver went away looking disappointed. With some difficulty Ronny managed to get them onto the bed and persuaded them to take most of their clothes off. Wendy told him that if he was man enough he could have her forward, backwards or sideways, as long as she could sleep afterwards, and he could use the new condoms . Ronny said that he would remind her of that in the morning.

Caroline was the first to wake up. She looked around slowly her eyes unable to focus properly. Her tongue was hard and tasted terrible, and she did not want to allow it back into her mouth; she reached out and felt someone next to her. She looked carefully at the partially clothed body of Wendy, She then looked at herself. She was undressed but she had no recollection of undressing. In fact, she had no idea where she was. Just then Ronny appeared with cups of coffee. "Drink this, you look as though you need it." Wendy opened her eyes. "Where am I?" she said looking around the unfamiliar surroundings. She looked at Caroline before asking her what Ronny was doing there. Ronny told them that they had spent the night at his place. He had arranged to leave the hospital for the night to see how he managed, it had been arranged with Amanda.

He had spent the evening with friends in town. Whereupon he had come across the two of them in a what he described as a bad condition.

"I have no clothes on," said Wendy in a tone of voice that expressed her surprise. Caroline realised that she also had no clothes on. She looked at Ronny. "Tell me you didn't, please Ronny, you wouldn't take advantage of us in that condition?" Ronny just smiled before asking them what exactly could they remember. Both shook their heads. "Then everything's fine, no damage done," laughed Ronny. "But I have no clothes on, what exactly happened here?" demanded Wendy. "Anyway you could not have..."

"Oh yes he could! And he would," said Caroline seemingly remembering some similar incident in the past. Not only that he could but he definitely would. Ronny was keeping a straight face and giving nothing away, he was enjoying himself. He then finally spoke in reassuring tones: he told them that they had nothing to reproach themselves over. They had behaved themselves properly, keeping up the traditions of their profession. "What does that mean, exactly?" asked Wendy suspiciously. "You didn't let the side down," said Ronny. "What the hell do you mean? Stop talking gibberish! Did you or didn't you?" said Caroline. "I might have," said Ronny, "but as neither of you can remember, let's just put it all down to fortune or fate, which might mean my good fortune and your fate, call it what you will."

"I can't think of anything less fortunate than waking up without most of my clothes on in your bungalow, knowing what a bastard you can be." Wendy looked at Caroline. "He wouldn't do that, really, would he, when we were in that condition?" Caroline thought about it for a while and decided that he might. Before it went any further, Ronny said that he had helped them out of a difficult situation and that he had looked after them like a father, and that they should be grateful. "You were both very demanding, saying that you were turned on and you were willing to do anything for me as I had rescued you from the clutches of two low life's who thought that they could have you on the cheap. Those were your very words, so I duly obliged you both." They did not say anything but looked at each other.

Ronny laughed, deliberately unconvincingly. Nothing happened he assured them, he had managed to get their clothes off and put them in the washer. He had spent most of the night trying to clean their clothes just so they could get home in a fit state. He said that he was really disappointed in the way they were reacting. Caroline said that she could remember most of what had happened. Wendy said she could remember being sick and hoping that she would die. Ronny said he had not been impressed with the two men whom they had picked up, "looked like used car salesmen," he said. "And the small one looked like an animated dwarf, or a hobbit, and the fact that you were holding onto their erect penis's was so off-putting, degrading is perhaps the correct word," he shuddered in an exaggerated fashion. "I washed your hands as well. God knows what you might have been holding earlier on that evening. I just feel slightly sorry to have observed you in such circumstances, it spoils any thoughts that I might retain regarding integrity and decency." Wendy looked at him and nearly choked before telling him what a shit he was.

Caroline had been listening and trying hard to remember. "That sounds bad, did we actually do that?" Caroline drank the coffee and she felt just a little better, Wendy said she felt unwell, as though she was sea-sick. Ronny told her that she looked rough enough to have sailed around Cape Horn. They decided that they could not eat breakfast, but thought it appropriate that they get into their clothes instead of wrapping bed sheets around themselves. Ronny agreed, but only after he had told them they looked better without their clothes on especially, when posing together. He could not stop himself laughing at that point, he then said that they would go back to the hospital together as they needed a minder to keep them from getting into trouble. "What a night!" said Wendy "I'm not doing that again – I'll never do it again, if I mention anything similar, please don't hesitate, just hit me hard."

"My legs still don't feel too good, they just don't seem to want to go in the same direction," added Caroline. "My bed's wet!" shouted Ronny, "one of you has wet my bed!" He looked at them both hoping to find the culprit. "I save you from those two creeps and all you do is pee in my bed, I can't believe either of you would do that." They looked at each other and at the same time said, "it was definitely not me."

"You do someone a good turn and that is what you get! A couple of drunken bed-wetters." Wendy was looking sheepish, "we're not perfect I'm the first to admit it, and we will pay for the sheets to be cleaned, won't we," she said nudging Caroline. He sighed in despair. Within a few minutes they were looking more respectable and their bodies had settled down to a more comfortable state. "What are you going to say when we get back?" asked Caroline. Ronny looked at her and smiled. "You don't honestly think that I'd mention this do you? Surely after all these years you must know me better than that?" Wendy looked across at Caroline wondering what she was going to say. She knew that Ronny and Caroline had known each other for years and that there was an atmosphere between them, but she had never asked Caroline about it, which was unusual as she had never been noted for her sensitivity. Caroline looked thoughtful before replying. And when she did reply she tried to choose her words carefully. She glanced across at Wendy as if to say this must not be mentioned again as it is too personal.

She looked carefully at Ronny before speaking. "I am grateful for last night, you helped us out of what was becoming a difficult situation, but I don't know what to expect from you, on the unit you seem to spend most of the time winding me up, or making me look foolish in front of the others. Why you do that the whole of the time, I really don't know." She continued while occasionally looking at Wendy. She continued to chose her words carefully, wondering if she should go ahead and say what she wanted, knowing that Wendy would be listening with her mouth wide open and enjoying every word. She decided that after last night's incident that she might as well be open and say what had been on her mind for some years. "When it was finished between us I was really hurt and you did nothing to help me. You just went off back to your wife calmly, as though nothing had ever happened. I just couldn't understand you, then you were supposedly getting divorced." She said the last few words as though she could still feel some of the pain she had experienced years earlier. Wendy's mouth was open wide, she wanted to ask a question but she dare not in case the subject might be changed, so she kept silent, she was listening intently to Caroline. Everything was falling into place, why had she not recognised this before? The night out together had proved more fruitful than she could ever have imagined. Ronny took a deep breath and moved closer to Caroline as though Wendy did not exist. He reached out and held her hand. To Wendy's surprise, Caroline did not remove her hand, it was as though Wendy was not in room with them. Ronny said that he had such feelings for her that he knew he would have to end the relationship, it was the last thing that he wanted, but he could do no other in the circumstances. Caroline told him that was not true. That if he had only asked she would have done whatever he had wanted if it meant them being together. But instead of that, he took the easy way out and went back to playing happy families. "You were comfortable and it was easy, in reality I was just something on the side," she added. She was getting emotional but she could not contain herself; the emotions had been suppressed for so many years and now they were pouring out. "I thought so much about you, and you made me believe that you felt the same about me," she started to cry. Wendy placed her arm around her. Ronny removed his hand and waited awhile before speaking. Caroline, he said her name again, "Caroline, it wasn't as you imagined, it really wasn't like that." He was trying to find the right words. "You were young enough to be my daughter, and at the time we laughed about it and we said it didn't matter, but it did and it was impossible. I knew deep down it really mattered. You were," he paused before continuing, "you are still the most wonderful woman I have ever met." "But it would not have lasted. We would have had nothing, I just had to be realistic." He raised his hand to prevent her from interjecting. "I know we said that we only needed each other, but that's not true, life isn't like that, especially when you're young. I thought that given a short period of time you would have tired of me, and would leave me for a younger man." Ronnie was now getting very emotional, while trying to remain calm and logical. "I could not contemplate that happening. I might have been weak and unwillingly to take the chance, but that's how I felt. I wanted you! I always wanted you, but I was frightened that I would lose you. That I'd be left with nothing. It might sound stupid and illogical to you but that's just how I felt at that time, I was bloody frightened and I will admit it, I was looking after my own interests. And, be honest, you've been here long enough to have seen similar situations that have turned out badly for the disabled person in the relationship; I divorced my wife, we had nothing in common, she didn't have any feelings for me, so we weren't playing happy families, it was a miserable time and it wasn't something I discussed or talked about."

Caroline tried to dry her eyes. "You never took the trouble to explain anything, it was as though no importance was attached to what we had, or what I thought we had." Ronny sighed a deep meaningful sigh. "I could not do that, knowing how I felt about you. It would've just started everything again and then what? Where would we have been? What would we have done? The world out there is still crap for many disabled people. You were better off without me, or so I thought at the time."

Wendy was on one side and Ronny on the other. She smiled

and then laughed in a manner that seemed almost uncontrolled. Suddenly they were all laughing but they were not sure why. Ronny turned to Wendy but before he could say anything she told him not to worry. That Caroline was her friend and she would not let her down, unlike him, the lousy bastard. Ronny laughed and Wendy gave him a hug and a kiss which surprised him. She had seen both Caroline and Ronny in a different light. 'And you think you know people,' she said to herself. "You promise not to say anything,?" insisted Caroline looking at Wendy in a manner that indicated that she would not forgive her if she did. "Can I just tell one or two friends?" said Wendy. Caroline was about to threaten her with bodily harm when she realised that Wendy was joking.

"Make her sign something, I don't trust her to keep her mouth shut," said Ronny. Wendy turned to berate him when he started laughing.

"I will make some more coffee, then we'd better get back to the hospital," said Wendy. Ronny looked at Caroline whose eyes were still red from crying. "Don't ever think that I stopped loving you, will you," said Ronny looking into her eyes. He continued. "We should have talked before, but I didn't know how, or what to say." Ronny's voice was full of emotion. "Perhaps we should have tried," he said. "Who knows, everything might have worked out." He was feeling sad at that moment. He said that in future they would always talk and they would be good friends. "I've left things too long," he said in a quiet voice. "Life isn't like fiction for most people, it's much more difficult and time is not always a great healer. Things don't always turn out right with happy endings. But we can now talk again, can't we?" he said while looking at her. He then leaned forward and kissed her tenderly. At that moment they both knew that they had made a mistake, and they should have taken the one chance that fate had granted them. Upon touching there was a sensation that was impossible to describe accurately, other than to say they wanted to stay together without moving.

Reluctantly he pulled away from her. "I'll get you a taxi and I'll follow later," said Ronny. He looked at her and said very gently, "Don't speak now, don't say anything, perhaps later." She smiled at him and suddenly felt relaxed as though a large weight had been taken from her. "We're good friends and we can now act like friends," he said.

In the taxi back to the hospital Caroline said that she was getting too old for nights like that where suddenly things get a bit hectic. Wendy agreed, with the reservation that they might have just been unlucky, she wondered how they had somehow become involved with two such creeps. "Luck had nothing to do with it," said Caroline "you were there, sat with him, your hand in his trousers ensuring that he had an erection, possibly his first for years, your expression and actions weren't subtle, you told him that he wasn't going to have to fight for anything. Your idea of being subtle seemed to be pulling his zip up and down while singing 'Danny Boy'." Wendy looked at her and said "I wasn't singing 'Danny Boy' I don't know 'Danny Boy'."

"Well, it sounded like 'Danny Boy'," said Caroline "but then again, I wasn't in a fit state to tell. For all I know it could have been something from Tosca!"

Caroline looked hard at Wendy. "OK, you've been dying to say something, so go ahead and get it off your chest. I can't stand the tension." Wendy gave what could be described as something between a laugh and a cough, "it's about you and Ronny," Caroline stopped her. "If one word of this gets out, or is ever mentioned, I'll never forgive you. I've already told you that," said Caroline who was now concerned knowing that Wendy loved gossip and for her to keep this to herself was going to be difficult. Fortunately Wendy realised that Caroline had meant what she said. Wendy swore that not a word would pass her lips. "Who else knows?" said Wendy lacking in sensitivity.

"Amanda, of course, she was on the unit at the time, but no one else. Well, yes, there is actually and I'd almost forgotten, Harry was on the unit at the time. That added to the difficulties as he fancied me and it put him at odds with Ronny, even now they don't speak to each other unless it's necessary, yet they are similar in many ways. Actually, I like Harry a lot, but he's always just a bit distant from me now because of what happened, although I still think he likes me, but because he's as difficult as Ronny it's hard to tell, Ronny's a real bastard though, but impossible to resist at times as he can be so nice and thoughtful, then quite the opposite.

"I went out a couple of times with Harry and I did fancy him, but for some reason he was bloody different, hard to understand and difficult to get to know. I know that he liked me because he confided in another nurse and she couldn't wait to tell me."

Wendy interjected, "I think Harry's basically a decent man, and not bad looking, but I agree that he's not easy to know, and he can also be bloody minded when he wants a bastard like Ronny. I must admit that he's interesting and he knows something about everything, I think that he has hidden depths and one day we might see the real Harry. That might be worth waiting for because he can either confuse or irritate everyone given time. I heard that his wife was quite attractive, one of the porters used to live by them before they separated, or to be precise, before she left him. There's something about him that's different, if it's something different that one wants."

"One is no longer sure what she wants," added Caroline enigmatically.

Then Caroline laughed out loud, "I was caught in bed with him once, not Harry, Ronny. Before you say anything, I know you can't imagine me in bed with a patient. I was caught with Ronny by an older member of staff who threatened to report me. I should mention he was in the side room at the time and I used to come back onto the unit most nights, depending who was on duty." She continued, "but I wasn't the only one, so no one took much notice until that particular time. It was later than I thought and this old battleaxe, a real cow, opened the room door and there we were, 'compromised,' I think is the term they use. She said that she was going to report me. Ronny told me to say nothing, he told her that she would look stupid when we denied everything. In fact, they might think she was senile and terminate her employment. She said something and flounced off. Ronny told me to just brazen it out, and if anybody said anything, he said he would ensure that she said nothing I sometimes wonder what he said to her. No one said a word, which surprised me as I was sure that not only would I be sacked, but I would be in the Sunday papers," she added.

Wendy smiled, "I'm seeing another side of you! You're a split personality! You've kept all this wonderful gossip away from me all of this time. Even I haven't been caught in bed with a patient, well, not by a nursing officer. Actually the last few hours have been a revelation. I've also seen a side of Ronny that surprised me. When he was looking at you and holding your hand, it was like a moment from a romantic film, it was so different, actually, it was wonderful, which might sound a bit over the top, but I felt emotional, I could have reached for my handkerchief. I felt as though I was party to something deep and meaningful. It was almost unreal, I almost wanted to throw up. If I had to write down the last hours events no one would believe me! It's a pure, romantic fantasy." Caroline looked at Wendy carefully wondering what she was going to say next.

"Are you winding me up? Because if you are, you're definitely succeeding," said Caroline. "If you start making strange remarks or hints in front of anyone, I'll never speak to you again, and that's after I've hit you as hard as I can, and I'll let it be known about the time you went out on that blind date with lurch, he was so ugly! I just couldn't believe anyone looked like that."

Wendy did not listen to what had just been said, she was lost in thought. She gave a large sigh and an intake of breath. "It's only then that you realise that you don't know people as well as you think you do. You just assume so many things without really knowing or understanding. Don't worry about it! None of us are what we seem to be," said Caroline. "Do you ever tell anyone your true feelings, your desires and aspirations? Of course you don't. Mind you, yours would be so disgusting that you wouldn't dare. We drift on, never really reaching out and touching one another. But deep down that desire to be close is always there. I sometimes think that's why I wanted to nurse, to be near people, to be just that bit closer, some kind of understanding, it's difficult to say really, it certainly wasn't for the money."

"Well you have surprised me!" said Wendy who then added, "and I'm not easy to surprise anymore although, I still find it hard to believe. You know, I didn't think last night was going to turn out so interesting, perhaps a few drinks and a few laughs. Then we met those two morons. "Good God!" said Caroline "we nearly..." Wendy stopped her, "but we didn't and thank God for that. I have to say it though, but yours was an ugly little sod, I just hope no one saw us with them, or we'd be downgraded in the social ratings. We wouldn't be in any social ratings if seen with them, whatever their names were." Wendy said something to herself before speaking. "I've just had a thought! What if we advertised in an upmarket magazine for two executive types with independent means?." Caroline looked at her in disbelief, before telling her that if she did that she was on her own.

"By the way, can I have those condoms back? They weren't cheap and, let's face it, last night didn't finish in the way I intended. I was wanting a really good seeing to, and look how it finished up."

"There are times when you sound incredibly common," said Caroline.

"That's because I am common! Hadn't you noticed?" retorted Wendy.

"Here we are, back at the ranch! Nothing seems to have changed," said Wendy. "I have to have a word with Andy sometime soon, he wasn't feeling too good yesterday." Caroline added that he was realising some of his limitations and he was not happy. Wendy sighed, then she added while smiling. "Perhaps he'll meet someone like you." Caroline was tempted to respond in a manner that indicated she was not in the mood to be teased at that moment, but decided that she would not give Wendy the pleasure of seeing her react in that manner. She said, "perhaps he will; who can tell?"

Wendy looked at her and was about to say something when Caroline said "I already know what you are going to say, but do say it, and then perhaps you might be able to leave the subject alone." Wendy thought for a few seconds then said. "It's about Ronny and what was said. I saw you both as I," she paused, unable to find the right words. "It was as though when you touched you looked almost in love, whatever that means," she quickly added. She continued before she was interrupted. "It looked special and so different, you were different people for that particular moment. I thought I knew you but I've seen a side of you that you've kept well hidden." She smiled at that point as though she was unsure as to what she should say next. She stared at Caroline in expectation. Caroline did not say anything and that simply was not good enough for Wendy. "What are you going to do?" she asked hoping for a detailed response. Caroline, who had been lost in thought, now smiled at Wendy. "I don't know why, really, but I'm glad you know what happened, I'm glad you saw us together." She continued, "it's been a problem for years, we could never talk and it was always there, festering like an open wound. It doesn't feel like that now, everything feels better for some reason, I don't even know why I'm talking like a schoolgirl at my age." "That's nice," said Wendy still smiling "I can't remember when you looked so content, if that's the right word." Wendy paused before saying, "I wonder if I am still, how can one put it politely? A bit pissed! It's all so bloody odd. You even look different now." 'That's silly,' said Wendy to herself. "Nothing has changed, we're back at work," but she was not convinced. "Ronny will soon be back in bed and we will still have a day's work ahead of us. Something has radically changed," said Wendy "and you know it has."

Wendy was becoming animated and her voice was getting louder. "You should reach out and take what is there. How often do you get a second chance? Just go for it, forget all the crap! Just grab it while you can."

"But what about Ronny? He was being sincere when he said those things, although he's not someone who I would trust for one minute normally."

"Exactly! You can't trust him."

"But it doesn't matter anymore! I honestly believe that the ghosts have been exorcised at last." Caroline, at that moment, felt as good as she had done for a long time, although her emotions and ability to think clearly were being bombarded by thoughts from the past.

It was a new experience for her, she felt so different. Her feelings for Ronny had changed over the past few hours, she knew that over the years her feelings had been distorted by events. She also knew that it was impossible to put the clock back, but it was true what Wendy had said. How many people get a second chance? She had been out with others, but somehow it was never a success. She now knew why. All these years she thought, I still loved him to some extent, even if it was far back in my subconscious. She started to laugh and Wendy asked her what was funny. "Just think back carefully, what the situation was when Ronny pulled up in the taxi." Wendy started to laugh out loud. "We had a narrow escape there! Yours was such an ugly little sod though, let's face it, they were both the pits!" they then both laughed out loud.

Rita was coming out of the office. She said "Ronny's just telephoned to say the film he took of you both last night has come out well, everything is crisp and in focus, and it will go down well when shown on the unit. What does he mean?" Caroline looked at Wendy and smiled, saying "I told you what he was like!"

"Will he really have a film of us?" asked Wendy with some concern. "That's one of the problems,: said Caroline, :with Ronny you can never tell, but we'll soon find out. He'll be smirking and referring to it throughout the day. It'll certainly add interest to the day, to the extent you'll want to damage him before the day is over." They both laughed out loud, "I think we'll find that Ronny has changed in the past few hours," said Wendy in her best motherly tone of voice. "Don't you believe it!" said Caroline, who was now looking forward to the day ahead. "He's not going to let us off the hook so easily." She knew that there would be plenty of banter and verbal fencing with Ronnie in the days ahead, but she was optimistic.

She was not under any illusions; she was no longer a girl going blindly into something, she would be positive and have control of the situation. She was clear in her mind that she would enjoy herself if the opportunity arose, while not looking for any form of commitment; if the situation arose that gave her the chance to have what she wanted, she would just take it. 'Life is just too short,' she said to herself 'just too short and we're so slow to learn that time is not on anyone's side,' she was sure that someone had said that to her, but she could not think who it was. For a moment she stared into space wondering if things would turn out as well as she hoped, then just as suddenly she thought to herself that it no longer really matters, a weight had been removed and she did not need Ronny, but she knew that she desired him. 'It's a strange turn of events,' she thought. 'I do not know what I really want but for some reason I feel as though I have a choice now which was not there yesterday, and Ronny can go into the back of my mind, it no longer matters, things are now in perspective.' For some reason she felt a freedom that exhilarated her. 'I'm my own person at last,' she thought. 'I did not know or understand why I felt and acted like I did, but now I think that I know, and I'm sure that the problem has gone forever. It was a strange night,' she thought' a very strange night. Bugger Ronny! It's time to move on,' she said to herself while smiling.

CHAPTER FIFTEEN

Caroline sensed that there was something wrong. She sat down in the office and looked at her colleagues who seemed far away, as though they did not want to talk to her. "Come on! Out with it! What's wrong?" she said in a tone that demanded a response. Astrid, who was new to the unit and had not worked alongside Caroline very often, decided that she would break the news regarding Bernard, she had little time for beating about the bush with such matters. As soon as Astrid mentioned Bernard's name, Caroline felt her heart miss a beat. Astrid continued as though she was enjoying imparting the information. "As far a we know, he died peacefully in his sleep." "What time?" asked Caroline, who was looking and feeling upset. "Does it matter what time?" said Astrid, while shrugging her shoulders. "It matters to me," said Caroline angrily.

Caroline walked out of the office down the corridor and across the drive to the area underneath the trees where Bernard had sat only some hours previously. Tears were streaming down her face. Wendy had started to leave the office to go after her, but then decided that at that moment Caroline needed to be alone.

She looked at the trees standing there, all seeing all knowing, 'you have seen it all before, from generation to generation,' thought Caroline. Then she suddenly thought of Amanda laying in bed, not having been told about Bernard. She realised that she would have to tell her. That was something that she was not looking forward to as she knew that Amanda was very fond of him. And while trying to treat all patients the same, Amanda had tried to spend some extra time with him, but Caroline knew that Amanda wanted to talk to him at length as they had only mentioned it the day before. She dried her tears knowing that it was not acceptable for either staff or patients to see that she had been crying. She decided that during her coffee break she would tell Amanda.

"What's going to happen today then?" said Harry pointing to Bernard's bed. "They won't leave that empty very long. We'll soon be having another cellmate," he laughed with a touch of irony. "Won't they try to keep it empty in order that it can be used in an emergency?" asked Andy. "I doubt it," said Harry, who looked as though he was concentrating upon something important. He was trying to think who he had spoken to who was waiting to come in. Could be him, he's already in another hospital waiting to come here. Could be someone I know who gets the bed, he's been waiting to come in."

"Is he OK, reasonable, will he fit into our elite little group?" asked Andy. "Sort of. hard to say with any certainty, depends on his situation, he's a bit of a ducker and diver type of person and he likes his drink and drugs, he'll do whatever he wants when he's fit enough, does not give a bugger! He's one person who was left by his wife with good cause, and not surprisingly."

"Sounds really nice," said Andy.

"Don't get me wrong; he'd give you every penny he had, then steal them back off you the next day," Harry laughed at that point, "but he's had a rough life, he had a rough life before his accident, in and out of prison for stupid offences most of his life. He never learned and he never will. Anyway, it might not be him, it could be anyone I suppose, as long as it's not Mildred."

"Who on earth is Mildred?" laughed Andy.

"She's a miserable old cow! Actually she's not that old really, from the back she's fine but her face is that of a well used brillo pad. She looks like a neglected country lane, which is rough and bloody miserable. She could drag you down to a state of doom and gloom within five minutes, believe me" he added in a serious tone of voice "we definitely don't want her."

"You don't want her simply because she has a soft spot for you," said Elisabeth who was listening.

"She has no soft spot for me or anyone else, she's a really hard b   u   g   g   e   r   .   "

Andy decided that he must get a look of Mildred, even if she did not come onto the unit. Anyone who Harry responded to in that vein, he thought, must be worth seeing.

"Last time I met her, all she could talk about was you," said Elisabeth. "She lusts after your body! Says that you could have been a film star, if you'd been in America."

Andy laughed out lout upon hearing the last remark. "A film star! Harry! She must have a brilliant imagination, that's all I can say." Harry was not amused. Harry winced as though in pain. He then quickly changed the subject, "what about Bernard's funeral? Will anyone go from here.?"

"Normally they would not, but I think Amanda and Caroline will, it seems as though they knew him better than we did. We should have spoken to him more often, but it's too late now. That sums up life really, always looking back thinking of what we should have done."

"I suppose that's par for the course," added Elisabeth, "we all seem a bit down this morning."

"It's the start of a new day! Who knows what delights it will bring us!" said Andy, without really believing it. Harry just grunted "It can't be much worse than yesterday, which started off OK, but as usual it finished on a low note. Just accept that such days come around and are there to try us. I've not forgotten that I have a few things to do over the next few days. The main one is to contact my daughter."

"You've not changed your mind then?" said Andy half expecting Harry to find an excuse that allowed him to ponder the situation in such detail that the objective would be forgotten. Harry unexpectedly snarled. "When I say I'll do something, then I do it. But I have to tell you, I'm not really looking forward to this, I really feel apprehensive about the whole thing."

Andy was trying to be supportive and positive. "We discussed all of this last night and you know that it's the right thing to do, this is something you want and you'll have to take a risk, but if you don't, you'll never know what response you would have got. On the other hand there is so much to gain."

Harry knew that Andy was right. "I'll give it my best shot! Who knows, it might really turn out better than I expect. Then I'll ask myself why didn't I do it years ago. I don't like being in a position where the outcome is so uncertain," said Harry while frowning. "It's as though I have one shot, and if things go wrong, that's it, there won't be another chance; that's how it seems to me."

Andy thought that with Harry you just could not win, that was his nature, 'he is never satisfied,' he said to himself. He hoped that in the same circumstances when he had to make a decision that he would be more decisive. Time would tell if this was the case, but at that moment Andy said to himself that he would try and be positive regarding whatever came his way. It was going to be a long journey and he already knew that the direction it was going to take would not be decided by him alone. But he also knew that he would not allow valuable time to slip by as he had observed had been the case with some of the other patients. "For some strange reason, I seem to have learned more this past twenty-four hours than I've learned over the past few weeks," said Andy. "One thing is certain and that is nothing remains exactly the same, the other certainty seems to be that once disabled, nothing comes to you on a plate, you have to go out and fight for everything."

"That about sums it up," said Harry who then added. "Just when you think that everything is sorted out and running smooth, something will go wrong, as long as you are aware of that then life will be easier. It's hard out there, just remember that, and you'll be out there soon enough, it's a different world as you'll soon find out. Most of the places you want to go to will not be accessible, most of the people you would like to know will not give you the time of day. You're really going to find it interesting," said Harry while laughing. "And just another thought, ignore what they say in here, they're used to us and our attitudes, out there we're aliens, only less threatening and what you say counts for nothing. Before you say anything, wait and see and if I'm wrong, and you're looked upon as the personality of the decade, then I'll say that I was wrong with great humility."

"That'll be a first!" added Elisabeth.

CHAPTER SIXTEEN

The wheelchair was tipped backwards and pulled up over what had been the single step which was now ramped by the laying down of a few pounds worth of tarmac. The ramp was hardly noticeable, but over the past few weeks it had taken on a level of importance that touched upon the surreal. The debate was centred upon the cost of the ramp and who should pay for it. A relative of Andy's had said that he would do it for nothing, but the offer was unacceptable, this was due to the Local Authority insisting that the ramp must be to the required specification. After numerous inspections, the cost of the ramp had gone from sixty pounds to somewhere between six and seven hundred, based on officers' time, administration, drawing up of plans, and provision of materials. Andy, when he was told, quickly said a sack of cement, a couple of hours work ,and the job would be done. But the authority was not going down the road of doing anything quickly or simply. "It has to be done right," said one officer, "we can't let people just do what they want, whenever they want."

After numerous meetings and debate, the issue was settled, and Andy was to be allowed to use the front door. From this experience Andy realized that he was entering into another world, where common sense was not something that was highly valued. On the contrary, cutting through the dross and getting things done only meant that there would be another similar job to follow, so why hurry. On entering the bungalow, Andy suddenly felt a wave of apprehension: this was it, this was going to be his home for the foreseeable future. Janice opened the door, which led into the kitchen area. She reached over the cooker and opened the window, letting in the fresh air. "It's a bit musty in here, but it'll soon feel lived-in," she said while forcing a smile for Andy's benefit. Andy looked around, "it smells of paint," muttered Andy, his voice lacked any enthusiasm. "The lounge area is through here, if you remember" said Janice as she opened another door. "They've already installed the furniture you chose, and it looks quite nice very cosy, I could move in here myself, given the chance."

" Move in if you want, presumably you're house trained, and I could do with a lodger with your money and skills." She ignored his remark and carried on looking around. "I checked on the bedrooms yesterday, and the extra bed for a carer had just arrived, but you need to buy some new bedding. We can do that later today." She looked in the bathroom and everything appeared in order. Andy looked around the room scrutinizing the furniture and the layout. "It doesn't look as though there's a great deal of room now that the furniture's in place," he said. "It was measured carefully - I did it myself, and I've made sure that you can get around without knocking into everything." She paused and looked around again carefully hoping not to miss anything. She had tried hard to get everything as right as possible knowing that Andy would find fault no matter where he lived, or what had been done with his needs in mind.

"I think they've done a decent job, considering how long some people have to wait for suitable accommodation." Andy grunted in a manner that suggested he neither agreed or disagreed. She was feeling almost optimistic, nothing appeared to be wrong, all the basics seemed to be there. "And someone has been thoughtful and stocked your cupboards and fridge. In fact I think we should mark the occasion by having a cup of coffee or tea. If in doubt resort to the tea, even if things aren't perfect the tea will make them appear better. Pure unadulterated rubbish, but we all do it!" said Janice while laughing. Andy hooked his thumb through the handle of the mug and sipped the hot coffee, which was originally going to be tea, he winced at the taste. "I can't drink this stuff," he said loudly, "it's disgusting! Bloody awful! Are you sure that they're not out to poison me and re-let this place?" he said. Janice had to agree the coffee tasted bitter. "You can buy your own later, we shouldn't grumble- it is free."

"I'd rather pay than drink this stuff," replied Andy. He looked around the room again. "So, this is it my residence, should I give it a name? 'Dun walking' sounds good," it amused him. 'It sounds better than 'Chez Andy',' he thought. He was finding it difficult to show any vestige of enthusiasm, he was not used to hiding his discontent although he had promised himself that he would try and be fair and reasonable. But he knew it was probably wishful thinking. He felt indifferent to his surroundings, it was as though he had little to do in choosing where he was going to live, or how. The system had taken over in a surreptitious manner and he had been sidelined. He did not attempt to increase his involvement as he thought it would make little difference to the outcome. The past few months had been a difficult learning curve for Andy, but he had learned and he was a wiser man. Knowing to some extent how the system worked provided him with no gratification at all. On the contrary, it increased his awareness of what little power he had over these mundane decisions. And to be fair, he had not assisted the process with any enthusiasm. Whatever someone suggested he had tended to go along with it, anything to make things easier and simpler. And on occasion he was just plain negative. He could not stomach the tokenism of everyone pretending that decisions were his. After a while, he thought, does it matter if the carpet matches the curtains? Or the settee is a three seater, or a two-seater? What does it matter? After all, he was not going to sit on them. And as for the carpets he could not have cared less, except he thought that he would have a problem trying to push his chair if the carpets were anything but smooth. He thought it fortunate that he would be able to get around in a powered chair. He had thought that with his luck someone would have bought carpets with a thick pile, making it impossible to get around on, but fortunately they hadn't.

"What about the television? It should've been here already." Janice said that someone else had been dealing with it, but she would telephone the shop to find out why it was not here. "Very well," she said to some unknown person, she then placed her phone back in her pocket. "Evidently they called around and no one was here, so they took it back. I've explained the situation and it'll be here in the morning. One day without television won't do you any harm, will it?" she said while smiling. Andy grunted something to the effect that he had no choice. "It was only a couple of hours ago you were complaining that there was only rubbish on television, and you'd thought of doing without one," said Janice. "I could watch videos or DVD's," Andy promptly replied. "Answer for everything," she said while forcing a smile, "but you don't have a DVD, do you?" she said looking confused and wondering if she had missed something. Andy was tempted to explain to her his reasoning but then thought, why should he? It was his place and his television and he did not have to explain himself if he did not want to. That was something he must remember, it is important. I do not have to explain myself. A bloody good point he thought. The time he had spent in hospital had dulled his thinking when it came to new experiences and situations, he had to get his act together and get his thinking right otherwise everyone would run rings around him, and push him from pillar to post without him having a say in his own existence. "Is there anything else you need to see before we go shopping? There are a few things we need to do." That's typical he thought, I'm already being told what I have to do. "I need to think what I need from the shops I'm not going to have you spending my money on things that I don't want or need." That should get the message across clearly he thought.

He looked around the room again. "It's very cosy, very cosy," said Andy sarcastically. "There is one thing missing, though." Janice for a moment looked concerned. "I need a couple of ash trays," said Andy, pleased to be able to find fault, even if it was something as insignificant as an ashtray. "Ashtrays are definitely not my department," said Janice quickly. "I gave up smoking when I was no longer a teenager and had obtained some sense."

"That must've been quite some years ago," added Andy who was not going to allow her to get away with such a remark. Why do all of these self righteous bastards who give up smoking jump on you, and can't wait to tell you how weak and degenerate you are. They pretend to be concerned about your health when all they are concerned about is that you are smoking and enjoying it and they are not. He thought that it was possibly a form of jealousy, that they really wanted to smoke, that they enjoyed smoking but the fear of catching dozens of smoking related conditions stopped them. He knew that smoking was bad, it was unhealthy and responsible for thousands of deaths a year. But so was sex, he reasoned. Why not try and ban sex, except for procreation. Thousands of abortions take place every year. Thousands of unwanted children are born. So, why not have a campaign against sex. We can manage without it. The bastards won't do that because they are enjoying it. Even the adverts for safe sex are a cop out. They don't say 'stop having sex it can kill,' they find away around saying you must get protection. His thoughts were coming thick and fast. Why not create safe smoking? With all the technology that now exists it must be possibly to make a safe smoke. He looked at Janice, and was about to make a comment showing concern over the dangers she was facing if she pursued an active sex life, but he thought better of it. The irony would be lost on her as was any attempt at humour.

Andy recognized that only a few shared his humour, and sometimes it was difficult for those who did not know him well to know if he was being serious or not. "Let's go to the shops then, before the excitement gets too much for me," he said, while trying to think if there was something he really needed and could not manage without. He knew that there would be something he had forgotten, because life is like that, but at that moment he accepted that nothing came to mind. There was the possibility that once looking around something might come into his mind and he would purchase it. Who knows I might feel light headed by the experience and by something that is frivolous.

The eager assistant descended upon Andy and Janice as soon as they entered the shop. "Have you had a computer before sir? Is there a particular model that interests you? What would you be using it for, mainly?" He was about to continue when Andy told him that he was looking for himself, that he understood how they functioned due to him being a senior software designer. And he did not want anyone trying to sell him something he did not want, his tone of voice indicated clearly his intent. The sales assistant continued to smile, while agreeing with Andy. Andy thought, 'why is he still here? Hasn't he got the message? Why doesn't he go away? He is hanging around like a waiter expecting a tip.' Finally the young man realized that his assistance was not yet wanted, but he would be called upon as soon as the situation changed. He backed away still smiling and thinking how badly he needed the commission, His mortgage had been fine, a good deal they thought, but now his wife was pregnant, and life was going to get harder. He would make sure of his commission as he needed it. He asked himself every day how had she become pregnant; she was on the pill, they had agreed to no children for a few years. Just his bad luck he thought.

"I didn't know that you were a software designer," said Janice.

"I wasn't, but he thinks that I am."

"That was just a blatant lie then! How could you look at him and tell him something which is totally untrue?"

"It's easy, very easy, but you don't lie to everyone, only certain types who deserve no better."

"That's unkind. In fact, it's worse than unkind I was willing to be objective regarding your character, but I'm no longer sure."

"Just stick with me, Janice my love, and before the day is over you'll appreciate me."

Janice did not know anything about computers and she hoped that she would not have to learn how to use one, but reality suggested otherwise. They were complicated machines that seemed to breakdown every few minutes. Their introduction had not improved anything as far as she could tell. All they had done was to provide the idle with an excuse that if something went wrong, then it was the computer's fault. Andy did not particularly like the machines as they seemed to have a grudge against him. He had used computers at university and at work, but he had always found it a battle between him and the machine, with the machine usually winning. He could never understand why the things crashed and you lost your work. Why couldn't they recognize when a problem was imminent and rectify it before it caused a real problem. Computers are stupid things if they are unable to repair themselves and continue operating. Why on earth can't they do that he thought, why do they break down so frequently. His eye was suddenly taken by a flat screen with a very good definition. He was impressed by the sharpness and the colour. He looked at the price and sighed, it was too expensive, he was not willing to spend such a large amount of money on a monitor. However, he was tempted and he started to think where he might be able to make savings in order that he might be able to afford the flat screened monitor. A few weeks ago he had been scanning through the magazines comparing prices, and trying to decide what he needed to buy, his budget was reasonable but he knew the technology changed so quickly anything that was thought of as state-of-the-art was almost obsolete before it was taken out of its wrapping. With this thought in mind, a sensible economic machine that would do the things he wanted would suffice. But he was impressed with the monitor he had just been looking at. He looked at the printers carefully while he tried hard to remember which ones had been seen as a good buy. They nearly all looked alike, except for the odd one that looked very different due to some oversight in the design and marketing section of the company. These odd ones were usually marked down as they had proved unpopular. Andy looked at the rows of printers and thought about it from an economic point of view. What would be the main use he would put the printer to? A mixture of things, he thought, text would take up possibly 75 percent of the work. He knew that he was just making an educated guess but it was the best he could do in the circumstances. He was hoping to take up photography but he was now unsure about it. He had tried various devices to attach the camera to a flexible mount on the arm of his wheelchair, none were very successful and he found this frustrating. For the time being he had decided that he would not invest in a digital camera unless it was very simplified.

He beckoned to the assistant who had been awaiting the call. He speedily moved into close proximity to Andy, but being careful not to invade his personal space as he had been taught in a recent training session. "What's the difference between this lot here, other than the price?" asked Andy. The willing assistant began to explain the differences in performance, speed, quality, etc. Andy was cynical but tried not to show his feelings to the assistant. He was also slightly bemused by the fact that they all seemed capable of doing more or less the same. "Let's simplify it, shall we,: he said. "Will any of these machines do...," and he expanded on his perceived needs. The assistant leaned back, took a deep breath and held out his arms. "How long is a piece of string?" Andy was tempted to tell him he wasn't intending to buy string, but he resisted.

"Which one would you recommend?" said Andy who then quickly added, "leaving aside your potential commission."

"This is the one I'd go for," he replied, fondling the printer with some affection, "she's a beauty, does everything you need."

"Why is that one better than the others?" Janice had been patient listening to the conversation, but she was now bored and she decided to wander away to see if anything remotely interested her non technical mind. She had used computers at work, but if they produced what she had intended she concluded that it was more by good luck than anything else.

She picked up a box that caught her eye. 'Design your own living space' was the title on the box. Janice looked at the back and read the contents. How to arrange your living space, design your room or your furniture, match the colour schemes, show different lighting effects. 'That could be very useful,' she thought. It would save time if she could look at the accommodation and the likely furniture from the beginning. She would recognize right away whether it was practical or not. She looked at the price and thought that it seemed reasonable if it did all of the things it had said it did. She placed the box down, deciding that she would consider the value to her of having such software. Perhaps soon, she thought. After a moments thought she had talked herself out of buying the software knowing that she would have to install it on one of the computers at work and that practice was frowned upon. She turned around to see what Andy was doing. He had moved away from the printers and was now looking at the various screens that were on display. She decided that she would leave him to it. She wandered down the aisles looking at the glossy software packages. Very soon a young man approached her and offered her his assistance.

Andy had decided that he definitely needed the flat screen monitor, and a more powerful computer than he had previously thought. After some prolonged discussion he had made his choice. He made his way to an area which had been set aside for the completion of such transactions. Janice soon joined him and asked him what exactly he had bought. After he had told her and explained the logic of spending more than he had intended she nodded in what he took as a sign of approval. He had been expecting some criticism having already told her how much he was willing to spend. "It's ready for you to take now," said the young man. Janice thanked him and took hold of the box. "What's that?" enquired Andy. "I've bought a laptop. It seemed the sensible thing to do as it was on special offer, and after all, I need one. I can't bury my head in the sand forever can I?" Andy started laughing, he now knew why she wasn't willing to criticise his purchase. He was still laughing when the young man handed her the extra software she had bought.

"We have a few more things to buy yet," he said, "probably won't fit them into the car if you buy any more software. You've enough stuff there to start your own publishing company." Janice tried to justify some of her purchases but gave up as she was only playing into his hands. And if she were to tell the truth, she did not have much of an idea what most of the software actually did. She had accepted the assistant's advice regarding what was essential. He had told her with some certainty that she would need to create her own web site. Janice did not know what a web site was, but it sounded important, and therefore as she was starting up, this was the opportune time to make sure she had one.

The pub doors were heavily sprung and it was difficult in getting the wheelchair through as the next door was set at a right angle. Andy went to the nearest table as the other tables were arranged in such a manner that there was insufficient space between them. "I'll have a pint and a...," he paused while he looked again at the menu which was scrawled upon a blackboard at the back of the bar. "What are Freddy's super sausages?" he enquired. The young women behind the bar said that she had no idea, not a clue, but they were large and they were popular and gave you wind. She added that they came with chips and either egg or beans. "I'll have them with both egg and beans," said Andy. The young women looked perplexed for the moment. "You can have them with either egg or beans for the same price, but if you have both, I don't know what the price is." She looked at him with some hope that he would settle for one or the other. "Ask someone!" said Andy sharply. "How much is it if someone wants beans *and* egg with the sausage?" she shouted through an aperture at the back of the bar. "No, he wants both beans *and* egg," she shouted again. She turned to Andy and smiled. "We don't a price for both, it's the breweries policy." "I want both," said Andy adamantly, not willing to be beaten by such a simple event. "Look at it this way if possible," he said with some impatience, "how much would beans and toast cost, and how much would toast cost without beans? Just subtract." She looked at him with a blank expression. Suddenly the light went on. "That's the cost of the beans," she said happily. "Well it might not be," said Andy. She looked disappointed at this remark. He continued, "it's a good indication though, as to the approximate price of a portion of beans, but it might be less in reality if I have them with the egg as I'm buying more." She looked bewildered. Andy was about to prolong the discussion when Janice started to glare at him. "Leave Freddy's sausages, and I'll have the scampi," he said. He quickly added, "does it come with peas?" The young women felt more confident with the scampi and told him that it came with chips and salad as well as peas, everyone smiled at this acceptable outcome. "I'll have a beef sandwich on wholemeal bread," said Janice. "Sorry, but we only have white bread unless you want it in a," she paused trying to think of the word. She gave up the effort. "One of those French long sandwiches" she said. I don't think those will be wholemeal," said Janice now wishing she had settled for the white bread. "Quite a lot of people are eating them nowadays," said the young women. "It's with everyone going abroad you know, they want something different nowadays, and French bread is really popular," she said, while for some unknown reason winking in an exaggerated manner. Janice assumed that there was some mystical significance in the gesture, but finally settled for the white bread with ham as it was soon discovered that the beef was no longer available for some unknown reason. "It was there ten minutes ago! I saw it with my own eyes, on the plate on the table. It's that bloody dog, it'll eat anything," she said sighing. Janice looked apprehensive and asked if the dog was still roaming around the kitchen. The young women smiled and said "of course not, you can't have animals roaming around where food is!" She added "he's just let in for his food, it'd be wrong to leave him outside in all weather." Andy wondered if the dog had a taste for scampi then dismissed the idea.

He tasted his beer and shuddered. "This beer is off," he stated loudly. "You're not the first to say that today, I've told him that there's something wrong, but will he listen? He sits on his arse in there doing nothing," she gestured in the direction of the door leading into another room. "He's playing about with the computer all day, he says that he has to keep up-to-date with modern international retail trends. If you ask me he has another woman somewhere, he's always in those chat rooms morning noon and night. Only comes into the bar when it's closing time." Andy groaned loudly, "I don't care what he does, but the beer is off," said Andy. "I'll get you another pint." Andy stopped her before she had chance to produce more of the offensive liquid. "I don't want another pint of that stuff." She smiled and said "would you prefer a bottle or a pint of larger?" "I'll have a bottle, it's probably safer," he said unable to contain his disdain. To their surprise the food was edible and they quickly consumed it, they were more hungry than they had realized. Andy looked around the large room, "I didn't realise that such places still existed! It's in a time warp! Nothing has changed here in years, and it's not very clean, is it? If we go down with food poisoning we'll know where we obtained it."

Janice said that they had to get some food in as he could not expect his carers to nip out shopping every day. "I thought that was what they were supposed to do," he said sarcastically. "What's the bloody point of having carers if they won't do what I want them to do?" "I didn't mean it as it sounded," said Janice. "Of course they'll shop for you, but remember that you've been assessed, and time has been allocated for specific tasks. Everything we could think of is down on the plan, there'll be things that need changing but for the moment, until you find out what needs changing, it'll suffice."

"What exactly does '**suffice**' mean," he said while over-emphasizing the word. "Don't you mean 'survive'? Everything will be fine if I survive the ordeal of not obtaining food when I need it." She did not respond to his outbreak, she was not unfamiliar with his attitude and the line he was likely to take in a given situation. "Your carers are the ones you interviewed, you chose them yourself and I'm sure that they won't let you down. Well, possibly not the first few days. And if one of them doesn't like the job then she'll not hang around. My experience with carers in this situation is that those who understand the job and enjoy it will stay with you. While the others, who did not realize what the job entailed when they applied it, might turn out good carers, or they will leave quickly, realizing it's not what they thought it was." Andy once again grimaced. He thought back a couple of weeks when Janice, a social worker, and himself had started interviewing potential carers.

Advertisements had been placed in the local press asking for carers who were interested in providing round the clock care for a severely disabled man. Internal adverts went out in the Local Authorities' magazine. There were quite a few individuals who sent for the application form and a more detailed job description. It was obvious that some had little or no idea what the job entailed and these were dismissed. It was agreed that Andy needed experienced carers who he could feel secure with. It was going to be a new experience for him and there would be some possible difficulties crop up that needed to be dealt with sensibly and effectively. "You're lucky to get decent carers! They're hard to find. No one seems to want the work. I suppose it's because of the poor pay and the lack of appreciation. The agencies pocket most of the money and don't really care who they employ. Local Authorities can't get suitable carers to work for them either. They don't put enough effort into allocating enough funding, that's part of the problem. The main problem is people just don't want that type of work anymore, which is bloody sad really, as they could obtain more satisfaction than working at some of the jobs that pay a bit more."

"You're really cheering me up, telling me that no one actually wants the job," said Andy. "If things start off right it's a whole lot easier for everyone concerned," said Janice. "You have to think of the basic practicalities."

"Which means in reality, Is this person capable of washing, dressing and toileting me, cooking and cleaning, and putting me to bed? They might appear to be simple things that everyone does for themselves everyday, but for some reason some people find it difficult to do these things for others in an acceptable manner. Even though they seem to want to be carers. I don't like saying this, but some applicants also think it's such an easy job that any standard is acceptable, and the client should be grateful for the assistance they receive. It's difficult to get across to some carers that the client is, in one way or another, paying their wages and a good job is expected as a right. Somehow, we have created a culture where good carers are not valued as highly as they should be."

The social worker agreed and added how good carers could improve the lifestyle of a client. Andy said that a good carer, in his opinion, should have nothing to do or say about his lifestyle. He wanted carers to do what they were told, that would be enough and as far as his lifestyle was concerned at the moment, he did not have one.

"Well, it's going to be easy then, isn't it?" said Janice "you're starting with a clean sheet, you can develop as you go along, you can learn together," she smiled at that point. This irritated Andy but he did not say anything.

Most of the applicants turned out to be better than they had expected. They finally chose four who, it turned out, had the most experience. They all said that they were flexible and would not mind working at anytime. Two said that they would like to work full time if possible. And they would work extra hours if and when they were needed. It was something of a disappointment when two of the people who they interviewed stated that they would love the job but now they had found out what the rate of pay was they just could not afford to do the job. They could earn more filling shelves at the supermarket and get their shopping at a discount. Andy asked about the possibility of them being on call for emergencies or holidays, but they both declined. "I can't attract decent carers if I can't pay a suitable rate," he said feeling very angry. "And who will I get for the money I can offer? Some morons who think it must be simple and easy, otherwise the pay would be better." Janice nodded in agreement . "There is one good point though, if they do want the job at the hourly rate we're offering, it could mean that caring is more important than the extra money." Andy looked at her as though he could not believe what he had heard. "Just forget that I said that," said Janice who could not understand why she had mentioned it in the first place. She knew how difficult it could be to get good carers. The agencies and the carers just seemed to work in a manner that was unreliable and took no account of the needs of the client. She also knew that social services departments were under funded and for some reason did not seem to recognise the effects a poor service had on the individuals concerned.

Many of her colleagues agreed that caring, while not requiring an IQ that would get the person a membership of mensa, it does require common sense and an understanding of people, but until the powers that be recognise the importance of carers we will not be able to pay them properly. She then said, "it's going to get worse with an aging population, unless society is quickly educated and recognises that we nearly all will, at sometime, require carers. It's a simple fact of life and we must learn to pay for it, there are no cheap options." Andy said he understood the situation, or he thought he did, but it did not solve his problems which existed there and then, and not at some future date. "Actually, you can't totally blame the local authorities for everything, the government doesn't really support care in the community, it just pays lip service to the problem and occasionally comes up with stupid, half-baked ideas that help no one in the long term. Care in the community is basically very simple. Money is needed and then a sensible structure that makes the job interesting and worthwhile for paid carers. For years, governments just cannot bear the idea that care costs money and most people who are being cared for deserve better, they are treat as though they're undeserving, as though society is doing them a favour. When they have worked hard and paid their taxes expecting a better retirement and a comfortable old age." Andy agreed with what she said, then added. "We younger ones are going to depend upon these services for most of our lives. Does that mean that we can expect a miserable, impoverished lifestyle for the rest of our lives? In a supposedly wealthy society don't we deserve a little better than that? Otherwise, all we can look forward to is going around like refugees for the rest of our lives. Reminds me of children, looking in the sweetshop window seeing all the wonderful things, yet not being able to go in and buy any of them, the only difference is, this will be forever." Janice said nothing.

After the interviews, Janice asked Andy what his thoughts were regarding the carers. Andy had taken the process seriously as he knew that he was going to be dependent upon these people to a large extent, and their abilities could dictate the quality of his life. What he did not want was a constant stream of new carers coming into his home, having to be taught how he wanted things doing. If that was to be the case, he could see all of his time being taken up with having to deal with carers. There would be little or no time for anything else. What a bloody existence! he thought. He had talked about carers with some of the other patients on the unit. One patient said that it was a bloody nightmare getting good carers at the price the local authority paid. All his days were taken up by the thought of being let down, although his care package was in the hands of an agency. Another patient said that he was lucky his authority had come up with a decent care package using their own staff, and he said that they had proved reliable and good carers on the whole. But he was aware of the problems, as a disabled friend of his had been robbed by his carer. Emptied his bank account and gone off abroad on an extended holiday. That's the problem, said another patient, they come into your home and you need them to assist you with everything, subsequently you have to trust them, you have no choice. It can make you feel very insecure knowing that the carer might go into your wallet on a regular basis. You need trustworthy carers who deals with your mail, and pay your bills. With some you will have no privacy at all within a short time, that's the reality, there is no way around it.

"A good carer is rarer than a penny black, so treat them with respect, a bad carer is a nightmare, get rid of them as soon as you can said," another patient. His mind soon switched to a more positive note as the carers who had been offered the job did appear to be normal, sensible people who wanted to do a good job. And there was the small bonus that he found two of them reasonable attractive. Nothing to shout about, he thought, but quite acceptable, as they would not curdle the milk or frighten the cat. That was something else he had to consider, getting a cat. He was not a particular animal lover, but he thought a suitable cat might be a reasonable addition to the household. He did not know if the house had mice or not but a good cat would solve that problem. He also thought that cats don't need walking or having things thrown for them. You don't have to exercise a cat, they managed these things by themselves. 'I'll definitely get me a cat,' he thought. As soon as he is established, it's down to the cats home to find some appreciative young cat who looks as though they might be loyal. Although he knew that cats were their own masters and loyalty was mainly concerned with regular food and curling up in front of the fire.

He would have preferred an older cat, but once out of the door it might go back to its original locality, so it must be a young cat or even a kitten. He then thought about training it to go outside and the tray of cat litter in the kitchen. For a moment he was unsure as to whether the idea was a good one. He did not like the thought of cats using his kitchen as a toilet area. He thought that he might get a few fish, it would be something to look at and fish were never much trouble, never really offensive to anyone. In fact, when he thought about it, he could not think of anything that fish actually did that was interesting. They eat, sleep, swim about and that's it. Not a demanding lifestyle, not creative in any shape or form. It's possible that fish never think and that they just react to basic stimuli, he thought. He wondered why that had not crossed his mind before. He then briefly thought about a Macaw. He had always wanted one but they were expensive and they would leave droppings all over the place. He new that he could not keep one in a cage as it was unfair and cruel. He felt strongly about having animals locked up, unable to fly around or walk around with inadequate space. While he was not interested in animal rights, he still thought it wrong to inflict miserable circumstances upon animals just for our amusement. In recent years he had also decided that animal experimentation was undesirable. Which brought him to a difficult question which he had discussed with Harry. Would you use animals for experimentation if it was probable that it would lead to a cure or solution to being spinally injured?. Harry said that when he was originally injured he would have done almost anything to have improved his physical condition, but as he grew older he had decided that he definitely did not want animals experimented upon in his name. Andy had argued the point that if we're willing to eat them, then what is the difference. Harry said it was clear to him that prolonged suffering of an animal was unacceptable and that was it. He added I would shoot them, go fishing, etc and eat them as a quick, clean death is as good as it gets for most animals, as they tend not to die of old age. But why should I or anyone inflict prolonged pain on an animal? It does not seem acceptable. Andy was unsure about it, although to some extent he felt like Harry. How many thousand experiments would be acceptable, asked Harry before it was decided there was enough information available?

"I see your point," said Andy while still unsure.

"We're only animals, and we wouldn't like some powerful creature experimenting on us," added Harry "it's as simple as that! It's wrong, and that's my position, but I can understand others who would sacrifice their own mothers if they could find a treatment that restored them to a non-disabled condition. But that's their choice." Andy said that he was possibly in agreement with Harry, but that he might change his mind after more thought. "I think that after serious thought you'll see it my way," added Harry. Andy looked back on such conversations and recognised that he had benefited from some of Harry's opinions although at the time Harry's dogmatic approach tended to force him into taking an opposing view on principle.

The supermarket was relatively quiet and parking was easy. "Don't forget my lottery tickets," he said, "You could all be redundant within twenty four hours this week! Could be my week!" he said with false enthusiasm. "Then it's me for the bright lights, fast cars and loose women. I'd be very popular! If I was a millionaire there'd be no problems getting suitable accommodation or carers."

"You wouldn't be able to trust them," added Janice quickly. "Are you saying that such people would only want to be associated with me because of my money?" he looked at Janice eagerly awaiting her response. "Some of them would, a few might not, they just might be genuine," she said while wishing she had said nothing. "Are you saying that people are not going to like me for myself? That my scintillating personality and my animal magnetism isn't going to attract people?." "If you were a magnet, you couldn't attract iron filings," replied Janice. "You have the personality of an amoeba." That was not quite the response he had wanted, but it amused him. He had started to like Janice as she seemed to understand him and rarely backed off if he confronted her with some provocative statement. "I won't bother winning then. But if I had, I would've seen that you were well looked after." She smiled but did not let him see her. "How would you look after me?" she asked. Andy thought for some time as though he was putting some serious thought into the situation. "First of all, we'd go and look at that little sports car you admire, then we would go to the estate agents to see what suitable property there was in a better part of town. While they were sorting this out, we could call in at the travel agents and book you that trip up the Yangtze river you've always wanted." Janice smiled again and briefly her hand rested on his shoulder. "You'd do that right away if you won?" she enquired. He looked at her sincerely, then he smiled. "In your bloody dreams! You'll get bugger all from me! As you just said, you'd be likely to be after my money." She withdrew her hand and resisted hitting him, although the temptation was considerable. She had fallen for it, and he had taken the opportunity to wind her up. He laughed out loud! He had enjoyed the moment. Almost instantly he felt a little guilty, he should not have said that he thought, she had been kind to him and considerate, she did not deserve it. He wished he had resisted saying anything but it was too late. He could not suddenly say he was sorry, he would feel foolish and saying sorry was not something he had become accustomed to.

He quite enjoyed going to the supermarket. There was something surreal about such places he thought. Kafka would have loved these places, food coming in at the back by container, consumers coming in at the front and taking stuff away, a never ending cycle. The nearest society gets to perpetual motion. He looked down the isles with their large display banners, stating boldly their objective. 'Buy one, get one free,' 'three for the price of two', 'twenty percent more free.' It's wonderful stuff he thought.. No one can remember the name of the minister of health but say the magic words "buy one, get one free" and everyone knows not only what it means, which is obvious, but also knows which store you are likely to be in. "Where are the fig biscuits?" he asked a young assistant who was smiling at him in what could be described as a simpering manner while she re-priced some items. "Don't know. Only started yesterday. They might be where it says biscuits," she smirked at her own remark. Andy grunted something unpleasant about her being over educated. Andy had not seen the sign some feet away. "I'll take some fig biscuits," he said hoping they were on some special offer. "What about some of these mixed ones?" Janice had seen some biscuits she liked, although if asked she would say honestly that she wasn't really a biscuit person. "I don't like them," said Andy quickly. "But what about your visitors? They might like fig biscuits." Andy produced a look something between amazement and contempt. "What visitors? Who's expecting visitors? I' not and if I had any, they can bring their own biscuits. You've not told anyone where I live have you?" he quickly asked. "Only those who need to know," replied Janice. "If you like those biscuits, why don't you just buy them? Why ask me to buy them? I'm trying to diet and if I buy them I'll eat them."

"Then don't buy them! Do without, punish yourself. Buy a good whip, self-flagellation is in for all those who diet. You can spend your life dieting and live miserable, or you can be sensible."

"Like you! You do mean be sensible like you?" she laughed at that point. "I do things sensibly, with forethought and logic. Important decisions are given plenty of thought and consideration. What about some tins of soup they always come in handy and a few tins of cooked meat. They keep well, so you don't have to throw them away." He was getting a little bit bored. "Just get what you think I'll need for a few days while I go and get a few things." He moved along the aisles slowly, looking carefully as if to find some hidden gem that had been overlooked by the masses. "Lamb burger steaks," he read it out loud then he shuddered. 'Let's have a look at the wine section,' he said to himself. He grunted as he moved along. 'All pasta and pizza's' he thought, 'and jumbo super burgers what a load of junk. There is little wonder that children can't walk any distance or undertake sport at school.' He suddenly stopped himself. 'Bloody hell,' he thought 'I'm sounding like Harry.' "Get a grip on yourself, Andy, or you're lost before you start," he said out loud.

Janice had partially filled the basket when she found him staring at a bottle of wine on the bottom shelf. He seemed transfixed by this object. "Do you want a couple of bottles of plonk?" asked Janice whose interest in wine was limited to the price and colour. "That gem laying there is definitely not plonk," he said trying to contain his excitement. "That is Haut Brion, a great wine, not as popular as it once was but a great wine. What it's doing here amongst this lot I daren't think. Pass me the bottle please I need to look at the label." After a few moments he sighed deeply. "Put that in the basket and don't shake it about.

I tremble to think how it's suffered, but a couple of years lying quietly will help it come together," he said with obvious satisfaction. "You're surely not paying that amount!" Janice was about to say more but he stopped her. "It's a fraction of its real value," he said while smiling. She could not see it, in her book wine was wine and you bought it and drank it, that was the end of it. An assistant who was walking past said. "I see you have the last bottle of Haut Brion, sir." Andy's mind froze for a moment. "You mean there were more?" "We had a case, it came in yesterday. I don't know why we received it but it was priced up. Anyway you have the last bottle." He paused, scratched his head and started to walk away. "Last week we had a Lafite, in fact, half a case of the stuff, don't know what happened to the other half."

"What happened to it?" asked Andy who was hot on the trail. "Manager bought the lot."

"Surely he's not allowed to do that! There must be a law against it." The assistant smiled, this small but pleasurable interaction had brightened up his day. "Not only that, sir," he added, "but he gets a discount on anything he buys." He walked away, pleased with his opportunity to impart such frustrating information. "That can't be right! I'm going to e-mail the chief executive about this. It's a bloody disgrace! And to think I nearly bought shares in this company, they're corrupt, totally without any honour or decency."

"It's only a bottle of wine, I just can't understand what you are going on about. If it's so important, I'll buy you one from an off license."

"You haven't a bloody clue!" have you he said in exasperation, "not a bloody clue! It's casting pearls before swine once again."

"I was trying to help and I offered to buy you a bottle I thought it was a nice gesture on my part but you're an ungrateful sod."

"To buy a decent bottle of Lafite would cost you your weeks wage and probably more."

"It's not worth it! No wine is worth a weeks' wage," said Janice sharply, as she walked away towards the checkout, "after all, it's only grape juice in a fancy bottle! It's all a con." Andy had not calmed down; I bet he does not even drink wine, he will sell it for a fat profit, the..., he stopped himself and thought, 'this is not sensible, after all it is only a drink. Perhaps Janice has a point. It's just a drink, it's grape juice, why not get things into perspective he thought. He just could not allow that to happen though. I bet the bastard's had dinner parties and bragged about it, he gave a large sigh and shook his head, life is like that he thought. Then it dawned upon him, life was good! After all, had not he just obtained the last bottle of Haut Brion? He smiled at that point a smile of satisfaction.

CHAPTER SEVENTEEN

"Just tell me once again what the plan is?" said Andy, with an expression that signified he was asking politely. Janice was patient and knew that it was important that Andy had understood the arrangements. She made sure that she did not sound patronizing.

"A carer will start coming in tonight at six o clock when she'll make your evening meal. She'll stay until about 10.30pm when another carer will assist in getting you to bed, she'll stay through the night. In the morning a carer will come to get you up and make your breakfast, etc. There are a few short gaps where you don't have a carer, these we agreed upon. During the first week or two it's more of a case of seeing how things go. If adjustments need to be made we can make them, but we've tried to think of most things." She was being serious and Andy knew that his care package was more important than anything else. He was not sure that every area had been covered but he had confidence in Janice. Or to be accurate he had as much confidence in her as he had in anyone who was part of a creaking system that was badly in need of a major overhaul.

She was as satisfied as she could be that he understood who was doing what. She continued. "I'm leaving you the week's rota, and my mobile number, if there's anything you need you can ring me, and you can ring me at home if you're really stuck, although I often switch off my mobile once I'm at home, otherwise they'd be calling me every few minutes to do something." Andy quickly assured her that he would not be ringing her. "You also have the numbers of your carers. Nothing should go wrong but just in case, ring if necessary. In the morning you're going to see if there are any employment opportunities. I have an appointment but I'll try and get here around 11.30am. Then we can see if it's possible to prevent you from living in idleness for the rest of your life. "

Andy said that he was unsure about seeking a job right away. Didn't she think that it was a bit rushed, that he had only just moved into his own place and suddenly she wanted him working? Janice thought carefully before answering. "In a sense you're right, it is early for you, and if you want to take your time then you can do. It's entirely your own choice." He could tell by the tone of her voice that he was stepping into an area which might not be of any short term benefit to him and that he was expected to show some degree of a positive response. He explained to her "It's not that I don't want some suitable employment," he said convincingly. "But It has to be right for me. I'm not going to take the first job that comes along just for the sake of it, I'm not going to go around begging for someone to employ me." Janice agreed with him which caused him to be suspicious. "What you must consider," she paused before continuing. "What you must consider is that there are not hundreds of employers queuing up to cash in upon whatever talents you may or may not have. It's sometimes difficult in getting potential employers to even consider employing a disabled person."

"What about the quota system?" said Andy while knowing that such a system had done little or nothing with regard to employing disabled people. "Unless there's a willingness to enforce any quotas then it's a total waste of time," she said, seemingly dismissing his remark. "What we've always needed are clearly defined rights for disabled people." Janice had been in her job for some years and she had been frustrated many times in the past when she had tried to assist people in gaining employment. It was during moments like this that she had to remember that Andy was not only new to his disability, but new to the whole number of issues concerned with disability and disabled peoples' rights. 'You have a lot to learn,' she thought to herself. She hoped for his sake that he would learn quickly. "On the other hand, there might be someone out there just waiting for you to come along and take the company from a sleepy, small concern to becoming a multinational. Before long you could be jet setting around the world keeping control of your expanding empire. You could have your own jet. Something in keeping with your new found status; nothing ostentatious, relatively small but tasteful, and of course your personal assistant." She continued amusing herself. "Plus the large company penthouse in Mayfair." Janice gave a little laugh before telling him to keep buying the lottery tickets. Andy had listened to Janice waiting for her to finish. "Just a minute! Before you go any further, I'm serious about this. Just because I'm disabled don't think that I would be grateful for any crap job that is offered. I do have some ability, I didn't lose it just because I had an accident. Those skills and variables haven't changed. So don't expect me to tug on my forelock and grovel will you, because you could be waiting a bloody long time." Janice sighed meaningfully, "that's definitely one thing I won't expect from you," she said. In many respects she was pleased that Andy had retained his self respect and some of his old values. She also realized that circumstances might force him to compromise, and she knew that he would find it difficult, but at least he would fight the system once he was aware of how it operated.

The door closed behind her, Andy looked around his kitchen area. "This is it! My own kitchen, my little 'chez Andy' my home," he murmured, "it's all mine!" he shouted mockingly, "'my horse, my kingdom for a horse'." He did not feel too happy at the prospect now the moment had arrived. He had wanted his own place, he wanted to be able to do what he liked when he liked, but it wasn't quite like that, for some reason it did not feel like that at all. There felt what he could only describe as an air of controlled desperation. He clearly remembered when going up to university everything was new to him then. It seemed like a continuous adventure full of interesting experiences. There seemed so much to learn in such a short time. But you knew that you were not alone and there were thousands in a similar position and if you did not get something right you were not automatically thought of as the village idiot. It was easy to submerge oneself below periscope depth and come to the surface when everything was going along fine. There was always someone there who knew less than you, and this was so comforting. For days the new students drifted around in shoals for protection while slowly gaining confidence as they overcame the numerous social obstacles that were placed in their way.

He could remember his excitement when he finally found a small flat that he could afford if another person would share the rent. It appeared dull, even dirty, but it was his and he was going to make the best of it. His mind jumped forward thinking about the possible drinking sessions he could have, and the girls who could stay overnight if they were good and compliant. That seemed not very long ago yet it was a different time, and so much had changed for him within the past few months. He prevented himself from thinking about it. He had to be positive, he had to convince himself that everything was possible. All he had to do was make the effort and use what common sense he had; he was intelligent and capable, others had seemingly done reasonable well and there was no reason why he could not do better than most.

The bungalow was different, the place was clean and tidy, there was a reasonable amount of space and it was furnished. Some people would be glad of this, he thought. He looked at the clock, in twenty minutes his first carer would arrive and make his first meal in his home. He had given no thought to what he wanted to eat. It dawned upon him that this was now his responsibility; he had to decide these simple things. He looked at some of the items he had bought earlier that day. He could not make up his mind, this caused him to feel a mixture of anger and bewilderment. Here he was starting out in his own home and he could not decide what to eat for his first meal. 'Bloody pathetic,' he thought to himself. Where has that positive aggressive approach he had promised himself, it had already gone. I must have left it upon leaving the spinal unit he thought. Or was it just bullshit. Was I trying to convince myself that I would do things in such a manner that I would ride roughshod over all obstacles. He thought that he had created a genuine positive attitude, that he had gradually got his act together. He had given a lot of thought to his situation and he was realistic about most things of importance. "We shall overcome, we shall overcome," he sang out loud. "I have a dream, I have a dream," he shouted "that all," he then paused while trying to think of the correct words. Was it men and women or all people. Bugger it, he could not remember the next line exactly and he stopped his outburst at that point. He pressed the large switch that heated the electric kettle, it had already been filled with water by Janice. She had also placed coffee and sugar in a mug, the milk was also near to hand. Andy had chosen such items carefully making sure that his thumb could easily get through the handles. My first cup of coffee made by my own fair hand, he smiled to himself. He drank his coffee slowly savouring each mouthful. He had decided to mentally make a note of these firsts in order to be able to judge over time what if any progress he had made. He was against such measuring devices if the truth were known, but he had hoped that after a period of time he would be able to clearly recognize any new skills he had acquired. He had set himself this task as some sort of yardstick to measure his general progress. Although he thought of himself as being logical and well structured, he also knew that he had the unfortunate tendency to neglect some important aspects of life if a suitable distraction came his way. Fortunately he knew that for the foreseeable future he had to concentrate hard and make sure that everything was going in the right direction. In some respects the previous weeks had been very difficult for him. He had to recognize the reality of his situation, and it had not been easy. In fact he knew deep down that many aspects of his situation were always going to be difficult to come to terms with. It was one of those inescapable facts of life that you might prefer to change, but you can't, it is not within your power. While logical and reasonable it had to be recognised that with some things it was the case that for a given time they remained beyond the horizon. Andy was intelligent by any standard, but some of his losses since his accident had been very hard to accept, and the more he thought about them the harder it became. He had reasoned that this should not be the case. If he looked at things sensibly and analysed the situation he should be able to take what decisions were appropriate to bring about the best results. He had found that no matter how hard he tried it did not always work, his mind kept leaping about in different directions distracting his more logical train of thought. But he had now promised himself that he had to be structured, he was on his own and if he failed, then it was down to him. He could not blame anyone else. Although he knew that if he really wanted to he could blame the system and no one would dispute it. But failing was not something he was used to and the thought of failure was perhaps the greatest of incentives. Throughout his life he had always worried about failure. Everyone had expected him to succeed and it placed upon him a responsibility that he could have done without. Now that he was disabled he could easily fail and no one would give a toss. They would sympathise and tell him how well he had done, that he had really tried hard and it wasn't his fault. He shuddered at such a prospect.

The doorbell rang, he turned towards the door where one of the switches was located that operated the intercom and the door locking mechanism. To his surprise he heard a key being turned in the lock. Fear suddenly ran through his veins. The door opened and a youngish looking women, whom he correctly presumed was his carer, entered the kitchen. "I didn't know who was coming into the place," he said controlling his voice while his pulse rate tried to return to something near normal. "I was given a key," said the carer looking slightly bewildered. Andy responded promptly and told her that he would decide who would have a key and who would not in the future. "For all he knew, half the district could have access," his voice was getting louder. He looked at the carer and knew by her expression that this was not the best of new starts. "Let's start again, shall we?" he said in a quieter voice that he hoped was reassuring for her. He then quickly added, "But I am annoyed that no one troubled to inform me that I was not the only person with a key; you do understand that, don't you?" he asked, "it was something of a shock to see my door being opened by a key." The carer just nodded her head and held out the key. Andy did not take it so she placed it on the surface next to the cooker. "It's Debbie isn't it?" said Andy smiling and realizing that shouting at your carer upon her first visit is possibly not the best way to start a good working relationship. "Don't worry Debbie, it's not your fault," he said while smiling in the hope that she would not regret starting the job as his carer.

Debbie was a small, youngish women of indeterminate age. If you wanted to guess you would probably say her age was between twenty-nine to thirty-six or seven. She had short mousy hair, small features and a slightly turned up nose that made Andy think she looked a little bit like a pixie out of those books he had as a young child, or possibly an elf. He thought that it summed her up reasonably accurately. "I'm sorry about the key," she said in a soft apologetic voice that was used to humility. "Don't worry about it," said Andy, "As I've said, it's not your fault Debbie." Andy had decided that he would be friendly and reasonable and see how things progressed. "Let's have a cup of tea Debbie, then you can start." She smiled again, reassured it seemed by this offer of tea. "You'll have to show me where things are, but I'll soon get used to things, and you must tell me if I'm not doing things the way you want them, won't you?" Andy promised her that he would tell her without delay, but informed her that nearly everything was new to him too, so it was a learning experience for both of them. This seemed to satisfy her. "You're my first," she suddenly said while pouring the hot water into the mugs "First what?" enquired Andy. She was about to reply when he stopped her. "There's a teapot somewhere, I prefer it out of a teapot. I can't stand drinking out of some receptacle and finding myself sucking on a teabag - it's disgusting!" "Oh! I'm sorry," she said quickly. "You weren't to know," added Andy. "And you'll soon get to know my likes and dislikes; the pot is over there, I think, hiding behind what looks like a strange frying contraption." "That's a slow cooker," said Debbie enthusiastically, "they're very good." "What are they good for?" said Andy with genuine curiosity. Debbie was on her own subject now i.e. domestic appliances, and she wanted to expand and impress her first client with her knowledge. "You can tell me about it later," said Andy crushing her brief opportunity to impress him with her advanced knowledge on most items for the domestic use of. It was difficult for her to hide her disappointment.

Andy had just remembered what she had said. "What did you mean when you said that I was your first? First born or what?" She laughed nervously, "you're my first client, this is my first day in this type of job. Don't you remember? You asked me at my interview about my previous experience, and I said that I had none. I thought that I wouldn't stand a chance as there are so many carers around with experience."

"I thought that we'd advertised for experienced carers," said Andy somewhat puzzled. "I believe you did, but I applied anyway, it's what I want to do, and I only live a few hundred yards away; it's so easy for me to nip round here."

What's the point of advertising for experienced carers when no one takes any notice, he thought. Andy had left the handling of the final short listing to Janice. He tried to recall the interview, he smiled to himself when he realized how, in the case of Debbie, past experience had been skirted around. It should have been one of the areas the social worker had dealt with, you just can't trust the buggers, he thought. He then wondered why the social worker had not asked the agreed questions, and how he had overlooked it. I should have taken more notice he thought, I'm in the real world again and I cannot allow that bunch to pull any strokes on me or the system will finish up controlling me and I won't have a bloody clue what's happening or why. This has got to be a lesson, he thought.

"This is something you wanted to do?" he enquired, "you wanted to be a carer?" he asked again while suggesting she might like a fig biscuit. She politely declined saying figs upset her stomach. That's a small bonus, thought Andy she will not be eating my fig biscuits. "There are some others, I think they're in a cupboard." "I won't bother if you don't mind, I've already had something to eat." "I don't mind at all," replied Andy. "You were telling me that you always wanted to be a carer." She smiled and leaned back against the cupboards. "I didn't always want to be a carer, not when I was young, but I always liked people and I enjoyed doing things for them. I used to run errands after school for some of the old people who lived near by, I really enjoyed it and my grandmother was involved in looking after the elderly, although at the time I used to think she was as old as they were," she laughed at that point seemingly more relaxed. "Sometimes I would go with her and she would give me small jobs to do."

"You were definitely born too late! They would have welcomed you into any household in pre-war times. You could have been a first rate scullion." Debbie looked bemused wondering if he was being offensive as she did not know what a scullion was. She continued, "anyway, after I left school I worked briefly in a shop but there wasn't any money in it, so I went to the machine works, making components for cars. It wasn't bad really, we had plenty of laughs, and the money was good with overtime." Andy was starting to wish he had not asked her why she wanted to become a carer. But he had plenty of time and he was not going anywhere, so there appeared little harm in allowing her to continue. "I then became pregnant so I got married, had two girls within a short space of time." Her tone suddenly changed at that point. "He was fine until then, but he was a real bastard, an absolute bastard."

"I take it you don't like him then?" quipped Andy. Like him, her voice suddenly changed, "I loath and detest the man. He was an animal, and he acted like an animal, he wouldn't leave me alone, there was definitely something wrong with him."

Andy had been hoping that whatever she said he would not encourage her, but his curiosity got the better of him. "Why did you marry him then?" She looked at him as if the question was ridiculous. "I was pregnant, that's why, and in our family if you became pregnant you got married just to get away from home."

"I can take it that you didn't like being at home," said Andy whose tone showed some degree of boredom, which fortunately was not picked up by Debbie. "We all wanted to get away, my father, he was a nasty violent man after a few drinks. He treat my mother awful, why she didn't leave him we'll never know. But she didn't, she stuck with him year after year . She never had any money, what little there was he always drank it. The only thing she received was blows and abuse. I swore that as soon as I could, I'd be away. And look what happened. I became pregnant to beech tree." At this point Andy must have looked confused to such an extent that even Debbie noticed. "They all call him beech tree because he's as thick as a plank of wood."

"Thank you for that explanation, I did wonder. But why beech? why not oak, or ash?" Debbie just ignored Andy's last comments as she was engrossed in her story, she continued "there's something wrong with him up here." She pointed to her head. "He's sexually incontinent, never stops. I knew he didn't go with me for my intelligent conversation or sophisticated wit. But I didn't realize how bad he was, although his own sister told me that he was no good. She was my bridesmaid at the wedding. Her boy friend was the best man, I borrowed my aunts wedding ring. We went for a drink afterwards to the 'Flying Horse.' I asked him why the 'Flying Horse' as we never go there. After a few drinks he went to the gents. He hadn't come back after a while so I went looking for him. Can you believe it? I caught him having it off with the landlady, on our wedding day of all days!" She said it as though she still found it difficult to believe. Andy's ears pricked up she had now regained some interest.

"What did you say to him? Or what did he say to you?"

"What could he say? I'd caught him red handed. Looking back I must've been so thick it's hard to believe it myself. I confronted him and demanded an explanation. Without hesitation he said that if he was nice to the landlady, he knew that we'd be able to drink all night for next to nothing, and as we were broke it seemed a sensible idea." At the time and in those circumstances it sounded a good idea. I did not like the idea, but it was practical. Only later did I realize what a lying, cheating bastard he was. He would go with anything that still breathed, could never get enough. I was glad to get rid of him. Her mood and tone of voice suddenly changed, "now then, what about something to eat?" She turned and smiled at Andy, who was still thinking about her partner and the pub landlady. No one could be so stupid, he thought not on their wedding day, or any other day. He found it difficult to believe what he had just heard. I suppose it takes all sorts, he said to himself. Hopefully life will have taught her a few things over the years. He pondered on the thought of her husband and the pub landlady, he smiled to himself thinking that if it had been written as a sketch for television no one would have believed it.

"I'm not really very hungry, to be honest, but I suppose that I should eat something." Debbie then took the initiative which surprised her. "Well, it's on my list of things to do as this is your first night. I'm here for only 90 minutes, as there's really nothing to do and it's all clean and tidy." She gazed around the kitchen making sure that everything seemed to be in its rightful place. "Anyway, I'll make you something to eat and if you don't mind, I'll be off after I have washed up. I'm off out tonight; it's a large jackpot at the bingo, and tonight I feel it could be mine." She gave a little twitching movement at the thought of winning a large amount of money. "I think that I'll make do with a sandwich of some kind," said Andy. "A sandwich? Oh no, not a sandwich!" she said while opening the cupboards to see what was on the shelves. By her expression it was obvious that she was disappointed.

"The venison is in the freezer along with the Dover sole, and the fois gras, well who knows where that is?" he looked irritated. "I've not tried to fill the place with food that I might never get around to eating. This is my first day here and I've had more important things to think about than food. I can eat almost anything, whatever you want to make me, I'll eat it." Debbie felt bad that she had annoyed Andy and that she had caused this outburst. She was upset and it showed. "I didn't mean anything, except that as it was your first day and mine, I wanted to cook you something a little bit different, something that you really like. I wasn't criticizing." Andy knew that she was trying to make things better and felt slightly guilty about his outburst. The fact that he had not given a great deal of thought about food was not her fault, and after all he liked food and once he was settled he would give it his attention. But for the moment anything would suffice. While in hospital he had promised himself during one of his infrequent periods of optimism that he would start off with as high a standard as possible and only compromise when necessary. And good food was one of those areas where he had decided that he would not compromise. His resources were limited but he had spent very little money while he was in hospital and he was in a position where he could exercise choice, if even in a modest form. Debbie still thought that it was her duty to provide him with something substantial and befitting a man of his age. In her mind she had been indoctrinated that the man of the house needed a hot meal after his days' labouring in the factory or in the fields. "What about a mushroom and ham omelette?" she asked. Andy thought about it and decided that it sounded a reasonable offer and agreed to her choice. This brought the smile back to her face. "I can't find any cream," she said while closing the fridge door. Andy wondered why she wanted cream but did not ask. He could no longer refrain from asking about the cream. Debbie told him that she was a decent cook, something higher in status than a scullion. It had taken her a little time but she had finally remembered the lowly status of the scullion in a household. "I cream the mushroom, of course half goes inside and the other half over the omelette." Andy had to agree that it sounded quite good. He thought to himself that if she was a good cook it would make his evening meals enjoyable and something to look forward to. He then thought that he should see what she produced first before becoming too optimistic and arranging dinner parties, he smiled to himself at that point.

"One other point," said Andy "you mentioned that you were here for 90 minutes and you'd go after you had cooked me something. This is something we need to establish from the beginning. If you're supposed to be here for 90 minutes, then you must do the 90 minutes, unless you have an emergency situation. You do realise that, don't you?" he said while looking directly at her awaiting to gage her expression. Debbie looked slightly bemused by what Andy had said and she could not remember implying that she would not stay for the full time allocated. Give them an inch and they will take a mile, wanted to leave early on her first visit, he thought, Anyway we will get that right from the start, it's unbelievable, he thought. "I didn't want to go before my time," said Debbie looking hurt. "I must have misunderstood," said Andy who was nearly sure that he had heard correctly.

"This is very good," said Andy, swallowing his third mouthful, "very good." Debbie positively beamed; she was unused to a man giving her a compliment for anything she did. "But it's not just ham, is it?" asked Andy. Debbie told him that she had added a touch of cheese, and a touch of onion, only a small amount but it makes all the difference. Andy agreed and asked if it required a specific type of cheese. Debbie had to think, but before she answered, Andy started laughing and told her he was not serious about a specific cheese. This allowed Debbie to laugh. The both agreed, without speaking, that they had got off to a reasonable start, considering that it was a new situation for both of them. Debbie extracted a cigarette from the packet, "would you like one now?" she held out her hand with the cigarette. Andy was about to say that when he wanted a smoke he would tell her, but he decided that he would let it go. He had enjoyed the food and they were getting on better than he had expected, so why say something that would make her defensive or even unhappy. You must remember these things, said Andy to himself, she appears the type who is eager to please, but like a child she could get upset if corrected or directed too forcefully. He had always recognized that with some people there will always be a good level of open banter, while with others it would never be acceptable. Some people are on a similar wavelength and the interaction between them will never be a problem while others try hard to communicate but never really make it. What was always a source of interest to Andy was that you could never tell just by looking at a person, or knowing their status, whether or not you could hope for that desired level of communication. And often it was a surprise who you could or could not relate to. He thought back at the times when he had met a girl who he thought was incredibly attractive, only to find that they just could not talk to one another, there was nothing there that interested both of them. He thought that it was just his luck that he had met the girl of his dreams and she might as well be speaking a rare Mongolian dialect for all he knew.

He enjoyed the smoke, he actually thought for a moment that Debbie appeared to enjoy watching him smoke as her expression indicated a level of satisfaction one obtains when you know that you have done something right. "I'd better wash up and leave you out everything you might need."

"I thought you said when you arrived that you'd be here until ten thirty."

"I did say that, but when I looked at my notes, I realized that they' only put me down for the shortened time today." She looked concerned and said that if he wanted her to stay longer she would do. Andy thought about it and tried to think if there was anything he needed. Everything seemed to be in place, he thought. "You might as well go if that was the arrangement."

"Here's my mobile number, I'll have it switched on, so if you need anything just call me and I'll come round." Andy thanked her and told her that he would not hesitate to call her if necessary. "I'll call the office in the morning and make sure that they get my rota worked out properly." She opened the door to leave, unexpectedly she moved quickly towards Andy and kissed him on the cheek. "We haven't done too badly for the first time have we?" she said, looking slightly embarrassed upon realizing what she had done. She did not know what Andy's response was likely to be. Andy smiled at her more out of surprise than anything. "I think we've managed quite well," he said, still smiling. The door closed behind Debbie. He looked around wondering if there was something he should do. He decided that at some time that evening he should ring home to his family but he would put that moment off for the time being as he already had an idea of how the conversation would go. His father would answer the telephone, he would then say that he could not hear properly and he would say, "your mother wants a word with you." This was the opening, which really meant your mother is now about to issue instructions from her command bunker. The polite voice of a women in late middle age would come over the phone.

"Is that you Andrew?" as if it could be someone else. "Are you alright? Is everything as it's supposed to be? Who's made your meal? What have you had?" And so it would go on; a prolonged question and answer session that went nowhere but always ended at the same point. "I don't like it at all, I'm not happy with the situation, how are you going to manage?"

"Don't worry mother, I'll manage."

"If there's anything at all you must call us, won't you? I want you to promise you will, otherwise I'll not be able to sleep." And Andy promised he would call. He decided that he would call later after getting used to his new surroundings.

That was Debbie was it, he mused. She had been better than he had expected, not playmate of the month but not too bad on the eye, which was a bonus. The more important thing was that she seemed a decent cook, and reasonably intelligent in a dopey sort of way. There was no reason why they could not get on and have a good working relationship. She would do he thought, then he pondered upon the word 'do'; is that good enough for me, someone who would 'do,' or should I try for something better? He gave this some thought as to the word 'do' was not quite good enough. I have not been fair with her, he concluded, she will probably be better than most carers, the evidence is limited, the jury is still out, and it's very unfair to arrive at conclusions at this time, he thought, a little later on it might be fair, but for the moment it's more of a matter of wait and see. He looked at his watch, that is something that I have not got, he thought, a clock, it's not a real home without a clock, he thought, he decided that was something he would rectify in the morning.

His thoughts then drifted back to the unit. What would I be doing now? We would have eaten and some of us would want to watch the news before any visitors arrive, for a moment the unit seemed a long way away, something that was separate to his present situation. The television control was difficult to handle; it had seemed simple when he had tried to hold it in the shop but now it wasn't resting properly between his fingers. He finally manipulated it until he had switched the television on, he found it reasonably easy changing channels; his finger had stiffened over the months and while this had worried him at the time he had been informed that by being stiff he would be able to do more and he needed to be able to wedge things in his hand. Once he got used to that it would allow him to do quite a lot of things, which while in a hospital bed had seemed totally impossible. The information for once had been correct, his stiffened, partially clenched fingers were suited to having objects wedged in them. He clearly remembered the first time that he had tried to feed himself it was a fiasco. He had been told that by putting a strap around his wrist with a zip it would be simple to put a fork or spoon in to it, this would then allow him to feed himself without help, except if he needed anything cutting up. He reached out trying to balance his arm while aiming for the pile of creamed potatoes on his plate, he had looked at the slices of beef and had decided that they seemed a more difficult option. He allowed his arm to swing across to his plate in a controlled movement. Eureka! The fork landed firmly in the potatoes, a careful extraction and then a careful movement to his mouth was required. Upon nearing the mouth his arm swung towards him out of control. The fork stabbed him in the left cheek below the eye, the potato fell off and dropped down the front of his shirt. "The fucking bastard!" he spluttered out angrily. "Now, now, patience is required," said a passing nurse. Andy did not at that particular moment feel patient, he shook his arm violently trying to rid himself of the strap and the fork. After a while the fork dropped out onto the floor. "I'll get you a clean fork and give you the rest," said Belinda, a young nurse who had only recently arrived on the unit. "Bugger off! I don't want it and take this with you," shouted Andy, indicating towards the plate,. Those close by burst out laughing. He realized that he was making himself look foolish but for the moment could not decide what action was appropriate. Belinda recognized his situation and came to his rescue. She pulled up a chair and started to feed him. He glanced around waiting for someone to say something, but no one did. In the days that followed he had learned to eat using the strap containing a fork, once he had really got used to that he decided that it would be better if he could wedge a fork between his fingers. This turned out a bit more difficult than he had first envisaged as it was something of a balancing act. Given time he was successful and it gave him some considerable satisfaction. The thought of being seen in public with a strap and a fork did not appeal to him at all. He visualized the situation of being in a decent restaurant ordering something nice and delicate then having to have his strap fitted, he had decided that he would not do that if he could find a better way.

Andy suddenly stopped thinking, his mind numbed over, it was as if a cloud that had the ability to obscure his thoughts had suddenly descended upon him, his mind had been put into limbo momentarily. He could not think properly and he felt a surge of fear but that quickly disappeared much to his relief, he shuddered as though a cold chill had passed over him. He started to think again but he was concerned about the last few minutes. He tried to look at things logically and he asked himself. Why had he so suddenly felt lost, almost helpless and unable to think? After some time he concluded that the past few hours had been such a new experience which he was unaccustomed to, and that for some inexplicable reason his mind must have been temporarily overloaded. He then wondered if that was possible, was there such a physiological state as an overloaded mind. He wasn't sure but it sounded plausible and he decided not to dwell upon the thought in case it happened again. He could not find anything on television although he was pleased that he had phoned the shop and insisted they brought one around without delay. He sat and thought some more about his situation but his heart was not in it so he gave up. This is it, he thought, I'm by myself and it's now up to me to decide my future, it's all down to me, and if I want anything then I have to make things happen. At the time such a thought was more important than Andy realized. Time passed slowly, but the clock eventually moved around to ten thirty, the carer was due to arrive.

CHAPTER EIGHTEEN

The door bell sounded and Andy shouted for whoever had rung the door bell to come in but realized that was unwise, he moved to the answering speaker system that had been installed, pressed the button and asked who it was. A female replied that it was Pat from the agencies. He let her in. Pat was quite tall and slim, she moved in what might be described as an athletic manner. She looked slightly tanned as though she had been away on holiday or regularly used a sun bed. She looks OK, thought Andy who then hoped that she would be a good carer, and not someone who rushed about doing things her way and sticking to any pre-conceived ideas that she might have formed. From his limited experience he knew that he had to ensure that she did things in the way he wanted, it was his needs that they were dealing with and he should not let her forget it. Start as you mean to go on he thought or she will take over.

"I'm sorry if I'm a bit early," said Pat while looking around the room.

"You're on time," said Andy who observed her looking around. "Do you want to look around the place or have you seen it before?" he asked in a voice that tried to obscure his sarcasm. Pat recognized that he had observed her looking around and not looking at him as she introduced herself. "I'm sorry," she said "it's just that I've not had a look around and I'm not sure what I'm supposed to be doing. But don't worry, I learn quickly," she smiled at him as though to reassure him. Andy groaned instantly, just as he had expected he thought. Everything is supposed to be set up correctly, everyone properly briefed and the carer who is going to put me to bed hasn't a bloody clue. He had somehow expected this, the system promises so much but once again somehow communications are not entered into properly because no one gives a toss, and he is left to give instructions.

"I thought you'd been told everything that you needed to do," he replied. "Actually I was told which makes me look rather silly, but that was a couple of weeks ago and due to some confusion as to when you were leaving hospital, it had slipped onto the back burner in my mind," she then quickly added, "but not to worry, it'll be fine, and I'll do what you asked." Andy said to himself that he had already had a similar conversation with the carer who had just left, hopefully things would soon be organized better, he thought. He then thought that this was his first night so to speak and he knew that it would not be smooth and simple, it was just too much to expect, promises, promises; it was always the same, a lack of communication, the left hand not knowing what the right hand was doing. He wondered how they ever organised anything, and what happened when they got things wrong. In business, someone would soon be on a warning, he thought or probably sacked.

"Have you had your supper?" she asked, "is there anything you'd like me to get you now?" she looked at Andy in expectation.

"Let me show you around the place as you'll be staying, you should look at your room first of all, after all, it must be strange for you coming into a strange house and meeting someone for the first time." That seems considerate on my part, he thought to himself. He had decided that he would be as considerate as he could as long as they did their job correctly. Knowing his own personality he realized that it was never going to be easy as he was not known for his diplomacy when things were not going right.

"It's a very nice room," said Pat wanting to strike the right note, "did you choose the décor?" she added. Andy said that he had suggested a few things but had not been totally involved the whole of the time as it did not interest him so much. He now realized that if he had shown more interest he could have obtained things more to his liking, but at the time when accommodation was being arranged he had not felt in the mood to totally involve himself. In truth, at that time he was unsure as to what he really wanted as his future seemed to be so uncertain. It was so confusing, one person said one thing and then someone else would say the opposite. It had reached the stage where Andy realized that there were no certainties, information changed on a regular basis. What was more confusing was trying to ascertain who was responsible for what. In the end he realized that he was at the mercy of the system and all that he could do was to keep asking appropriate questions with the hope that someone would clarify the situation.

The telephone rang, much to Andy's surprise. He was pleasantly surprised that it was Belinda who was calling. She apologised for calling so late but she wanted to know how he was managing. He tried to explain that everything seemed fine and much as he expected it to be, but he admitted that it was a daunting experience being in the real world without the comfort of the back up that was available to him when he was on the unit. He quickly added that if she mentioned that to anyone he would not forgive her. She said that she could understand that, and she would not want him to loose what little credibility he might have, he could hear her trying hard to stifle a laugh at that point but he let it go for the time being. She then asked him if it would be OK if she called around in the morning as she had a few days off. Andy was pleased to be able to say yes. He asked her to bring some decent coffee with her. He smiled to himself, for some unknown reason he was glad that Belinda had phoned him, it made him feel as though he had not been totally forgotten, it is trivial really, he said to himself, but it was a nice feeling to be thought about.

"What would you like me to do now?" asked Pat. Andy thought for a while and decided that he should go to bed, although the prospect was not something he was looking forward to. He was unsure as to what skills or knowledge Pat had. Therefore he thought getting into bed and undressed might take more time and effort than it had while he was in hospital. Andy decided that whatever happened he must remain calm and reasonable, and not allow himself to display any frustration as it would probably transfer itself to his carer, and he did not want her to find anything difficult the first time she stayed with him. He asked her if she was familiar with the tracking system that lifted him out of his wheelchair into bed. She said that she was used to them. Andy was in bed and undressed in less time than he thought would be the case. He recognized quickly that Pat was used to handling disabled people with confidence and he found this reassuring. He explained that he would press his call button if he needed to be moved or required a drink. She insisted that he must call her if he needed anything as that was what she was there for. Andy settled down in bed and thought about the days events.

Surprisingly everything had gone better than he had expected. He had decided to expect the worst, but it had been much better. For the moment he had to expect that some time something would go wrong, but if it did not then it was a bonus. He allowed his thoughts to drift back over the past few months. He was feeling tired and his thoughts came and went as though they were part of a badly edited film where there was little continuity and no real story but just a mélange of distorted events. He then thought about Harry and smiled to himself. He had come to like Harry a lot over the months they were together; he had learned quite a lot about Harry, but also about himself. He knew that being disabled was not something he liked or would ever really accept, but he also knew that there were no cures or miracles as Harry often had told him, and he had to get on with his life. He remembered clearly Harry saying how much time and effort he had wasted through his ignorance and through the complexity of the system. He had said, without trying to camouflage his feelings, that time was so important. Andy had learned to listen to what Harry had to say on these matters. Don't waste time, go out and get the things you want, involve yourself in obtaining those things that you feel are important, otherwise you will never get them. There are no magic wands, no one is waiting out there to sort out your life or make it easier, you have to do it yourself and the quicker you learn how to do this the better you will be. That was the basic message that Harry always returned to. Andy thought that he understood clearly what Harry had meant, because Harry had talked at great length on these matters once he thought Andy was genuinely interested and capable of understanding some of the more subtle aspects.

One point that Harry did reserve until shortly before Andy was due to leave hospital was his views on satisfaction and appreciation. This item was something that Andy had enjoyed listening to, much to his surprise. Harry had said "that unless you can do many of the things that you always really wanted to do previous to your accident it can make life lacking in satisfaction. The same applies to achievement, you might want to climb Everest or something, and it's not going to happen, you have to try and come to terms with some of those things. But the thing that will probably irritate you most is that if you do something worthwhile, the rest of society will dismiss it as being of no importance. You'll not be looked upon as an able bodied person, you'll not have their status, that sounds sad and almost illogical, but believe me, your efforts will not be valued, or even recognised by most people, so don't expect it. Actually, that's one of the real reasons some of the sporting types stick with the sports, their medals and trips away gives them a little status, even if it's only amongst a small minority of their peers, they would never admit it though."

To his surprise Andy was feeling less tired than he had previously thought and he was also surprised how easy it seemed that he could recall his conversations in some detail. He valued those conversations as he had learned more than he had realised at the time. Harry said that if he listened he might save himself making a few mistakes, on the other hand it depended upon his ability to recognise and retain the information that he was given.

Harry had explained that it was so easy to let things drift along at their own pace as though there was all the time in the world. But after some years, and a number of major incidents in his life, it had dawned upon him that you cannot sit back and just allow things to happen, you have to make them happen yourself. Harry said that such a statement might sound arrogant, but if you don't do it yourself nothing will happen in the way or manner you would like it to. He went on to say that realities have to be faced, only then can you adapt yourself to a situation. Andy said that he thought Social Services would help and ensure that some basic things were available. Harry gave a cynical laugh and continued holding forth on the subject.

"Let's look at reality," he said as though he was about to give important instructions to a group of students. "The major problem is simple. You're very dependant, and you need the physical assistance of others every day of your life. It's an inescapable fact, therefore you operate within those parameters. Once you accept that fact, you can then start to stretch those parameters as far as is in your interest. You have to be self centred and selfish to an extent, without being totally objectionable, which in your case might prove difficult." Andy did not rise to the bait. Harry had paused at that point in order to gather his thoughts and to try and explain himself a little clearer.

Harry was muttering under his breath, it was as though his brain was ticking over like a tractor, quite slow but attempting to get to a specific point. "I'm not saying that you should use people in a manner that you would find unacceptable if you were the able bodied person. In other words, don't act like an idiot and piss people off just for the sake of it." Andy resented the possibility of Harry even considering that he might act like an idiot. Harry continued, "it's a fine line in getting people to assist you in the manner you want, when you want. It's all too common to hear them saying how demanding a person is. When I hear this, it really pisses me off," said Harry. "But on the other hand I've come across disabled people who treat their carer's or partners like slaves, and then can't understand when they find that those who are there to help dig their heels in and withhold their support. And instead of helping they just make life more difficult in some situations." He quickly added, "if they're paid carers, I know that shouldn't happen as they're paid to do a job in a professional manner, and they should recognize the situation you are in and why some things are important to you. The trouble is, it does not tend to work like that. Carers come in all shapes and sizes when it comes to their ability to provide good care or any level of care. Don't expect too much from them as you're likely to be disappointed. On the other hand, you might come across carers who are very good, also bright, perceptive and really caring. Such carers are a rare breed believe me, they're always in demand." Harry gave a large sigh at this point. "The trouble is that the system sends out masses of information that is complex and seemingly contradictory. It should be simple for social services and the health service to be able to sort out your care needs without any problems as it's not rocket science, it's so bloody simple. But the skill is in how the system can complicate something simple. They have it off to a fine art. More people are employed to do less and especially less hands-on-care. There are so many do's and don'ts it's difficult to ascertain what carers and nurses are allowed to do." He took a large breath at this point as if to emphasis what he was about to say. "This now brings me to an interesting point." Andy knew that

Harry had moved himself gently along into a position where he could go into considerable detail at great length. This is going to be boring in the extreme, thought Andy. He wondered if there was an easy way of getting Harry's thoughts onto a different subject before he was in full flow.

"I was thinking about Bernard last night," said Andy.

"We should really have gone to his funeral," said Harry quickly interjecting.

"I didn't know him," said Andy excusing himself.

"Well, I suppose so," said Harry, trying to quickly think of something that might justify his non-attendance. "To be honest, I didn't know him all that well, really. I knew of him, mainly through others who had mentioned him. I can't remember who told me, but it seemed as though Bernard had a number of lives. Or to be more precise he compartmentalized his thoughts and experiences to the extent that it was difficult to know what he'd done, where he'd been and what he knew." Harry was disappointed in his own thoughts and went on. "People like Bernard have often lived a very full life that makes our lives look so ordinary, and we never make the effort to find out what knowledge and understanding they have gained over the years."

Harry held up his arm in a gesture to stop Andy from interrupting. "Before you say anything, I'll admit that I had little or nothing to do with him just because he didn't appear as though he wanted to talk. After all, he was very ill, or he wouldn't have died, would he?" Harry thought that he was unconvincing, and he knew that he just had not bothered to enter into a conversation because Bernard was old, and age was not respected or valued. Harry was not pleased with himself knowing that he was as guilty as those individuals in what he called the system. He had not given a toss for Bernard, he had not taken the trouble to give him the time of day and this made him feel guilty. He was angry because of the guilt he had brought on himself. How many times over the years had he gone on and on about a caring society and people's needs. Yet here he had been just a few beds away from an old man whom they could not bother to talk to, and it was for no other reason than his age. "I judged him on the grounds of his age as though he was not worth my attention." Harry felt embarrassed at this point and decided that he would change the subject before Andy said something that would make him more uncomfortable.

"He did get up out of bed his last day," added Andy.

"That's not much to write home about is it? He got up and then died. What kind of sentiment is that?"

Andy told him that it was just a fact, he had got up for the first time that day. Harry was feeling irritable as the conversation was not making him feel any better, on the contrary. "We didn't go to the funeral because we didn't know him well enough, and because we didn't bother, I feel guilty for some reason as he was probably a very decent person who had no friends left, which is bloody sad, and that sums it up accurately," added Andy.

Andy smiled to himself when he recalled how uncomfortable Harry had looked. Andy recalled how the days passed slowly after Bernard's death; it had temporarily cast a shadow over those few who lived in proximity to him and had not given him any meaningful consideration. One morning it somehow felt different, the atmosphere that had pervaded the room had gone. "It's the big day today," said Harry trying to be nonchalant, Andy said nothing so Harry said it again. "It's the big day today."

"What's happening, is the Queen visiting?" asked Andy pretending he did not know. "My daughter's coming to see me, and I'm getting up for the occasion as I think it'll look better if I'm not in bed, being in bed would give a totally wrong impression."

"How can it give a wrong impression? You spend most of your time in bed, it's no big secret, or are you somehow ashamed of being in bed?" said Andy, trying to make Harry uncomfortable.

"I just don't want her to think that I'm a bed-fast worn out old fart, and that this has been my life."

"That's fine if you don't want her to know the truth!" said Andy sarcastically. "If you want to create a good impression give her some money for clothes, and take her to the pub." Harry looked shocked for a moment. He then laughed, believing that Andy was trying to annoy him. "My daughter will not be used to pubs and such like," added Harry.

It was Andy's turn to look bemused. "She's sixteen, all girls are used to pubs at sixteen," he said with some emphasis, "she'll be out clubbing at weekends, drinking triple whatever is on offer, and possibly going out with someone years older than her with a good expense account. I can see him now, a cocky middle class type who drives a small car with an oversize engine." He was about to expand upon his experience of sixteen year old girls when he thought better of it. "You'll be telling me next that she knows nothing of boyfriends."

Harry glared at him. "This is my daughter you're talking about; she's not like the rough stuff you are used to picking up when they're so stoned that they don't know what the hell they're doing."

"She's old enough to be married!" retorted Andy, who had no patience when it came to Harry's sudden blind belief that his daughter must have the manner and purity of the Madonna.

"Take it from me," said Andy, by the time they reach sixteen they have been around the block a few times. And if my memory serves me correctly, didn't she go to a public school? A bunch of young lesbians will probably control the place. And you should know that my friends and I used to date some of the sixteen year olds from a nearby girls school, little ravers all of them, they couldn't get enough, they knew that if they did not come across with the goods we could easily find someone who would, they loved being seen out with us simply because we were a few years older and we could always find a few pounds to buy them a couple of drinks."

"Don't talk such bloody rubbish," said Harry, who thought suddenly that Andy might have a point. He had no idea what his daughter was really like. He could hardly think what she might look like although her mother had said that she was growing tall. But that was quite some time ago and was does growing tall mean, and people change so quickly when they are young. He sighed and then reassured himself that she must be reasonable and sensible. After all when he had written to her she had replied quickly and had said clearly that she would like to meet him. And now the day had arrived.

Looking back Andy decided that it was one of the more interesting days on the unit. He smiled to himself when he recalled the performance that Harry went through before the arrival of his daughter. He changed his tie at least five or six times before he settled upon a plain, dark red one that seemed to enhance nothing that he was wearing.

"It looks fine to me, totally bland and non-descript," said Andy.

"It looks very nice," said Elisabeth trying to be helpful, "it's nice to see someone wearing a tie in this place. Standards have gone down over the years. The only kind of clothes anyone wears in here are t-shirts and jeans."

"I agree!" shouted Harry "someone has to try and regain the standards." Andy groaned before telling them that they were living in a different age, that the young were no longer trapped by such conformities as wearing ties, etc. This gave Harry the opportunity to tell Andy to look around him carefully. "Everyone in here seems to be wearing almost identical clothes. You're conforming more than we ever did. In fact, you're at the mercy of the labels. You dare not buy anything until you've made sure that it has the right label, it's pathetic you have no mind of your own, you all follow the morons on television. Elisabeth now wished that she had not said anything, she should have known better, it just gave Harry the opportunity to sound off, but she recognised that he was under some stress wondering what to say upon first meeting his daughter.

Andy was surprised at how easy it was to recall these conversations. He decided that he was thirsty and looked to ascertain the position of his water jug. It seemed within reach, and there was a long flexible straw secured in it. With a bit of shuffling around he managed to get the straw in his grasp. He was then able to slowly move the jug towards him. It was a delicate exercise but he had done it successfully many times in the past while in hospital. Now that he was at home he was determined that he would not lose his ability to do something so simple.

He laid back and smiled when he thought of Harry's face when he met his daughter. It could have been one of those moments in life that makes you cringe at the thought of it. Or it could be a moment that should be cherished by all those who were aware of its significance. Harry had gone along the corridor to meet her in the hope of eliminating any possible embarrassment that might come his way. He knew that this meeting meant so much to him and hopefully to her. Andy had managed to get himself someway along the corridor so he could observe the proceedings. After sometime he decided that he would return to the unit and that no matter how tempting, he had no right to intrude in anyway. He did think at the time that he would have liked to have seen her if only out of curiosity. Harry was looking pleased upon his return. "Went alright then?" asked Andy. "It was fine!" said Harry keeping firm control over his emotions. Elisabeth and Andy waited for Harry to expand on the meeting. "I hope we don't have to drag it out of him bit by bit," said Elisabeth. Harry decided that they were ready and primed to listen to what he had to say.

"First of all, she's a very nice girl, or to be accurate, a young women." He could feel the emotion welling up inside him already. He continued, "she's very attractive,"

"Oh god! Here we go! How come I'm surprised at that?" said Andy.

"I'm being as objective as I can," said Harry ignoring Andy's comment. "She's still at school and hopes to go on to University. We talked about general things and she did remember me better than I expected. Evidently her mother had told her quite a lot after her stepfather died, more than I thought she would" ' best thing he ever did,' said Harry under his breath. "Evidently little was said about me when he was still around as he wasn't comfortable discussing such things."

"I bet he wasn't!" said Andy "it would make him look a right bastard stealing someone's wife and daughter, with her husband stuck in a wheelchair, unable to go around and give him a kicking."

"Be that as it may," said Harry who could not disagree with Andy's sentiments "that was the position." Tears were forming in Harry's eyes and a lump was in his throat. "You'll have to excuse me," he said. He tried to cough but he couldn't, "the thing is," he paused trying to pull his thoughts together. "She's coming again next weekend. She wants to see me regularly and she said that there was so much to catch up on, then she cried and put her arms around me. It was something I'd often thought about. But with my luck I never thought it would happen." At that point Harry could not continue. Both Elisabeth and Andy decided not to say anything. Andy thought that it was such an important day for Harry, a day to remember. Harry insisted that they should look at the photographs she had given Harry.

"She's very nice," said Elizabeth. "She's an attractive girl," said Andy who was pleasantly surprised. The young women on the photograph had long dark hair, parted in the middle, her features were fine, almost delicate, she looked tall and slim. 'She's a very good looking type,' he thought, definitely someone he would have paid quite a bit of attention to if he was given the opportunity. Harry seemed to know what Andy was thinking and asked for the photographs back. "She didn't bring one of her mother then?" enquired Andy. Harry did not say anything for a moment, he was undecided upon his next action but he thought that the day had gone so well there was little that could be done to spoil it.

"Well, actually, she did," said Harry tentatively. "She left one with me, for some reason she didn't explain, I didn't particularly want it, but I didn't want to offend her, after all it must've been important to her for some reason." Both Elizabeth and Andy waited for Harry to produce the photograph. When he did Andy had to admit that Harry had been correct in his description, she was a good looking woman.

"How on earth did someone who looked like that marry an ugly sod like you?" asked Andy. At any other time Harry would have come back with a verbal tirade upon hearing such a remark but this time he did not bother, he was not interested in Andy's comments.

Andy smiled when he recalled the events. He then thought that it was about time he tried to get some sleep, it was another big day waiting in the morning. And he was no longer in hospital on the unit where he would be awakened by the clanging of linen trolleys being pushed around, and the loud voice of someone telling them to keep it quiet, or words to that effect.

He then realised that the community nurses had not got in touch with him. I knew that there was something that I should have done. Hold on a minute, I was told that all of this had been arranged. Who is going to do my bowels? Who will change the catheter? Pat asked him if he was awake and would he like a drink of anything. Andy said that he would have a drink of water right away as he needed to keep up his fluid intake, but he would also have a cup of coffee which he would drink afterwards. When he finally drifted off to sleep he had slept better than he expected. "Your other new carer will be arriving in about an hour, would you like to have me make your breakfast now or wait while you get up?" Andy was confronted with a choice and this pleased him. He decided that he would wait until he got up.

The new carer was called Kath, she was a homely type of person who was always smiling, very easy going. And as she said, there was not much that she had not experienced when it came to care. She explained that she had been working as a carer for some years. She had worked in residential establishments and hospitals, but working in the community was best. She added that she was able to spend more time with the individual clients and get to know their needs. That was important to her. "The happier the client is the better I feel," she said. Andy took a liking to her right away. She seemed so easy to get on with, he then thought 'what you see is what you get' and that makes life easier. Pat and Kath washed and dressed him together although both admitted that it was often easier to work by oneself. "When are you having your bowels dealt with?" said Kath. "I think it's been agreed for Thursday morning, the district nurse is coming in to do them." Thank god I have remembered' he wondered why he could not remember the agreed arrangement the previous night. "I could do them if you want," said Kath "it's no trouble, you have to keep regular you know, and I'm very good at manual evacuations even if I say so myself. In fact, everyone sent for me to do them when I used to work at the old hospital."

"I bet you were really popular," said Andy. "And at parties when asked to do your party piece did you put on rubber gloves and ask for a volunteer?" They laughed at that point. Pat nodded as if to agree, "she's good at dealing with bowels though everyone knows it. My first husband had terrible problems with his bowels, either could not go or could not stop. I had to learn how to deal with them, he didn't like the idea at first but he soon got used to it. Anyway, if you have a problem or you need to get an extra one in, then just ask me. I'll bring some gloves that fit me better than the ones you have here, I might as well leave them here just in case." Andy thought that he had better sound appreciative as the offer might have to be taken up at a future date. "It's very considerate of you, and I appreciate the offer but I'd better not upset the system the first few days that I'm home, very touchy some of the nurses." Pat and Kath nodded in agreement again. "The offer is there though, if you need your bowels doing at anytime I'll do them. Keeping a good bowel regime is important as you'll always feel better if things are working as they should. We can both change catheters as well, if you want us to, I don't know if there are any rules that say that we can't do that," she said looking at them both in order to ascertain if they knew of something that might prevent them undertaking such a task. "As I'm employing you, there's no reason for you not to do those things if you're willing. I'll decide who can deal with my requirements," he said firmly. They soon had Andy out of bed and sat at the table awaiting his breakfast. Evidently Pat had worked with Kath before and they had respect for each others' ability which made it easier for everyone concerned. Pat said goodbye and reminded him that she would be back late evening, Andy thanked her and said that he would look forward to seeing her. What surprised him was that he actually meant it, she is efficient and attractive, also sensible, it could have been worse, he said to himself.

"We'll have a smoke now," declared Andy, who had enjoyed his breakfast. Kath said that if he did not mind she would like to get on and clean his bedroom and make his bed first. "Get the work done first, relax later," she added. "Quite right," said Andy in a loud voice "but I'll have a smoke anyway." Under his breath he muttered I wonder if you will have stuck to that idea in a few weeks time. He promised himself that he would remind her if the opportunity arose. He looked at the clock and realised that Belinda would be arriving soon. It then dawned upon him that Janice was going to take him around to see someone about the possibility of employment, the idea did not please him, it seemed all too hurried. He decided that the employment could wait and that his time would be better spent with Belinda. He telephoned Janice who told him to go out and enjoy himself, looking for a job could wait. She then told him that someone had come around to show her how to operate her new computer, but she had already crashed the thing and the screen was black and nothing seemed to happen whatever key she pressed. He apologised for laughing and told her what to do to get it functioning again. Andy suddenly felt a wave of what could only be described as freedom. He realised that he had made a very simple decision yet it pleased him. He had decided to go out with Belinda instead of job hunting, or to be more precise talking to a few people who might suggest or arrange for him to see someone else. Kath said that she had done the things that he had asked her to do and was there anything else he needed doing. He could not think of anything in particular, everything was new and clean as he had only just moved in. Kath suggested that between them they should work out what needed doing on a regular basis, "some form of rota or system is required regarding shopping and going out, doing ordinary things," she said. Andy thought that this sounded sensible and suggested that she should work out what needed doing and when, and he would consider it. He decided that he had better not just tell her to get on with things or she might take over. He decided that he had better mention to Kath that she might be careful not to tread on the toes of the other carers. If they thought she was taking over they might not like it. When Andy had explained this to her she thought about it for a moment and said, "I'll leave it for you to decide what you want doing." Andy had half expected such a response. "You work out what needs to be done and I'll tell them, using your notes then we won't upset anyone, will we?" he added a smile. "That seems fine with me, I don't want to upset anyone. I was just trying to help," she said looking slightly put out. Last thing I need is a bloody oversensitive carer, he said to himself, what is the problem with being told something, why do they take it as a personal insult? Can't they just do something without trying to complicate life, anyway bugger them ,they are employed to do a job not run my life, he said to himself. "Everything's fine, you work out what needs to be done and between us it'll happen," said Andy with an enthusiastic tone that seemed to appease Kath, who then started to smile in a distinctive homely way that is only seen on women who enjoy organising other people in the interest of others concerned, and for the benefit of all. Thank god that seems settled, he thought to himself. One thing he was sure of was that he was not going to have a paid carer telling him what to do and when. He would not have accepted that if had been married and no matter how well meaning someone might be, he knew that he had to make decisions, if he allowed others to make decisions then he would lose the ability. He also knew that it was not difficult to make decisions, having them implemented was the difficulty. "Everyone seems to know what's good for you," he said while sighing, "if they could get their own lives in order they might inspire more confidence."

CHAPTER NINETEEN

The bell rang and it was Belinda, she was a little earlier than expected. "I couldn't wait to have a look at the place," she said. Her eyes quickly went around the rooms looking at everything and not wanting to miss anything of importance. "It's very nice, very nice, a bit upmarket and middle class I think, well almost middle class but not quite, but it's much better than my place," she said. "Even your furniture and carpets are new and of what might be called a reasonable quality." Andy had not bothered getting too involved with the choice of some of these items but he felt the need to say something appropriate. "I'm not intending to live in squalor you know, I do have a few standards left," he said pretending that his feeling had been hurt, "and besides, I do have decent taste, the furnishings are tasteful. If I lived elsewhere then they might be more lavish but I think that they are in keeping with the surroundings." Belinda was unsure as to whether he was being serious or not, so she decided to be diplomatic knowing how argumentative Andy could be at times. Andy said that he would like to go down to the garage, he had telephoned a couple of weeks ago, he wanted to look at a few cars. "I've never had a brand new car," said Belinda, "I think that's a good idea," she said, "you've never mentioned that you were going to learn to drive."

"I already drive," said Andy quickly, "I past my test years ago but it's going to be a bit different now. I'll have to learn a few new moves. Should take me all of thirty minutes with my ability," he added while smiling and awaiting a response, non was forthcoming - Belinda knew him too well. "Before I forget, I've brought you a plant as a house warming present." Andy expressed his thanks and told her that she should not have gone to any trouble. She went outside and came in with the plant. Andy took in a deep breath. "That looks bloody good stuff!" he said out loud, "I'm assured it's good quality, it cost enough." Andy could recognise a good thriving cannabis plant when he saw one. "Look at those buds!" he gasped, "we must get it in the right temperature and with plenty of light, we have to treat it right at this point otherwise we'll bugger it up."

"I'm assured that it's quite hardy, it's not been forced too quickly and it does provide a good crop."

"You are a wonderful woman!" he said, while holding out his arms. They gave each other a long and affectionate cuddle. "Would you have given me a cuddle if I hadn't brought you the plant?" enquired Belinda. "I might have, said Andy who was still laughing at the prospects of some good smoking and the relaxing of his spasms. "I have to admit I wasn't expecting a present from you of that nature, it was very thoughtful. Just out of curiosity, how much was it? Because there's quite a lot there if the buds are anything to go by."

"I'm not telling you how much it cost, and it's bad manners of you to ask," said Belinda with some indignation. "You didn't have to sleep with anyone or do anything perverted did you?" he asked while smiling. She just ignored the remark. "For a plant like that I'd sleep with anything that was still breathing."

"You'd do that for nothing!" remarked Belinda who took the opportunity to show him that she had no illusions about him. "Some of those types you went to the pub with from off the unit I don't know how you could sit across from some of them."

"Those are your wonderful, caring colleagues you're talking about, defenders of the sick and all that crap."

She sighed a deep sigh and told him again that she still could not understand him going out with some of them. She then quickly informed him before he had a chance to say anything that he had even gone out with big Lucy. "She was bloody grateful and she was fine, nothing wrong with Lucy that a few drinks can't fix!" he said while laughing. "She doesn't drink," said Belinda.

"I know that, what I meant was she was fine after I had taken a few drinks, before that she wasn't easy on the eyes I will grant you that. But she was easily pleased, she didn't ask for much out of life."

"It's a good job her expectations are low, otherwise she's going to be disappointed," added Belinda. "I didn't realise how unkind and mean you could be to someone less fortunate," said Andy while giving the impression that he was being totally serious. She looked at him directly hoping to catch some small sign that would tell her if he was being serious but his face did not display any clues. "She was good when you got her going, went like a train," he said, adding a few physical gestures. Belinda laughed out loud, then suddenly stopped. She looked directly at him again. "Not with Lucy you surely didn't." He stopped her from saying anything else. "Give me some credit! She was definitely a bridge too far, no matter how much I'd drunk."

"If I remember correctly you fell out of the chair while trying to get back on the unit quietly and she picked you up in her arms and carried you the rest of the way." It was Andy's turn to sigh. "She was a big girl wasn't she? I think she was a man in drag."

"If that was the case, why go out with her?" Andy told her that he was not prejudiced, if he, or possibly she, was a man or a woman it did not bother him. And with Lucy there was no way he was going to attempt to find out. "Just think of offending her, one swipe from her and I'd be dead! She could crack Brazil nuts in the palm of her hands, I think she intimidated me, that's why I went out with her. That's a good, non-sexual reason. don't you think? I'm pleased that I've just thought that up, I'll always use that if the subject ever arises again but I will admit she was not a pretty sight on an empty stomach. Have you ever thought what happens to girls who look like her?" said Andy. Belinda waited for him to continue. "They just grow larger and drift through life without any real aims and they meet a mate only by accident. Like icebergs drifting around and occasionally touching, that's how they appear to me. We had one in our class at school and even then I wondered what sort of lifestyle could she expect being the size of a young whale. Who would ever ask her out? And imagine trying to be romantic? For a moment I was going to mention sex but I just couldn't envisage her having sex with anyone." He wondered what had happened to her as he had not seen or heard of her for years. "I bet she's living in a commune with some strange types, who constantly pretend that they're tolerant of each other and all the world's creatures, but secretly they wonder why God made them as they are. That sounds awful doesn't it, poor sods. When you look around at people you often wonder what they are doing with their lives, what do they really want and why are they so miserable."

He continued, "they're trapped, most just drifted into a job they didn't like and a relationship they soon disliked, they feel trapped, destined for a life that's dull and tedious. They can see their future and they don't like what they see, but they can't make the effort to do anything about it, so they drift on in a state of limbo."

"You're not going to let that happen to you then! You're going to be positive and outgoing, doing the things you want and going to the places that interest you." Andy thought for a moment before replying. "I'll give it a bloody good try and if I fail it won't be through lack of effort on my part." Belinda smiled instantly she was pleased with what Andy had said.

"Would you like any assistance?" said the young man while looking at Belinda. "Yes, I would," said Andy in a manner that made it clear that he was the person that the salesman should be talking to. The salesman turned towards Andy and smiled again. Andy explained that he was hoping to obtain a car using the mobility scheme. The salesman suddenly seemed to lose his initial interest while still remaining polite. He explained that they had a number of models that were popular and well priced at the moment that he might find suitable. "We do have a service that provides any adaptations you might require," he added. Andy looked around for some time, asking questions that he thought he should ask, but he was not sure which car really interested him. Then the salesmen came up with an important point. "Will you be using an ordinary chair or an electrically powered one?" Andy had not thought of that. He had given a lot of thought to obtaining the best electric chair he could obtain out of the system. This had caused him a considerable amount of arguments with the members of staff who thought it better for him if he used a manual chair. "The exercise is good for you and you'll keep your strength," said one enthusiastic type. Harry had discussed this with him on a number of occasions and Andy had listened carefully realising that it was an important issue. Harry's line was: "It's OK keeping fit, in fact, it's a good idea, but you have to consider the stress it's putting on your body constantly trying to push up hill and dale. How long can you do it without doing damage?" And another point said Harry, "How far can you get before you're tired, and then what? Pushing yourself around is not the holy grail, it's simply getting from point a to point b and you can do that better in a powered chair, it's common sense, so why waste your energy when you have only a limited amount. Look at it this way, we use cars all the time to travel in and about in. We choose not to walk, so why should wheelchair users push themselves around when they don't need to? It's stupid. These sporting enthusiasts will have you buggering yourself up if you aren't careful. Look after your body and decide the things you want to do, then you'll know what sort of chair you want. If you sit around the house that's fine, but if you're getting out and about you need your energy, that's common sense."

Andy had to agree with those points. He was annoyed with himself that he had arrived at the car showroom without thinking it through. He thanked the salesman and told him that he would go away and consider the situation. "Why hadn't I thought about the bloody chair?" he said in an angry tone, "I looked really stupid, I'm supposed to know about these things as they are not accessories, but essential items that I'll use every day." He continued complaining about his stupidity until Belinda appeared to agree with him which then stopped him.

"I'm a bit disappointed about you forgetting which chair you would be using. I thought you were going to get something really up market with a bit of style," said Belinda. "I don't think I can afford much style at the moment, but who knows," he gave her a knowing wink that left her bemused wondering what he might be contemplating. He then added, "if I get something with a bit of style will it really impress you?"

"That all depends upon how much style we're talking about," she said while laughing. She then said that she was not easily impressed by cars although she would like one for herself that was a little bit out of the ordinary, an old Triumph Stag would be fine. She then changed the subject. "By the way, I've found a nice little pub that does good food," said Belinda. Andy thought and hoped it was better than the strange establishment he had eaten in yesterday.

Belinda was driving along the country roads as though she knew where she was going. Andy remarked that he was not familiar with the area, she did not say anything but headed up a steep hillside that brought them out onto the edge of the moors. She turned into a small car park that badly needed repairing. "Bloody rough place," said Andy grumbling at the sight of the broken tarmac, "it's out in the wild a bit isn't it? I think I can hear the banjos playing. If I see grits on the menu I'm leaving, they probably eat strangers around here. I bet they're all inbred, the only thing that's the norm around here is incest. I bet they all look related in there, just take note, all slightly strange with staring eyes."

Once out of the car he was quickly pushed through the side entrance which was the only one accessible and into a lounge area. To Andy's surprise, but obviously not Belinda's, Harry and his daughter were already sat at a table waiting for them. "It's about time you showed up, frightened of putting your hand in your pocket?" retorted Harry. Andy was pleased to see Harry and his daughter but deliberately did not show his feelings as it would seem at odds with the character he had created for himself, although now that he was out of an hospital environment it should be possible to act in a less defensive manner, he thought that he cold modify his image when he finally decided what his image was going to be.

"I'm not going to be the over-modest, shy retiring type," he had told Harry who fully agreed with him upon that point. "If you don't speak up they'll walk all over you," said Harry, although he never actually said who 'they' were.

The establishment was better than expected. They were enjoying the meal and talking about the unit and the patients and the staff, recalling the more ridiculous episodes that they were party to, when Harry suddenly said, "I'll tell you before you get around to asking, Petra's mother is coming up north next week to stay with her brother, and I've decided to meet her." Andy decided for once not to say anything as he recognised that this must have been even more difficult than when Harry had decided to contact his daughter. Belinda said that it would be nice for him to see her again, she continued, "after all, some things are best left in the past and time moves on." Andy coughed hoping she would say no more. He knew she was just trying to think of something to say but she had no idea what Harry has gone through over the years. And it would be better to respond carefully without adding anything that might illicit a negative response from Harry who would not need much of an excuse to change his mind.

Andy recalled the long conversation they had which wasn't really as much a conversation more a monologue. I don't really want to be there when they meet, thought Andy, it could go either way. "We were wondering," said Belinda looking first at Harry then at Petra and back at Andy "if Harry could meet her at your place, it's neutral territory if you see what I mean." Andy was about to state that he had no intention of letting them meet at his place for their first meeting, and was annoyed that they had even thought about it. They might tear the place in bits, he thought. He then realised what had just been said. Obviously Belinda had spoken at some length with Harry about the situation. Therefore, knowing the background, and knowing Harry's feelings, he agreed with some reluctance, which he tried to hide. There is just one condition he added, Harry sighed expecting something unusually strange. "What is it?" asked Harry. "I'm not going to be there. I'm going out for the day, and don't wreck the furniture." Belinda gave him a hug, Petra hugged him and kissed him. For a brief moment Andy was distracted but his mind fixed itself upon what he had just heard, he decided to say nothing and just let things take their course. "I really appreciate it," said Harry while half smiling, "I told these two here you were not totally self-centred. And beneath that rough exterior their beats a heart of lead!" Harry could not prevent himself from laughing at that point. "We need some place quiet and different." Andy was about to say why different, what do you propose to do? Hopefully nothing strange or violent on his new carpets, but he refrained. "I'm taking you out for the day," said Belinda "you deserve something very special as you've been so considerate, I haven't made my mind up where, just yet but somewhere nice, perhaps the job centre." Everyone laughed, including Andy. "In your dreams!" said Andy "I was supposed to be looking at employment today and I thought 'bugger it'."

"There's plenty time for that," added Harry quickly, "there are more important things in life at the moment." Andy nodded in agreement. Belinda and Petra smiled to each other knowing that the outcome was inevitable. Andy thought that it was surprising how quickly things can change either for good or for bad. For a moment he almost felt optimistic. He finally asked, "Who's paying for this meal?" They turned and looked at him before laughing. "No, I'm bloody not," he said, "if Harry is using my place, rent free I should add, then he can pay for lunch." Harry was about to argue but decided that paying for lunch was a good deal really.

Belinda took Andy back to his accommodation and she invited herself in. "That was nice of you letting Harry use your home for his meeting."

"Nice! You both manipulated me into a position where it was almost impossible for me to say no without looking bad." Belinda said nothing but looked around the room. "It doesn't look too bad to me," she said not wanting to display too much enthusiasm as she knew Andy would not be able to resist telling her in great detail what was wrong with the place. They had a coffee and a smoke, although Belinda did not smoke very often she thought it was a suitable occasion where smoking along with Andy seemed acceptable. "What do you think about Harry and his ex-wife?" she asked, wondering what Andy's response would be. Andy looked thoughtful for some short time before answering. "It's difficult, a very difficult situation," he said. "While in hospital we talked at length about it, one night he gave me a full history of events, and I could see that it had caused him a lot of pain. But I recognised that he still had feelings for her although they were a mixture of love and hate, well perhaps not hate in the normal sense of the word. There was so much hurt, I was surprised because Harry is normally as hard and as cynical as you can get. He knows the system and he doesn't get thrown by anything usually. But that night he was perturbed to say the least. I'm wondering if she wants to see him because she somehow feels guilty, or does she still care about him, or what. She hasn't shown any caring feelings in the past, so why now?"

"They do have something important in common which she might want to talk about," said Belinda. Andy looked bemused. "They might want to talk about Petra."

"I hadn't thought of that on the grounds that she obviously never wanted to before."

"It must've been difficult when she was married, it's often harder for a women."

"Just a minute!" said Andy in a harsh tone which signified he was going to disagree with Belinda's last statement. "Don't make

401

excuses for her actions. She took the child and went for an easier, or better option, the option has changed and now she'll talk with Harry, is that a really nice, considerate woman?" laughed Andy.

"I'm not making excuses for her, but let's be honest, we don't know all of the circumstances, do we?" Andy admitted that they did not. "All I know is what Harry told me and it was the truth, believe me it was bloody hard for him to talk about it, that was until he got going then it was impossible to stop him. He'd been bottling it all up for years. You should have seen him the day he made contact with his daughter. He was like a child one minute, then he would go into a strange mood asking himself if he had done the right thing. He was hard to communicate with because whatever I said he somehow took it the wrong way. Now that his wife is coming up he'll be a total wreck for the next forty-eight hours, anyway we'll see what materialises when they meet. It's worth remembering that Harry is not the same person as he was when she left him. He's done quite a lot since then and he will look at things differently now, she might be in for a surprise as he's almost sophisticated in some of his attitudes and tastes. When she left him he was probably still the ordinary, working-class type of young man she had grown up with, and going away with her boss, who wasn't short of money must have seemed like moving up socially in the world. Well she has now descended and Harry has moved upwards, so it'll be interesting to watch the interaction, as long as I haven't to watch it," he said while laughing.

He wanted to emphasise the point so he said it again. "Let's face it, he's no longer the innocent, quite type, struggling along anymore. And he's done reasonably well for himself, he is not, as I have just said, the poor miserable sod that she ran away from. Anyway, at the end of the day we'll see what happens, one thing is certain it will not be dull, and to be honest I just can't predict which way things will go. One minute I think that I know, the next minute I'm unsure. These events certainly come from out of the blue it seems. In his position I'd simply meet with her and listen carefully to what she had to say, then tell her to fuck-off. I think she's just coming up to see him out of curiosity and to ensure their daughter is in his will. Or she could be wanting help financially if Petra goes to University. "That's cynical," added Belinda looking surprised. "What you've just said sounds awful as though everyone is just out for what they can get," she looked disappointed and her expression conveyed her disappointment. Andy seemingly had not listened and he ignored her. "Mind you, I must admit Harry had got it right, she's a good looking women and that surprised me." Belinda took the opportunity to interject, "Harry's an attractive man and interesting, most women who give themselves the opportunity to get to understand him would like him. I know one or two nurses who like him quite a bit." Andy looked surprised at her statement. "Whatever you do, don't tell him that or we'll never hear the end of it." He thought for a moment, then asked her, "are you sure that they like him?" Belinda said that she was positive, "he's really interesting, not your ordinary dull fellow who lives for drinking and football." Andy thought about it for a minute, "I suppose that's true," he said, "but he's not the easiest person to understand at times."

Belinda looked at Andy and carefully chose her words. "In some ways you're like him, cynical, difficult and argumentative. Harry the younger," she said. She smiled a wry smile before saying. "And you're a bit different." Andy was about to say something but he was not quite sure if he was being complimented or insulted, so he said nothing in case he got it wrong. "And going back to an earlier point when you stated that not all women are constantly thinking about money and their best opportunity, I agree," said Andy "it's just that it appears that way when you look at things objectively. Look at the unit! See who's married a nurse or a physio in the past, and what percentage of them have received a large amount of compensation. Look at the individuals very carefully and think about it. One thing is certain, it's not the poorest or the most severely disabled who seem to be the most desirable. Women are very selective in their distribution of warmth and compassion."

"That's a horrible thing to say and if a few do go for the money then it doesn't mean that we're all the same." Belinda turned and looked at Andy before speaking. "Just one question," she said seriously. "What is it?" asked Andy in all innocence. "Have you got a few pounds tucked away in the building society, or a good insurance policy, stocks and shares, property, anything that can easily be turned into cash?" She burst out laughing at that point and Andy had to laugh. He suddenly stopped laughing and said, "Harry's not been talking has he, he's not mentioned my auntie's recent death?" Belinda looked uncomfortable at that moment. "He's not said anything to me, I didn't know that you had an auntie who died."

"That's fine then." They were quiet for a moment until Belinda broke the silence. "I'm sorry about your auntie, what did she die of?"

"Oh ,she isn't dead, I just wondered if you thought she was, you can't be too careful." He burst out laughing as she hit him on the shoulder. "Actually I don't have an auntie, I wonder if I could get one, or if there is some organisation that supplies people who want to be someone's aunt? It was just a thought," he said in a distant meandering manner.

"What are you doing tomorrow?" asked Belinda changing the subject away from Harry. Andy replied. "I've been thinking about that and I have no plans. I'm definitely not looking for work yet, to be honest, I'm not sure that I have the energy to work fulltime." Belinda asked him if he was seriously thinking about work but he did not answer. "Why don't you come round for lunch at my place and then we could talk about a few other things that I need to buy?" He continued, "you'll have to make lunch, though, if you want something cooked, as I'd probably just have a sandwich." He had told Belinda what she had wanted to hear. "I might as well move in with you if I'm going to be doing domestic work," she replied. She quickly added while laughing that It could save her a lot in rent. Andy was not sure if she was just saying that for the sake of it or if she was testing the water, in which case he would be very interested, as he had liked Belinda from their first meeting, and their friendship had grown over the weeks until they had become close to one another. "You've had worse ideas," said Andy smiling. "By the way, how much do you pay in rent?" Belinda was about to dismiss what she had said and laugh it off when she realised that Andy seemed serious. "It's only a one bed-roomed flat but it's costly to run and it's not really in a good area," she was going to add a few more negative aspects when Andy said. "How about you stopping at my place for a week, see if it works as there's a spare room and you can contribute to the rent."

"I thought you didn't pay any rent, you're not working." That's true thought Andy who then wondered if he could charge Belinda some rent and not lose any benefits. "And you have to consider your care package, if my living there would effect it."

"You wouldn't be providing care, so no, it wouldn't. I have carers who do that for a living and I'm not going to take their living off of them. I've only been employing them for a few hours. Looking at things logically I can't see how it can effect anything and it's only for a week, just to see if it's workable, you'll be a non-paying guest for a week and damn the expense! I'll live dangerously. Let's give it a try and see how it goes." Belinda smiled to herself, she knew that it would work out successfully, it was one of those things that rarely happens in life. When you just know, deep down, that something is right. Andy was smiling. Belinda asked him what he was smiling at. He replied that if he had a larger place he could take in lodgers and it would be better for him than looking for employment. Belinda told him that he had been with Harry too long as that sounded like his thinking, although it was not a bad idea. Andy laughed and said within a short time Harry's thinking will be turned upside down, the poor sod will not know what has hit him, his former wife will see to that, and the strangest thing is I know deep down it is what Harry wants, it's odd how some things go in a circle, he thought. I have been out of the unit only a matter of hours and things have changed, and the strangest thing is that most of it is none of my doing. He had decided years ago that he was not a fatalist but he also on occasion recognised that some things just seemed destined to happen. He usually put this down to coincidence but he was never quite sure at those odd times; he decided that he would resist displaying any optimism whatever the situation, well, for the time being anyway.

"We might as well call at your place and you can collect some clothes and any other items you might need for the week. Just one point though." She looked at him not quite knowing what to expect. "You can contribute to the food as I'd hate for you to feel guilty by living off of me for a week." She smiled at him and told him not to worry about that as she had already put some food in a large bag. Andy looked at her and realised that he had already been out manoeuvred, he started to laugh, soon they were both laughing.

"It's a good job that I like you," he said. She enquired why. He told her that he was just thinking about her contribution to his rent, if he ever got around to paying any, if she was good he would be generous, but if she wasn't then she would be paying a proper rent. She thought about what he had said for a short while before replying. "How good do I have to be before I witness this generosity of yours?" she asked. "We'll just have to see, won't we," said Andy, who thought that his first couple of days out of the unit had not been dull. I might even look for some work if I get bored, he thought. Then he decided that he would not rush into that. And in future he should put the thought out of his head as there were better things to do than work.

Belinda leaned back and stared hard at him. "What's wrong? Have I said anything?" he asked in a voice that showed concern. Belinda laughed before replying. "I know it's all a bit quick, and what I say might seem strange, and you can always say no." Andy held up his hand, "stop there! Just tell me what it is, as I can't stand the suspense and when someone says that I can always say 'no' then I start to worry." Belinda smiled in a way that Andy clearly recognised, that warm gentle smile which means this is what I want and you are going to be in agreement with me. "I think things will be fine when you get used to my little quirks," at that point she burst out laughing. Andy could only agree while wondering what her quirks were. "I think I should point out to you that you might think that I have a few 'quirks' as you have put it, but there is a difference." Belinda looked surprised and apprehensive for the moment before she asked him about the difference. "The difference is," said Andy "that if you don't accept my quirks that's tough, but if I don't like yours then you're looking for other accommodation." She sighed to herself, relieved upon realising Andy was just being Andy. "I'm sure we'll be OK," at that point she kissed him tenderly. Andy was not slow when the occasion warranted it. "Does this mean I'll require a larger bed?" he said, while wondering what her reaction might be, "and in case I get distracted I must tell you that you do have wonderful legs," he continued, "I was going to tell you that before but I hadn't got around to it." She smiled at the compliment. "You might have to get a double bed but then again, it depends how good you are, doesn't it?" she replied while smiling. "I've never had any complaints!" he added quickly. "That's because you have gone out with unsophisticated, low-life types who're happy with a bag of chips and their bus fair home after a night out with you. But I expect a little more than that, but we'll see if you measure up to the standard I require to satisfy my needs."

"I hope you have a good vibrator and plenty of batteries," said Andy while laughing. Belinda pretended to look shocked. "A vibrator! Why do I want a vibrator? Don't tell me that you're paralyzed or something! My god, can't you have sex like a normal person? Must I remain unfulfilled?"

"That's bloody insensitive!" said Andy "if I wasn't so thick skinned you could have hurt my feelings with a snide remark of that nature. Makes it sound as though only a very fit able bodied type is good enough." She looked him right in the eyes and said. "Do not go all sensitive on me because you and I both know that it's not like you at all."

"I might have become sensitive on leaving the unit," he replied in his defence.

"You'll be telling me next that you'll want me to turn out the light while I undress."

"My god!" shouted Andy "you brazen hussy! You're not intending to undress in my presence, surely not?" She smiled a knowing smile but did not say anything.

"Do you think that I did right in having the catheter out before I left the unit? I feel a little bit clammy at times, as though my bladder isn't emptying properly." Belinda looked at him and said, "for a brief moment I thought that you might have had it out for other reasons, but that was foolish of me, wasn't it?" Andy thought that he had better be careful with his next answer. "Well, actually, it did cross my mind, but I didn't want to appear to take anything for granted," he said while smiling. "You lying sod! You never thought anything of the kind, you must think that I'm simple! I made a simple statement leading you on and you trotted out a smarmy response. I have you sussed out already," said Belinda. I'm going to have to be more careful if she can read me so easily, thought Andy. "Just one point though which you might or might not be able to answer. How long can you retain an erection?" Her question surprised Andy and he had to think about an answer. "With appropriate stimulation it'll stay around for quite sometime, but it can also just disappear quite quickly. It's not something that I have experimented with as I've only had the thing out a few days, and I had it put back in before I left the unit thinking that it was something that I could get used to dealing with later."

"Well, perhaps when you feel inclined we should experiment a little and just see what we can do. I'm always willing to experiment in a good cause," she said. This is better than I expected thought Andy. He was glad that she was open about it as he was not quite sure how hard to push things.

While they had become very friendly Andy realised they had not spent a full night in bed together and he suddenly felt very concerned, or to be more accurate he felt afraid, afraid that he actually could not satisfy her sexual needs. He then thought it would be OK as she had nursed him and it wasn't as though she was unaware of his physical condition. And they had on a number of occasions spent sometime fumbling about on a hospital bed after they had been out for the evening. It is not quite the same thing, thought Andy, he then thought that all he could do was his best, and that they were both sensible adults and therefore they would talk, and ensure if something was not right then they would work at it and put it right, that seemed to satisfy him. She is so attractive and so bloody nice, I don't want to screw it up by being inadequate or insensitive. I must make sure that I get it right, he thought. 'Inadequate' isn't the right word, and she will not see me as inadequate, he said to himself.

Andy's thoughts suddenly drifted back to a discussion that he had with Spike. Although he did not go to Spike and Luna's wedding, he was invited, along with Harry and any other patients who were on the unit, to meet with Spike and Luna the month after their wedding. They had realised that by getting married at such short notice they had not allowed their friends to attend or celebrate with them. Spike came up with the idea of a post-wedding celebration which could be held anytime after the usual reception. Luna told him that she had never heard of such a thing, but it sounded a good idea or at least a good reason for a party.

At the party Harry introduced Andy to Spike. It seemed as they had known each other for years, they enjoyed talking and laughing about things that amused them, but for some reason seemed to amuse know one else. That was when Spike mentioned the cottage he had rented for their honeymoon. His detailed description had stuck in Andy's mind. Small traditional cottage on the coast, but by itself with superb views and all modern amenities, while still retaining its character. "You would enjoy the place," said Spike "it's everything you need if you enjoy something a little bit different, and you can actually get down onto the sand as it's not the loose sand you get at holiday beaches, it's smooth and firm. Having said that, it's very difficult in some places even, for the best outdoor powered chairs, but worth a try. The views from the large window are something special, especially when there's a storm. You can hear the waves pounding on the rocks and the lightening flashing out of the clouds shooting down to the water. If you enjoy such things it's perfect. And there's the remains of a Roman camp nearby." He was about to expand upon the Roman camp but then thought better of it. "You wouldn't be interested in Roman History, would you," enquired Spike. Andy thought about it for a while then asked, "what particular period?" then added that he was interested in Roman history in general, especially the military side. "That's excellent! We must talk sometime soon," said Spike with enthusiasm, who promised himself that they would get together as soon as possible as Spike had the idea that he might persuade Andy to go on a dig with him and they would take Luna and Belinda, that way the two young women would not be bored as they would have each others' company.

Andy told Spike that it sounded like the sort of place that he might want to go to in the future. He remembered that somewhere he had put down the telephone number, he had put it into the back of his wallet. He then thought about the last time he had been at the coast, in a cottage some years back with his mother and father. They had looked along the beach every day for driftwood, they had looked amongst the rocks and the small pools left behind when the tide had gone out. They had collected fossils, wild flowers, pebbles, almost everything had been interesting. That was a good holiday, he thought, he even managed to get through the week without arguing with his mother. He looked at Belinda and thought, if this does work out, then it might be worthwhile renting that cottage, if Spike and Luna managed there should not be a problem. Then the thought occurred to him that he might be just moving things forward a bit too quickly. He knew how easily he became enthused with an idea once he started to look into something. He definitely did not want Belinda to think he had just automatically assumed that he would make some arrangements and she would follow. But at the same time he knew that she had made plans that had ensured she was staying with him for a while. The trouble is, women are not logical creatures and what she thinks is good or acceptable if she initiates it, might not be acceptable if I initiate it. Bugger it, just see how things go and don't look upon it as being complicated, he thought.

He turned to Belinda and said. "D'you know anything about sea fishing?" She looked at him as though he was speaking some obscure language, "what did you say?" she asked, not sure that she had heard him correctly or not. He repeated the question. "The only thing that I know about fish is that it either comes frozen or from a fish and chip shop."

"Just as I thought," said Andy. "in that case you have a real treat in store for you. You'll love sea fishing." Belinda seemed to take a long time thinking about Andy's last remark before replying. "I can't think of many things that I would like to do less than sea fishing. The thought of fishing in general seems to be an exercise in boredom."

"That's good!" said Andy enthusiastically. She looked bemused again wondering what was going through his mind. He continued, "if that's how you see it, then when you actually experience it you'll be surprised at how pleasurable it can be." She stared hard at him and then said. "Have I missed something somewhere? How did we get onto sea fishing?" Andy smiled and told her. "Don't worry about it for now, but if you're lucky I'll teach you all you need to know. We might be going to a cottage for a few days, but that depends upon how you and I get along."

"I see," said Belinda, her voice expressing her disdain. "It's like a prize, if I'm good then you take me to a cottage in order to teach me how to fish at sea." Andy said "yes, that's it! It's a good idea isn't it? It's brilliant! You'll love every minute of it!" She sighed, wondering if it was worthwhile having a conversation with Andy as he was definitely not listening. "It's very thoughtful of you, particularly as I've just told you the whole concept of fishing is boring."

"I thought you liked the idea," he replied with some disappointment. "I don't even know what you're talking about, one minute it's sea fishing and a cottage, or a few days away, just explain it to me in a structured manner." Andy explained his thoughts as logically as possible. When he had finished she sighed. "And there I was for a moment thinking that you were taking me somewhere to pamper me and indulge me."

"There's no pleasing some people," said Andy looking hurt, "most people would jump at the opportunity. Anyway that puts you on a yellow card as far as I'm concerned, so you're going to have to be very careful, anymore transgressions and your rent goes up." At that point they both laughed. Andy then asked her if she had ever collected fossils. She replied while laughing, "Only you Andy, and I'm not sure which period in the earth's history you really belong to."

"Well, that decides that issue, a week away together and you'll know all there is to know about me and sea fishing." She stared at him carefully, he looked back at her and asked her, "what is it? What do you want to say?"

"I was just wondering," she said, then paused.

"Don't bugger me about! Just come out with it," said Andy. She deliberately took her time before answering him. "I just thought, how are you going to get in a boat? I'm sure you'll have thought this out, but I'm curious to hear it directly from you, especially if you're in a powered chair." Andy groaned, then suppressed the sound before she could hear it. "That's a good point you've hit on there, a very good point, which I'll get back to. Now then what about fossils, do you like fossils?" She smiled to herself and was about to come back at him with a witty reply but decided against it, as she realised that Andy was trying to find something that was of interest them both. "Fossils? I can take them or leave them," she replied. "What about country

411

houses and castles and such like?" he said with an air of desperation. "I enjoy those," she said enthusiastically. "Fine, that's something to remember, I'll avoid going to those places until I think of a suitable way of getting safely into a rowing boat."

"I do have a few favourite places that I tend to keep to myself, but for some reason I'd like to take you to see them. They mean a great deal to me and they feel different, it's hard to explain; it's like going to a new place and suddenly feeling that the whole atmosphere is not only different and good, but far above those normal sentiments." He smiled at her and told her that it would mean a great deal to him if she felt the same about these places. "I have a few places that I also think are special, so we'll write down a list and see if we have any places in common, and that way we'll decide which to see first." Andy thought that sounded sensible. He was looking forward to the time ahead as it appeared that Belinda was not only level headed, but probably shared many of his tastes, except for sea fishing. He leaned back and grunted in a manner that indicated a form of contentment. "You know, if I tried, I think that I could really get to like you and to prove it, I'm going to do something for you that I save for very, very special people." Belinda was taken by surprise, "that's a really nice thing, Andy, I feel embarrassed for some reason. What is it you are going to do? Don't keep me in suspense." He smiled at her in a knowing kind of way. "Come on, tell me! Don't have me guessing - what is it you're going to do?" Andy cleared his voice and looked at her. She looked back in anticipation. "I'm going to do my best, my very best impression of Elvis for you." She sat back in the chair, her jaw dropped momentarily, "that's good of you! I just can't wait! In fact I think that I'm overcome with emotion at the thought of witnessing the event."

"My Elvis is bloody good! Everyone says so. Now, what do you want? You have a choice of 'Jailhouse Rock' or 'Return to Sender'."

"This is just too much for me! I actually have a choice? I don't like either, so let's put Elvis away or wherever he comes from."

"Don't say that I haven't offered, will you, as I don't make such offers to everyone," he said. "Perhaps some other time, when the time and place is more conducive," she said. "Well, OK then, but don't let me forget as you'll really like it, well everyone else seems to."

"What about his hip shaking and all that stuff? How do you manage that?"

"You're deliberately being insensitive again. OK, what if I do," he paused for a moment. "I was going to say Stevie Wonder but you'd probably insist on poking me in both eyes. Leave them for the moment, I'll find someone whom you can't come back at me with a snide reply. By the way, who do you like?"

"I thought that you might get around to asking sometime."

CHAPTER TWENTY

Harry had arrived at Andy's an hour earlier that expected. Belinda had opened the door thinking it was the carer who had returned having forgotten something. "I'm a little bit early," he said apologetically, "but I wanted to make sure that everything was acceptable to Andy, and that he'd not had second thoughts about me meeting Judith here." Belinda said that there was no problem as Andy had changed the habits of a lifetime and decided to spend some money. "He's actually booked us into a hotel for the night," she said expressing surprise, "so there's no hurry for you to leave here, take all the time you need." She leaned forward and kissed Harry on the cheek. "And don't get upset before she arrives, everything will be fine, you're older now and you can handle these things." Harry told her that he wished he was as sure as she was. "I don't mind admitting to you that I'm still not sure how I'm going to handle the meeting, my mind has been in a turmoil thinking about it, there are so many contradictory thoughts going through my mind. I do want to see her, but it's not going to be easy as I can feel myself getting angry when I think about the past."

"You've moved on since then Harry, and you're successful, you've made something of your life, whether or not you think you have. So don't worry, just think of who you are today and not who you were in the past." She kissed Harry and Harry smiled at her and said something that sounded like thanks.

Andy appeared and told Harry that he should not take any shit from her after all these years. Belinda quickly interrupted him before he had the opportunity to make Harry more insecure. "That's right Mr. Sensitivity just make things more difficult." Andy was about to explain to her that he was only looking after Harry's interest when he thought he might just as well say nothing, because Harry would only do what he wanted in any case. "We're ready for going now, but the kettle has boiled, so you can make yourself some tea or coffee, and there's a bottle of whiskey on the shelf if you think you might need something stronger." Harry did not smile at Andy's offer of whiskey. he was occupied with his own thoughts. Suddenly he remembered where he was,

"I didn't ask you where is it you've booked in, somewhere romantic and tasteful, I presume?" He then looked across at Andy and said, "knowing him, it's a B and B in some back street that's dirt cheap, where you have to have injections before you dare eat anything." Belinda quickly arose to Andy's defence. "He's booked us in at an hotel actually, but only for one night, I had to give him some valium though because the price sent him into an instant state of depression. I've told him that I'm worth every penny, and I'm definitely not going away with him to some scruffy establishment in some back street as I'm used to better things. And I'm not going fishing. Can you believe it? He actually wanted to take me sea fishing, thinking it would be so romantic. So we decided upon a decent hotel, although I left it entirely up to him."

"I'd better get my money's worth, and it's not whether you are worth every penny, if it was just pennies it wouldn't worry me," Andy muttered. "What exactly do you mean by that remark?" said Belinda attempting to look indignant. "Well, let's be honest, a bed is a bed and breakfast is breakfast isn't it? How much can you increase the cost by and justify it?" he said while looking towards Harry for some show of agreement. "It's the location and the ambience and everything about a place that makes the difference, and if you can't understand that then it's impossible for me to explain it to you." Andy smiled at her remarks and told her that he agreed with her and it did not matter how much it cost. She smiled and then gave him a quick kiss on the cheek. He looked at Harry and said "don't worry, I'll put it on her rent!" Harry laughed out loud, then Andy laughed. "You've not done badly there, she looks pretty good. If I was a few years younger I would've asked her out myself, in fact, when she returns dissatisfied, I might just do that." Belinda came out of the bedroom with a suitcase and wondered what the cause of the laughter was. "Just one point before I leave, this hotel is costing me a fortune so I hope that you appreciate me letting you use my place without a down payment or contract or anything."

"That's my boy! You're learning fast," said Harry while laughing.

"Where is it we're going?" she asked. "I'll gave you the directions and you just follow them and I promise you that you'll enjoy the place."

"We're not going to do anything stupid, like fishing, are we?" she said while looking at him carefully in order to ascertain that fishing wasn't something he had planned. "No fishing, nothing at all that might disturb the tranquil and beauty of the experience," he said somewhat enigmatically. She was now very suspicious but decided not to say anything as she followed his instructions and headed north towards the A1.

"You turn right here, then left to the top of the hill."

"I seem to have been driving forever, are you sure that you know where we are?" she asked. "Just around the corner and through the gates, and follow the drive as it winds its way down towards the river."

Suddenly the hotel appeared in front of them. Belinda took in a deep breath in surprise, "it looks wonderful!" She could not find the appropriate words right away it was far better than anything she had envisaged. The building had previously been in the ownership of a wealthy family who had ensured that the grounds and the building were both tasteful and grand without being ostentatious in any way. Belinda was even more impressed when they went into reception, she looked around like a child who had suddenly been given the keys to a magic kingdom that only existed in someone's imagination. Once they had checked in and Andy had told reception that he had asked for a room with a good view, they felt comfortable, as though they had returned home after a long trip to distant parts. "It feels right, doesn't it?" said Andy looking around. The porter asked them to follow him and he led the way towards their room. "If there's anything at all you require, don't hesitate to ring reception and I'll come right away," said the porter as he placed the suitcase on the stand next to the bath robes. "A bit of a grovelling type," said Andy when the porter finally left them alone in the room. "Only because you were slow at tipping him," she added. "Look at the view of the river," said Belinda loudly in her excitement, "there are ducks and swans down there! It's fabulous! How did you know about this place, have you stayed here before?"

"I tend to know about such places," said Andy pleased with himself, "the important thing is do you like it and what about the bed? It's not a four poster, but it is impressive; it's on the large side even for us, as you know I wave my arms about a great deal when I'm trying to get to sleep."

"Surely you've not gone to all this expense and trouble to waste time on sleeping, have you?" she said. She sat on his knee and started to kiss him slowly at first but gradually more passionately until they started to relax with each other. Andy could feel himself getting aroused, he did not want to exert any control over his feelings, yet he was still insecure wondering what his capabilities were and would they be adequate for his present situation. He was soon to find out. Belinda got off of his knee and stood in front of him, she slowly started to undress herself. "I know you like tradition, so I have my sexiest black underwear on, and stockings," she said huskily, her voice heavy with longing. She teased him carefully and deliberately as she took her clothes off. "Leave your stockings on," said Andy, who was mesmerised by her performance. His mind was turning over rapidly as thoughts quickly moved in and out of his imagination. In the past they had kissed and cuddled, and he had fondled her and enjoyed it, although it was sometimes difficult to physically obtain a suitable position due to the circumstances, but now he saw Belinda in another light, she was almost a different person. She had carefully stripped for him while breaking off to kiss him and then she posed briefly and explicitly. He loved it and the feelings it aroused within him.

"Do you like me, Andrew, really like me? Do you want me now or do you want to wait, but I can assure you I have a large appetite, so don't worry." Get the cushion from the settee and place it on the table he told her. She did as she was told, she wanted him to take control of her, it was something she had desired for a long time. She lay on the table with her legs apart as he reached down to her. She moaned a soft gentle moan that signifies a deep seated pleasure. Andy was intoxicated by the taste of her and he soon realised that he had little to feel apprehensive about at that particular moment. They moved to the bed, and made love, long and passionately and time slipped by without them noticing it. She held him close and told him that he had made her feel incredibly good and that she loved him. She went on to tell him that she had fallen for him the very first time that she had seen him, but she had not said anything in case nothing materialised or he might not have wanted her. Andy was briefly about to say something amusing, but realised that she was being very serious and a similar response from him was required. To his surprise he did not find it difficult, everything seemed so simple and natural.

"You do look fabulous in those black stockings!" he said while laughing.

"Men have such simple tastes," she said while placing his hand on her thigh.

Andy asked her if it would be acceptable if he chose dinner for both of them. Belinda said that she would be honoured if he would take the trouble to do that and she would reward any kindness of his in any manner he chose. They laughed at each others quips and played up to each other in a manner that neither of them would have thought possible only a few days earlier. "Let's start with something light and pleasant, smoked salmon strips with asparagus and quails eggs. That sounds quite good," said Andy, reading from the extensive menu, "we'll have that, then what about Beef Wellington?" He could see that Belinda was not enthusiastic about the beef. "I'd prefer something a little lighter to be honest." Andy felt disappointed for the moment. "What about a lobster salad? That's light and," she stopped him. "To be honest, I'm not very hungry for food. I'd like to go back to our room as soon as we can, that is, if that's what you want," she added. Andy said that he could think of nothing better, but said that they might as well have something very simple and then they would use room service if they needed anything during the night. He called the waiter over and explained that they both wanted something relatively light and simple and could he suggest anything. The waiter said that the chef has a very special salad that might interest them. It was cornets of thinly sliced venison filled with a mild cream cheese, laid upon a bed of cold cooked spinach that had a hint of crushed lime added. "That sounds very good to me," said Andy, looking forward to seeing the salad in front of him. The waiter looked pleased due to his suggestion being taken on board. "I think we'll have a decent white Burgundy," added Andy "I was going to have Champagne but I didn't want to appear vulgar," he added while laughing. "Please, be as vulgar as you want! It sounds good to me," said Belinda. "We'll get a bottle out of the bar in the room," he said, "drinking in bed always feels nice and decadent."

"I just can't believe this!" she said "it's unreal!" Andy laughed and asked her to explain. "Well, here we are in this wonderful room, I'm astride you in bed wearing only my dark stockings, and we're drinking and smoking as though it's something we've always done."

"It's bloody good, isn't it?" added Andy, they both laughed as she leaned forward and embraced him, "come on then, let me feel that tongue of yours again, and if you can keep this up, I'll get it insured."

"I'm going to lick you all over, as though you're covered in chocolate," he said while laughing. "I'm not sure if I can melt the chocolate for you at this moment, but I noticed some strawberry yoghurt in the fridge and I'm sure you'll like the taste of it."

"Go on then, if you insist, but if you can find blackcurrant that would be better," she pretended to be offended but she carefully smeared on the yoghurt as he watched, "that's so bloody sexy watching you do that." he said.

"It cools down parts that are over heating," she said while laughing.. They made love throughout the night, sometimes tenderly and then with a passion that neither of them had experienced before. The morning soon arrived and surprisingly they both felt fresh as though they had slept well and rested well. Neither of them spoke, they kissed one another and again made love passionately. "I don't want to leave this place, it's paradise!"

"Don't worry, we'll be coming back here. I've made a reservation for us for next month, it's just for two nights, but it'll be special."

"You are a wonderful man," said Belinda, "and more thoughtful than people give you credit for, but they don't know you like I do." He felt very good upon hearing her say those words, any insecurity that he might have envisaged did not materialise. "You've given me more than you'll ever know! Just one incredible night has changed my life," he told her.

"I knew that it would be like this," she said, "I somehow expected it. It might sound strange after such a short time, but I have to tell you that I do love you. I can't explain my feelings, they overwhelm me, that's the only way that I can put it." She caressed his face with both hands. "You're so special Andy, and you don't understand how I feel about you yet, but you will very soon."

"I think that we'd better get back now and see if the house is still standing." Andy laughed and said that he was sure everything would be fine. "But before we do that, I want you one more time, or perhaps two."

"You can have me as many times as you want," she said while pressing her lips to his.

The door bell rang and Harry answered the door. Petra kissed him and stepped back in order that Harry could greet Judith. He was not sure what to say so he just asked them to come in. It somehow seemed inadequate for the occasion but he could not think of any other greeting that might sound any more suitable. He asked them to sit down and offered them tea or coffee, which they both refused, Petra asked if there was a coke available. Harry told her to look as he had no idea what Andy had in stock.. Petra then said that she was going into town and would bring back a few items for lunch if that was agreeable. Harry agreed that it would be as he had already said that he did not know what food Andy had in the house, and he did not want to impose upon him any more than he had to. Petra left them and Harry looked across at Judith. Time has been good to her, he thought, although she looks older she basically looked little different than he had imagined. He was about to ask her how she was when she asked him first. "I'm fine," he answered, "a little older and wiser but I can't complain really." Her voice quivered briefly with uncertainty. "I wanted to see how you were and to talk about Petra." Harry interrupted, "she looks a really fine girl, she's a credit to you," he suddenly felt very uncomfortable not knowing what to say, as the small talk was not his style, and over the years he had never thought that he might be swapping meaningless pleasantries with Judith if he ever met her again. "Yes, she's a good girl, and she's done well at school so we expected her to go on to University." Harry did not like it when she said 'we', but he refrained from making any comment. Judith took a deep breath as though she was going to say something of importance. She started tentatively. "It's been a long time Harry, and many things have happened to both of us, some good and some not so good, and it's no good pretending that the past didn't exist, it did and there's nothing that we can say or do about it." Harry thought that there was a lot that he could say, and was likely to before the day was out, but for the moment he listened.

"When I left you I just didn't know what to say to you." She paused as though she wanted to retract those words and start again. "First of all, I want to say thank you for seeing me, after all that has happened it was more than I expected, you'll have to forgive me if I can't find the right words, it's difficult." Harry nodded and waited for her to continue. "I feel the need to explain things to you." Harry stopped her and said that it seemed a little late to be doing that as he had wanted an explanation years ago. "Do you know how I felt? How desperate I was wanting and trying to understand?" he said, while trying not to raise his voice. He had decided that whatever was said he would keep control of himself. "I had no idea, not a bloody clue! You left me and took Petra and it almost destroyed me. I could not believe or accept that you would do that. I'm not stupid and I realise that these things happen, especially to disabled people who were married before one of them became disabled. But perhaps I was just stupid after all, because I never imagined that it would happen to me. I didn't understand any of it, least of all you." He was about to tell her that she had expressed her love for him the night before she had left him for another man, but something stopped him for the moment.

Judith was very uncomfortable and searched for her words carefully. "I don't know what to say really, except that I didn't feel good or happy about leaving you like that. I just couldn't think of anyway that was easy."

"Easy for you or easy for me? Which do you mean?" said Harry his voice starting to rise. Judith stood up and said that she had better go and that it was probably a mistake in them meeting again. This was not what Harry had intended and he realised that if she left now he would never be in a position to tell her all the thoughts that had passed through his mind. He wanted her to know and understand his pain. He wanted her to feel the way he had felt, only then would she understand, he said to himself. He knew that he was not going to see or experience such a situation, his ideas and plans of how the scenario would develop was not going to plan, and if Judith left his only opportunity would be lost. He had years of anger and frustration stored away which he had hoped he could one day bring out and finally lay to rest, but it was not going as he had hoped. "Please, sit down, there's no need to go. It's just this situation that I find a little bit difficult, like you, and you must appreciate that," he said in a moderate tone of voice which he hoped sounded reassuring. She sat down and Harry decided that he would allow her to talk if she wished, he was hoping for an explanation that was acceptable, while knowing that whatever she said it would never restore his trust. But he still wanted her to explain.

Her voice was soft and controlled. "Over the years I've given it a lot of thought and I have tried hard to be honest with myself, and I can tell you my thoughts, but if it's only going to lead to us shouting at one another then there's little point, is there?" she said, looking at him and awaiting a response. Harry half smiled, the type of smile one makes when you are not happy with a situation, but for the time being you accept it. "We're adults, and a considerable time has passed and I think we can conduct ourselves as adults, so please continue." She half smiled and nodded before talking. "All I can say is that when you had the accident I was devastated and I couldn't come to terms with it. Both families impressed upon me the importance of being there for you and giving you the support you needed. You were so ill it seemed, and I loved you so much, but you were distant and different, you weren't the same person and although I loved you there was a difference, and you weren't the man I had married or fallen in love with. When you left hospital I was so happy to have you home, I wanted to do everything for you and to make you happy, that's how I felt. But you were so different, you might not have recognised it but you had changed, your thoughts and ideas had changed, and although you expressed your love for Petra and I, you were so wrapped up in your condition it seemed as though it was only you and your needs that counted."

"I wasn't like that at all!" said Harry "are you sure that your conception of me at that time has been created in your mind over the years? I had no idea that you thought like that, nothing was ever said, so why didn't you tell me or say anything?" He paused for a moment as they sat looking at one another. Harry was starting to feel emotional and he did not want to feel anything but logical and controlled. He took a deep breath before allowing her to continue.

He did not believe what she had said as it seemed too glib and simplistic but he did not contradict her . "You weren't yourself and it was almost impossible to speak to you as your mood swings made every issue into an argument. When I started work it wasn't for the money, it was to get out of the house."

"What you mean is, you got out of the house to get away from me." She looked at Harry carefully before replying. "That was the reason. I just could not put up with your attitude day after day, it was totally negative and self-centred." Harry interrupted her, "Just a minute! Before you say anymore, I was in love with you. I would have given you anything I could, and you knew that. So all of this self-centred bit, while seemingly plausible from your point of view, just doesn't seem to be as I remember things. And let's not forget one other point which might seem small to you at the time and even now. You didn't leave me to go and stay with your mother, you went with a man much older than yourself who had plenty of money, which seems clear to me that you went for a better option! That's the long and short of it, and you took my daughter with you. That's something that I find even today difficult to accept. And there's one other point that has crossed my mind upon many occasions. I slept with you and we made love, and you told me how much you loved me, and always would. The following day you left me. That I do not understand. You didn't have to lie to me, you could have just left me, but instead of that you had to lie and deceive me right to the end, and you must have known how I would feel. All I can say is you didn't give a toss for me, at that time you went for something better. You couldn't cope with my disability despite what you said at the time, so you saw your opportunity and you were off to pastures new! That's how I see it. If that's upsetting to you, or distasteful in any way, then I'm sorry, but that's how I saw it, and still see it' and over the years I've looked at the situation time and time again and I have always arrived at the same conclusions. I've been honest with you, as there's little point in pretending that I felt different."

Harry was expecting her to get up and leave at that point but for some reason she didn't.

"You make it sound so simple! But it was not like that. Of course I loved you! But as I've said, you were not the man I had married, you had changed and that wasn't your physical condition, but your personality and your attitude towards everything and I couldn't go on living with that any longer."

"So, you found yourself another man! You could not leave me and live with your mother, or was it all a wonderful coincidence?" said Harry sarcastically. They stared at each other not really sure what either of them should say next. Harry had calmed down to some extent although he could feel his pulse racing. "Perhaps it would be a good idea if we had a coffee or something." She agreed and asked where Andy kept his coffee. Harry had to explain to her that he did not know as this was the first time he had visited. Eventually they found what they were looking for and it gave them the opportunity to break off the conversation and return to a few pleasantries that soothed the situation.

"It's been a long time, hasn't it?" said Judith. "Sometimes it seems like yesterday, other times it does seem a long time. I suppose it depends upon what you're doing and your circumstances at the time," said Harry. "I must admit, you still look very good and you look well." She thanked him, and told him that he did not look bad and she hoped that his health was OK. "What are you thinking of doing then," he asked believing that he might as well get right to the point. She paused for a short while before replying. "I was thinking of coming back up here to live, but I'm not sure, my mother died and left me the house, my brothers agreed to the situation and as they were doing quite well, they didn't need it. Petra will be going into the sixth form somewhere, her results are good and it's a matter of finding her a suitable place with good standards. I can no longer keep her in the school she attended as the fees are quite high."

"I've never believed in public schools," added Harry "they breed the wrong attitudes." She ignored his remark and carried on. "I'll find myself a job and we should be able to manage as I did obtain a few skills over the years, especially with computers."

"Almost everyone uses a computer nowadays. I've used one for years, taught myself," said Harry. Judith tensed, realising that whatever she said Harry would attempt to treat it in some form of a derogatory manner if possible. "Actually I'm a programmer and quite good at it. I worked for a software company for three or four years."

"I thought that you had enough money to ensure you never had to work again!" said Harry surprised.

My husband became ill and the business had a few problems and I needed to work. We obviously had savings, but those went on maintaining a standard and school fees, of course. I had to find carers for Jim as he became progressively more ill, so I worked full time until I stayed at home to look after him."

"It's a pity he didn't make provision for you," said Harry. Her tone of voice changed suddenly. "He was a good man, and he did everything that he could, and I will not listen to a word said against him. He spent a lot of time and money on Petra," she said with genuine passion. Harry laughed out loud at that point. "I'm sorry Judith, if I can't see it the way you do, but in my book he was the man who buggered off with my wife and daughter, so try and understand if I see it differently; he's not a good man in my book." Judith was pragmatic. "I can understand that," she said "but all I'm saying is that he was good with me, and he was also good with Petra, he made sure that she wanted for nothing, and she has a trust fund for when she is twenty-one, which will be considerable. She doesn't need any money from you, in case that possibility is causing you some concern."

Harry could feel himself getting angry when the outside door opened. "I've brought back some fish and chips," said Petra, "mother was always going on about how they can only make good fish and chips in the north."

"That's a good idea!" said Harry "I could just eat some." Judith agreed and forced a smile, "at least we can agree that fish and chips are better up here." Petra recognised that there was a considerable amount of tension in the air but she did not say anything. "Have you contacted anyone regarding a sixth form?" asked Harry. "Not yet, we need some advice as to which is best, and whether or not we can obtain a place." Harry took out his diary and tore out a page and wrote a name and number down. "Telephone him and tell him it's my daughter who's wanting a place and you should have no problems." Judith looked vague for a moment. "I used to teach there, he's a friend of mine and he owes me a few favours, you'll not have a problem, believe me." Petra kissed him and thanked him. Judith asked him if it had a good reputation regarding its results. "What better reputation could it have, I worked there didn't I?" Both Petra and Harry laughed but Judith didn't. "I'm being serious, it's important that the sixth form is good and ensures that the students obtain the required results."

"I would not have mentioned it if it hadn't been suitable. It is my daughter's education that we're talking about," said Harry indignantly. "That's fine then, we'll telephone them."

"I'll have a word with him this evening, then he'll be aware of what's needed. It's a few miles away but it does have a good record, and it's in a decent area as I know such things are important to you." Judith let his last remark go .

"I wasn't aware that you were a teacher," said Judith "I thought my mother would have told me."

"Why should she tell you? She couldn't stand the sight of me, so she wouldn't tell you anything about me, unless it was derogatory." Judith nodded in agreement. "What else have you done that I'm not aware of?" she said while looking at Harry. This pleased Harry as he realised that in the circumstances he had not done too badly, and many would say that he had done quite well. "I suppose over the years I've done a few things and looking back, I think that it's fair to say that circumstances did at times drive me on. But it wasn't all fun and games, far from it. I do have a decent place of my own and I don't work at the moment, but I might go back and do some teaching if I feel inclined, it all depends how I feel really, and at the moment I can afford not to work as I've made a little progress financially. All in all, I suppose that I've done as well as most would have expected of me. After all, people didn't expect much of me, did they?" he said in a tone that could not disguise his anger. "I did improve my education and became a little more sophisticated. I would no longer drink out of a finger bowl, or pass the port the wrong way." Petra burst out laughing at that point, but Judith stared ahead and said nothing. "When were you thinking of moving up here?" asked Harry. Judith said that she would move once she was sure that Petra was going to get on with her studies, but now she had a number to ring she would do that, and then go over if possible, for a look around. "We're staying in a small hotel for two or three nights because my mother's house needs decorating, and some modernisation, but once that's sorted then we'll move in, it doesn't have to be perfect, but it has been neglected a bit over the past few years. Where do you live now? I know you no longer live where you used to, as I wrote to you some months ago but received no reply." Harry's curiosity was aroused "What was it about?" he asked, while not wanting her to notice his curiosity. "It was mainly to tell you about Petra and her education."

"I see," said Harry. Judith suddenly stood up, "I think that we should go now, we've taken up a lot of your time, and it was very nice of your friend to allow us to use his house. Will you thank him for me?" Harry realised that he did not want her to leave at that moment, but there was nothing that he could do about it without seeming too eager for her to stay, and he did not want to give her that impression. He showed them to the door and he then insisted that Petra must call around to see him, he gave her his telephone number. She promised that she would see him as soon as they moved. Judith was deliberately very polite and thanked him and said that meeting him had been difficult, but she hoped that he did not feel, she suddenly stopped herself realising that what she was about to say was unlikely to convey what she really meant. To her surprise, Harry had not ranted or raved or threatened her with God knows what, time changes everyone and his circumstances have been different to most, she thought. At that moment her mind took her back to the night that she had left Harry, and she felt sad at recalling how she had really felt, if only we could change things, she said to herself. She had loved him and his disability by itself did not affect her love, he was, on the surface, the man she had married, but deep down he had changed. He was always happy and laughing, willing to help anyone, nothing was a problem to him. His disability hardened him without him realising it, she thought. She was capable of being honest with herself after all these years. She had chosen an option that was easier, more comfortable, less hard work. She did not like his disability, it restricted them both, she thought it did not matter to her that he was disabled, but she often contradicted herself as though the truth, or some aspects of the truth, were too hard to accept. She had left him for another man, seemingly a better option, it was so simple. She did not leave him to live by herself, and she knew how much he loved her, but her needs and desires outweighed her love for him. All of her family agreed with her when she left, she was not short of support. Her mother had said that she did not know how she had put up with him for so long. "There are lots of men out there who would give a great deal to go out with you, you won't have to look far to find a decent man if you want one." Her mother's words rang in her head. Harry was a decent man she thought, I should have given it more time, we should have talked more. I walked out on him, he deserved better, but it's gone now and, her thoughts drifted out of her mind, but she was not happy with herself at that moment. She suddenly changed and concluded that in the long term it had been better for Petra.

She turned to Petra as they walked to the car. "Your father has changed a lot since I last saw him, he seems to have mellowed quite a bit."

"I like him," said Petra, "I like him a lot." Judith smiled, "for some strange reason I thought that you would, and in all fairness you should get to know one another, if that's what you want?" she said while carefully looking at Petra trying to determine her feelings. "It's early days yet," she said while giving Petra a quick hug, "but he was a nice man and he is your father, and you have quite a few of his ways, but don't worry they're not so bad." Petra looked closely at her mother, it was obvious that her mother had not been looking forward to her meeting with Harry. "What do you think of him now that you have met him again?" she asked innocently. Judith thought before answering. "He was very special and as I've said, he was nice," she stopped herself from expanding upon her statement by saying, "but that was a long time ago and much has happened since then, and I don't know what he's been doing, or what he's like now."

"Well, I like him, I like him a lot," said Petra. "He's not bad looking for his age, is he?" Judith laughed at her statement, "he was a good looking man, I suppose he still is, for his age, as you have said." Petra gave a little cough that indicated to Judith that she was about to ask a difficult question. "If he was good looking and nice, why did you leave him?"

"I was wondering when you was going to ask me that. Because life is sometimes more complicated than that, being good looking and nice isn't always enough. After his accident he changed, he was difficult to live with, it was as though he was totally concerned with himself and nothing else, it's hard to explain, but he was so negative and unwilling to do anything." She could feel her emotions were becoming difficult to control, "it should have been different, but you don't know that at the time; there's no one there who you can really talk to, everyone seems to have their own ideas and they never seem helpful." She shrugged her shoulders. "We might discuss it later if I remember, but we have a few things that require our attention now."

"I'm glad that he's my father, it feels right for some reason." She was about to add that she would not have left him. She had more sensitivity than her father and stopped herself realising the pain that such a statement would cause her mother.

Harry was feeling a bit bemused by the experience, he had expected a blazing row, with Judith running out and slamming the door once he had said what he had planned to say. It just did not work out like that he thought, he felt slightly cheated but he looked at the events philosophically. He was pleased that they were moving back up north as it would give him the opportunity to see Petra on a regular basis. Suddenly he felt sad realising how he had missed her growing up. He then sighed, and remembered that it was not of his doing, but Judith's. His thoughts moved on to Judith and the things they had said, although their meeting was brief. "I suppose I said some of the things that I wanted to say," he said to himself. He also realised that whatever he said it would never compensate for what she had done to him and the years he had lost with Petra. One has to be pragmatic about such things and after all, at the end of the day, what really counts is their daughter's wellbeing, and the stability that he thought that he could add to the equation. He made himself another drink and thought about Judith. She still looked good, and very attractive. Only time will tell, he thought to himself. He then thought that he should prepare himself for all the questions that Andy would have waiting for him. And what about Andy and Belinda, he thought, they have all of this ahead of them, at that point he laughed to himself wondering if they would be any more successful.

The telephone rang and it was the worst news that Harry could have received. He asked the caller to give him a few minutes and he would be ready, he slowly placed the receiver down. Harry was shocked, he was shaking, he could not believe what he had just heard. He answered the door, it was Caroline. "It's is true; he's dead, I'm sorry to say, and Belinda's in intensive care, but they think that she'll recover, but they can't be sure if she will be the same. I mean they're not certain, nothing is certain," the words poured out in a torrent. "What the hell happened? I just can't believe it that Andy's dead! It's not staying in my head," he said in despair. "I find it difficult Harry, but it's true."

"What are we going to do? If he's dead, what are we going to do," he asked again. Suddenly Caroline was lost for words. "I don't know, it just did not occur to me, all I could think of was coming round to see you and tell you. I'm sure that we should do something, but I can't for the moment think what it is."

"Who told you?" asked Harry. "The police contacted his family, but I heard from a friend who works in casualty, she knew of Andy and Belinda, and thought that I should know."

"I just don't know what to say or think," said Harry "one minute he's here, the next gone, it's bloody unreal."

"There'll be a funeral, which you'll attend, I presume?" Harry did not hear the question, his mind was wandering, going through various scenarios.

"What happened? How did it happen?"

"I don't know yet, but I'll find out. That's all that I know."

"What about Belinda? Is she gong to be OK, is there anything we can do? I feel helpless."

"I'll see her this afternoon and find out what her condition is. We can only hope, and then we can do whatever we can." Harry nodded and sighed, he felt as though a large part of his world had crashed. He had not known Andy very long but they were close friends, they had built up a special friendship that they both knew would last for as long as they did. Now it had ended tragically. He was bemused, he just could not understand why the world worked in such a way, kicking and hurting ordinary people, inflicting pain on those who did not deserve it, he felt sorry for himself. Then his thoughts turned to Belinda and tears formed in his eyes. Harry cried longer than he had ever cried before. He wanted to shout and to rant, he wanted to blame someone. He had something to look forward to, he had a life in front of him and suddenly it's gone, taken. Harry held his head in his hands, his usual inhibitions had disappeared. He felt as though the world had become empty and there was no explanation, no reason no logic.

CHAPTER TWENTY-ONE

The sky was seemingly losing its light and the group of people moved towards each other and slowly shook hands, they said a few pleasantries to each other in what appeared to be a well rehearsed ritual. The sky had darkened in a manner that was conducive to the occasion. Harry shuddered although he was not really cold, "it seems as though it has suddenly come cold," he said in a manner that did not warrant a reply. He looked at Caroline for a moment. "Are you ready to go and see Belinda now?" She nodded her acceptance, this was something that they were not looking forward to but someone had to do it, and Harry thought that it was something that he should do. In the preceding months he had become close to Andy and he looked upon him as a younger, but kindred spirit. Times and events can change so quickly, he thought to himself, one minute things are looking positive and the next minute everything has changed, he shook his head slowly as though in disbelief at the recent events. They moved away from the graveyard towards the gates and the parked cars, occasionally nodding in recognition to those who had attended. There had been no conversation or small talk amongst those who knew each other so well, everyone appeared shocked and unable to find the appropriate words.

The journey to the hospital was not a long one and although Harry wanted to say something he was lost for words. It was as though somewhere in his mind he knew that he wanted to say something which was important, something that rationalised the whole complex situation, but he did not know how to do it, he felt unusually confused. "What are we going to say, exactly?" he asked. "Let's deal with the situation when it arrives," said Caroline in a manner that was unusually abrupt for her but she did not feel that she wanted a prolonged discussion at that moment, and she was not feeling sensitive to what Harry might have said or was feeling.

Caroline and Harry made their way to the unit where Belinda had been a patient for the past week, they had visited regularly but it was only yesterday that she had started to regain consciousness. When they approached the bed they realised that she did not at first recognise them, but the sound of their voices brought a smile of recognition to her badly bruised face. Caroline asked her how she felt and almost at the same time insisted that she did not reply if it was difficult or painful. Harry thought to himself that it was going to be a very difficult visit, irrespective of whether Belinda could talk or whether she could not, he hoped that Belinda did not say anything, or to be precise, ask any questions. Caroline did not wait for a reply but drifted into what seemed like a well practiced routine of platitudes and generalities interspersed with a few obvious facts. "You've had an accident, but don't worry, everything's under control and you'll be fine, but you need to rest and you need to look after yourself." Harry looked at Belinda and thought to himself, this is the rubbish they churn out to all patients, surely Belinda will recognise this and suspect that something is wrong. Belinda seemed as though she was attempting to speak but before she could say anything Caroline interrupted her. "You've been here a few days and you had a bang on your head and unfortunately some broken ribs, but you'll soon be up and about." What on earth is she saying that for, thought Harry, she was not expected to live and she is lucky to be here, and it will be a long time before she is up and about, it will not be so easy with her legs badly broken. "Everything is being taken care of so, don't worry, you're being well looked after, and most of the nurses know you anyway." Belinda attempted to smile as she heard what Caroline was saying, although it did not really register, it sounded kind. "We're going to let you get some rest now, but we'll be back." Harry said that everyone was asking about her and looking forward to seeing her.

Harry closed the car door before asking Caroline why she had not told Belinda anything. Caroline was about to dismiss his question, but then seemingly realised the effect that the situation was having on Harry. She explained that It was not the right time, she would not have taken it in, or at best it would have confused her, and at worst well, who can say. "It doesn't seem right somehow, I think that she has a right to know," said Harry his voice lacking in conviction. Caroline turned and looked at him before speaking. "Consider this carefully, I don't like the situation, and I don't like any deception in normal circumstances, but what would the truth do to Belinda at this precise moment?" Harry muttered something. "Exactly," said Caroline "it wouldn't help her at all, there'll come a time, perhaps tomorrow or the day after, when she'll need to know, but until then let's save it until she's capable of understanding what we're saying."

"You're probably right," said Harry, while at the same time sighing "it's just that somehow it doesn't feel right, does it? In fact, I feel bloody helpless, stupid, and lost for words." Caroline placed her arm around Harry and gave him a hug, she had never seen Harry lost for words or so emotional because of someone else's predicament, "these things happen Harry, all of the time, it's just that they've happened to friends of ours. I suppose that's a fact, but it doesn't help, does it?" she added. "We' better get you back home and have something to eat," said Caroline. Harry replied that he had already prepared some food, thinking that they would go back there as he did not want to go back to Andy's parents house. "I told Judith and Petra to go back to my place, Petra was very fond of Andy, in fact she had a crush on him."

"She couldn't have helped but like him," said Caroline, "we all liked him." Harry nodded in agreement.

"It's nice to see a real fire," said Caroline, everyone agreed. "I have a full central heating system installed as well," said Harry, "fires are good to look at, but you're always throwing a log on or cleaning the things out." Why on earth are we talking about fires, he thought, when we have just been to the funeral of a good friend, and then visited another friend in hospital who has just had her legs broken badly and does not know it yet. Somehow Judith seemed to recognise what he was thinking and asked. "Do we know what really happened?" Caroline said that according to the police Andy and Belinda were driving normally and swerved to avoid a tractor pulling out from a field onto the road. They had to swerve across the road to miss it, they went through a hedge, dropped down a banking and hit the side of a building which then fell on the car trapping them inside. When the ambulance arrived and the fire brigade, Andy was dead and they had to get Belinda out as quickly as possible as she had a bad head injury, and she was trapped by her legs, both of which are broken. "That's all that they could tell me." Harry was looking into space focusing upon nothing in particular. He turned towards the others. "We talked them into going so that we could use their home, they wouldn't have gone if it hadn't been for us," said Harry getting emotional. "Life is not like that," said Caroline "and what happened is nothing to do with you, you're more sensible than that to even start to think along those lines, it could happen to anyone at anytime. I've seen too many people blame themselves for things that they have had no control over, so leave that to others who enjoy feeling guilty." Her carefully chosen words had the desired effect. "I am not enjoying this!" retorted Harry loudly. "None of us are enjoying it, but let's think about Belinda, because she's going to need support from all of us in the very near future. I'll visit her when I go off duty tomorrow and see what the situation is after talking to whoever is in charge of the unit. If she's alert and she asks me, I'll tell her the truth, because she's bound to find out quickly. There are some nurses on the unit who are insensitive enough to question her, just in order that they'll have something to gossip about during their lunch break." Judith said that it was hard to believe that anyone would do that. "Oh believe me, they would!" said Harry "they would not be able to wait some of them, women wallow in passing on bad news, in fact, they'd really enjoy the situation." Caroline glared at Harry feeling that his remark was somehow directed at Judith. "It's better if it comes from me," said Caroline who then added, "I'm not looking forward to this, in the past I've had to give bad news to many people and it's never easy, but giving such news to a friend is a new experience and quite honestly I just don't know how she'll react."

"Perhaps it might be better if someone else did it," added Harry.

They did not need to worry with regard to who it was who might be appropriate to tell her the bad news. When Caroline arrived she could tell that Belinda had already been informed. Her face, which was already badly bruised, had not been improved by the tears and the red eyes that accompanied the tears. Belinda burst into tears as Caroline sat down, she wanted to reach across and comfort her but she knew that touching her would only give Belinda physical pain. To watch her in her grief was so painful and Caroline just could not think of anything sensible to say. Belinda solved the problem by speaking first. "It appears as though my body has been kicked around a bit, I asked them, and they've told me that my legs are broken, both femurs, and a few ribs, with a bad knock on my head, but they scanned my head again this morning and they've said that it seems as though I still have a brain." At that point she attempted to smile. There was a long pause before she spoke again, when she suddenly started she burst into tears, "I know about Andy," she gasped out between sobs, She looked at Caroline and asked her why did it happen, her tears ran down her cheeks uncontrollably. Caroline looked at her and held her hand tightly, she said that she did not know why these things happen, suddenly she also was crying. This is unprofessional and I must not do this, she tried saying to herself, but the tears would not stop. She moved closer to Belinda and said. "There's nothing that I or anyone can say that will make it easier, he loved you, and you loved him, your time together was so short, but no one can take those moments away from you, you'll always have those thoughts and feelings." Both of them attempted to stop crying but they failed as they shared their grief with an outburst of emotion. "We're nurses," said Caroline, trying to smile through her tears "we should show an example to others."

"What does example count for?" asked Belinda quietly. "Absolutely nothing," said Caroline, "if you were someone else I could say all of the things we're supposed to say in these circumstances, but I can't say anything that'll make you feel better." With that she leaned over and gently kissed Belinda who started to cry again, a gently sobbing cry that would have touched the heart of the most hardened individual. "I'll come back this evening and bring Harry with me, if you want him to come." Belinda nodded and closed her eyes in a vain attempt to shut out the world. Her memory was returning and her thoughts were confusing but she was now remembering the accident.

She tried to shake Andy but he would not move, she tried to move him but found out that she was unable to move, she was trapped and then the sudden pain struck her, she felt the intense pain in her legs and her body. She knew that blood was running down her face, she could feel it warm and unpleasant. But she was concerned about Andy, he would not respond, she felt for his pulse but she could not find one, she looked around for help but she could not see properly, everything was confused, some objects were out of focus. She then realised that Andy was not breathing and that he was dead. Strangely she did not shout or scream or do anything in particular, for a moment she sat there, her mind lost in the enormity of the events. She vaguely remembered someone pulling the door off of the car and talking to her, but she could not remember what they said. After that she remembered Harry and Caroline talking to her, but she was not sure if that was yesterday or the day before, she was not sure of anything except that Andy was no longer alive. She was alone and without the man whom she had fallen in love with. She drifted into a troubled sleep.

"How's she doing now nurse?" asked Harry in a cheerful voice that belied his feelings. "She's not the best of patients," replied the nurse laughing, she knew Belinda and had found time to spend extra time with her. Unlike some of her peers she genuinely wanted to help, she was more sensitive than most and this was proving beneficial. Belinda was familiar with the routine and she fully understood what was happening but somehow being a patient made it all very different. She realised that it was not quite like she had imagined, it was for some inexplicable reason more difficult, you were no longer a person, despite what the staff said, you were a case who had to follow the procedures even if you felt they were wrong. I will make sure that I remember these things, she said to herself, she thought that she might write an article for the magazine, she then changed her mind, thinking that it would only make her enemies and solve no problems. The last thought annoyed her and she was angry with herself. She then decided that she would write down her thoughts and perceptions as she did not give a toss at that moment for potential enemies. We're all too concerned about making waves, she thought, and due to that attitude nothing changes for the better, too many people say nothing when they know that things are not right. She was definitely recovering, she thought due to her belief that only a couple of days back such thoughts what not have entered her mind. She lay there wondering how long it would be before she would be allowed up and out of bed. She had worked on orthopaedics during her training and she was trying to remember the timescale when it came to treating the differing problems. It is going to take some time, she thought subsequently she had better get used to the idea. Looking at it from one point of view, it was not a bad thing as it would give her time to think and to give some thought to recent events. She had shed more tears these past few weeks than she had shed during the rest of her life up until that time. Her grief could not be hidden, although at times she tried in the belief that being a nurse, somehow, could exclude her from the grieving process. Fortunately Caroline recognised this and told her that everyone grieves differently and she should allow herself to do what her heart demanded and not her head. Belinda took the advice and allowed herself to feel the emotions that she had on occasion tried to suppress.

"She's ready and awaiting you," said the young nurse, who then added, "she can't wait to leave us, even though she's had preferential treatment, we even made sure that the liquid was exactly the correct temperature when she had her enemas."

"What enemas?" asked Belinda with a contrived look that indicated she either had not experienced enemas or she had given little or no thought to them. "She wanted one every day, said it was better than colonic irrigation. We were getting a little but suspicious at one time then we just thought that everyone has their sensual preferences."

"You cheeky devil!" said Belinda in a voice that was much louder than she normally used. "Yes, I'd be wondering," added Harry "you have to keep an eye on the anal retentive and their opposite numbers, they could give the place a bad name, or on the other hand create a demand."

"Come on! Stop there before you get worse," said Judith. She looked at Belinda carefully wondering if she could manage on her crutches. Before she could say anything Belinda said that she could get to the car if Judith would carry the few items that she was taking out with her.

"Well, what d'you think of the place?" said Harry. Belinda looked around carefully knowing that this was expected of her. "It's impressive Harry, it looks really nice and I didn't realise how large the place was, it could be called 'Harry's castle', it's very nice." Harry was pleased with her comments and indicative of his feelings he sighed in a manner that displayed a modicum of contentment. "I've kept adding bits on and reshaping other parts as ideas came to me," he said while tilting his head back and smiling for a moment, he was pleased at Belinda's reaction. He looked around him and thought that everything looked good and substantial. That's the correct word for it, thought Harry, 'substantial'. "Your rooms are through the door to the left. I think that you'll find everything that you need," added Judith, "if you need anything, just let me know and I'll get it for you and Petra will bring it around." Belinda looked bemused for a moment, "I assumed you were living here with Harry." At that point Harry made a cough-like noise, which indicated that he wanted to say something that would be clearly understood. "Judith and Petra live in the house they obtained when they came up here, which seems the best idea at the moment."

"So it's just you and I who'll be here?" said Belinda looking surprised. "Don't worry," said Judith "Mrs. Briggs comes in three or four mornings a week, and Harry has a carer or personal assistant, as he prefers to call them, come around everyday to ensure that he's up and out of bed and everything is functioning."

"Mrs. Briggs was originally going to do the cleaning and my washing, but to be truthful she's not really up to it, but she's a good cook and she's so considerate that I don't have the heart to let her go, besides I don't pay her very much so it's sensible to keep her on." He made an arm gesture which signified that he had justified his reasoning to his satisfaction. "That's the Harry we know and love," said Belinda, "for a moment I thought that you'd become soft in your old age." He nodded as though he was receiving a compliment. "Anyway, the point is that you have all the space that you need for the moment, and I want you to feel as though this is your home until you're fit and well and able to get back to work. I have plenty of space and you will not feel as though you're encroaching upon someone else's space, so just treat it as home," he paused and smiled before saying that if she wanted to do anything in the way of cooking or cleaning in the way of therapy, then he would not stop her, "work will do you good," he said and then added, "I can always find you something useful to do."

"She has not come here to work for you for free," said Judith. Harry looked a little put out at such a suggestion. "That could have hurt my feelings if I'd been oversensitive," he said. "I've discussed this with your parents who weren't happy when you told them that I had invited you to stay here, but I explained that it was near the hospital and useful regarding your physiotherapy, etc. They seemed to accept that, and I clearly told them that they're welcome here anytime, so there shouldn't be a problem." Belinda suddenly started crying, Judith led her to an armchair and helped her to sit down. "Everyone's been so nice to me," she said between sobs and tears. Judith placed her arm around her and told her that they were her friends and that is what friends were for, to be there for each other. Harry was on the verge of saying something sarcastic, but stopped himself realising that the small amount of pleasure that he might obtain at Judith's expense would not be balanced by the possible distress that it might cause Belinda. After a coffee, which tasted so much better than that served in hospital, Belinda went to her bedroom and lay on the bed, staring up at the ceiling her mind turning over leaping uncontrollably from one thought to another, all of which added to her existing emotional state. So much had happened in such a short space of time that it seemed unreal. She felt as though she was in a dream and suddenly she would awake and everything would be back to normal. She held back her tears realising that this was normal, this was real life and these things happened to other people, not just patients. And that patients and their families were not a separate race that frequented her place of employment but ordinary people like herself. Her thoughts once again raced through her head, out of control, there was no logic or clear positive thinking at that moment as she surprisingly fell asleep while still fully clothed, her mind and body were exhausted, and leaving the security of the hospital had placed a strain upon her.

Judith said goodbye to Harry and insisted that if he needed anything, or if Belinda needed anything he only had to telephone her and she would be around right away. She added that he could also contact her at work if necessary as she was sharing a job in the information section in the Town Hall and it was no problem receiving calls. He nodded in appreciation, he then thanked her and told her that without her help the past few weeks would have been very difficult. Judith smiled and replied that Caroline would have made sure that everything that was needed to have been done would have. She quickly added that Wendy was also a decent sort who would have helped if necessary. Harry knew what she had said was correct but he was pleased to be able to thank her, a few weeks earlier he would have found it almost impossible. "Life never ceases to surprise me," said Harry. "Who would have predicted the recent events?" he sighed a sigh of regret that Judith understood. "It's not been easy for you, I know how close you were and how much he meant to you." Harry held out his arms in exasperation, "he was like a younger brother and a friend, we got on so well despite the age difference. I have quite a few acquaintances but only a small number of true friends, and when you lose one it not only hurts but it emphasises your mortality and produces irrational feelings of apprehension. Life is so bloody short, I feel as though I have been saying that forever, but it is so true. There are things that I want to do, really want to do and most of them are not possible if I'm to be honest," he said looking at Judith. "You have plenty of time yet, and you have plenty of friends, remember, I've met a few of them these past few weeks and I doubt if they'll let you down."

"There are friends and friends," said Harry unsure as to whether that comment was in the correct context. She smiled at him while feeling that somehow Harry was getting at her even if it was unintentional. "Andy liked you a lot, from what others have told me, he wasn't a bad judge of character Harry," she smiled at him. As she was leaving Caroline arrived. "She seems to have managed to progress rapidly under your supervision," said Caroline sounding surprised at the physical progress that Belinda had made in a relatively short space of time. Harry grunted as a form of appreciation. "I'm a very good teacher, you forget that I'm a trained teacher but I also have the experience of being disabled, therefore I know how far and fast that I can push her, and she knows that I'll not take any bullshit from her when it comes to putting effort into whatever she is supposed to be doing." Caroline laughed out loud, "you never put effort into anything that you didn't want to. I bet you're really enjoying every minute of it, having one of us on the receiving end for a change." Harry was not slow with the banter. "I would gladly have you on the receiving end any time that you feel the urge," he said while trying to look serious. "Who knows, but one of these day it might be your lucky day," she replied. "You might just have got that slightly wrong," said Harry, "it might be your lucky day, in fact it would be your lucky day!" at that point he laughed. "You've not lost the modest approach, have you?"

"I have very little to be modest about, if one is objective," he added in a serious tone that indicated he possibly believed what he was saying. "But what, if anything, is happening between you and Judith?" asked Caroline deliberately and provocatively changing the subject. "You've nothing to worry about, I doubt if she'd be concerned or give it any thought, besides it's nothing to do with her." Caroline told him to be serious as he knew exactly what she meant. Harry snorted in the manner that only Harry could manage. "We're bordering upon being friends and we're slowly getting used to the existence of one another, we're polite and that keeps the interaction civilised, I suppose." He shrugged his shoulders in a somewhat bemused manner. "I don't know what might or might not happen, and if my past judgement is anything to go by I wouldn't see the warning signs, would I? Because I get swept along with enthusiasm, Oh yes, I bloody well would," he added. He started singing, "I still get that same old feeling."

"Knowing that song shows your age," said Caroline who was not amused at Harry's attitude. She had known him long enough to know that he could be difficult and irritating when he was in that type of mood and she did not want to allow him the pleasure of seeing her annoyed. At that moment Belinda entered the room and smiled on seeing Caroline. "You've done really well and made progress faster than expected," said Caroline. "It's Harry's cooking, well really Mrs. Briggs, she insists that I have to be built up, whatever that means."

"It means," said Harry. Caroline stopped him as she recognised that he was about to hold forth at some length. "We're expecting you back on the unit next week. I'm not supposed to tell you this, but I've heard that you can do a few mornings at work on the unit and then some clinics just to ease you in gently, it's almost fulltime and it'll provide you with an income." Belinda said that the income had not been a problem as she was in a scheme that paid her when she had to stay in hospital, so with that and her sick pay she was better off than when she was working. That part of the conversation captured Harry's attention, which was not lost on Belinda who turned to Harry and said that before she left she needed to know how much she owed him as she could not bring herself to live in his house without contributing. Harry smiled and was about to say something after quickly calculating her income, when Caroline said, "In the circumstances he would not dream of taking any money from you." Harry said, "oh yes I would!" Caroline said that he was only joking and that money counted for little when friends were helping one another. That's bloody news to me, thought Harry has she just made that up? It's not her money that we're talking about, it's easy when you are spending someone else's money. He realised that if he pursued the matter it would not look good, so with some reluctance he decided he would let the matter drop although it went against the grain. He then started to think correctly and realised that having Belinda there recovering had provided him with so much emotional sustenance and he had benefited a great deal by the experience. He thought that it would feel strange living by himself again as he had become used to Belinda being around. They had carefully given each other space and consideration. This was a new experience for Harry and he recognised that somehow he had mellowed. They had talked at length on most nights and they had explored their feelings. They found that they could talk about Andy and what they had hoped for the future without it being too distressing. "It's good to talk openly and honestly," said Harry. "We loved him and we still do."

"It'll feel strange going back on the unit, I'll not know what to say if anyone says anything," said Belinda in a voice lacking in confidence. "Such as what? What would anyone say?" said Harry whose voice was raised at the thought of anyone saying anything that might be insensitive. "Don't worry, only Harry would be likely to ask you anything and he already is aware of everything," laughed Caroline trying to make light of Belinda's concern. "Everyone has been concerned and we want you back with us," she gave Belinda a hug and then they both shed a tear. Harry groaned and invited them to have a drink to celebrate Belinda's return to work. "Just a moment! There is one item that we haven't discussed and that is your future accommodation and what alterations that need to be made. Choose whatever decorations you want and we'll get them done, it's no problem." Both Belinda and Caroline looked at each other and then at Harry. "Don't tell me you've made other plans, I was a bit presumptuous," said Harry "but I never thought that you might have other plans. It was stupid of me," he said while feeling disappointed. At that point Belinda threw her arms around him and kissed him. "Steady on! I could get to like that," he said. "You've been wonderful, Harry, I just could not have managed without you, and these past few weeks," she paused trying to think of the correct words. "I don't know what to say, except you've done so much for me and I'll never be able to repay you." She turned towards Caroline and said that she owed them both so much. Caroline did not want Harry to be hurt or put out in anyway. "Actually, I've asked her to stay with me now that she's mobile, it would have been difficult before due to the steps but now she can manage them without difficulty. And we get on well together' we make a good team." Harry knew that Belinda had thought of leaving but he had, in his way, clearly given her the option of staying. Harry had become used to having Belinda in the house, they had their own space and they liked each others company, he reluctantly agreed that it was a sensible idea, and that one had always got to look towards the future. That last phrase did not strike the right note but it did not seem to matter. Harry was no longer feeling pessimistic but he did not understand why as he had not had the best of days. "We'd thought of moving sometime tomorrow, if that's possible and if it fits in with any arrangements you might have. But it is up to you and we do not want to…" Harry quickly said "It's fine, there isn't a problem, it'll take that time to work out your rent."

"I was wondering how long it would take you before you threw that into the equation! laughed Caroline, at that point she kissed him more tenderly than he expected. She looked at him while smiling before she spoke . "You know, Harry, there are a lot worse than you around." Harry winced, "is that supposed to be some form of compliment? Because if it is, then I'm not impressed. Bloody hell! To hear that there are a lot worse than me around, that's really impressed me. Is that as good as it gets?" he said loudly. "You could at least offer to sleep with me and work off Belinda's rent which you were so quick to dismiss when it wasn't costing you bugger all."

"Don't be like that Harry, you know how much we all think about you, even when you're being difficult. And just think of your image, everyone will be impressed you'll go down in history as 'Harry the generous', and not 'Harry the mean bastard'. At that point even Harry burst out laughing. "Anyway, I mean this," he said while clearing his throat. "I don't want to say this in front of others so this is the opportunity now that you're leaving, you are leaving aren't you?" he said quickly. "That's good, I don't want to be stuck with you forever although you'll always remember that I did make the offer regarding you staying." He coughed and then added. "I definitely made some kind of generous offer I believe, perhaps in a moment of weakness, who knows, but I did make it." He looked around in case anyone disagreed. "Now, this is important and I'll not say it again." He looked slightly bemused before he spoke as though searching for words that he was unfamiliar with. "What I want to say is that the past months have been complex in the extreme, and that's an understatement." He paused again and gave a meaningful sigh. "I just don't know what has happened recently. I know what has happened, but I don't know why, and it'll take me a long time to come to terms with events. However, leaving that aside and this might sound contradictory, I want to say it has been one of the best times of my life, and one of the worst. I don't need to go into any detail or say anything at length. I just can't at this time talk about you and Andy in the depth that I need, although you and I have talked at length and with emotion," he said while looking at Belinda, "because I think I have some idea of what you have felt and are still feeling." He could not find words that did not sound insensitive or too emotional. "What I'm trying to say is that my life has been enriched by knowing you both, whatever happens in the future, this is an important part of my life and you'll always be a part of my life. I loved him like a brother," Harry started sounding emotional. "Does that sound, or make, sense?"

Caroline smiled and Belinda said "we understand Harry, and I'm so glad that we met, I also can't explain my feelings yet, but the pleasure of knowing Andy even for such a short time is something that I'll think of every day of my life. And I know people say it gets easier and better, but I don't want it to get easier, I loved him and still love him, and that's how I feel. And I love you Harry," she tried to laugh at that point as she told him that he might have to wait for his rent unless Caroline would oblige him by offering him her sexual favours but even if she didn't, then she would always be in his debt. "You were never in debt and you never will be," said Harry. They laughed while at the same time a feeling of sadness pervaded the atmosphere. "I remember talking to Andy and saying that it was a strange life. I said that he would find it interesting. I didn't think at the time what happened could happen. When someone has had an accident you never think that it can happen again." He felt uncertain again but he shook it off as though he would not allow any such thoughts to destroy that moment. "Let's never forget," he said. "And let's remember this friendship, and what we've shared, because it's something so rare and so special, and it's ours to hold onto and to cherish."

"That sounds as though you've read that bit somewhere." Harry looked hurt for a moment. "We can't go on talking like this, we're suppose to keep a stiff upper lip now and put things behind us," he said while trying to steer the conversation knowing that his emotions were getting the better of him. "I don't want to sound pathetic and I wouldn't want anyone to know of this." He paused unsure whether he should continue. They looked at him in expectation. "Sometimes I think that I can almost hear him talking. It's strange, isn't it.?" Belinda was quick to speak. "No, it's not strange. I talk to him every day, sometimes I know what his reply would be and I sometimes feel better. I'm not religious in the normal sense and I can't honestly say that I believe in an afterlife, it doesn't seem sensible, whichever way you look at it. But I do so much want to see him and to hold him again." Harry was not sure what to say, so for once he said nothing. "We know how much he loved you, and he'll always be there watching over you."

"I'm not particularly religious, but I do believe that we're more than our mortal bodies," said Caroline. "I'm ready for something to eat and then I'll leave you until tomorrow," said Caroline. "I've already made a casserole, well actually Mrs. Briggs made it and it's been cooking slowly so I'll get that arranged and we can eat." Caroline sat with a smile on her face. Harry asked her what it was that was causing her to smile. She said that she was not sure that she should tell him. This annoyed him considerably. I will say it but promise not to get angry. He promised. "Well, I'm betting you," she said deliberately slowly, "I'm betting that next year, at this time, Judith will be cooking your dinner." Harry gazed at her thoughtfully before speaking, He was unsure if there was a follow-up comment awaiting, dependent upon his answer. "Do I have a choice between you or Judith? Because you could do a lot worse, move in with me and I'll be the envy of every man around here, I'll treat you like a goddess. I've always said, to those of a discerning nature, that you have a body to die for, and that black silk underwear really turns me on." He looked at Belinda for confirmation. Belinda, while smiling, nodded in agreement. He laughed out loud at Caroline's expression, "it's back to 'Harry the bastard' again, isn't it?" Caroline looked at him somewhat enigmatically and said that she might give it a little thought if she was destitute, then quickly said that the casserole was very good. She looked across at Harry and smiled. At that moment Harry was totally confused and could not make up his mind if his prospects had improved or not. "Don't wait until you're destitute, think about it. I might find it hard to live with if you only take up my offer because you're desperate." Caroline looked at him carefully before telling him that she really would give it some thought. Harry poured himself a drink and wondered if he would be better off with Caroline or Judith, he enjoyed contemplating each of them carefully and their individual assets. It's a bloody fantasy, he said to himself, it would never happen, both would need to be convinced that it would be a good move for them. Then there was Petra, whom he decided must come first in his thinking. God it gets confusing, but it will work out this time, surely I deserve a bit of good luck, he thought. He also knew that it would not be simple plain sailing, life was not like that, at least his life wasn't, and luck did not seem to follow those who might or might not deserve it.

"There is some good news Harry, and it could effect you," Harry shook himself for a few seconds, he had been staring into space his mind drifting. "What's the good news?"

"Well, some months ago it was decided by someone to have a nurse of the year award, and to my surprise I've been voted nurse of the year! Please don't applaud," said Caroline excitedly. "I realise it's only on the unit, but isn't it nice when people actually vote for you because they respect you? And this is the bit that you'll like, the other good news is that the first prize is a weekend for two in Paris. It has just occurred to me," she said while putting her arms around him, "you've been so nice these past weeks, would you mind if I took you to Paris with me?" Harry was lost for words as his mind clouded over in a painful way that he had rarely experienced. He had totally forgotten about the nurse of the year award that he had discussed with Andy as a brilliant idea. It was months ago that he had arranged for some unsuspecting type to announce the idea and the prizes, although the person had taken a little convincing that such prizes had been made available by friends of the unit and they did exist. But Harry soon convinced him by telling him that he could announce the competition in a dignified manner, much better than anyone else of course, and he could present the prizes, which would feel as though he was doing some good. He would be doing something worthwhile, and just think how the winners will react? They will be oozing with gratitude, and they will remember who gave them the prize. That convinced him that giving the prizes was not only a right and proper thing to do but it was a service to humanity.

Harry's mind switched back to the present. "When were you thinking of going?" he asked tentatively. Caroline said that she could go almost anytime as she had a few days holiday to come. "One small point though, we can't fix a definite date at the moment. The snag is, that for some reason they don't seem to remember where the prizes or the details are, but that'll soon be sorted out as I'm going to ask one of the managers to look into it. Her face once again broke into a large warm smile. "And what's more, I believe that the prize is for a weekend stay in a five star hotel, who knows Harry, we might get the honeymoon suite. Do you think that you could cope with such a hectic weekend?" she said while tenderly kissing his forehead. Harry desperately wanted to say something but he kept his mouth shut knowing that whatever he said would only be to his disadvantage. She looked at Harry carefully before speaking. "When we get to Paris, Harry the past is non-existent, we'll enjoy ourselves as though the rest of the world doesn't exist. Before you say anything, I do mean that it's a fresh start, I think that we need it." Harry looked to the heavens and swore under his breath that he would get even with God if he ever had the opportunity. His mind was working over regarding how he might retrieve the situation. If it ever came to light that it was he and Andy who had thought the whole thing up his life would be unbearable and he would not be forgiven by Caroline. There is only one option he thought and it was drastic.

He decided that he would say that he had the trip to Paris donated anonymously and he would have to pay for it in the short-term as the money has been laying in an account awaiting the winner and he could not remember who had donated it, but he had the information somewhere. That sounds plausible enough he thought. "We could go very soon," said Harry "I just have to make a few financial arrangements. You do realise that the prize was only for the flights and the hotel don't you? There are no evening meals or any extras. I think it stated somewhere that the weekend was subject to availability but it had to be taken within a time period."

"I can't remember that!" said Caroline looking bemused. "Definitely," added Harry who thought that he was starting to think a little quicker once again. "If not taken within a specific time the prize was lost." He saw Caroline's expression change so he quickly added. "In case that happened there's still a prize though." He tried hard to quickly think of something suitable that might be acceptable, but cheap. He need not have bothered as Caroline said, "It's got to be Paris! I have set my mind on it." Caroline could hardly contain herself, for some reason the prospect of going to Paris had opened a door for her. "Let's go as soon as possible, while I still feel excited at the thought of it. Have you seen the price of those five star hotels? I just can't wait! I need some luxury," said Caroline. Harry groaned quietly and wondered if he was going to get his money's worth. Caroline looked at Harry and asked him what was he thinking about. Harry just smiled and said that in his opinion, nothing was too good for her and if she enjoyed herself then they could do it again whenever they wanted. "That's really a nice thought Harry, who knows, you might get into the habit of spending money unless you're very careful." Harry forced a smile, "you could be right. I think that I might need therapy, or something of that nature, I don't know what has come over me. Aversion therapy to prevent unnecessary and foolish expenditure, that's what I need urgently."

"Don't worry, once in Paris sightseeing during the day and going to the famous night clubs at night will be superb. I really am getting excited at the thought of it and once excited, who knows, you could see a different side of me. The Ritz or the George V, that's the type of hotel that I could become accustomed to."

"Not on my money you couldn't, no matter how excited you might get," added Harry quickly. Harry mumbled under his breath. "Let's see how you go on with this trip first."

"Sometimes it almost sounds as though it's your money that you're spending," laughed Caroline. "What if we ask Judith and Petra to join us? That would be really special, and I know that Petra would enjoy spending some time alone with you." Harry was starting to panic he could see a double loss looming on the horizon. No time alone with Caroline and the extra cost of taking two more along. "Just a minute, let's clarify this situation as it's getting just a little out of hand, unless you want to invite a few dozen of your friends along or everyone on the unit."

"I thought that the intention was for you and I to enjoy a few days luxury by ourselves, away from all the usual stress and distractions, or have I missed something?" Caroline smiled, gave him a squeeze and told him that it was she who had won the prize and if she wanted to invite people then she would do that. Harry winced, realising that if he was not careful he would not be going to Paris. It's just typical, he thought, bloody typical. A good scheme had been devised, everything had nearly worked out as planned, but then that hidden variable came into play and he was now having to foot the bill. Not only that, if he wasn't careful he would not be going, which would mean that there would be no recompense for him. "I am going to enjoy this weekend away, aren't I?" asked Harry while looking carefully at Caroline in order to ascertain any change in her expression that might clarify things to his satisfaction. "Of course you're going to enjoy it, and don't worry, we'll spend plenty of your money on entertainment, visiting the best nightclubs in the city. I wonder if Paris is still full of artists and such like?" Harry thought that might be a cheap option if he could induce her artistic side. "We'll look for some left bank weirdoes if that's what you want." Harry could feel the perspiration on his forehead. "Let's be realistic, let's take things steady, there's no reason to go mad and throw money about as though it's going out of fashion, is there?" She sighed then said, "it all depends upon how good a time we want, Harry," she winked at him. I think that I'm being set up but I can't be sure, he thought. Harry was in a difficult position, he did not want to waste money yet he wanted to ensure that Caroline had a good time as he definitely wanted value for his money.

Caroline switched off her mobile telephone and smiled. "That was Amanda, she's coming back to work at last, we've all missed her telling us what to do and where we're going wrong. When she left after her surgery and was accepted upon a senior management course I thought that she'd be moving on to pastures new once the course was over. Along with the other two sisters, I've been trying to run the unit in an efficient manner, but I realise that I'm not a good administrator. Well, to be more accurate, I should say that I don't enjoy the paper work, there's too much of it and it takes you away from the patients. " She continued, "there's a party next week, it's Wendy's Hen night and I'll be going, it might be a good idea if I take Amanda along and she can meet some of the new faces before she has to meet them in a work setting." Harry coughed to indicate that he wanted to say something serious. "Are you sure that it's a good idea? Have you thought it through carefully? Have you thought that most of you there will be rolling around pissed when in attendance at this function, and I'll call it a function because…" Harry held out his arms in exasperation, "what else can you call a pub full of nurses getting as much alcohol down their throats in the shortest possible time? It won't be similar to a Royal garden party will it? And what about little Mavis? She can drink an unbelievable amount and she still looks sober as though she's immune to alcohol. Which is a waste of money if it has no effect, but she does take all her clothes off and sing when she gets to that stage. Having said that, I wouldn't want to see her without her clothes, she's not a pretty sight with them on."

"That is very unkind, but true," added Belinda. "I think Amanda will observe you lot and quickly decide that she'd better re-think the situation and look elsewhere for a job." Caroline dismissed the comments while recognising that there was some logic in Harry's words. "She's not like that when she's out, she can differentiate between work and play, in fact she's another person once she's had a few drinks, she would surprise you." Harry looked slightly hurt, "I was just giving you an opinion. I'm not so bothered, I was just suggesting that it might not be a good idea. I was also going to ask you, what's the fellow like that's marrying Wendy? It's all happened so quickly, I knew she was desperate for a fellow but it's all been something of a rush. I hope that she doesn't regret it as she jumps in with both feet." Caroline shrugged her shoulders, "I've only met him a couple of times and he seemed fine for Wendy. What I mean by that is that he was not strange or abnormal." Harry winced, "what you really mean is that you wouldn't want him at any price." She said nothing which told Harry everything.

"I have sat here listening to you two talk as though you were an old married couple," said Belinda. "I'm sorry," said Harry "but it was the thought of going to Paris for a dirty weekend with Caroline that has made me lose all sense of time." Caroline laughed out loud. "I think that you might be in for a disappointment if you're expecting 'a dirty weekend' as you so crudely put it. I'm wanting to experience some of the finer things in life, art and culture." Harry scratched his head, he was now confused, was she winding him up and being obtuse, or was she being honest. He wondered if he had heard it all wrong. He was sure that she had implied that they were going to live it up and indulge themselves, everything she had said appeared to be suggestive. She had quickly hugged him and kissed him while telling him these things, she said that she, he paused, unable to think clearly for the moment. Before he had time to regain his thoughts Belinda said that both Caroline and herself really appreciated everything that he had done, she gave Harry a squeeze and kissed him. "You're OK Harry, despite what the others say about you."

"I must agree, you're not so bad," said Caroline. Harry was becoming more bemused, "A few minutes back I was a prince amongst men, I was Mr. Wonderful on my way to Paris, possibly having the honeymoon suite in a great hotel. What the hell has happened to change it? Something has happened and I have definitely missed it!" They just smiled at him enigmatically. "This needs some thinking out," he said to himself. They closed the door behind them, out of earshot they both burst out laughing. They laughed until tears ran down their cheeks. "That was cruel," said Belinda, "that was really cruel to lead him on like that. When did you know about the nurse of the year scam?"

"I knew right away, as soon as dopey Alec mentioned the idea, it was obvious he hadn't thought of it. It was either Harry or Ronny and as Ronny left the unit quickly it was then down to Harry, it was just the sort of thing that he would do. Once I knew that I asked around and observed the comments, it didn't require a genius to work it out. Anyway, it'll do him good to spend some of his money, he's been careful with it for years. It seems a little unkind somehow, as he's been such a good friend, and these past few weeks that I've stayed with him has also made me see him in a different light, he's a really nice person when you get to know him. I'll admit that getting to know him is not all that easy though, he keeps a great deal to himself, although he talks a lot when he is in a talkative mood." Caroline nodded in agreement. "Harry's often like an iceberg, there's more hidden than exposed, and if we ever get to France I'll try to ensure that he has a good time, besides, I have to work off your keep, someone has to sacrifice themselves."

"Would you really do that for me?" asked Belinda. "Of course not! Don't be stupid!" said Caroline, "but I'd do it for me, and it would really shock Harry if I seduced him." Belinda laughed and said that she had no doubt that he would not play hard to get. And she could imagine his train of thought. 'If she wants me so much perhaps we could have stayed at a cheaper hotel'. "That's definitely Harry," said Caroline while laughing.

The day had started bright and clear, the ground was covered in a white frost, and the air was cold and sharp. Belinda carefully parked the car just off the road and near to the footpath. She walked along the path through the trees until she came to a stream. The water was high for the time of year and the stream ran fast over the rocks causing the water to break up into white foaming rapids but on a miniature scale. On the other bank the reeds were turning colour awaiting the winter, and the fields were straw coloured as the remaining tall grass had died back while laying a warm blanket upon the frost covered ground. The fields stretched back, rolling away into the distance, only broken by the odd tree or bush that had somehow survived the enlarging of the fields.

She sat down upon a large stone by the bank of the stream. For some inexplicable reason she looked to see if there were any fish protruding from under the rocks but she could not see any. Her mind then switched from looking at the water to remembering the last time that she had been there, it looked familiar but did not feel the same and she wanted to capture the feeling that she had treasured. The summer was hot and humid, too hot to be really comfortable. They had sat talking about their childhood and Andy had told her that he wanted to show her one of his favourite places. "I used to play here with friends when I was young, we always stole matches and lit fires, it was a magical place. We dammed the stream and always fell in, we made camps in the trees and we loved it. We thought that it was our place, a secret place where our gang, our small band of brothers, could live like Robin Hood away from adults and the strange rules that were imposed upon us, we wanted freedom to be ourselves, every day was an adventure." He kissed her cheek with a gentleness that caused her to sigh. "The days were always long and sunny then. I just wanted you to see the place," he said while smiling in a manner that seemed to indicate contentment, which was something that Andy very rarely displayed.

She looked around her, all was quiet and peaceful, she thought that she had heard a sound although she could not make out what had caused it. A slight breeze suddenly appeared and birds flew out of the trees and landed in the fields.

Belinda thought that she was privileged to be allowed to visit this mysterious place where Andy and his friends had enjoyed their childhood. "I miss you so much," she said out loud. Tears ran down her cheeks. She arose from her seated position, gazed once more at the stream and then slowly, as if reluctant to go, turned towards the path that led back through the trees. The sun was brighter than it had been all day and it felt warm upon her face, she would not forget the stream or all of the other things that they had shared. The time that they had together was all too short but it was a time that she would never forget. Her life was better because of those few months together and she was not going to let herself feel sad or despondent. What had happened had happened. It was painful but it was not within her power to change anything. I will love him forever, whatever happens in the future will never change those thoughts and feelings, she said to herself. He was special, he was different, and I loved him more than life itself, tears formed in her eyes again as she reached the car. She looked back at the woods and decided that she would never return there again, she had felt something that it was impossible to describe as she had sat by the stream and she did not want to return only to find something had changed, no matter how small. Some things are best left just as they are, there is nothing or no one that can improve them. And to retain that clear memory is what is important. Life moves on and it takes you with it, only your memories are there to sustain you. She was unsure as to how she had arrived at such a conclusion but she knew that it was correct. She would not forget, whatever the future held for her. She had heard many people say that time heals everything, which in her mind meant that memories fade and lose their importance. The memories she held would never fade, she had given her love to Andy and she had felt the depth of his love and she knew that nothing would ever feel better, and such thoughts and feelings could not fade whatever happened.

She thought about the past few months and tried to put them into perspective, but it was impossible. So much had happened to her it was just too much to rationalise. One day it might make sense, one day I might understand why such things happen. It is possible that we will never really understand what the world has in store for us, what paths we have to take. She shook her head and sighed deeply. It is so painful, so bloody painful, she said to herself. But I would not have wanted to miss those times we had together, I felt more alive than I had ever done before. I now know what being alive feels like even if I do not understand what has happened or why. She closed her eyes hoping to dream.

Printed in the United Kingdom
by Lightning Source UK Ltd.
111113UKS00001B/1-6